ASCEND
SPECIAL EDITION

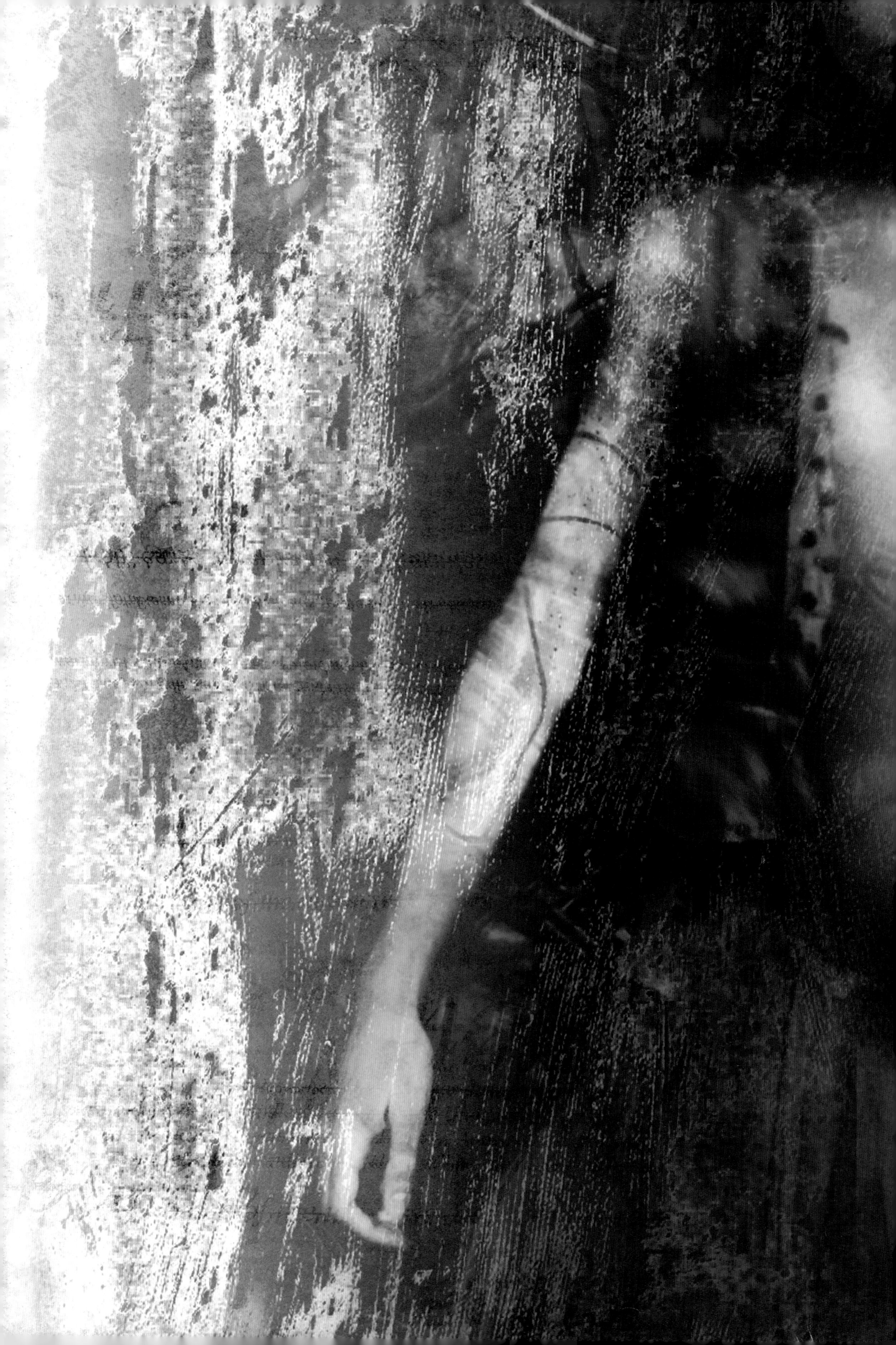

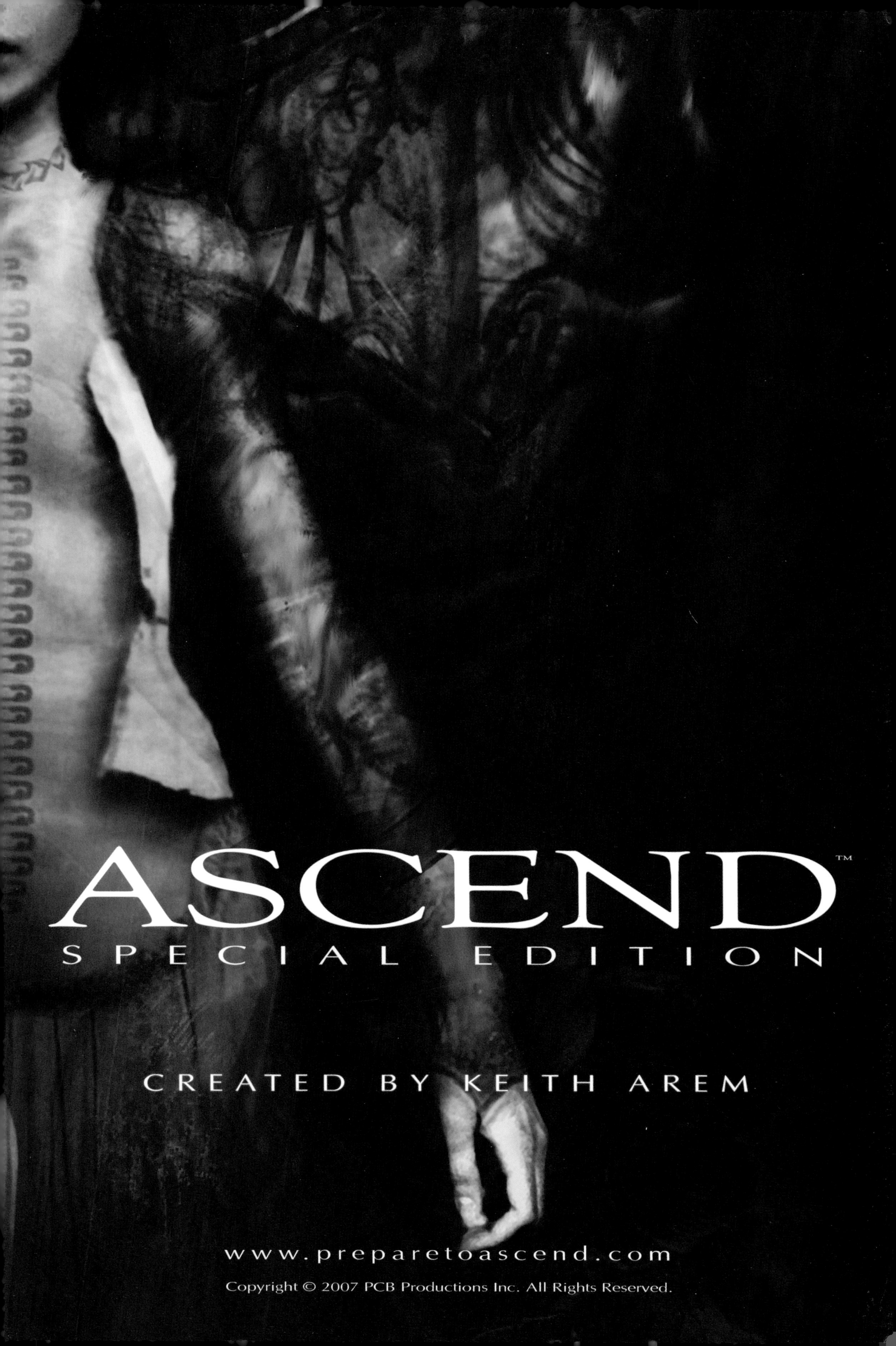

ASCEND™

SPECIAL EDITION

CREATED BY KEITH AREM

www.preparetoascend.com

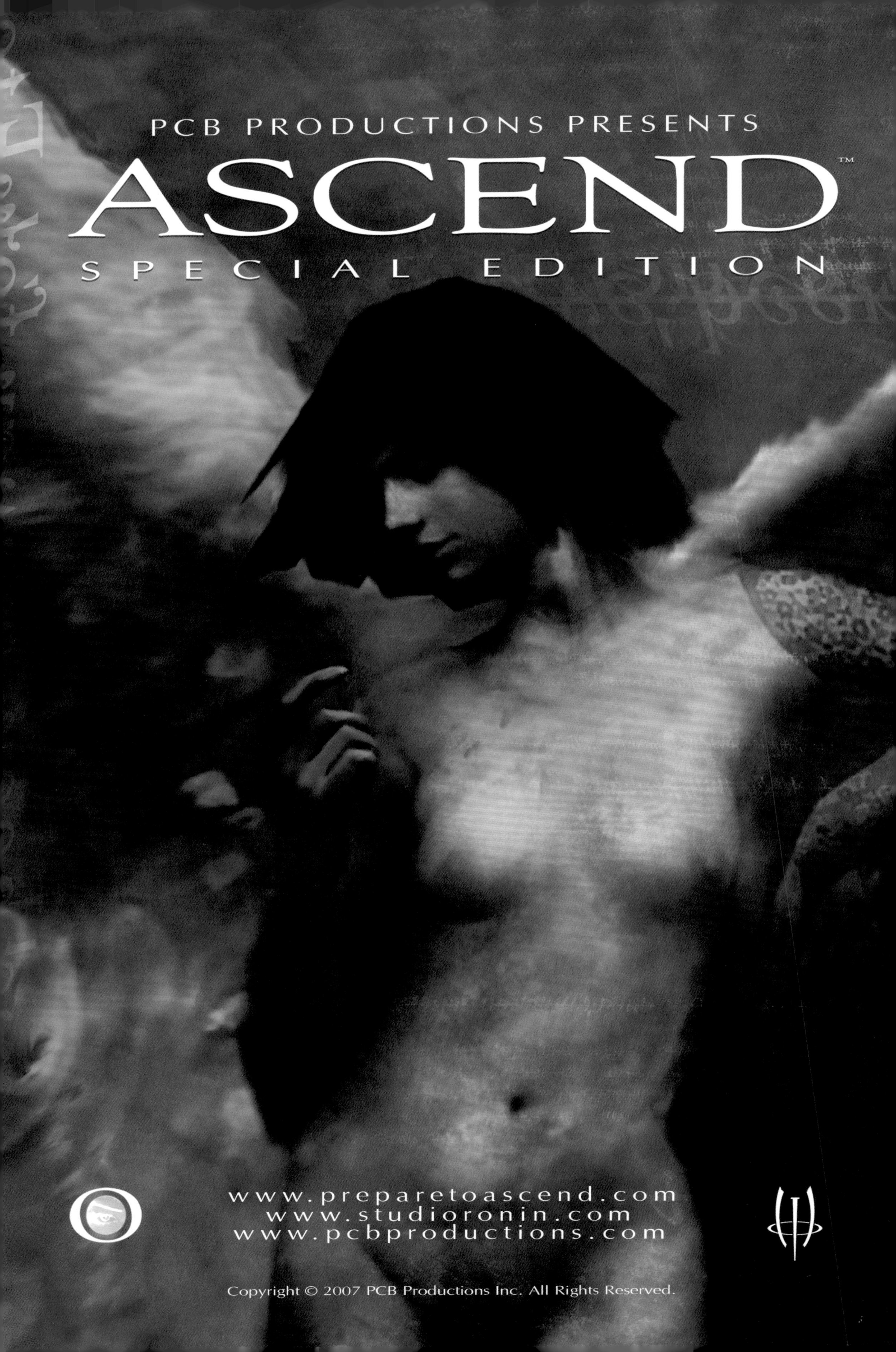
PCB PRODUCTIONS PRESENTS
ASCEND™
SPECIAL EDITION
www.preparetoascend.com
www.studioronin.com
www.pcbproductions.com
Copyright © 2007 PCB Productions Inc. All Rights Reserved.

WRITTEN AND PRODUCED BY
KEITH AREM

ARTWORK
CHRISTOPHER SHY

ADDITIONAL WRITING
SCOTT CUTHBERTSON

POST-PRODUCTION
KRISTIAN K HEDMAN

SPECIAL THANKS
Valerie Arem, Arnold and Cynthia Arem, Pam Bowles,
Brandon Humphreys, Howard Abramson, David Markus,
Laeta Kalogridis, Sam Gottlieb, Jimmy Palmiotti,
Ed O'Ross, Marcus Nispel, Yuri Lowenthal, Tara Platt,
Liam O'Brien, Kari Wahlgren, Brian Bendis,
John Orlando, Russell Binder, Rob Prior,
Krystyn Ingram, Leslie Cuthbertson, Dasha Shy

For Julia and Kyle

PCB PRODUCTIONS

Author Notes

"This is the only innocence you will ever have".

The truth is that I never gave much thought to Angels until the dream.

I'm not a religious person, although I have a strong respect for nature and the world,
and whatever it is that makes us all individuals. I've always been disappointed when someone
claims a tragic event is "God's will" or that their personal success or failure is in "God's hands."

I believe we all have free will, and if a god truly exists, it is an energy that lives inside everything,
rather than a bearded "Zeus", calling down orders from a mighty throne in the sky.

A lot changed on May 23rd, 2003. I had been traveling with my wife, when I awoke from the most
powerful dream of my life. In one night, I dreamed the complete story of Ascend.
It was like watching the most amazing motion picture, in which I experienced the lives of Sebastian,
Gideon, and Seraphine.

I woke up Valerie, and told her the entire story before it drifted away. She was stunned
and insisted I write it down before I lost the vision. But even after I wrote it down,
the dream was so powerful, I couldn't shake the images from my head. I had to get the
images out of my mind.

Six weeks later, I flew down to Comic Con in San Diego to find an artist. After meeting with
several fantastic and talented artists, I finally found Christopher — and Christopher's art found me.
Chris's images were exactly what I was seeing in my head, and when we started on the book together,
his paintings were finally able to express the visions that were plaguing my mind.

Christopher and I became extremely close friends over the course of the book.
Christopher and I both went through a really tough year, losing our Grandparents and family members,
which only strengthened our determination to make this book a statement about appreciating life.

"An artist never really finishes his work; he merely abandons it." -Paul Valéry

Since the release of the original printing of Ascend in February 2005, we have received a tremendous
amount of support and recognition for the book. There were so many concepts and story elements that
never made it into the first printing, so Chris and I wanted to use this re-printing opportunity
develop a Special Edition of the novel that would incorporate many of these ideas.

Also, in the original release, there were several panels that were misprinted with rough production
artwork, and the last 2 pages were accidentally lopped off during the printing.
All of this has been updated in this printing, along with several new enhancements.

Kristian Hedman, who had developed the amazing trailer and website for the first book, came on board to enhance the pages with new artwork, panel borders, text effects, and layout concepts.

Since the original book and panels were initially developed as storyboards for the upcoming motion picture, I took this opportunity to further flesh out the characters and dialogue, and help explain the complicated world of Ascend. The artwork was actually not intended to be a published as a graphic novel, so the biggest challenge has been to develop the characters and epic story only through art panels and dialog.

I was very adamant that the book should not to have text ballons and narration throughout, since I felt it was important to let the visuals to tell the narrative, and not to spoon feed the story..

The most significant addition to this edition is the linear progression of the story. In the original release, the cause of Angel's banishment was shrouded in mystery, and eventually revealed through a flashback in Act Three. For the Special Edition, I decided to go back and establish the main character, Sebastian, as a human, and follow his ascent into the war. The book introduces Rebeka, the assault and soul havest by Gideon, and the reasons why she took her life. We also understand Gideon's betrayal of his family.

Admittedly, the book is a lot to take in. The story and universe is based on the combination of the world religions and classic mythology. The characters are stoic, complex, and do not express outward emotion. The artwork is stunning and intricate, yet dreamlike in nature.
One of the reasons for this, was to establish a universe that feels enormous, yet slightly out of reach. I've always been drawn to films and books, where I don't completely understand what's going on, but I still love the world. Many people can get frustrated by this, but I've always found that what we don't see, or what we don't know, is more intriguing that something tangible in front of us... "Alien" was much more terrifying when we couldn't see what it looked like, and when we did get a glimpse of it, our minds filled in the rest.

For those who do want to know more about the story and background; I've included several pages of story notes, background information, and research, explaining the world of Ascend.
The following pages detail the story synopsis and original treatment for the book, and describe what I saw in my dream.

May You Never Know the Wars of Above.
- Keith Arem

July 2007

ASCEND: STORY NOTES

A dream:
A young man, SEBASTIAN, struggles to open his eyes. His face is covered with blood. He is crucified on a towering cross, amidst a field of sacrificed corpses. Suddenly, a bright shaft of light announces the presence of an angelic form. As SEBASTIAN trembles from the heavenly image, the Angel unfolds enormous wings to envelop Sebastian's soul. The angel is both beautiful and horrific at the same time. A small glowing green vial dangles from the Angel's neck. The Angel tells SEBASTIAN that the "MASHIACH" must awaken, but as the Angel begins to feed on SEBASTIAN'S soul; SEBASTIAN screams.

Sebastian awakens from the nightmare. It is now present day, and Sebastian tries to shake off the upsetting dream. Around his apartment are family pictures of Sebastian's deceased brother Gideon, and his younger sister Seraphine. Sebastian is rattled from the dream, and reluctantly answers the phone. His sister, Sera asks to see him.

Later that morning, Sebastian meets Seraphine for coffee. He is still grieving over the loss of Gideon, and Sera tries to console him. Sera tells Sebastian that she has been plagued by dreams of Gideon, and she has seen him as a vision of an angel, fighting in a horrific war in Heaven. She is haunted by his image, and believes she still sees him everywhere...almost stalking her.
Sebastian, who has given up on religion, criticizes Seraphine for her belief in an afterlife.
After Seraphine leaves the restaurant, Sebastian finds himself caught in the silent gaze of a beautiful waitress, Rebeka.

Sebastian walks through the streets, and boards a commuter train...unaware that something is stalking him. Something is disturbing about the train ride, and as the train increases speed, Sebastian sees images of Gideon around the train. Suddenly, the train derails, throwing it from the tracks onto the streets below. As Sebastian lies dying in the street, a bright light appears above each of the dead passengers around him. Angels have come here to feed. As Sebastian looks up, an Angel rises before him — its wings fully extend to absorb his soul. Just as in his dream before...this time it's real. Sebastian screams. Fade to black.

Sebastian emerges from a dense white fog, in the midst of an epic battle. All around him are thousands of Angels, locked in brutal combat with enormous, vicious beasts from the Underworld. Confused by his role in this brutal war, Sebastian realizes he is outfitted in battle armor. A flying demon descends, knocking him to the ground. Dazed, and disoriented, Sebastian, grabs a fallen broadsword and realizes he must fight to survive. Sebastian is surprisingly strong, and slays the beast. The war spans endlessly, and it is apparent there can be no victory in this war.

Ultimately, Sebastian and his fellow angel warriors are victorious in their battle, but the war is as far from over. As Sebastian recovers from the encounter, he is embraced by his brother Gideon. Gideon is a General in the Angelic Wars, and he is a respected leader among his soldiers. Gideon explains that they are fighting in the fields of Purgatory, and the war has destroyed Heaven. With no guidance or formal leadership from the Angelic Council, Gideon is bitter about the ongoing war, and muses that the peaceful tranquility of human religious "afterlife" is a myth.

Gideon avoids Sebastian's questions about the circumstances of his death in the train wreck, but tells Sebastian that he has an important mission for him. Gideon explains that he needs Sebastian to join the "Harvest" to recruit souls for their war. Angels serve as shepherds, to ensure human souls are protected on their ascension into Heaven's army. Gideon elaborates that the wars have not only destroyed Heaven and the Underworld, but they have also disrupted the natural cycle of life, since souls can not migrate from Heaven, through the surrounding "Guff", to be reincarnated back on earth. This endless soul "deforestation" of earth has denied the return of the fabled "MASHIACH", who is the only being capable of ending the war and restoring balance to the natural cycle of life. Gideon criticizes Heaven for its never ending cycle of robbing from Earth to replenish their armies, yet Sebastian senses there is a plan that Gideon is not revealing.

Sebastian agrees to join the Harvest and returns to Earth as an Angel. His decent back to earth is a fantastic and stunning journey, as he travels to his former home. His excitement is shaken when he lands in the midst of a horrific plane disaster, with burning wreckage and bodies all around him. Thousands of pleading voices fill his head, and Sebastian is "called" to a dead passenger in the wreckage. As he approaches the human soul, he realizes that this victim is his sister, SERAPHINE. He is devastated by this personal tragic loss of life, and is abruptly lost within his own memories. Gideon approaches to comfort his brother, but callously explains "now we can all be together again".

Suddenly, enormous wings painfully emerge from Sebastian's back, and he is stunned as they instinctively enfold around his fallen sister. SERAPHINE is absorbed in a brilliant wash of light, as Sebastian "harvests" her soul, and absorbs her soul's energy. A blinding beam of light blasts Sebastian, and the soul is ascended to Heaven. As Sebastian recovers from his First Harvest, a woman's cry catches Sebastian's attention, and he finds a survivor from the crash, still alive in the wreckage. He is fascinated by this beautiful mortal, and recognizes her as REBEKA, the waitress from the coffee shop. Frozen in thought, Gideon pushes Sebastian aside, and begins to Harvest her soul, even though she is still alive. As her soul is pulled from her body into Gideon, Sebastian snaps back into reality, and is suddenly furious. Sebastian restrains his brother to defend the innocent woman. As rescue crews arrive, Gideon reluctantly yields, and the tribe of Angels ascend home, leaving Rebeka alive in the wreckage.

Back in Heaven, Seraphine, now an angelic warrior, is reunited with Sebastian. Gideon embraces her, although there is a cool distance between them. Gideon has reunited his family, and explains that their Clan is now complete. Gideon leads them into many powerful battles, and each of the siblings proves to be skilled in combat.

Gideon expresses his frustration over the war, and proclaims that his legion could stop the endless battle, if he was granted the command to lead Heaven's armies. Gideon realizes the irony that the only the Mashiach can stop the cycle, however Heaven has denied his return since their relentless "Harvest" has depleted humans souls from replenishing the Guff and Earth.

Gideon persuades Sebastian and Seraphine to lead their Legion in rebellion by diverting Harvested souls for themselves. Seraphine and Sebastian are not comfortable with the idea of mutiny, but are torn by their loyalty to their brother. Suddenly...they are banished.

BOOK ONE

A cataclysm erupts in the still night of the dark metropolis. Three naked bodies are thrown to earth out of a dark storm. It is a re-birth, an event that is at once cosmic, terrible, glorious, and altogether organic and elemental in force. To the mortal, heads-down populace of humanity, they are invisible.

Sebastian, Gideon, and Seraphine rise from a daze and salvage their regal demeanor. They are strangers in their former home, powerful beings suddenly exiled to a Purgatory on Earth. Disoriented, they approach an abandoned cathedral, which does little to shelter then from the rain.

The three argue, although it is not immediately clear why they have been banished. The argument is vague, precise and biting. We do not understand exactly why they are here, however it is apparent that Gideon's insurrection in Heaven is the cause of their banishment. In a rage, Gideon leaves the other two behind.

Sebastian and Seraphine seek shelter in the abandoned cathedral, but soon learn they are still at the mercy of their angelic instincts. Despite their banishment, the two are still drawn to Harvest humans about to die. Seraphine, who has never been part of the Harvest, is "called" to a mortally injured woman in an auto accident. As she approaches the dying woman, she harvests her soul, and the two are engulfed in blaze of flame and light. Seraphine ascends the woman's soul, and she is embraced with a blinding white energy as she guides the soul to ascension. Because of her banishment, the soul is immediately ripped from her, and she is thrown back to earth.

As Gideon travels the back streets of the city, a human "believer" is drawn to Gideon. He sees Gideon as a "vision from god", and begs for his salvation. To Gideon, the hypocrisy of human religion is foolish and short sighted, and he mocks the believer "This life is the only true innocence you'll ever have. You have no idea what awaits you in the afterlife." Gideon tries to wave off the believer, but due to his unrealized power over mortals, he inadvertently murders the human. A savage darkness rips the man's life force from his body, and Gideon takes in the man's soul. As Gideon's wings transform into tentacle shaped appendages, he realizes he can harness this mortal power for himself. Gideon has found his new calling.

Sebastian is alone in the abandoned cathedral, and feels his situation is hopeless. Suddenly, he is called to a dying mortal. Sebastian is drawn to a woman who has taken her life, having slit her wrists in a bathtub. As he approaches the dying woman, he recognizes that this the survivor REBEKA from the airplane harvest. Instead of ascending Rebeka's soul, Sebastian makes a decision to sacrifice his life energy to restore her soul. This exchange of energy begins to slowly transform Rebeka into an Angel, and Sebastian begins to lose his powers...he is becoming mortal again. Seraphine follows Sebastian's trail to Rebeka's apartment, and rushes to tell Sebastian about her experience with the dying woman. She finds Sebastian embracing Rebeka, and without a word, retreats into the night.

Seraphine finds the decimated remains of the believer, killed by Gideon. She is deeply troubled by her dark visions, and knows Gideon is the cause of this mortal's death. Seraphine, a "Watcher" from the Angelic Wars, suddenly prophesizes her own death, and Gideon's rise to power. She realizes that humans are powerless to stop him, and she sets out on his path to uncover his intentions.

Rebeka knows there is something extraordinary about Sebastian, but she does not comprehend his true nature. She welcomes his presence, and already begins to show signs of changing into an Angel. Sebastian explains that he has sacrificed part of himself to save her, and that he no longer wants to be part of the Angelic Wars. Sebastian sees this as his opportunity to become mortal again, and stays to protect Rebeka.

Realizing his power to create a new legion on earth, GIDEON begins to stalk new victims, mocking his prey. Gideon grows stronger, as his dark energy grows with each victim's life force. Seraphine spies on Gideon and follows him as he stalks another victim. As Gideon kills again, Seraphine watches the human's life force ripped into Gideon. Gideon has become skilled at the art of killing, and grows even more powerful. It is a terrible vision and Seraphine gasps, a rare display of emotion that reveals her presence. Gideon turns and looks right at her, and realizes she is aware of his secret. Seraphine hides behind the wall and turns to run... but Gideon is already standing in front of her.

Gideon grabs Seraphine, and tries to convince her of the "good" he is doing for the universe. He explains that their survival requires this infusion of mortal souls to rebuild their legion on earth. Instead of allowing souls to ascend to Heaven, he is amassing an army of souls to storm the gates of their former home. As Gideon speaks, it becomes obvious that his personal crusade has made him insatiable and unbalanced. Gideon regards himself as the future ruler of Heaven and Hell, and explains that Heaven can not interfere, since they hold no power over their banished family. Seraphine manages to escape Gideon's grip, and he briefly smiles as he watches her go....Seraphine is the enemy.

The exchange of life energy has begun to affect Rebeka and Sebastian. Sebastian falls in love with Rebeka, and resigns himself to becoming a mortal. Sebastian's wings begin to decay, while Rebeka begins to develop the markings of an angel. Sebastian does not seem at peace with his new environment, however he begins to accept his fate on earth.

Meanwhile, Gideon has become a brutal killer, stalking his prey, and continuing to reap souls by the hundreds. He has acquired a thirst for religious worshipers and their congregations.

In her search for answers, Seraphine is approached by a blind prophet who acknowledges her presence. This is the fallen angel ESDRAS, a former warrior in Gideon's army, who prophesizes Seraphine's demise and Gideon's rise to power. The blind prophet alludes to Gideon's approaching war of Angels, and reveals the existence of a biblical weapon with the power to weaken him. ESDRAS cryptically describes that the last mortal soul must leave the earth for the MASHIACH to return. Seraphine sees the prophecy of what is happening to both of her fallen brothers, and runs off to warn Sebastian. As Seraphine departs, Gideon descends and murders Esdras.

Seraphine returns to Rebeka's apartment, and finds her transforming into an angel. Seraphine is appalled by Rebeka's transformation, and criticizes Sebastian for altering their species. Sebastian explains that he has abandoned his former existence as an angel, and wants this opportunity to become human again. Seraphine explains that Gideon has become a monster, but also that there is hope for them to stop him. She describes what she has learned about Gideon, and the existence of a biblical weapon, a vial with the power to stop Gideon and his growing army.

SEBASTIAN wants no part of this new war, and believes that killing Gideon is impossible. Seraphine criticizes Sebastian for bringing Rebeka into their lives, and he suddenly lashes out against Seraphine. Despite his mortal transformation, Sebastian is still very powerful, and his energy blasts Seraphine from the room. She is devastated by her brother's attack, and runs off into the raining night. REBEKA is frightened by Sebastian's actions, but encourages him to follow after her. Reconsidering his outburst, he realizes that he cannot hope to defeat Gideon alone, and chases after Seraphine. Rebeka goes after him.

As SERAPHINE runs down the street, GIDEON, who has been stalking them, silently descends from behind, and murders her. Sebastian arrives seconds later, finding Seraphine's slain body. He does not have the strength to save her, and cries out into the night, embracing her, vowing to avenge her death. Sebastian now understands he must stop Gideon, even if he must murder his own brother.

Rebeka chases after Sebastian, and finds him holding Seraphine's body. After Sebastian's recent ferocity, Rebeka questions if he murdered Seraphine. Rebeka runs away, leaving Sebastian alone with his slain sister.

BOOK THREE

SEBASTIAN is alone, and quests for guidance. He knows that without Seraphine, he cannot face Gideon alone. Sebastian leaves the metropolis and journeys into the deep desert.

Along his personal Walk of Judgment, Sebastian questions the value of life, the meaning of love, and comes to realize that the Earth is the only true innocence... not the idealist notion of Heaven. On his quest, Sebastian observes images of the best and worst of humanity, almost as a flashback to his previous lives throughout time. As he sees images of his mortal life, we realize Sebastian has walked the earth before. Seeing images of human life and death, he experiences a final flashback to the horrors of the angelic Purgatory Wars. During the flashback, Sebastian sees the similarity of human wars with the tragedy of the Purgatory Wars. Images of WWII, combined with the brutality of the Underworld creatures, Roman gladiators, and the hatred among the Angel warriors. Sebastian begins to weep at the wasted human life, sacrificed in the name of religion.

At the conclusion of his flashback, he finds himself in the deep desert. Sebastian enters an ancient cave where he is greeted by the banished angel General BARAK. Sebastian recognizes the glowing green vial around BARAK's neck, from the angel that harvested him on the Cross in his earlier dream. BARAK explains he was expelled from Heaven, just as Sebastian and his siblings were. BARAK was known as the legendary ANGEL OF DEATH from the bible, and warns of the impending holocaust if Gideon completes his army. BARAK explains that he once believed he could end the war himself, but his greed cost him his banishment.

Barak gives Sebastian his VIAL - an ancient biblical weapon, capable of weakening Gideon and his army.
The power of the small vial will not harm Gideon, but it will release all of the mortal souls from the earth.
BARAK explains that only the last Mortal Soul can awaken the MASHIACH. Gideon will try to consume
the souls for himself, and he will become vulnerable immediately after attempting to devour their energy.

Sebastian, who is becoming mortal, has fallen in love with Rebeka, refuses to commit mortal genocide.
Sebastian also understands that if he does not kill Gideon, there is no one capable of stopping him. Sebastian reluctantly
takes the vial, however, since he can not accept the further loss of life, and decides to confront Gideon directly.

Sebastian returns to the metropolis to face Gideon, and finds that he has become more powerful
than ever. The city has become a graveyard of consumed souls. Sebastian confronts Gideon and
accuses him of being responsible for their exile, and the murder of their sister Seraphine.
Gideon criticizes Heaven's endless war with the Underworld, and claims that
their harvesting of souls is no more justified than his recruiting soldiers for himself.
REBEKA hides in the shadows, a silhouetted figure, watching the two brothers clash.

Sebastian and Gideon struggle, using their ethereal Angelic powers against each other. Gideon's strength has become far
superior to Sebastian's, and he toys with Sebastian. Gideon soon impales Sebastian using his tentacle wings - mortally
injuring him. Gideon reveals that SEBASTIAN is actually the fabled "MASHIACH"; however his Angelic sacrifice made him
incapable of stopping him. Gideon accuses Sebastian of sympathizing with mortals, and claims Sebastian's love of Rebeka
has blinded him to the fact the Mashiach could have defeated him earlier. Gideon reveals that he murdered
and harvested Sebastian to recruit him into the Angelic Wars, hoping to awaken the Mashiach's powers in Sebastian.
Gideon further reveals that he caused the plane crash to harvest Seraphine, making both of their murders
the second death at their brother's hands. As Sebastian dies, Barak's green VIAL falls from his hand.

Rebeka, who has heard the exchange, appears and picks up the biblical weapon. Sebastian objects, but understands the vial
is the only way to stop Gideon. Rebeka detonates the weapon in a massive storm cloud of death, surrendering her
own life to weaken Gideon. The power of the Angel of Death coarses through the destroyed metropolis,
launching thousands of souls into Gideon. Gideon is weakened by the blast, and begins to distort by the gluttony
of mortal energy. Gideon becomes a towering beast, caused by the consumption of so many souls at one time.
Sebastian uses the last of his energy to release his own soul, the last mortal soul, and destroys Gideon.
Sebastian's sacrifice fulfills the role of the MASHIACH, as the one who would restore balance to the universe.

Sebastian lies dying on the ground, as the last of his angelic
markings fade. Sebastian summons the last of his energy to release his own soul, the last mortal soul, which
travels upward directly into Gideon. Gideon, unable to consume the last mortal, explodes in a blast of flesh
and light. The blast envelops the battlefield, consuming all of the warriors, as the skies about the metropolis
open to the heavens. An enormous shaft of light ascends every being from the city, leaving nothing behind.

As Sebastian's body lies in the fallen rubble, SERAPHINE descends from the
Heavens and appear in their full Angelic splendor. The war has ended, and having regained their place in
Heaven, they have come to bring her family back. Sebastian, Seraphine, and Rebeka ascend together.

As the clouds dissipate, the city lies in ruins. In front of the abandoned cathedral
that had once sheltered the angels, a ray of sunlight has illuminated a small green plant emerging,
and in the foreground lays Barak's vial. A small child crouches and picks up the fallen Biblical vial.
The young boy studies the weapon, and appears fascinated by the ancient weapon.
As his face comes into view, we see that he bears the tribal markings of an angel...The markings of Gideon.

AND THERE WAS WAR
IN HEAVEN:

THE ANGELS FOUGHT
AGAINST THE DRAGON;
AND THE DRAGON FOUGHT
THE ANGELS,
AND PREVAILED NOT;
NEITHER WAS THEIR PLACE
FOUND ANY MORE IN HEAVEN.
AND THE GREAT DRAGON WAS
CAST OUT, INTO THE EARTH,
AND HIS ANGELS WERE CAST
OUT WITH HIM.

FOR THE ACCUSER OF OUR
BRETHREN IS CAST DOWN,
WHICH ACCUSED THEM BEFORE
OUR GOD DAY AND NIGHT.

WOE TO THE INHABITERS OF
THE EARTH...
FOR HE IS COME DOWN UNTO
YOU, HAVING GREAT WRATH,
BECAUSE HE KNOWETH THAT
HE HATH BUT A SHORT TIME.

REVELATIONS 12:7-12

There is no way for you to comprehend how long our war has raged.
Eons... Millennia...

...mere teardrops in the ocean.

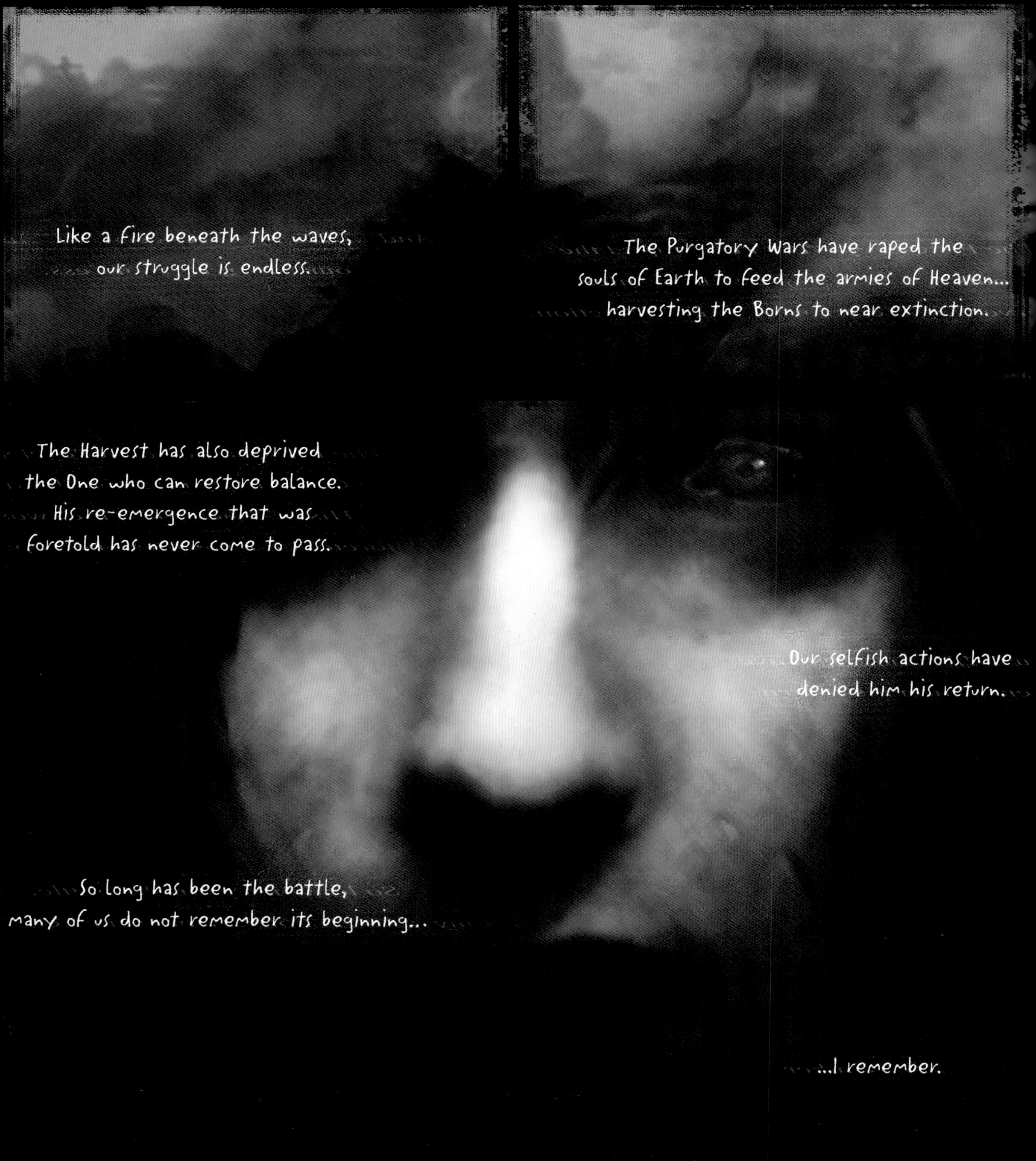
Like a fire beneath the waves, our struggle is endless.
The Purgatory Wars have raped the souls of Earth to feed the armies of Heaven... harvesting the Borns to near extinction.
The Harvest has also deprived the One who can restore balance. His re-emergence that was foretold has never come to pass.
Our selfish actions have denied him his return.
So long has been the battle, many of us do not remember its beginning...
...I remember.

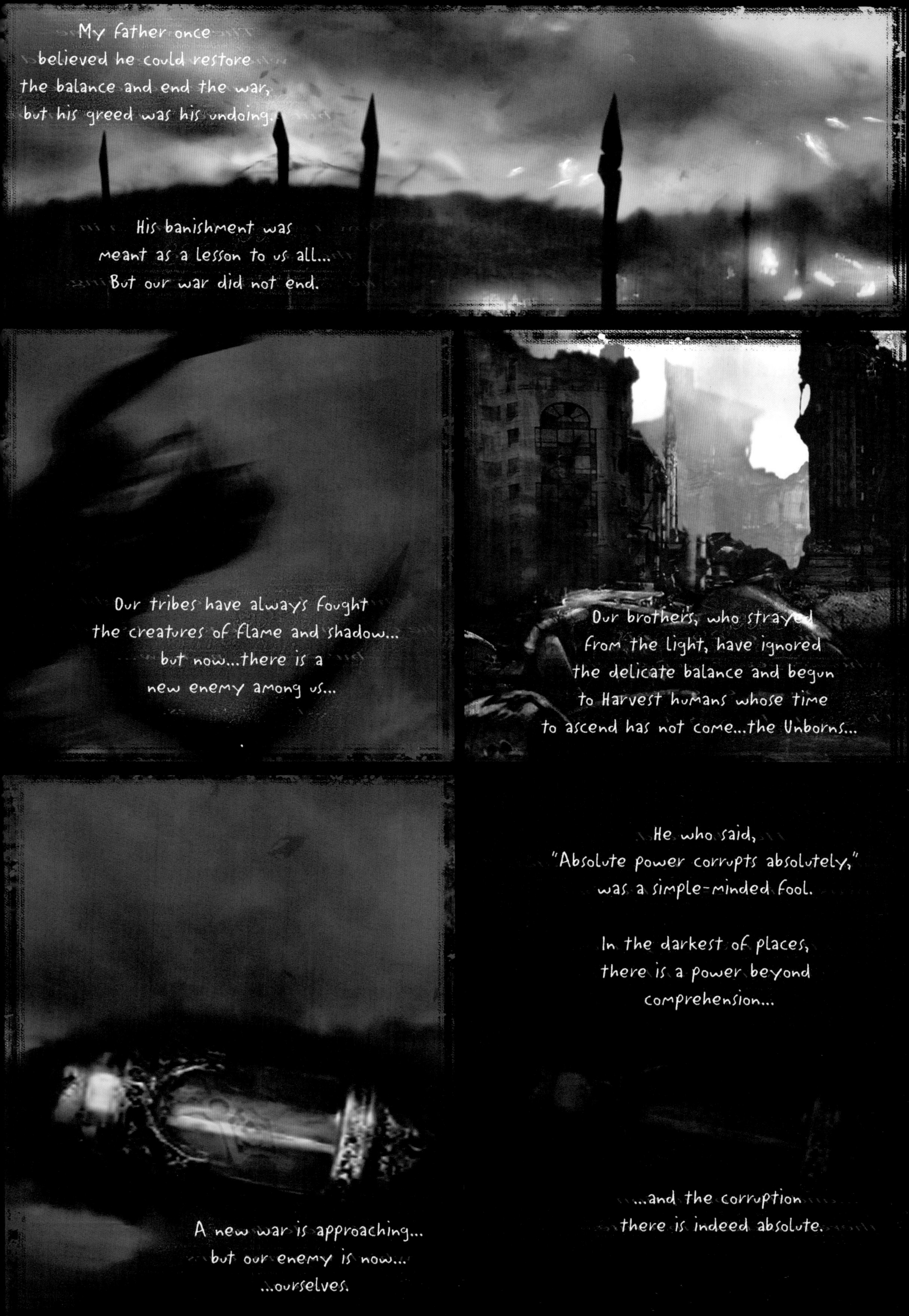
My father once believed he could restore the balance and end the war, but his greed was his undoing.
His banishment was meant as a lesson to us all... But our war did not end.
Our tribes have always fought the creatures of flame and shadow... but now...there is a new enemy among us...
Our brothers, who strayed from the light, have ignored the delicate balance and begun to Harvest humans whose time to ascend has not come...the Unborns...
A new war is approaching... but our enemy is now... ...ourselves.
He who said, "Absolute power corrupts absolutely," was a simple-minded fool.
In the darkest of places, there is a power beyond comprehension...
...and the corruption there is indeed absolute.

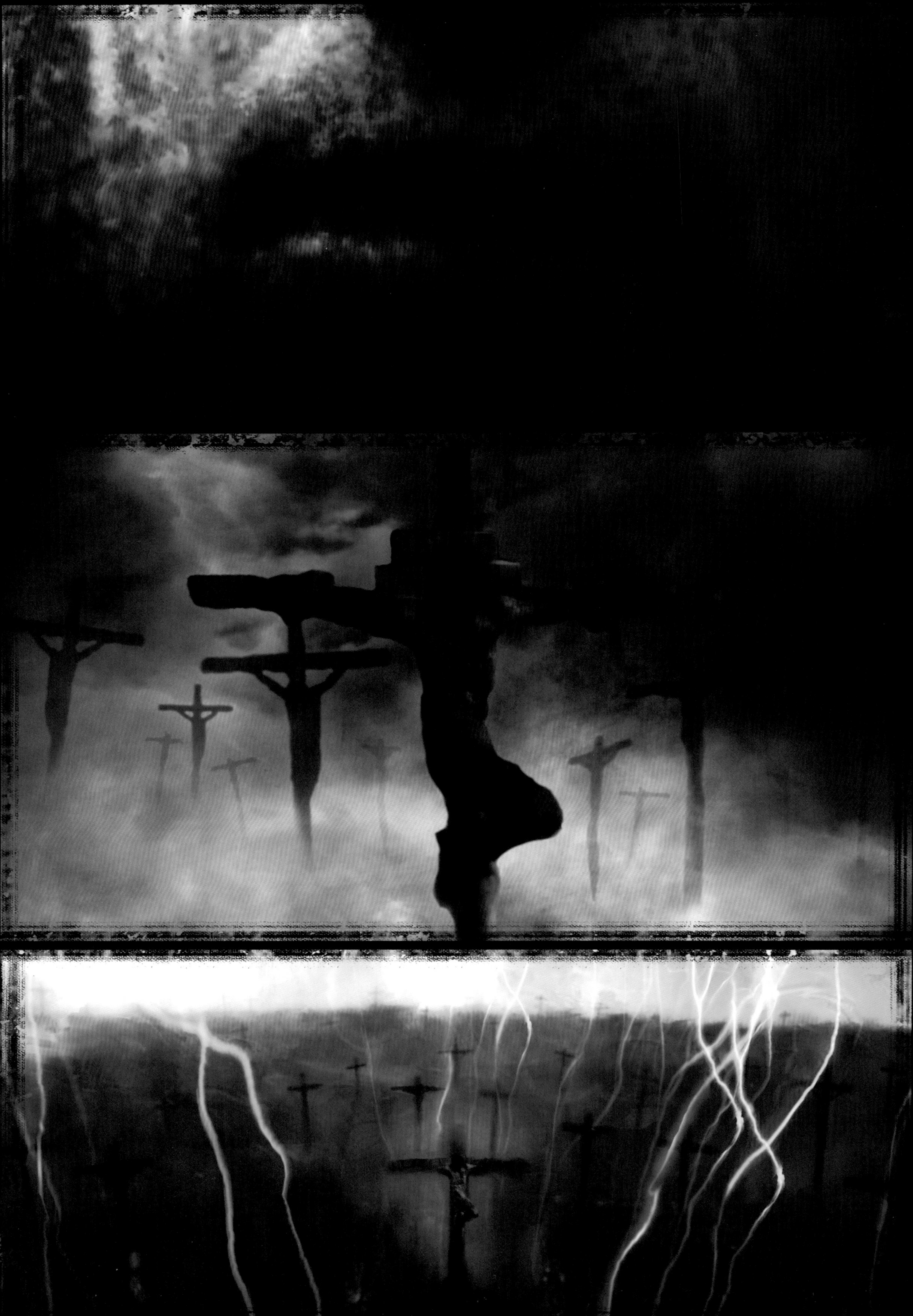

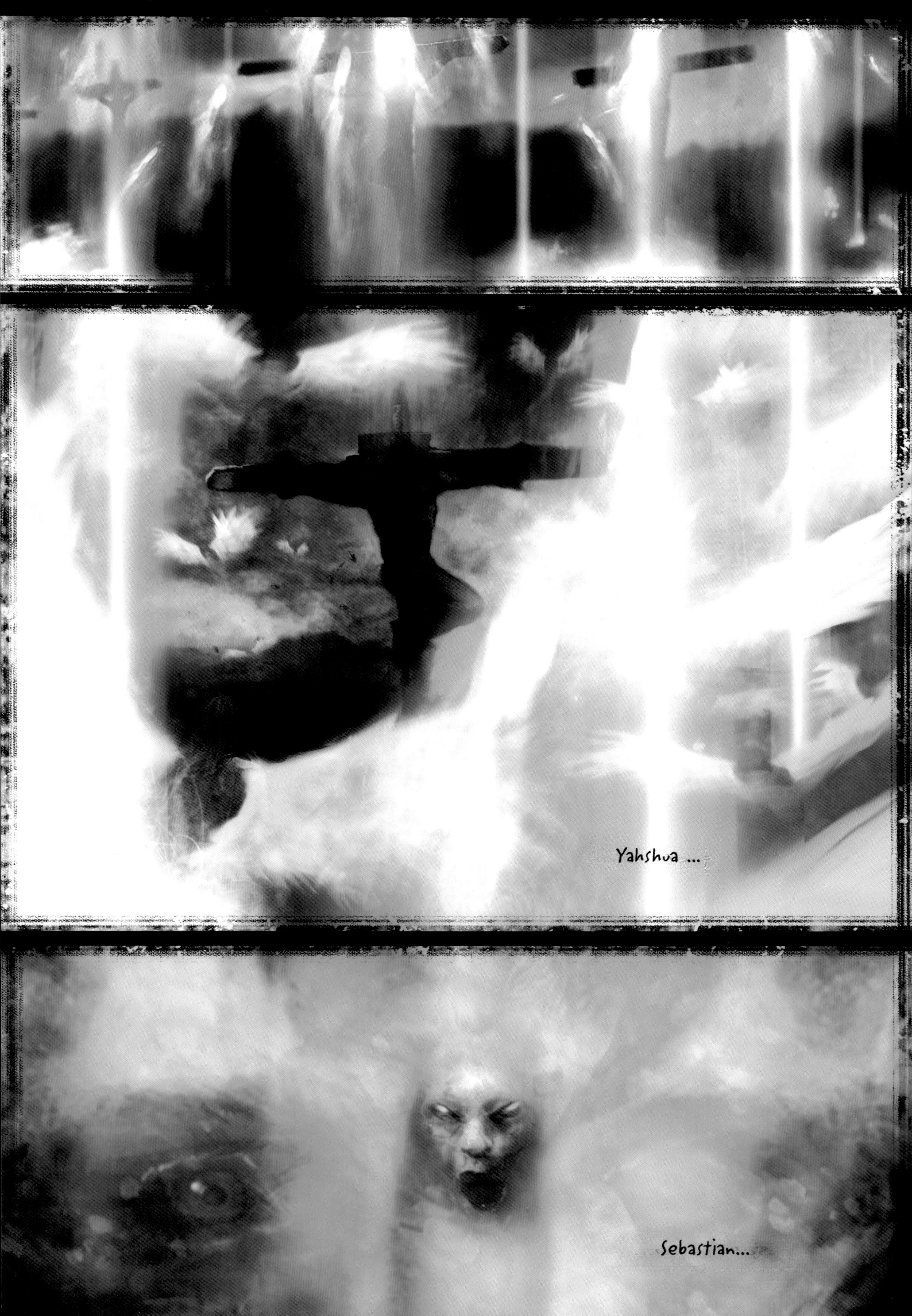
Yahshua ...
Sebastian...

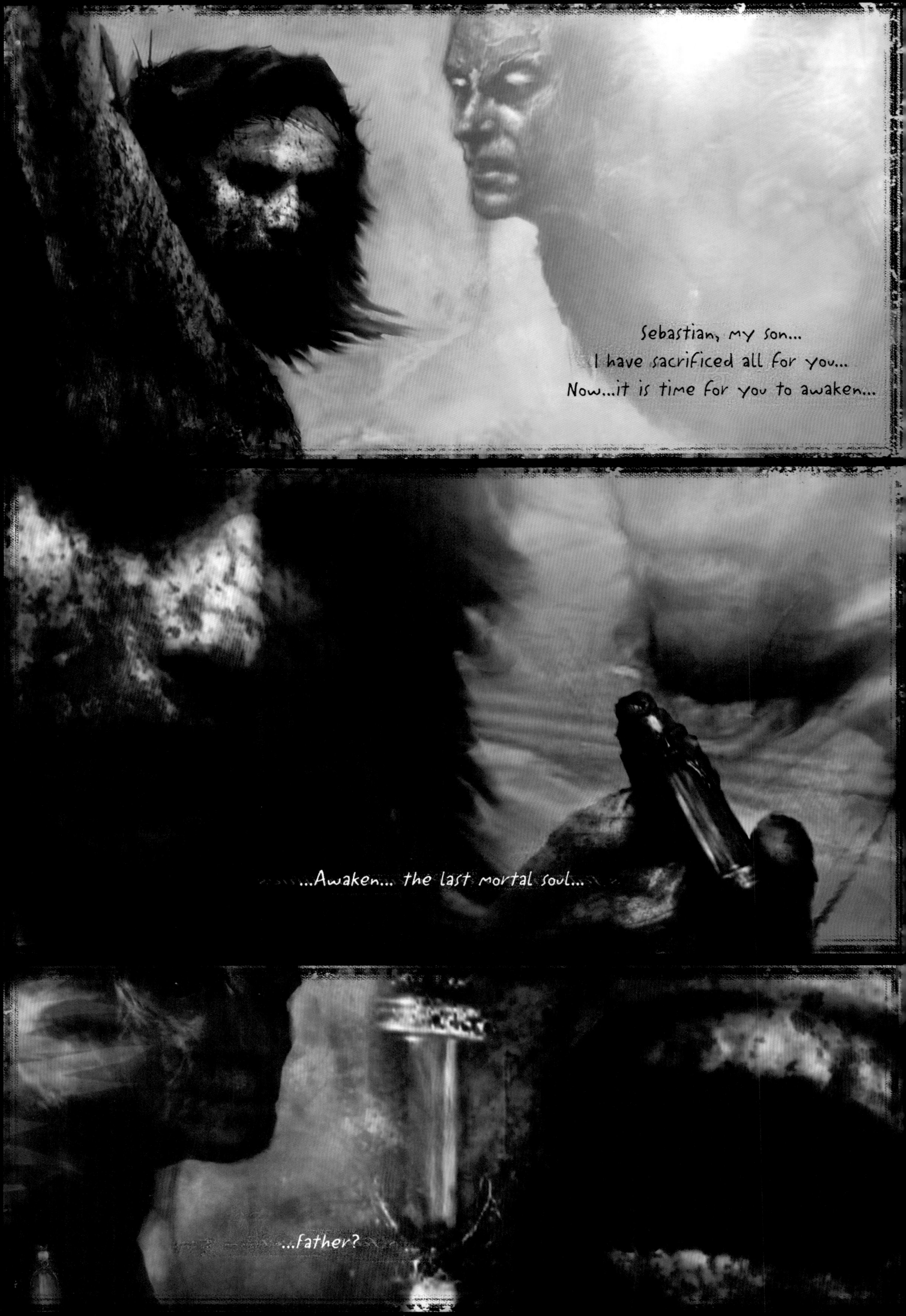
Sebastian, my son...
I have sacrificed all for you...
Now...it is time for you to awaken...
...Awaken... the last mortal soul...
...father?

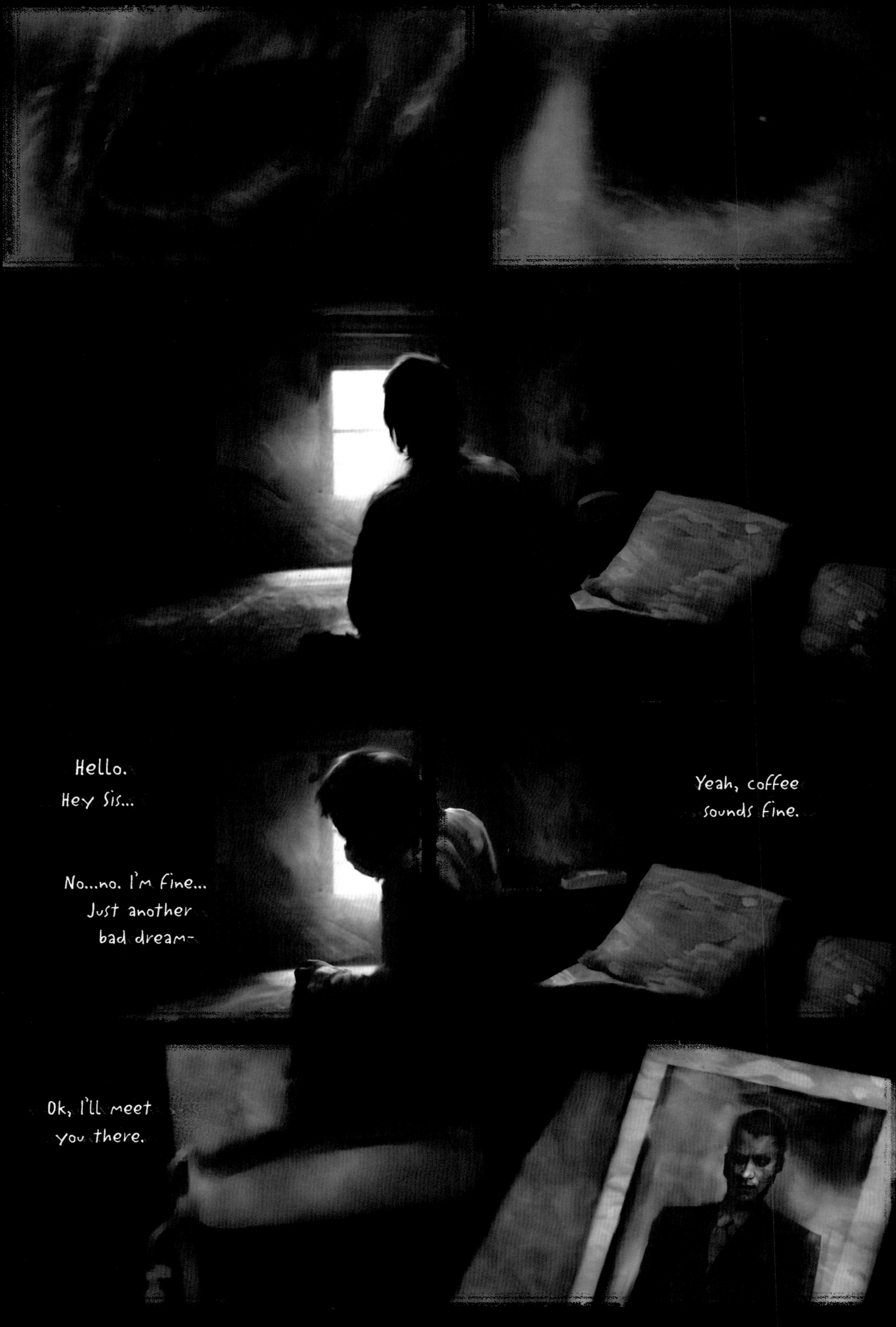
Hello.
Hey Sis...
Yeah, coffee sounds fine.
No...no. I'm fine... Just another bad dream-
Ok, I'll meet you there.

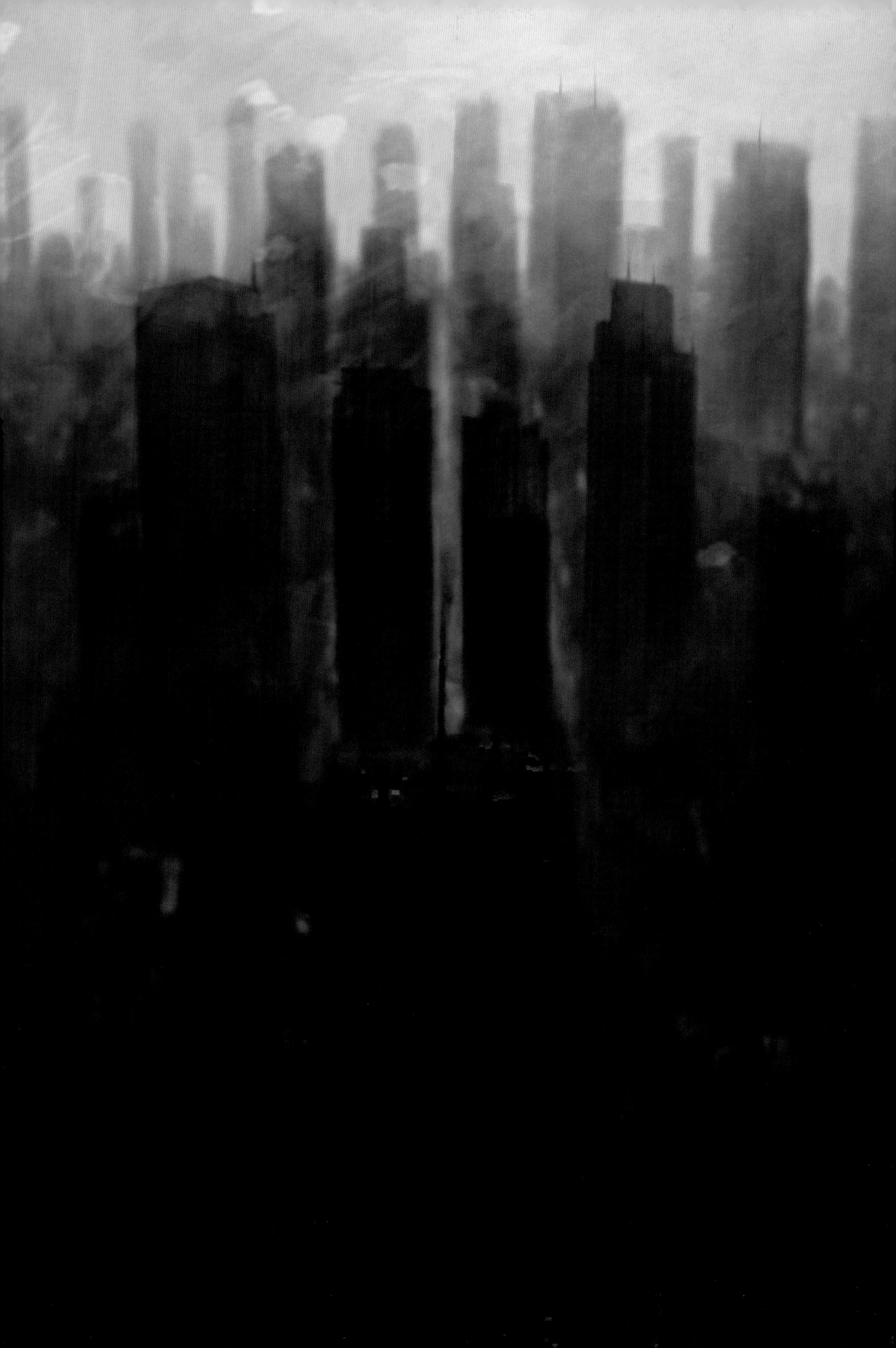

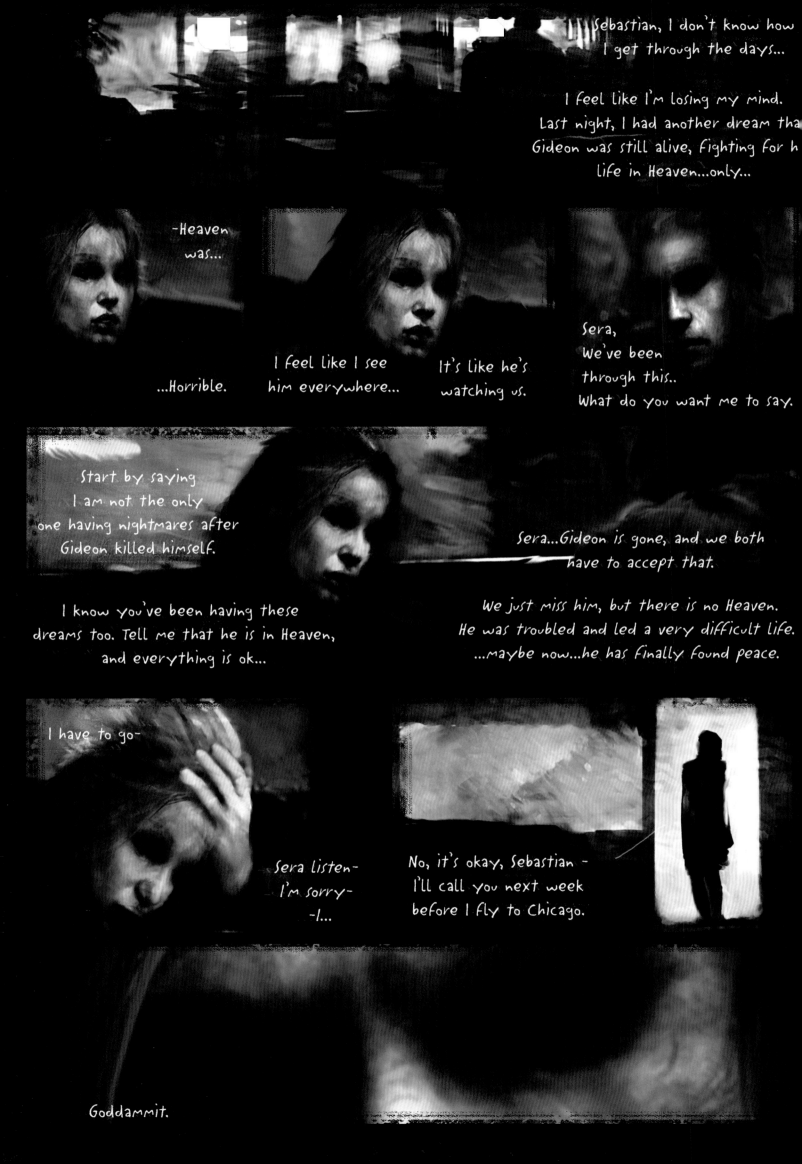

Sebastian, I don't know how I get through the days...

I feel like I'm losing my mind. Last night, I had another dream tha Gideon was still alive, fighting for h life in Heaven...only...

-Heaven was...

...Horrible.

I feel like I see him everywhere...

It's like he's watching us.

Sera, we've been through this.. What do you want me to say.

Start by saying I am not the only one having nightmares after Gideon killed himself.

Sera...Gideon is gone, and we both have to accept that.

I know you've been having these dreams too. Tell me that he is in Heaven, and everything is ok...

We just miss him, but there is no Heaven. He was troubled and led a very difficult life. ...maybe now...he has finally found peace.

I have to go-

Sera listen- I'm sorry- -I...

No, it's okay, Sebastian - I'll call you next week before I fly to Chicago.

Goddammit.

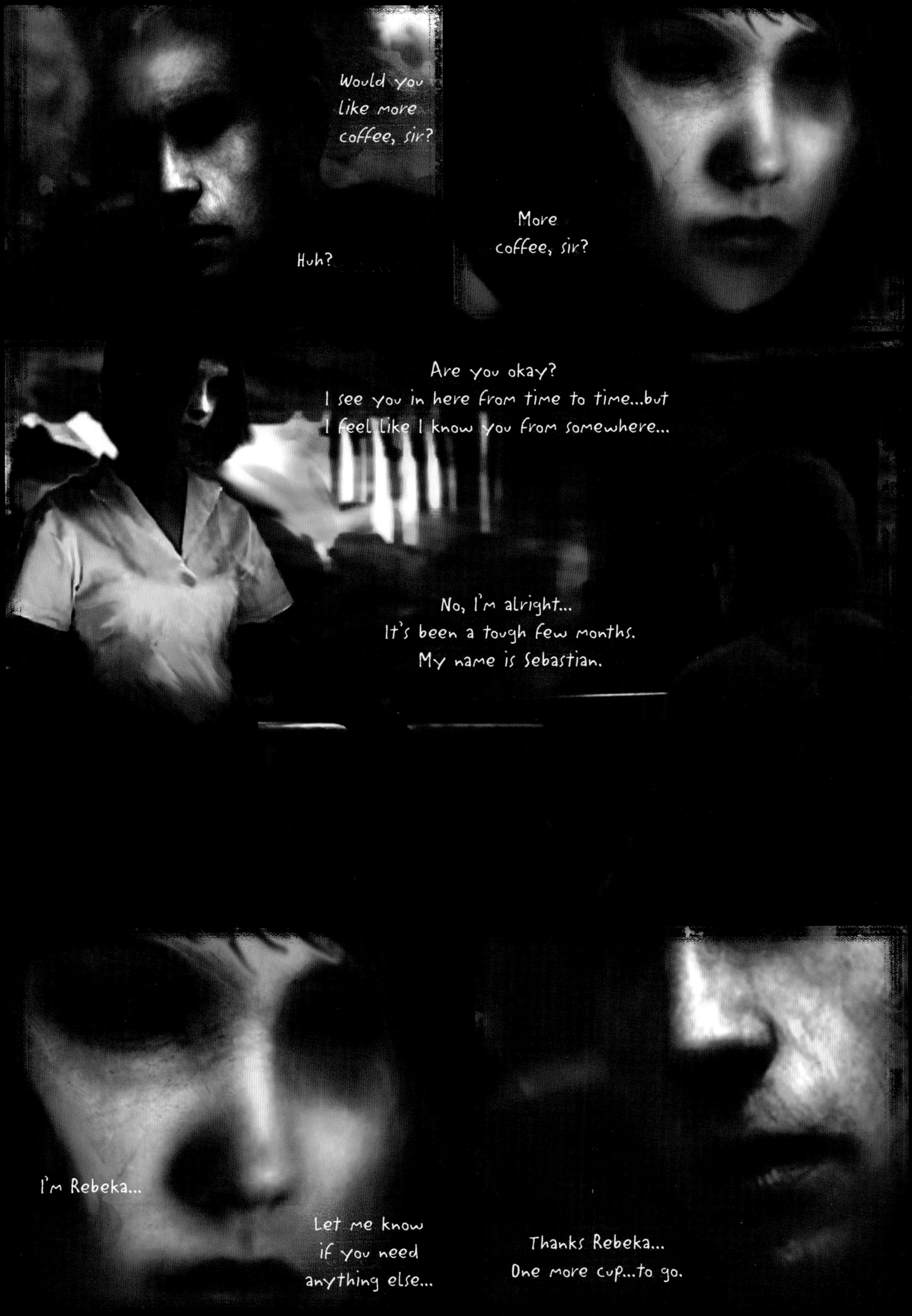

Would you like more coffee, sir?
Huh?
More coffee, sir?
Are you okay? I see you in here from time to time...but I feel like I know you from somewhere...
No, I'm alright... It's been a tough few months. My name is Sebastian.
I'm Rebeka...
Let me know if you need anything else...
Thanks Rebeka... One more cup...to go.

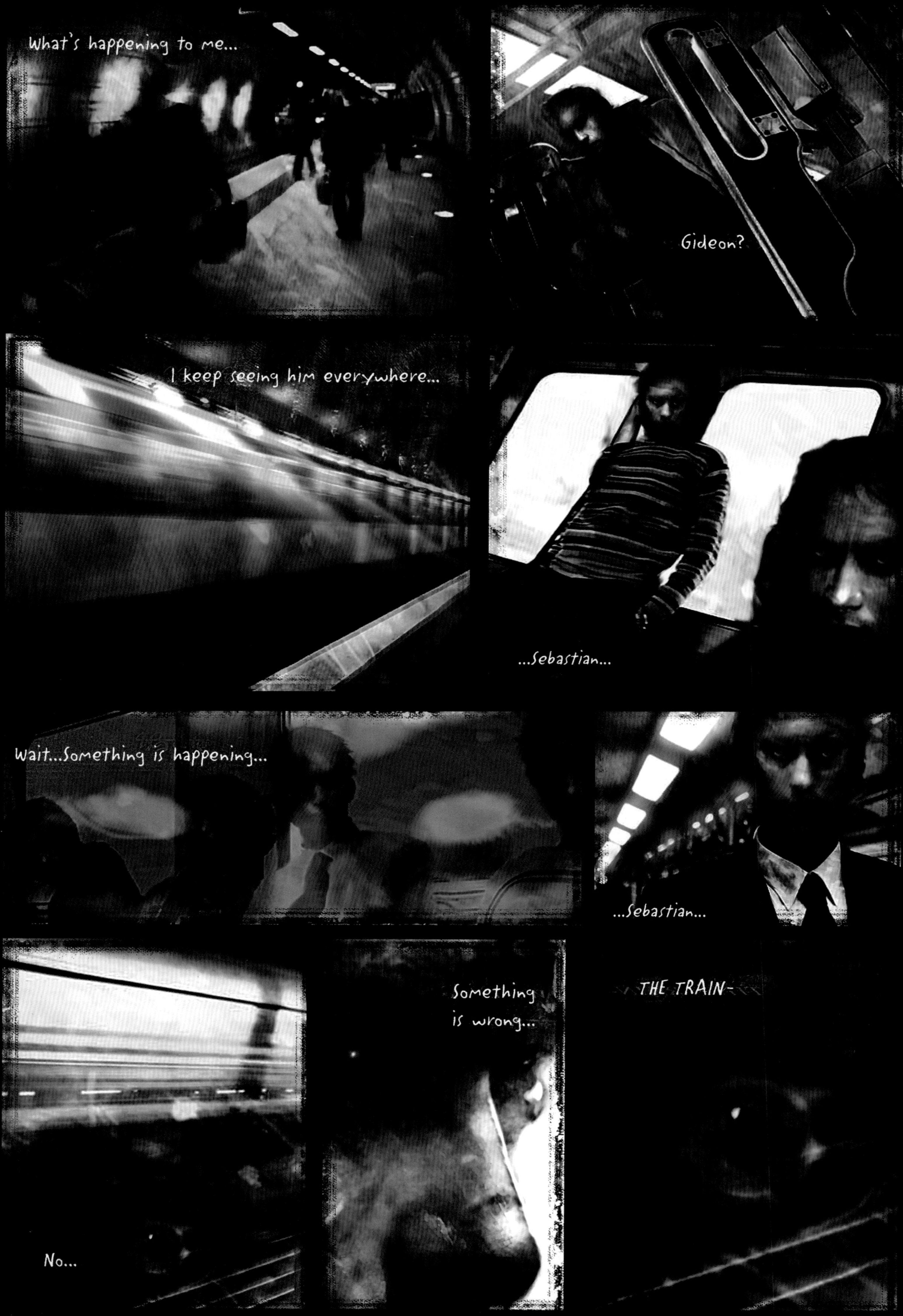
What's happening to me...
Gideon?
I keep seeing him everywhere...
...Sebastian...
Wait...Something is happening...
...Sebastian...
No...
Something is wrong...
THE TRAIN-

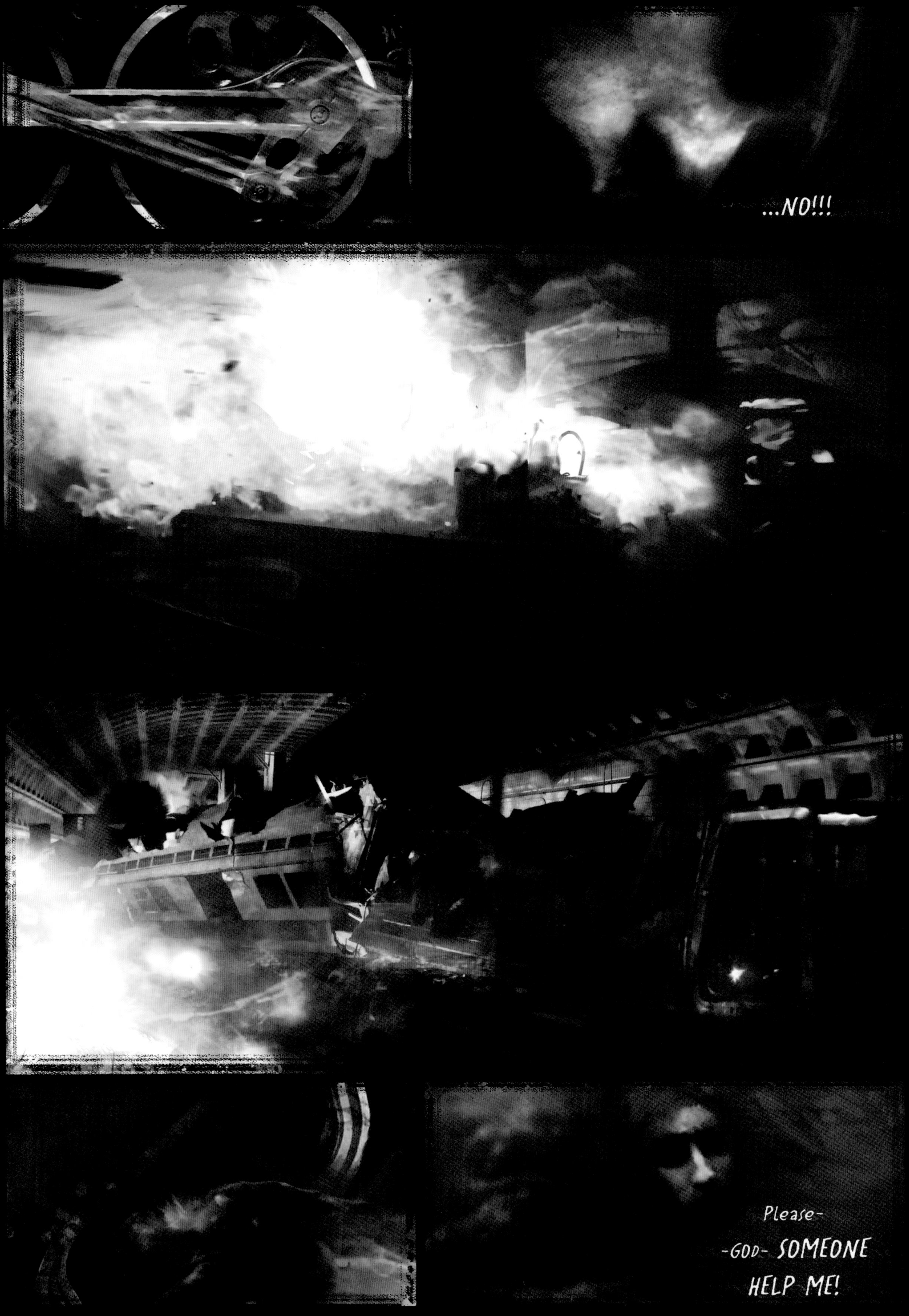
...NO!!!
Please-
-GOD- SOMEONE
HELP ME!

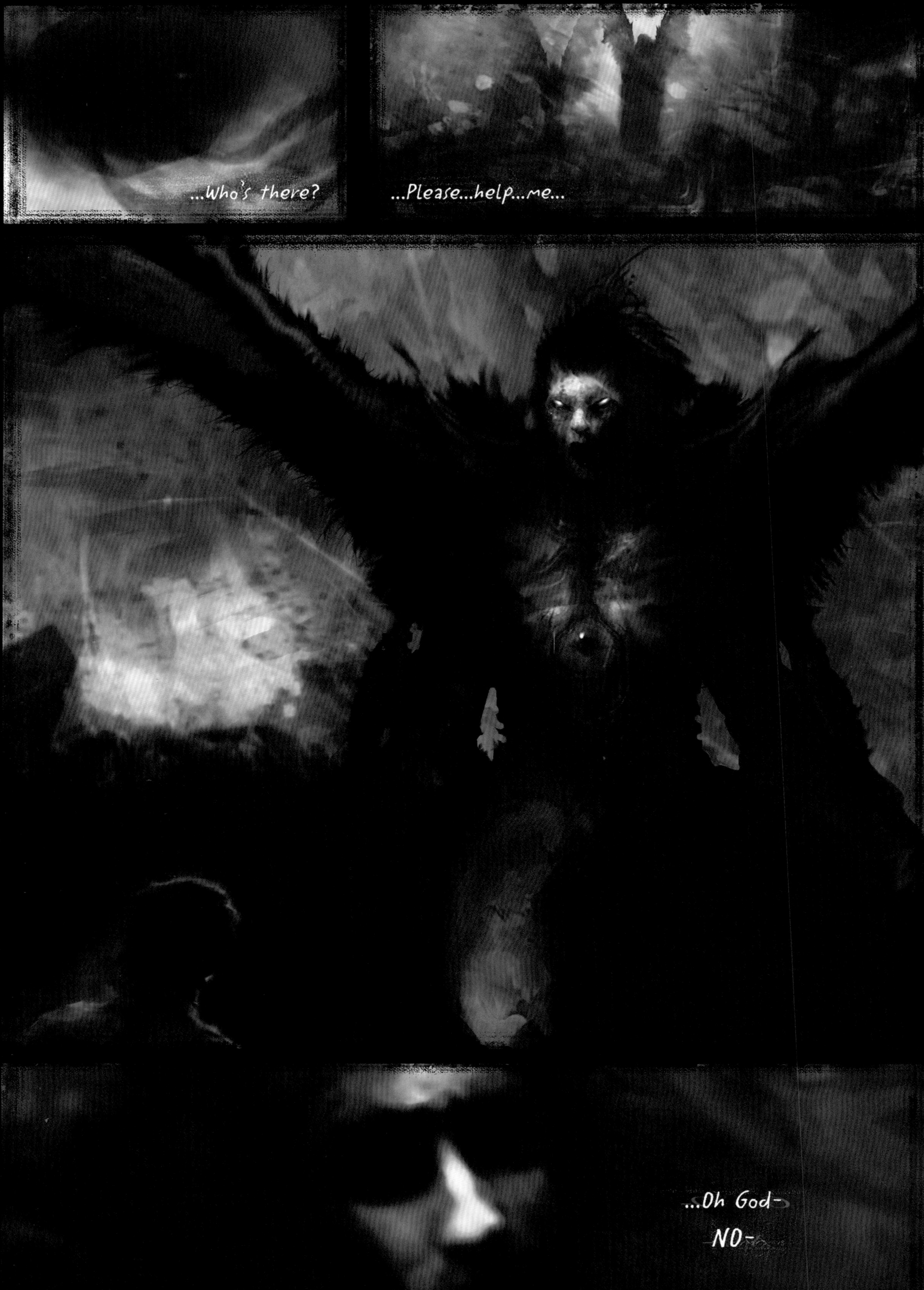
...Who's there?
...Please...help...me...
...Oh God-
NO-

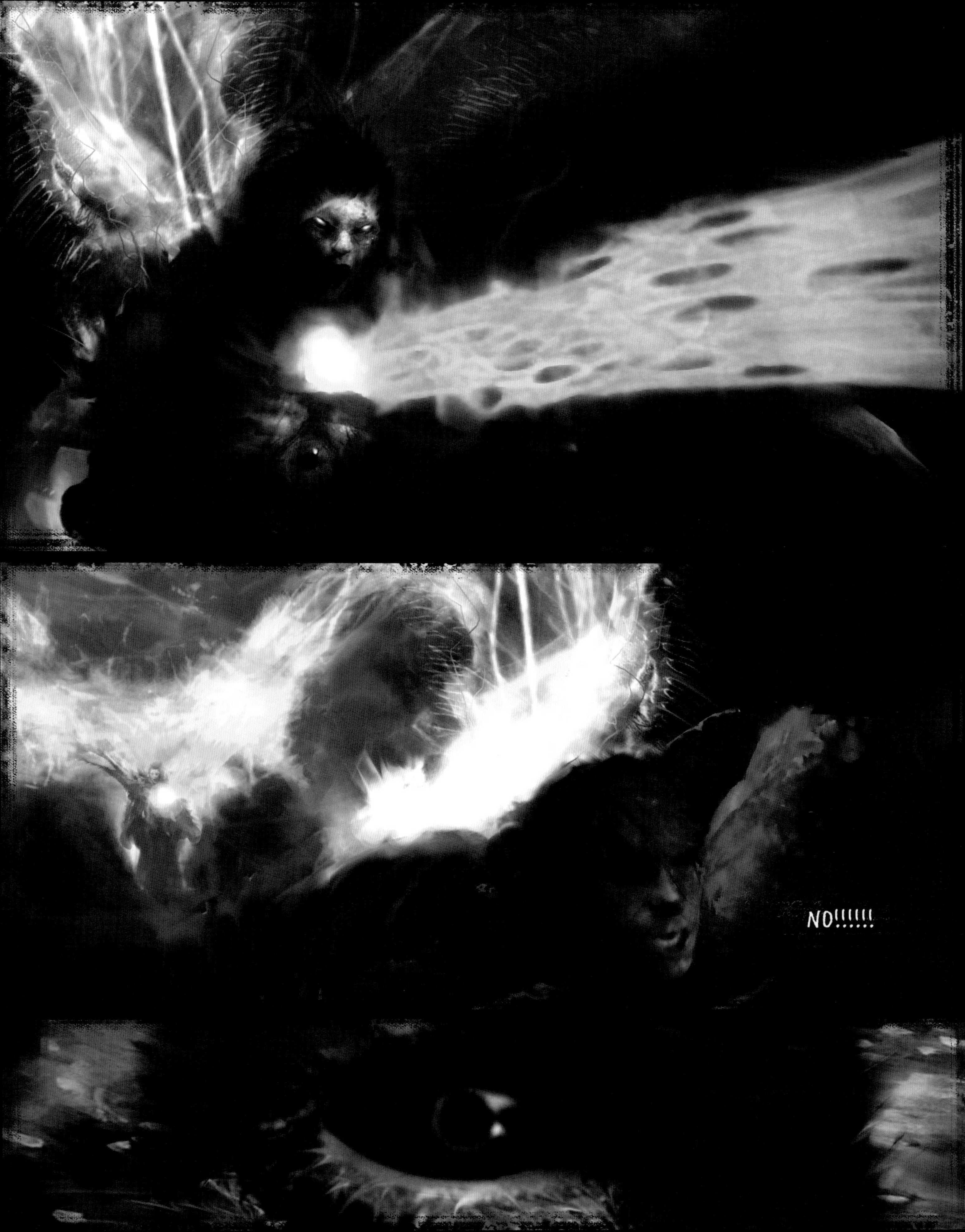
NO!!!!!!

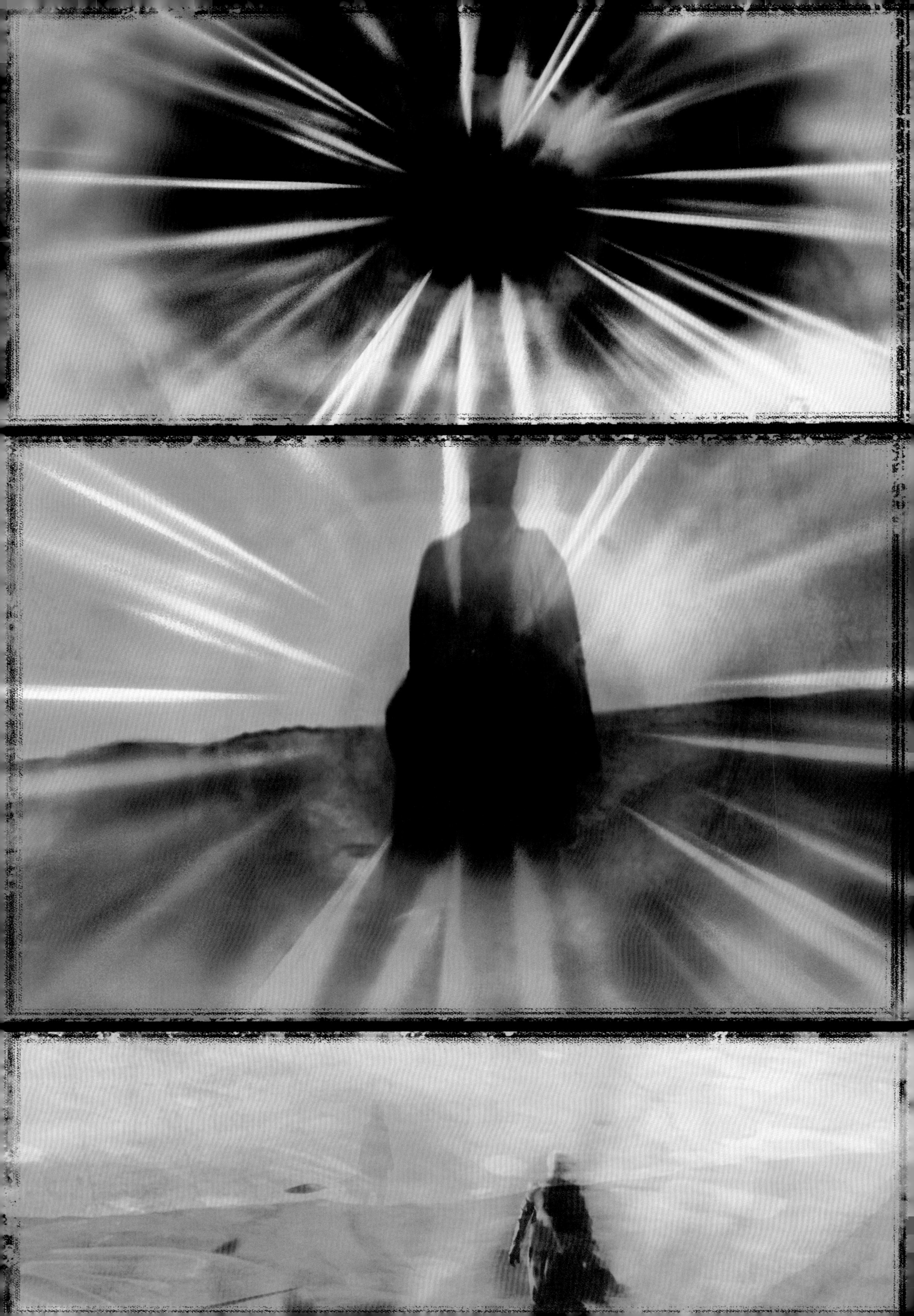

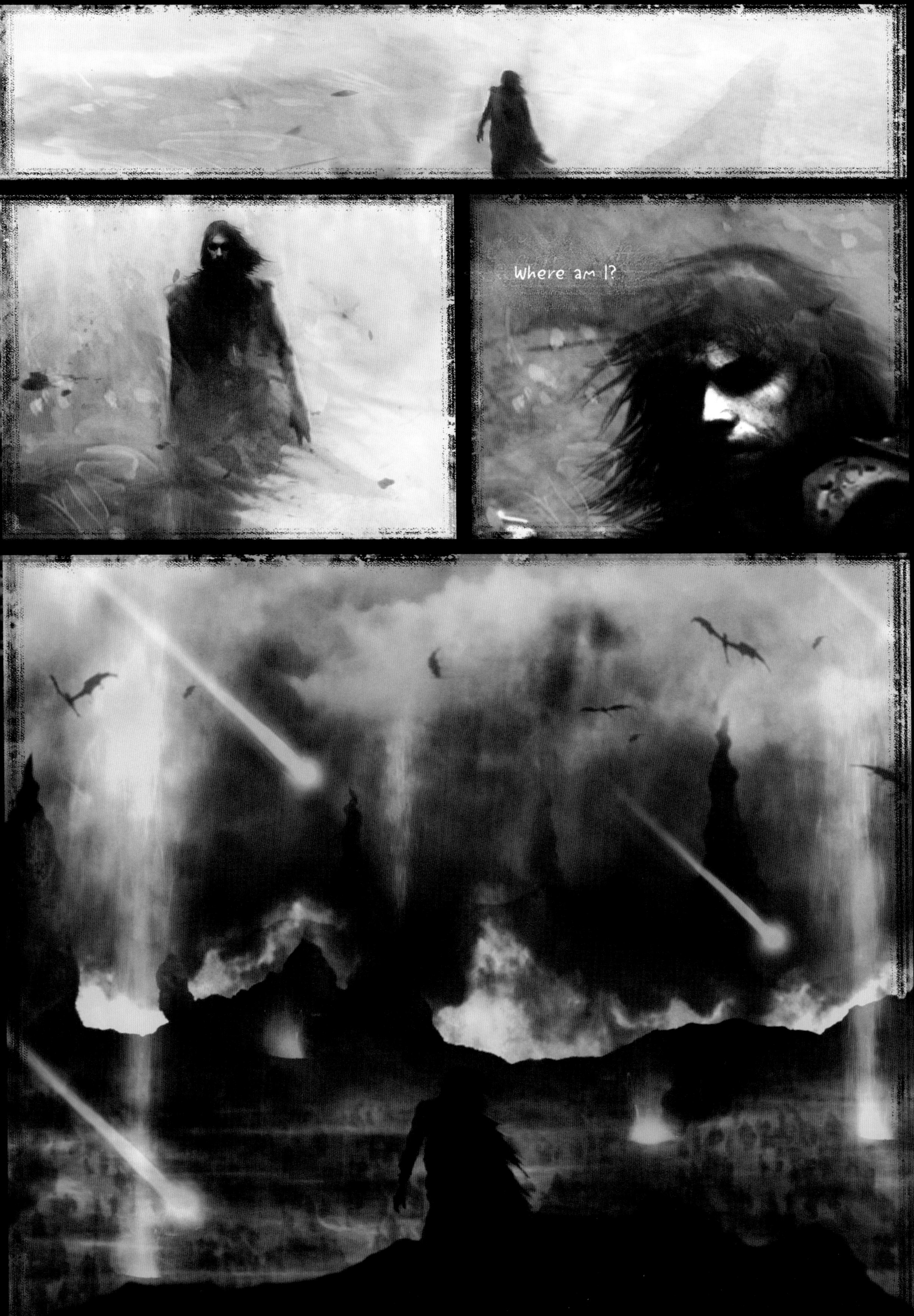
Where am I?

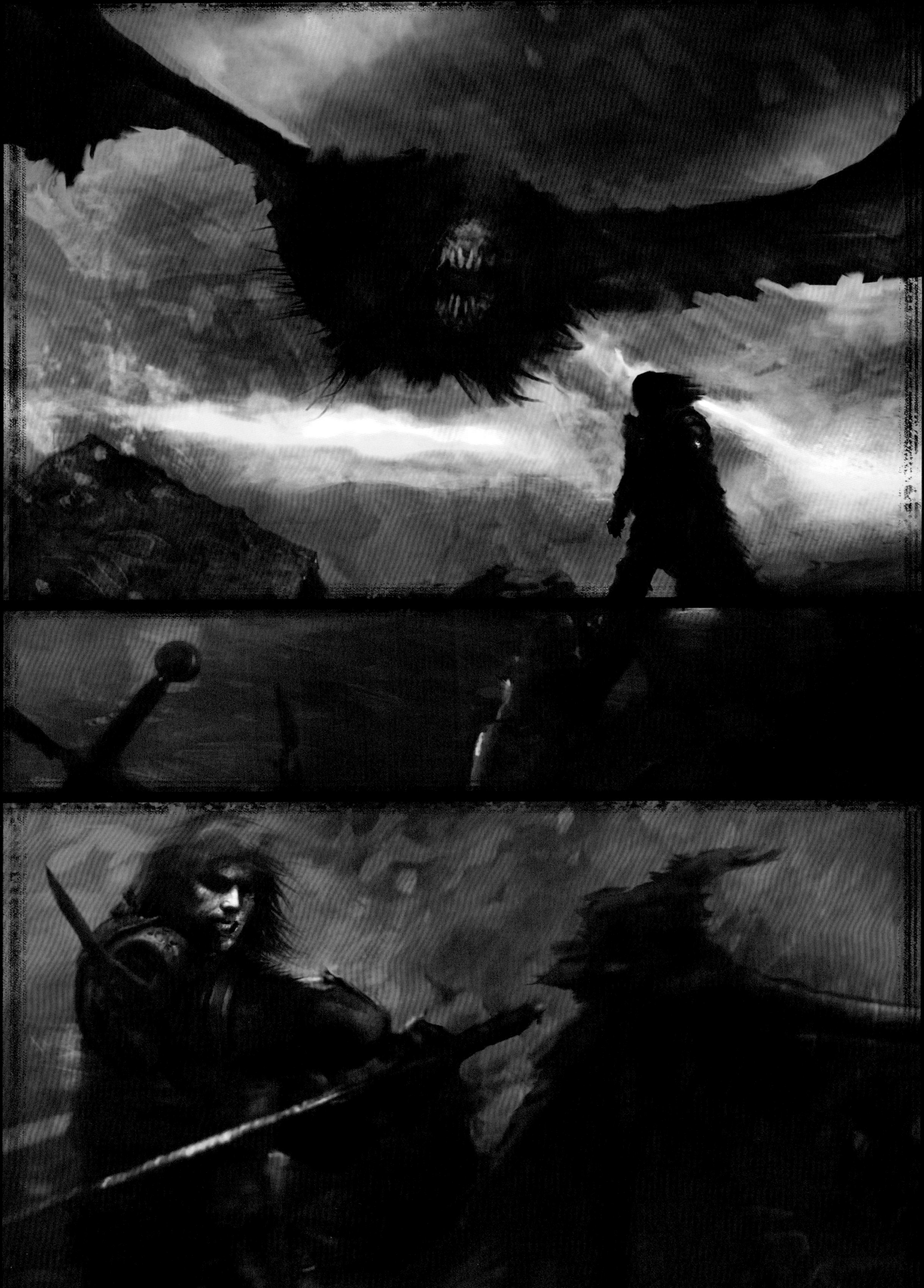

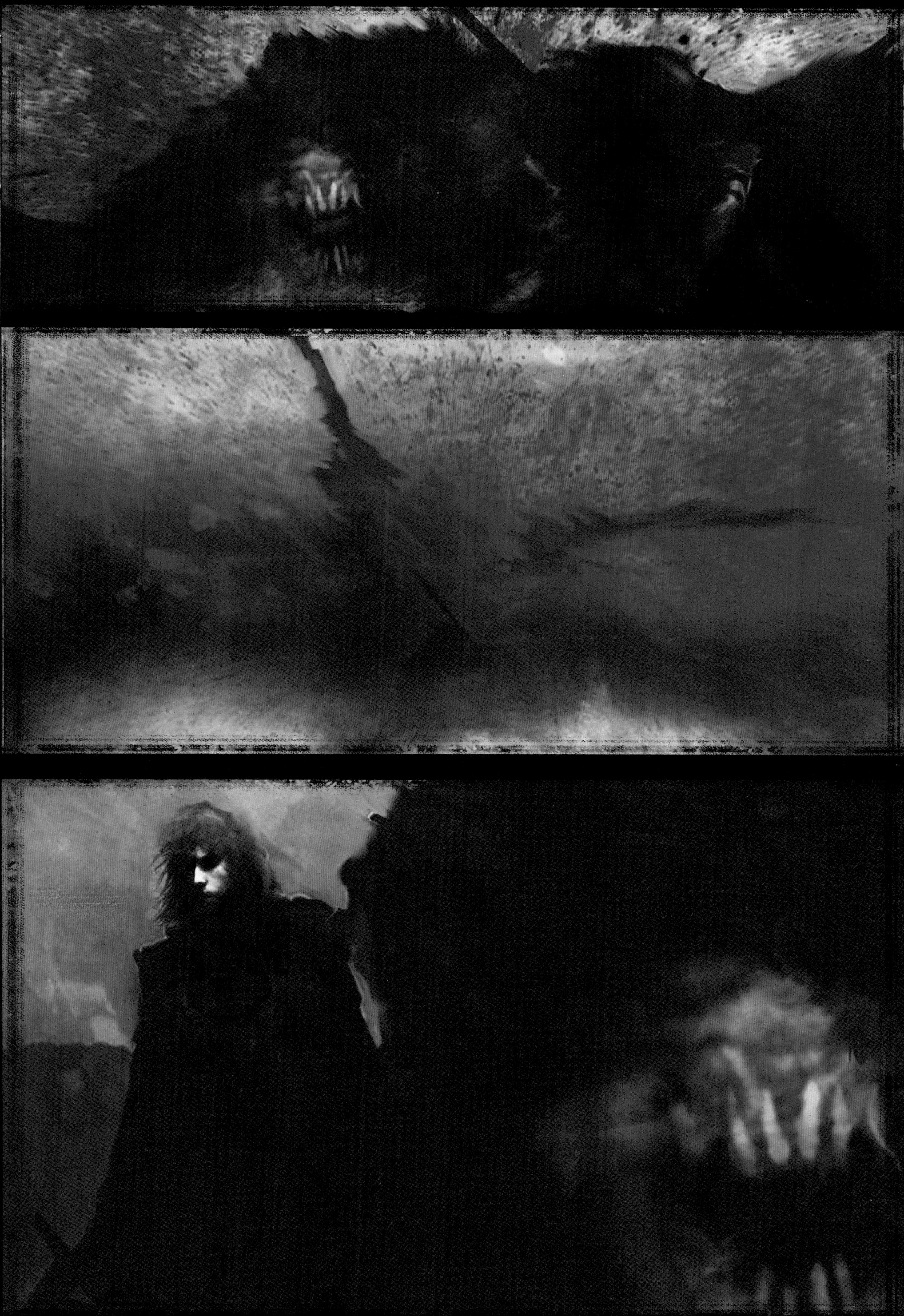

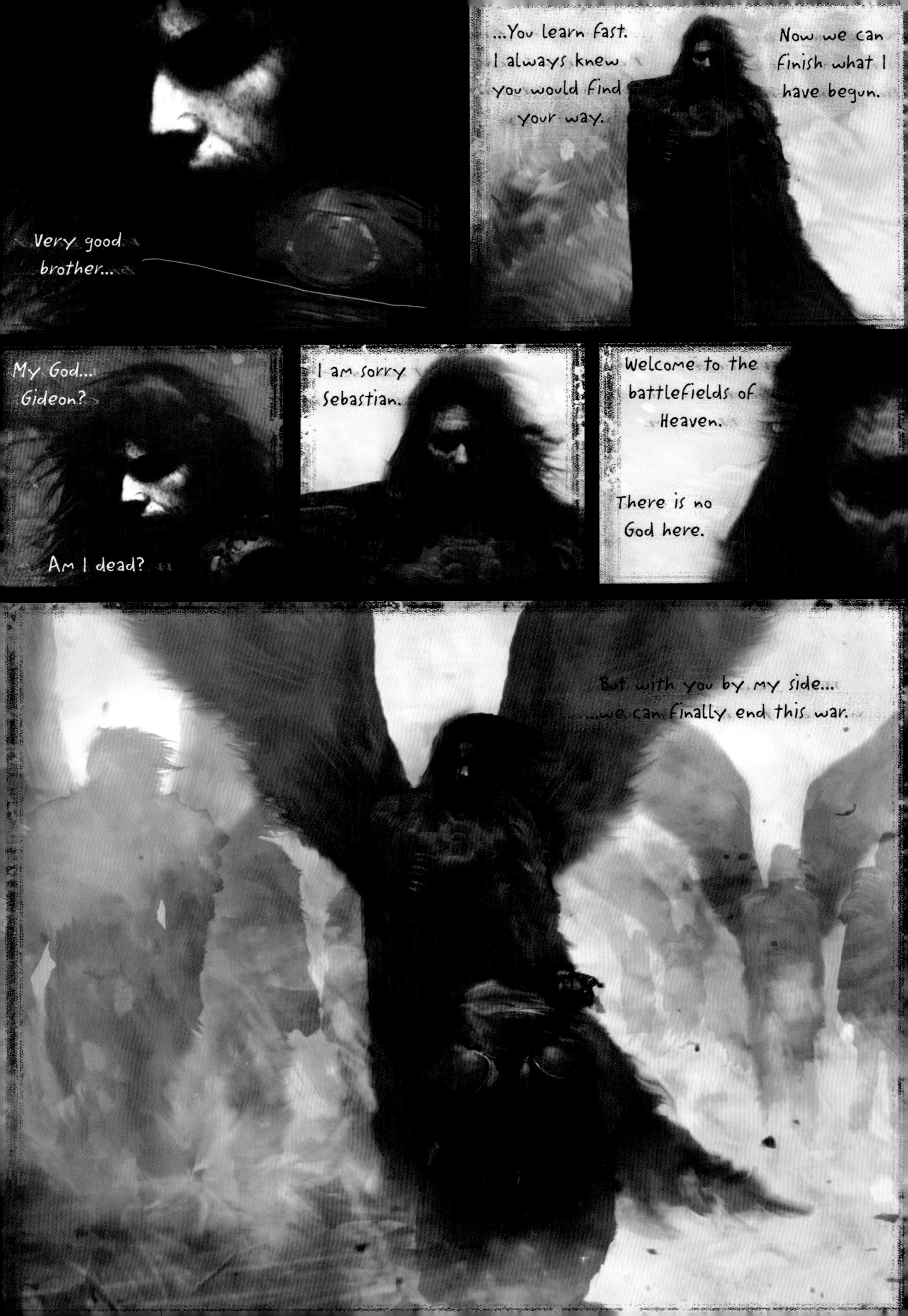
Very good brother...
...You learn fast. I always knew you would find your way.
Now we can finish what I have begun.
My God... Gideon?
Am I dead?
I am sorry Sebastian.
Welcome to the battlefields of Heaven.
There is no God here.
But with you by my side...
...we can finally end this war.

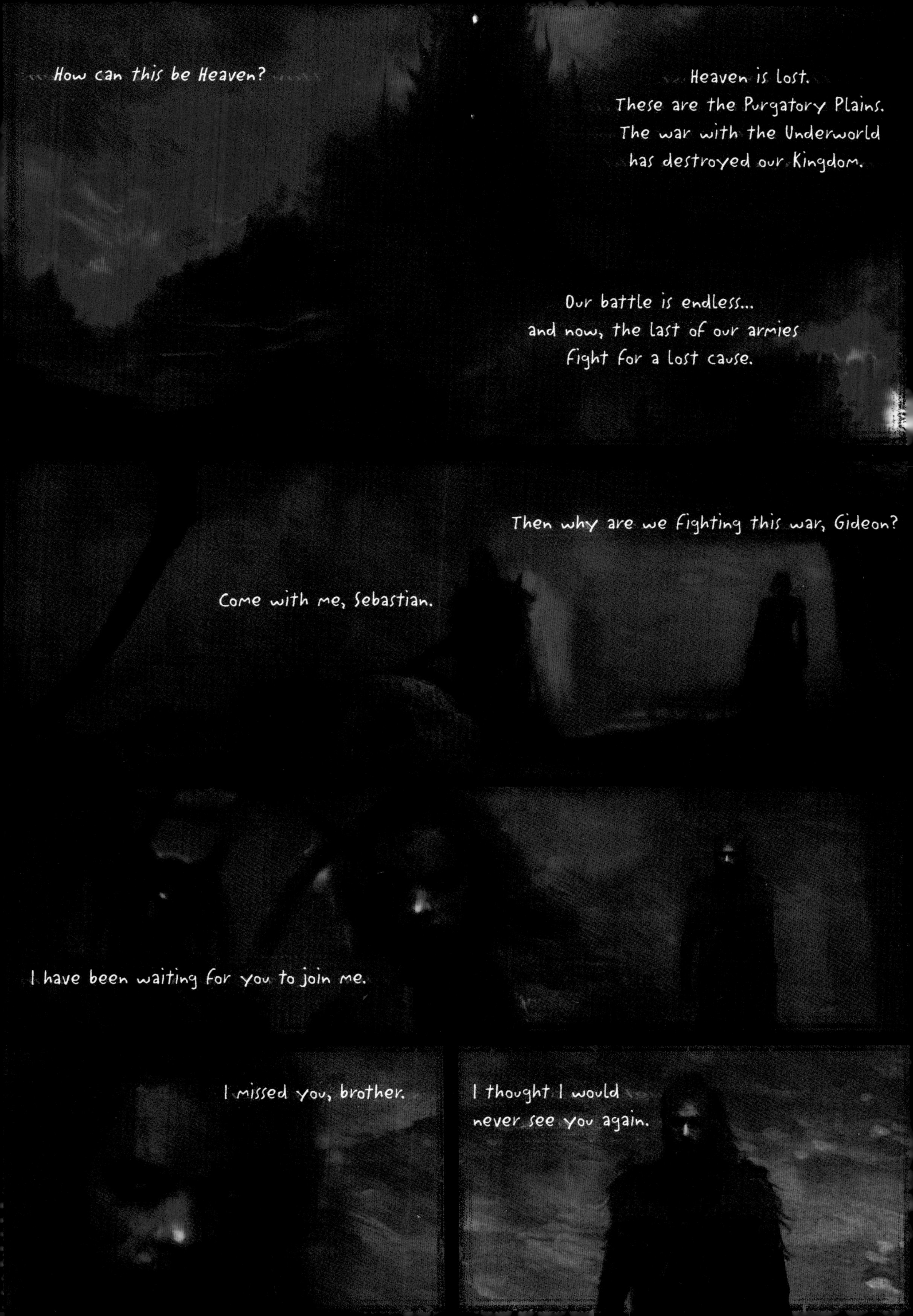
How can this be Heaven?
Heaven is lost. These are the Purgatory Plains. The war with the Underworld has destroyed our Kingdom.
Our battle is endless... and now, the last of our armies fight for a lost cause.
Then why are we fighting this war, Gideon?
Come with me, Sebastian.
I have been waiting for you to join me.
I missed you, brother.
I thought I would never see you again.

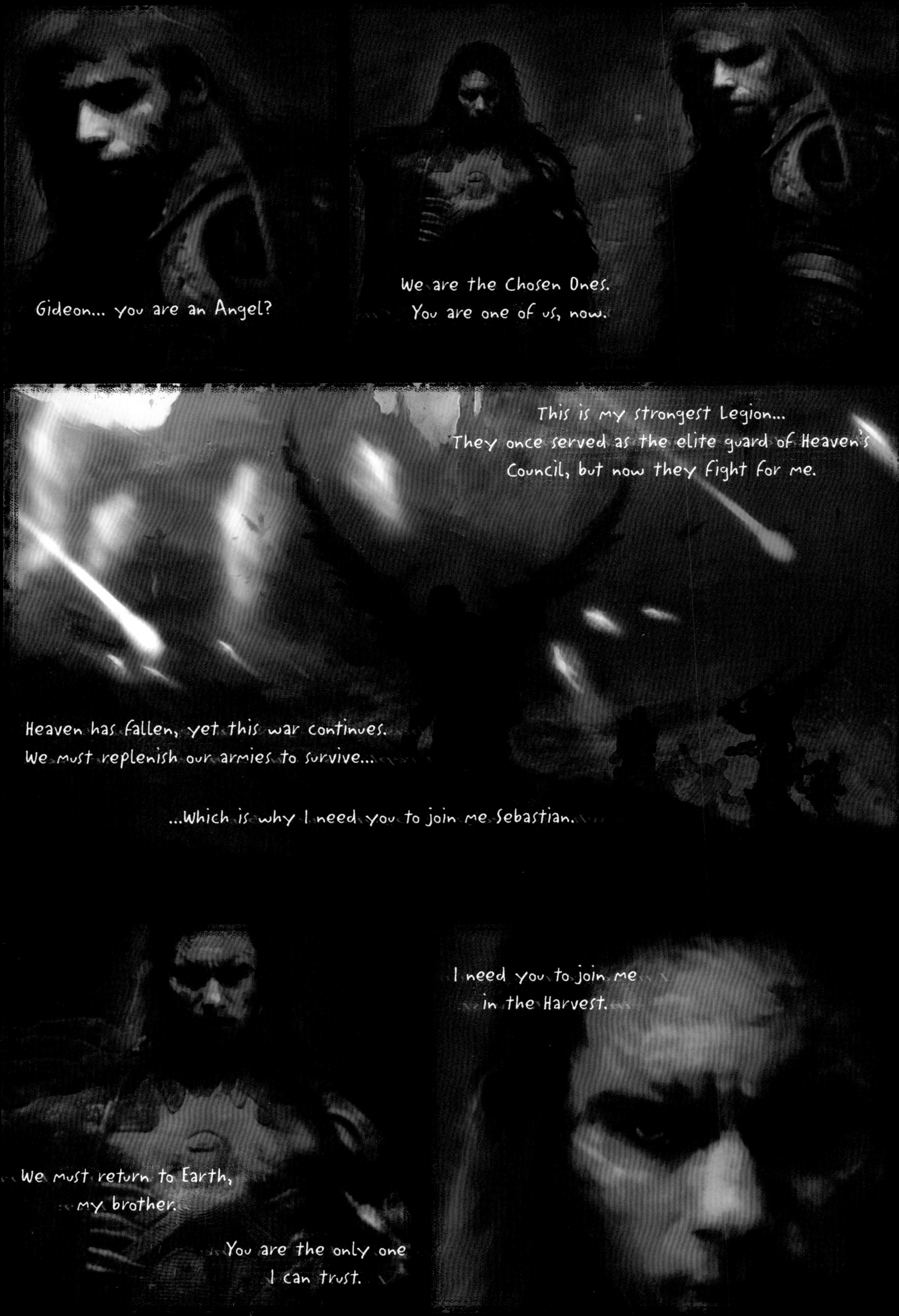

Gideon... you are an Angel?
We are the Chosen Ones.
You are one of us, now.
This is my strongest Legion...
They once served as the elite guard of Heaven's Council, but now they fight for me.
Heaven has fallen, yet this war continues.
We must replenish our armies to survive...
...Which is why I need you to join me Sebastian.
I need you to join me in the Harvest.
We must return to Earth, my brother.
You are the only one I can trust.

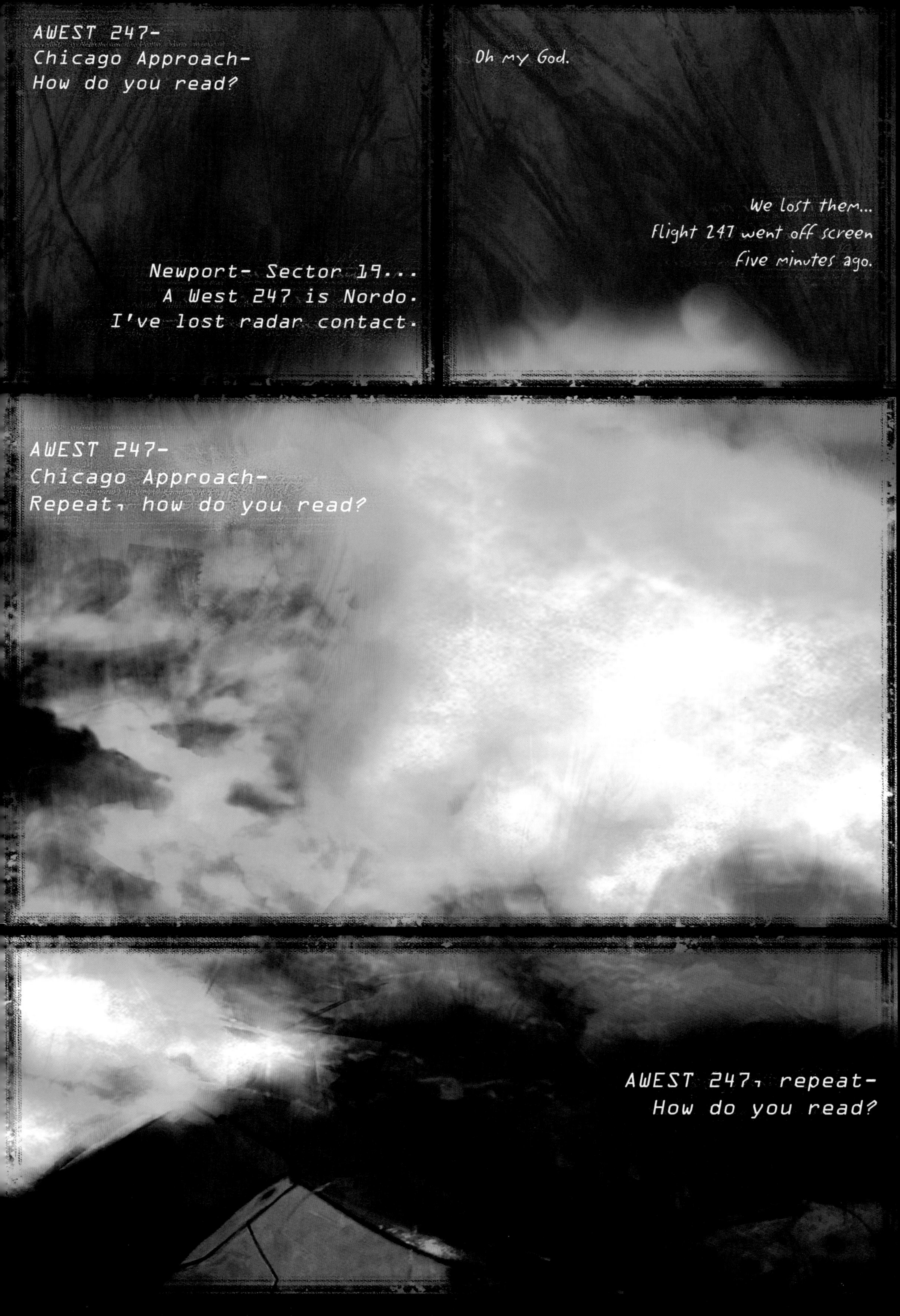
AWEST 247-
Chicago Approach-
How do you read?
Newport- Sector 19...
A West 247 is Nordo.
I've lost radar contact.
Oh my God.
We lost them...
Flight 247 went off screen
five minutes ago.
AWEST 247-
Chicago Approach-
Repeat, how do you read?
AWEST 247, repeat-
How do you read?

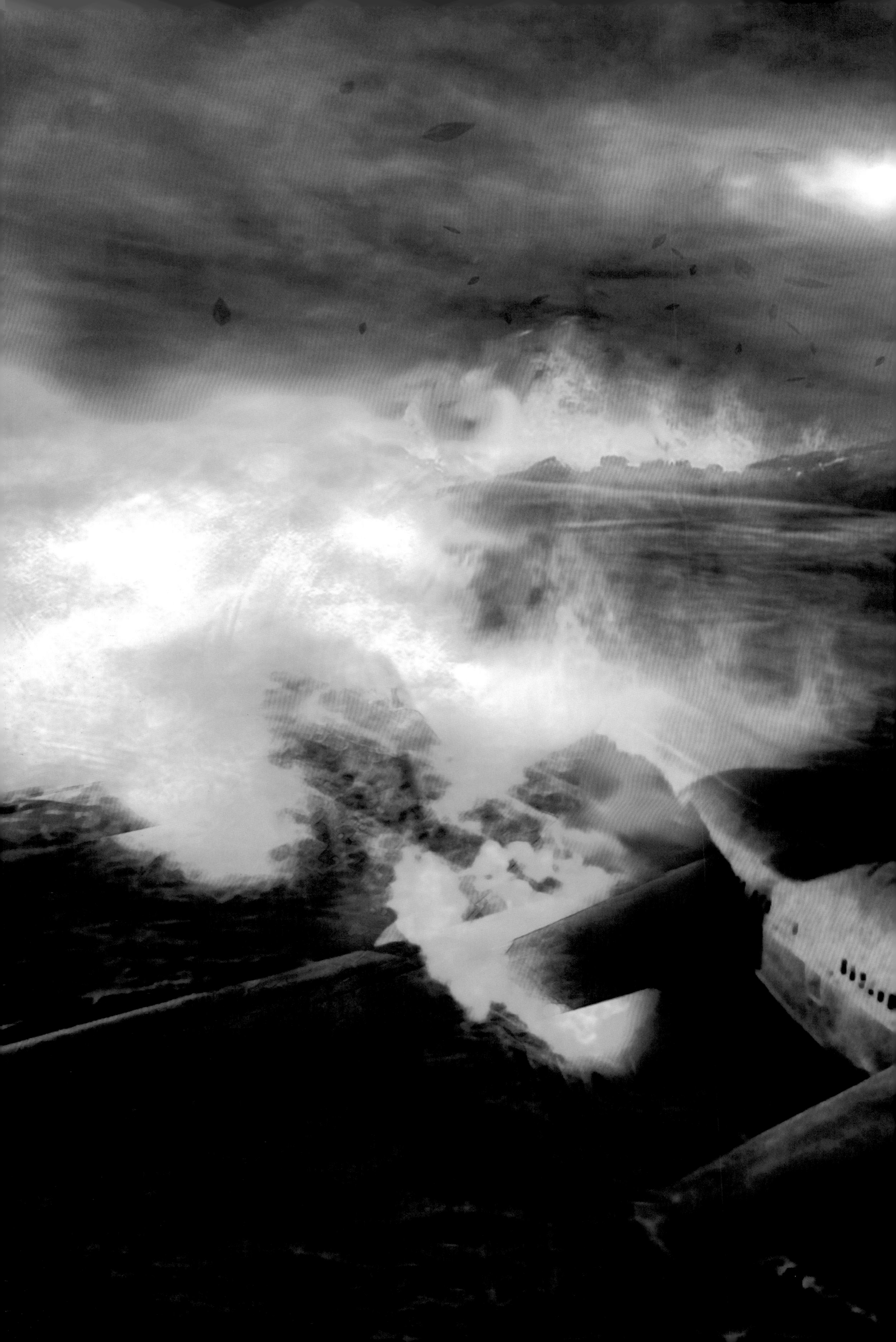

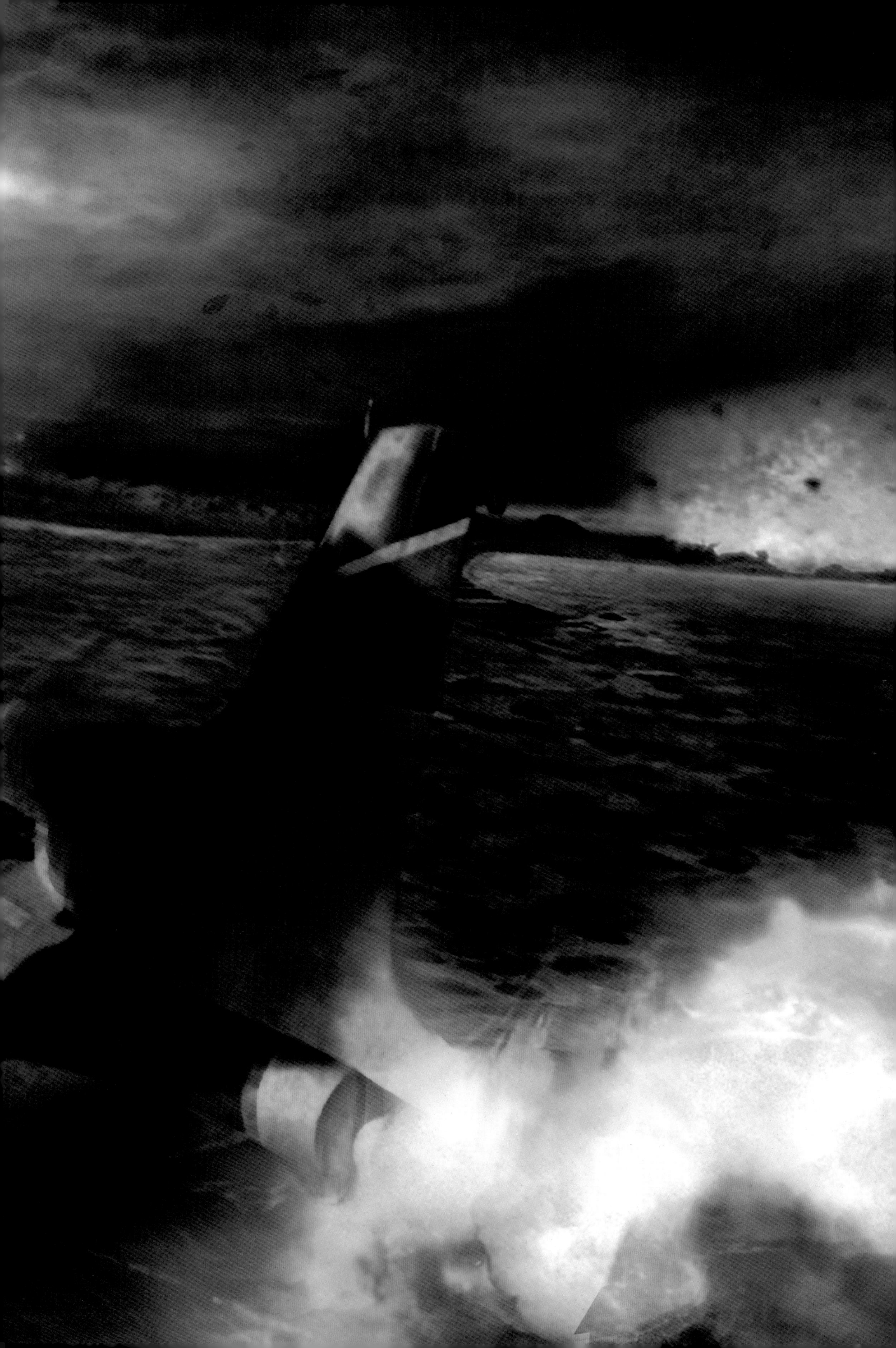

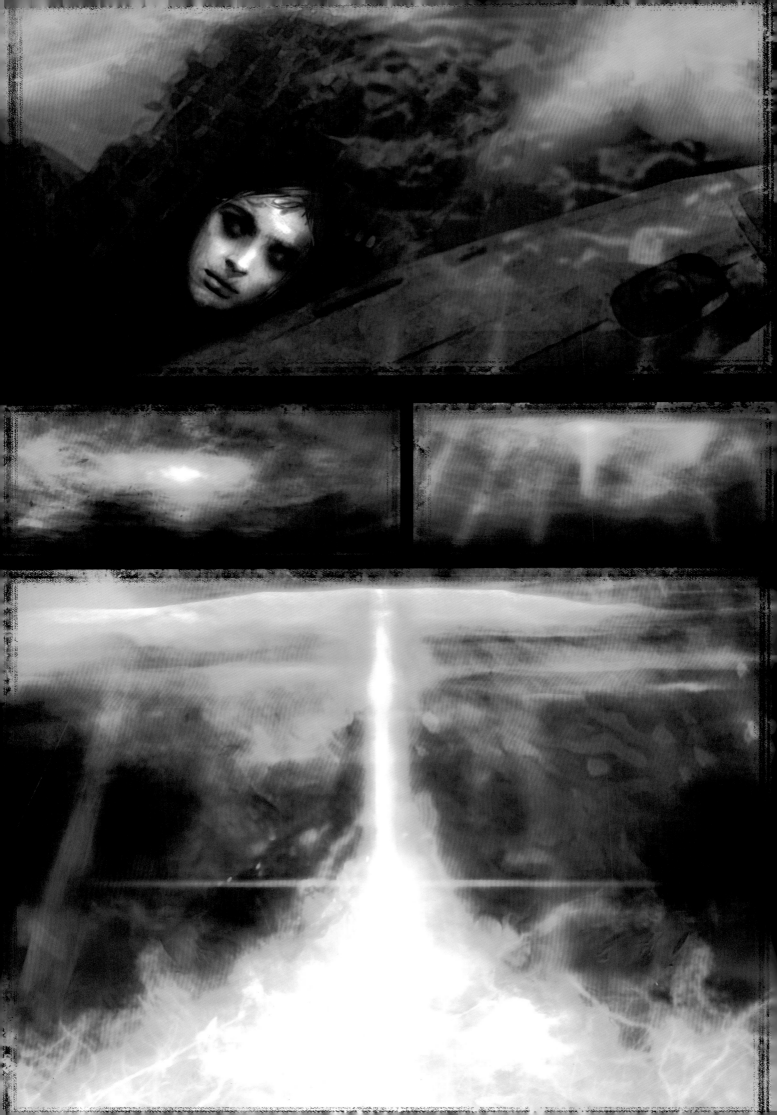

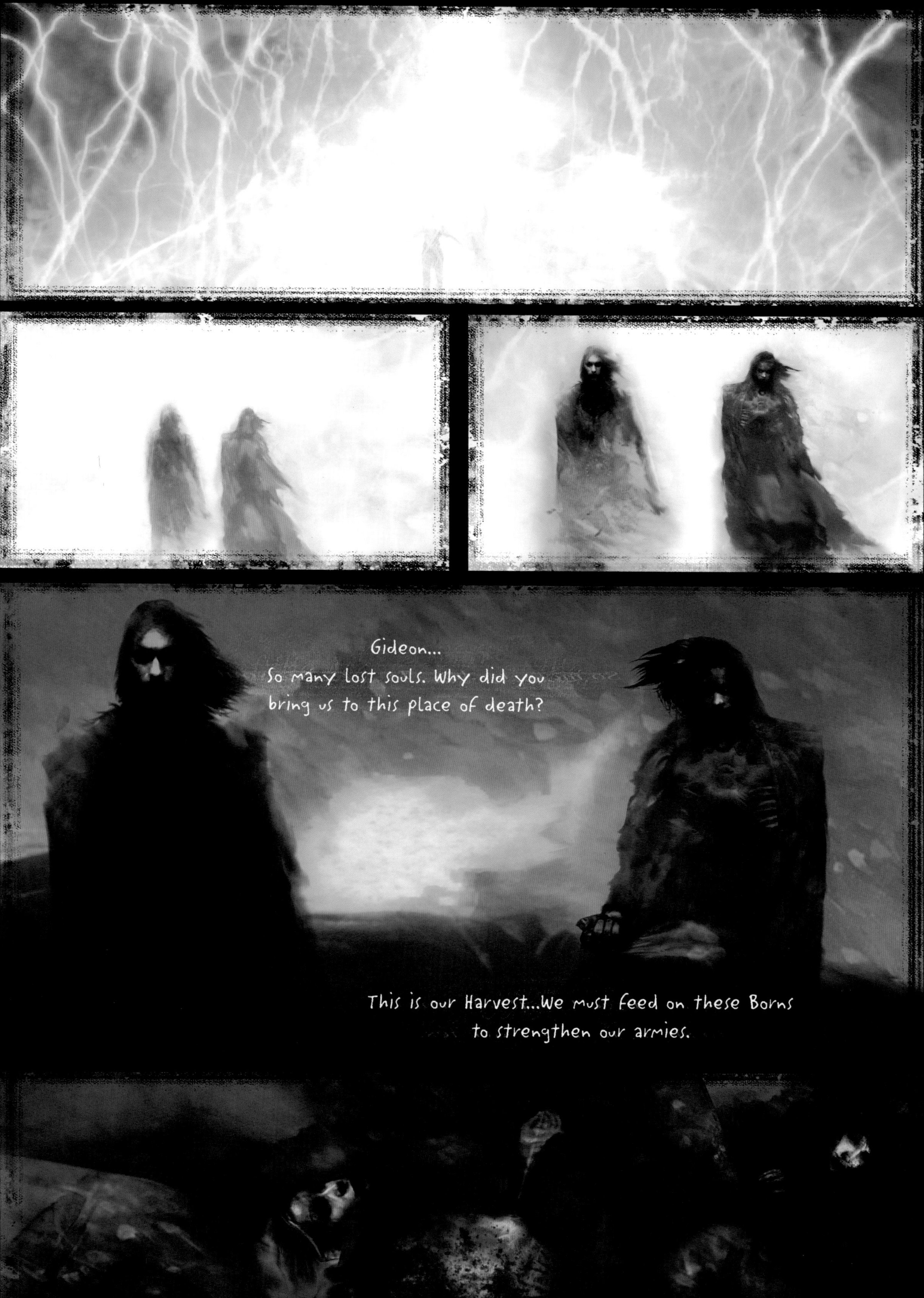
Gideon...
So many lost souls. Why did you bring us to this place of death?
This is our Harvest...We must feed on these Borns to strengthen our armies.

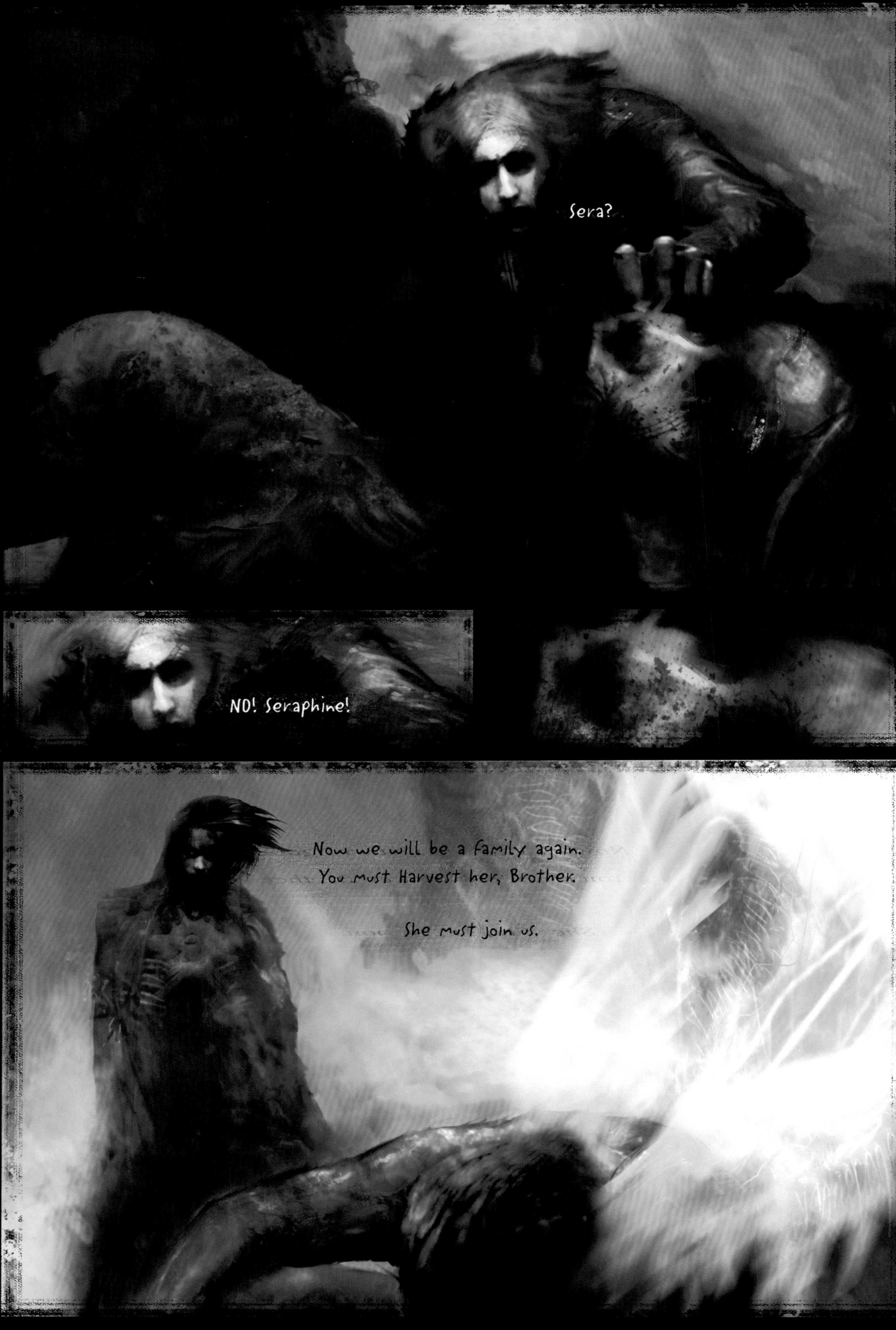
Sera?
NO! Seraphine!
Now we will be a family again.
You must Harvest her, Brother.
She must join us.

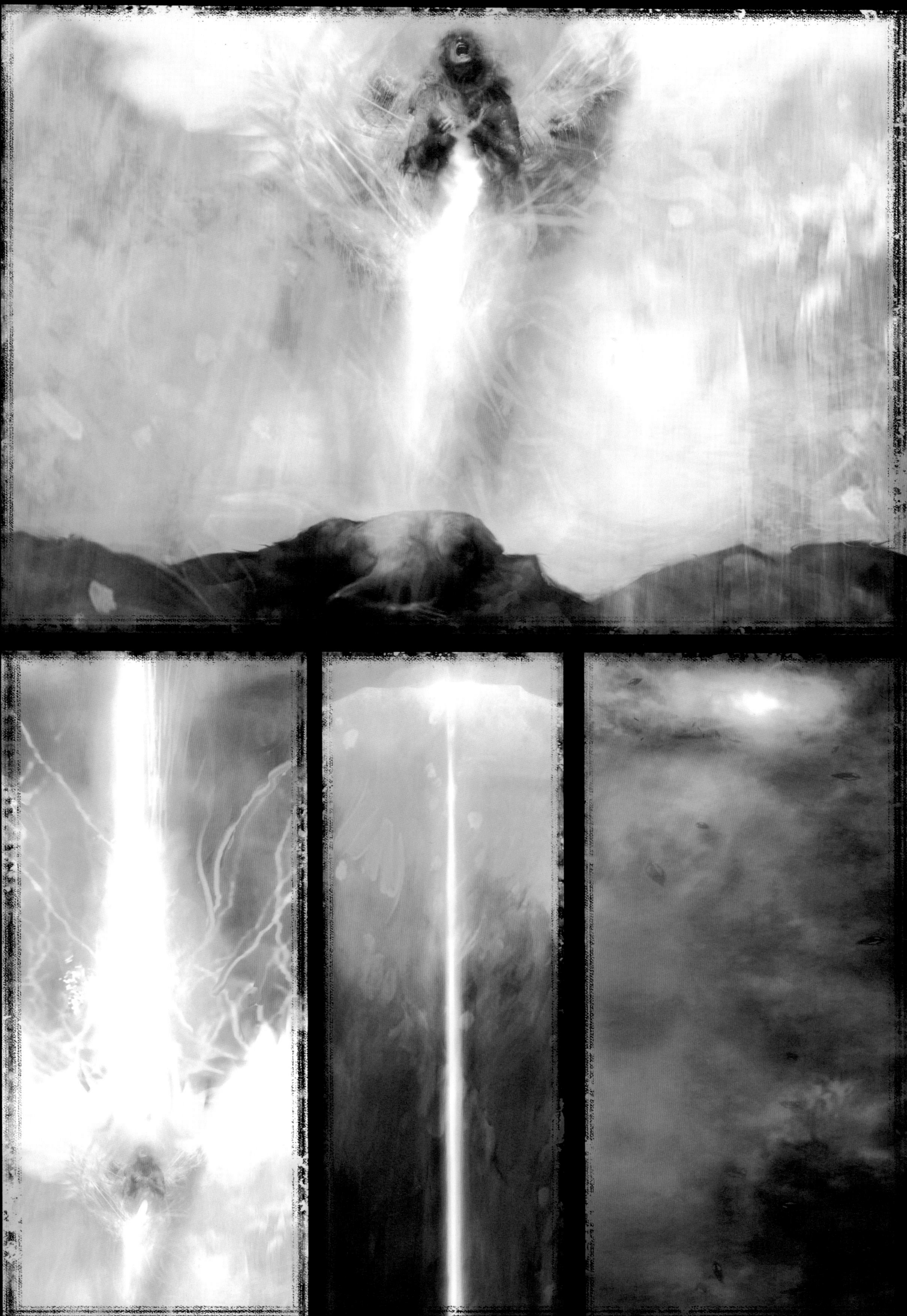

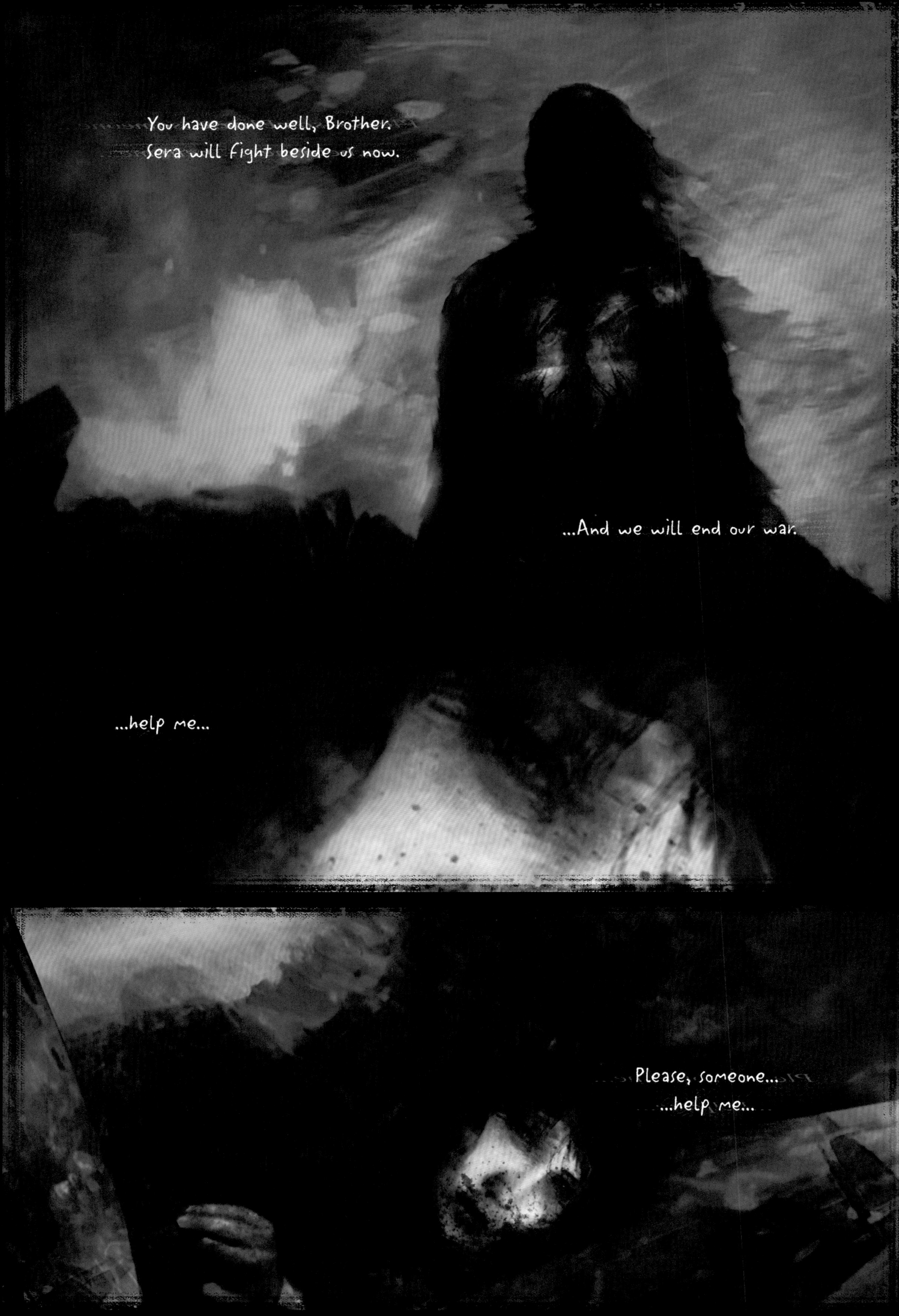
You have done well, Brother.
Sera will fight beside us now.
...And we will end our war.
...help me...
Please, someone...
...help me...

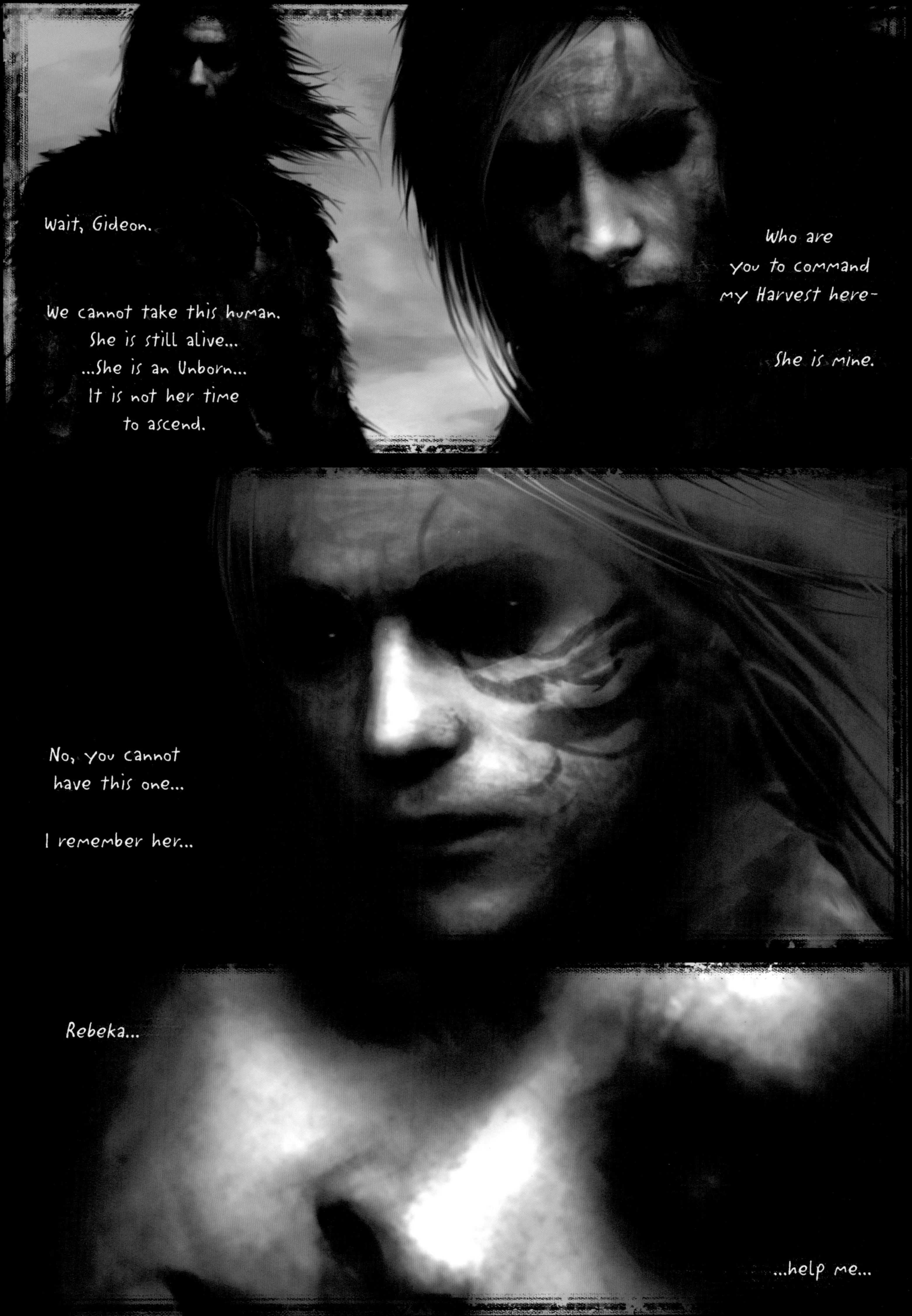
Wait, Gideon.
We cannot take this human. She is still alive... ...She is an Unborn... It is not her time to ascend.
Who are you to command my Harvest here-
She is mine.
No, you cannot have this one...
I remember her...
Rebeka...
...help me...

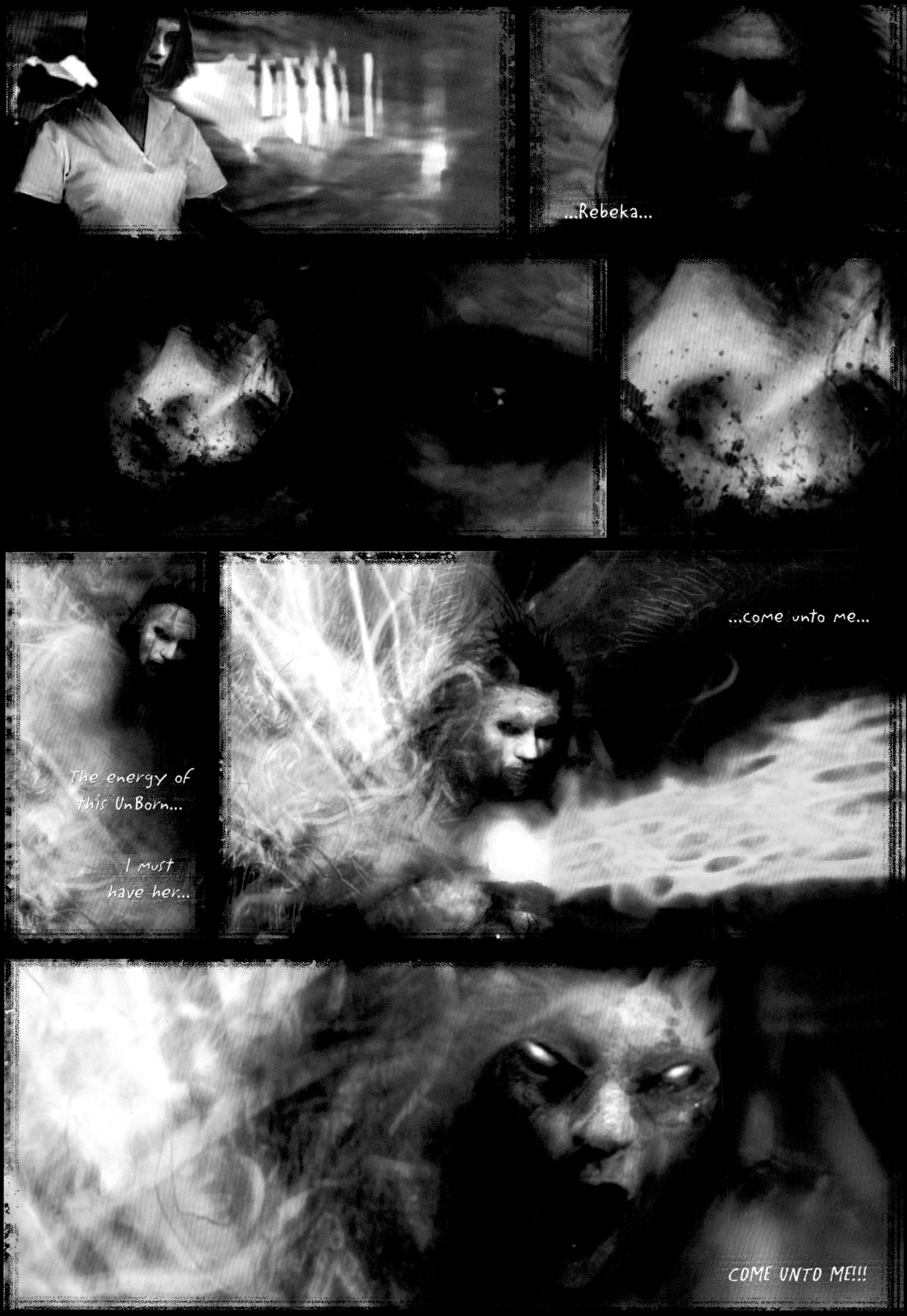
...Rebeka...
...come unto me...
The energy of this UnBorn...
I must have her...
COME UNTO ME!!!

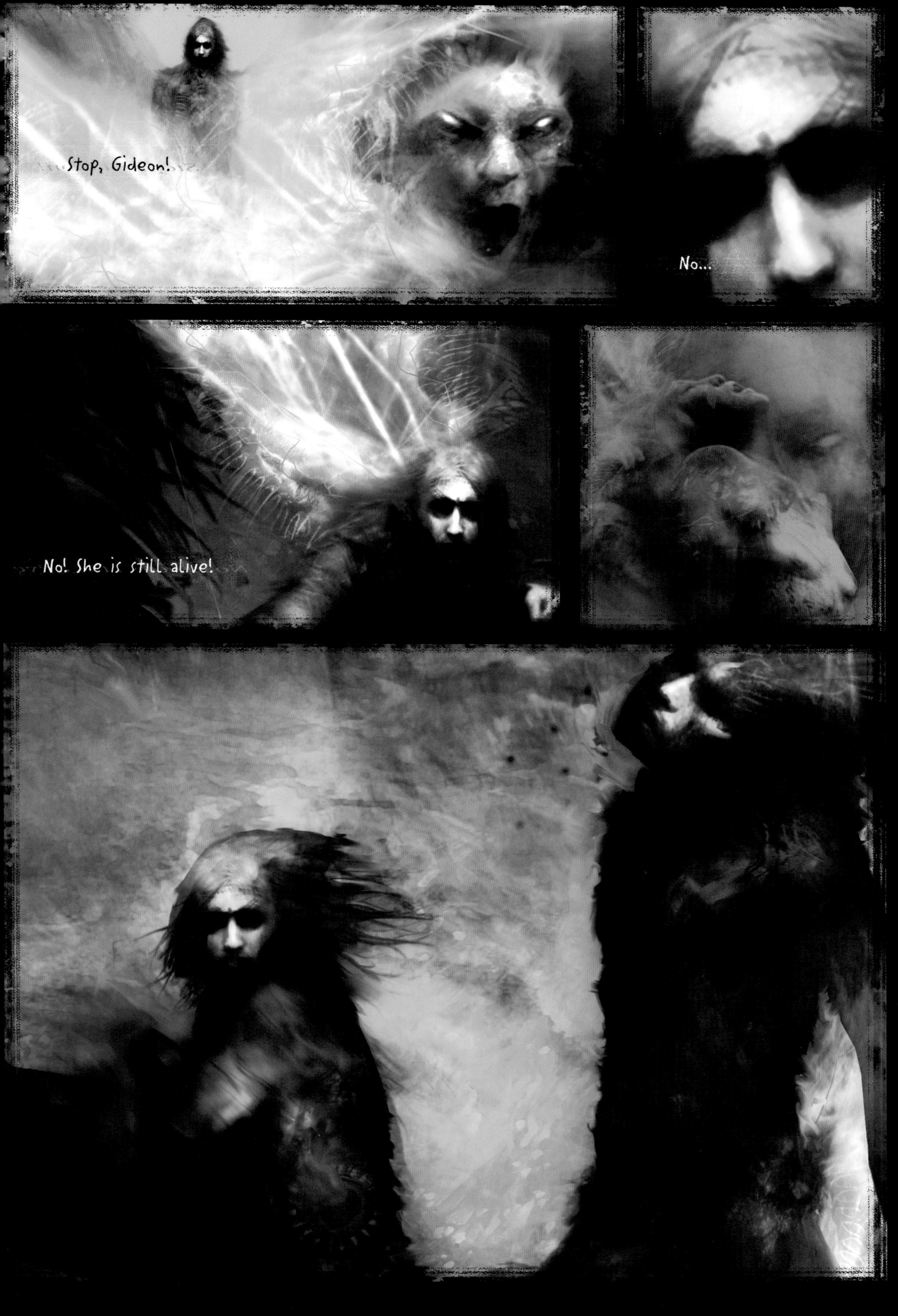
Stop, Gideon!
No...
No! She is still alive!

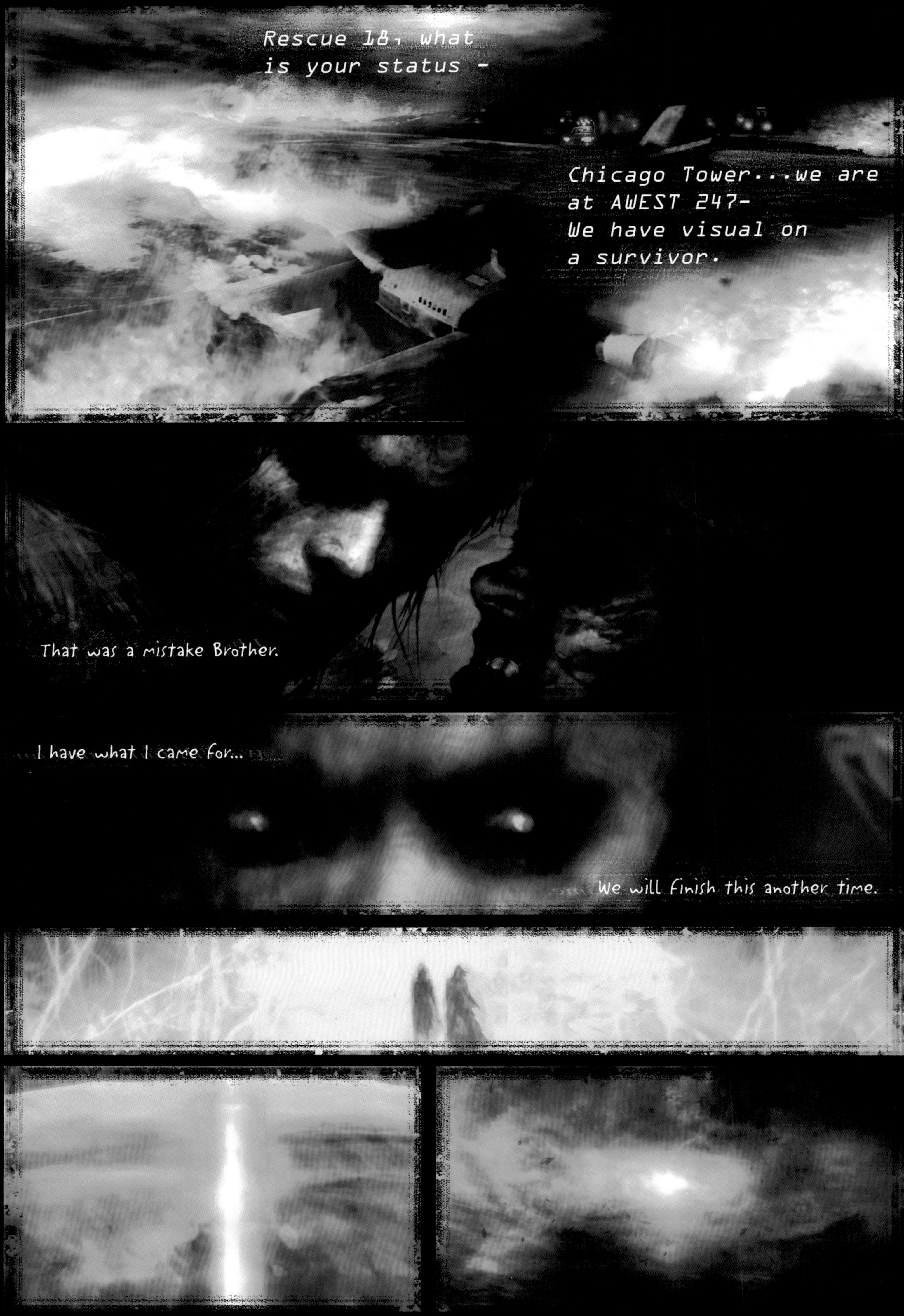
Rescue 18, what is your status -
Chicago Tower...we are at AWEST 247-
We have visual on a survivor.
That was a mistake Brother.
I have what I came for...
We will finish this another time.

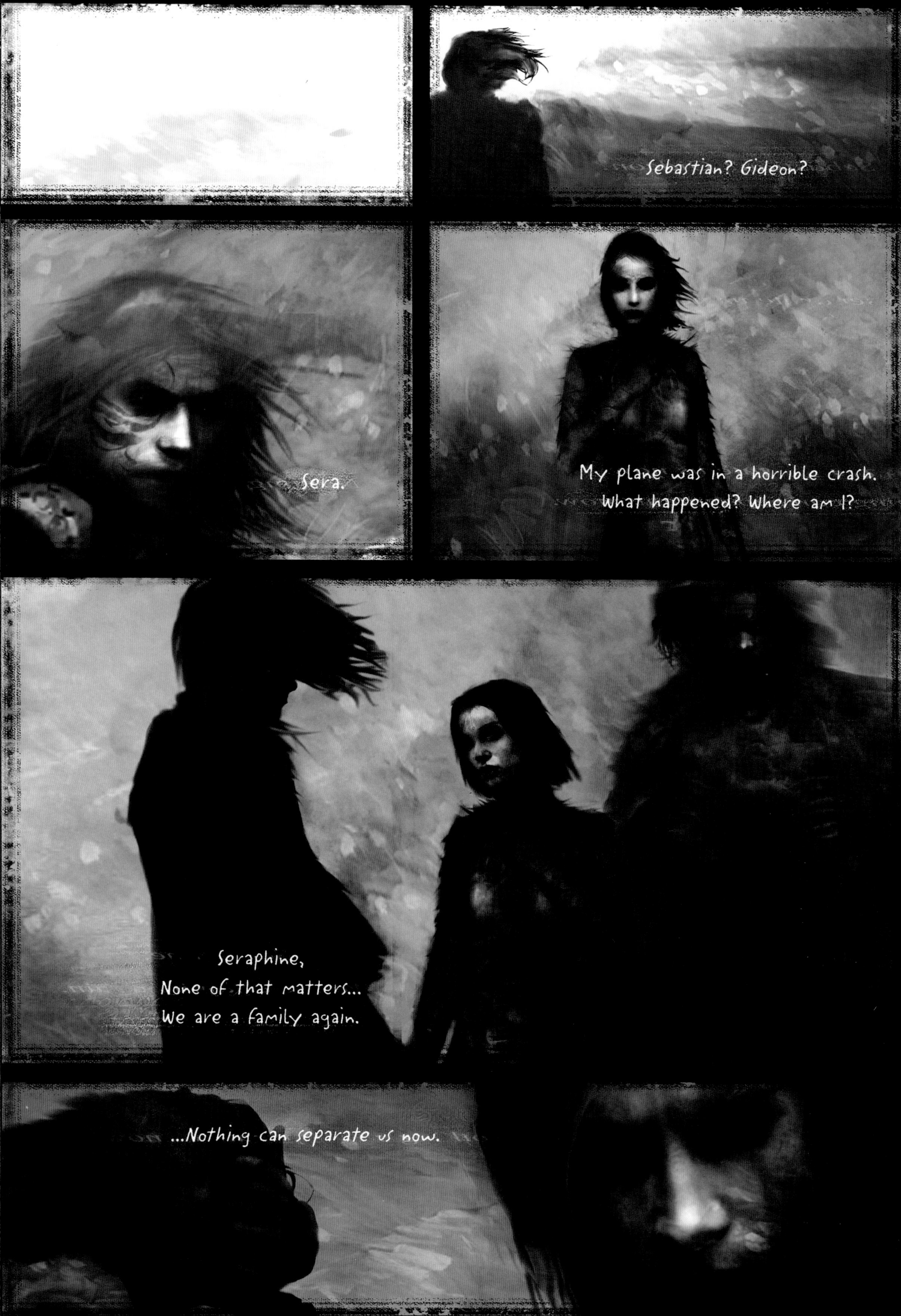
Sebastian? Gideon?
Sera.
My plane was in a horrible crash.
What happened? Where am I?
Seraphine,
None of that matters...
We are a family again.
...Nothing can separate us now.

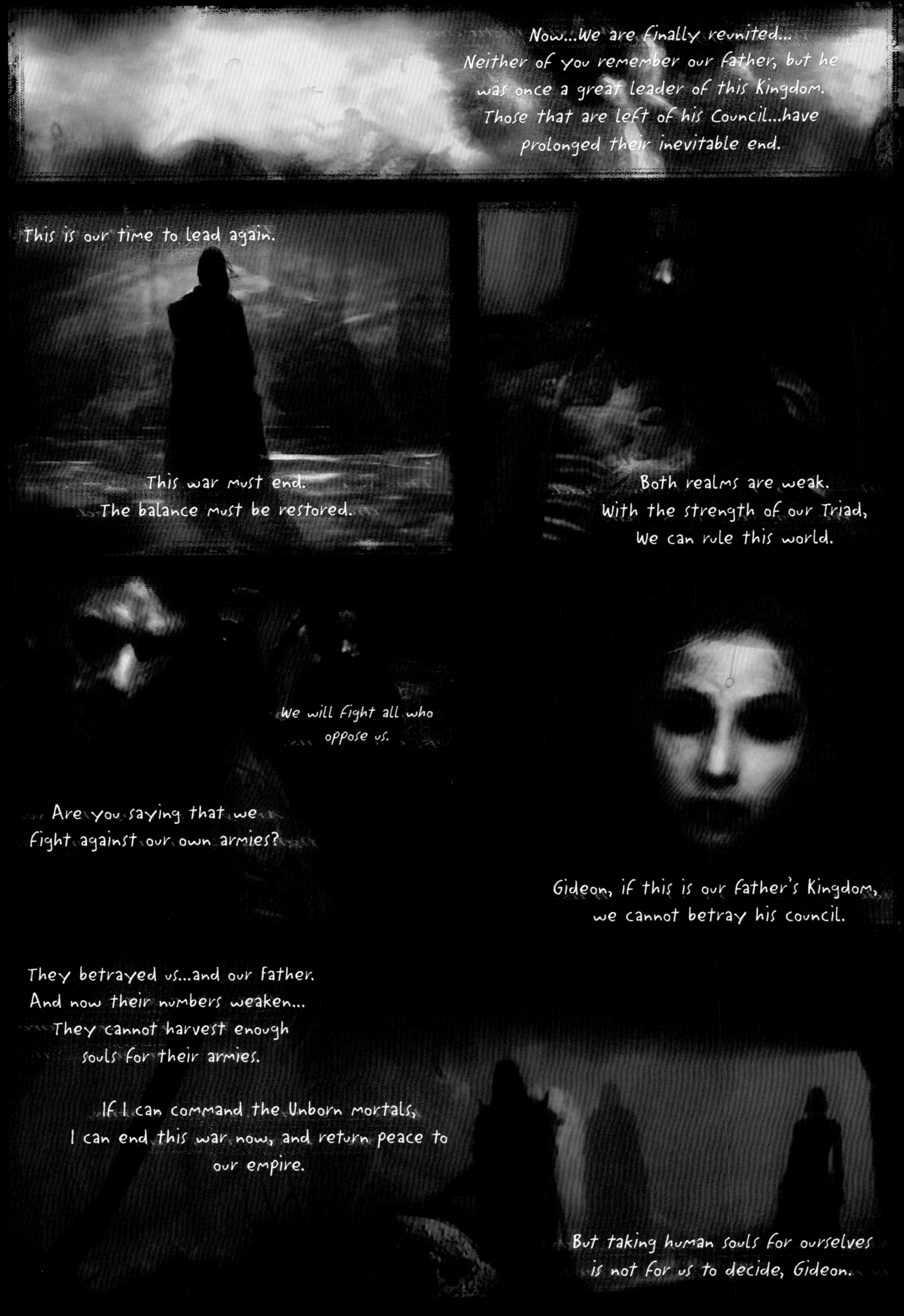
Now...We are finally reunited...
Neither of you remember our father, but he was once a great leader of this Kingdom.
Those that are left of his Council...have prolonged their inevitable end.
This is our time to lead again.
This war must end.
The balance must be restored.
Both realms are weak.
With the strength of our Triad, we can rule this world.
We will fight all who oppose us.
Are you saying that we fight against our own armies?
Gideon, if this is our father's Kingdom, we cannot betray his council.
They betrayed us...and our father.
And now their numbers weaken...
They cannot harvest enough souls for their armies.
If I can command the Unborn mortals, I can end this war now, and return peace to our empire.
But taking human souls for ourselves is not for us to decide, Gideon.

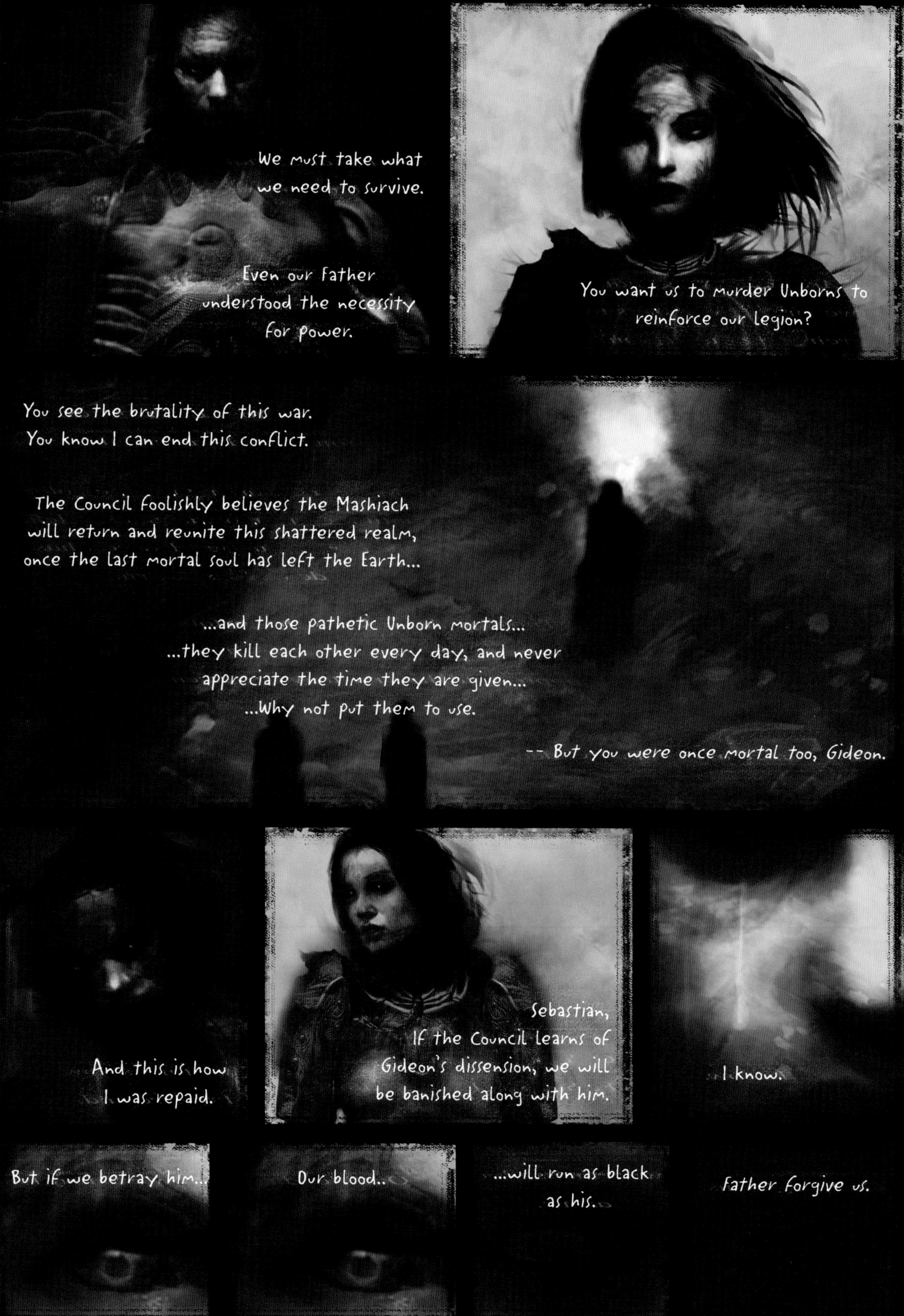
We must take what
we need to survive.
Even our father
understood the necessity
for power.
You want us to murder Unborns to
reinforce our legion?
You see the brutality of this war.
You know I can end this conflict.
The Council foolishly believes the Mashiach
will return and reunite this shattered realm,
once the last mortal soul has left the Earth...
...and those pathetic Unborn mortals...
...they kill each other every day, and never
appreciate the time they are given...
...Why not put them to use.
-- But you were once mortal too, Gideon.
And this is how
I was repaid.
Sebastian,
If the Council learns of
Gideon's dissension, we will
be banished along with him.
I know.
But if we betray him...
Our blood..
...will run as black
as his.
Father forgive us.

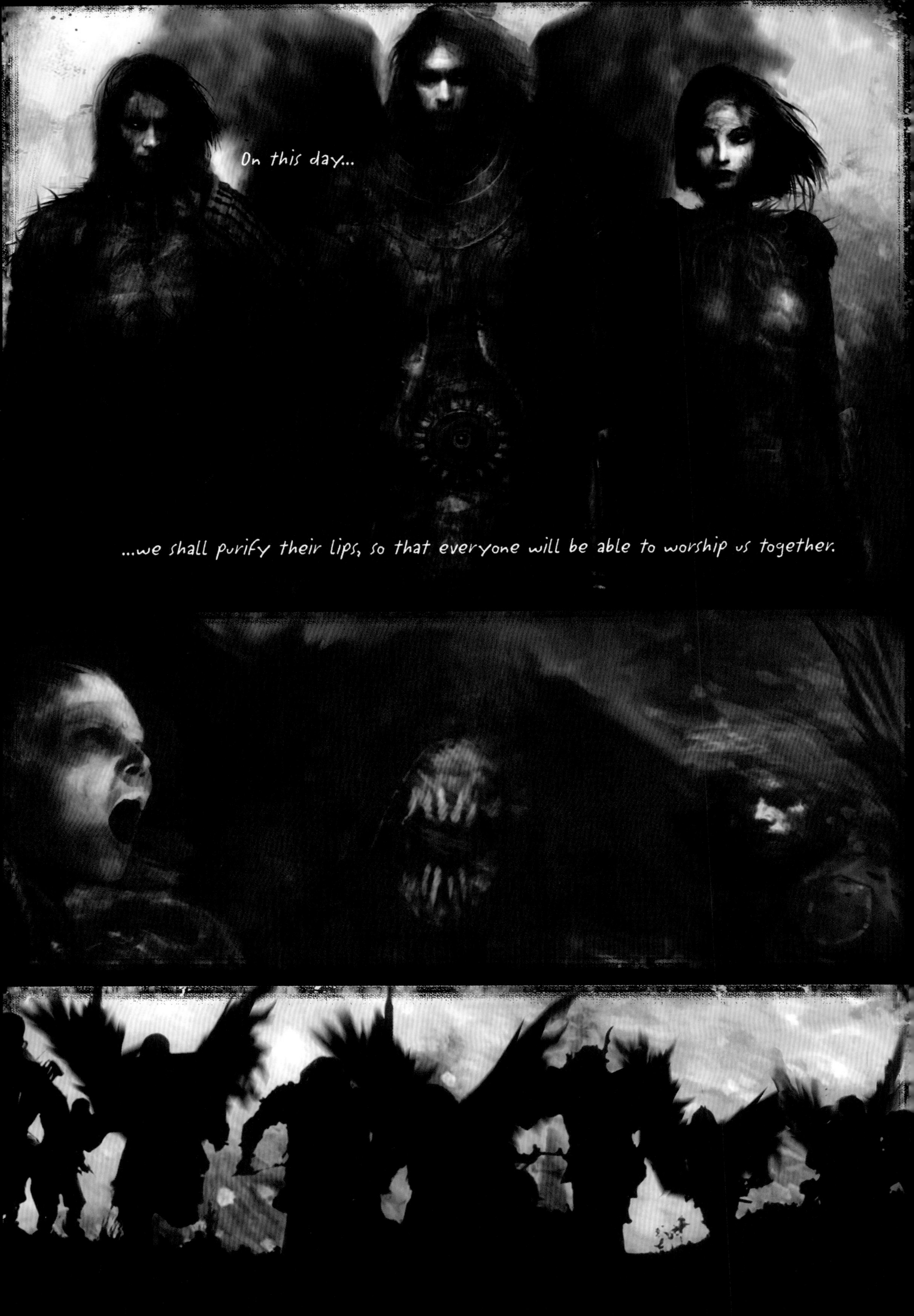
On this day...
...we shall purify their lips, so that everyone will be able to worship us together.

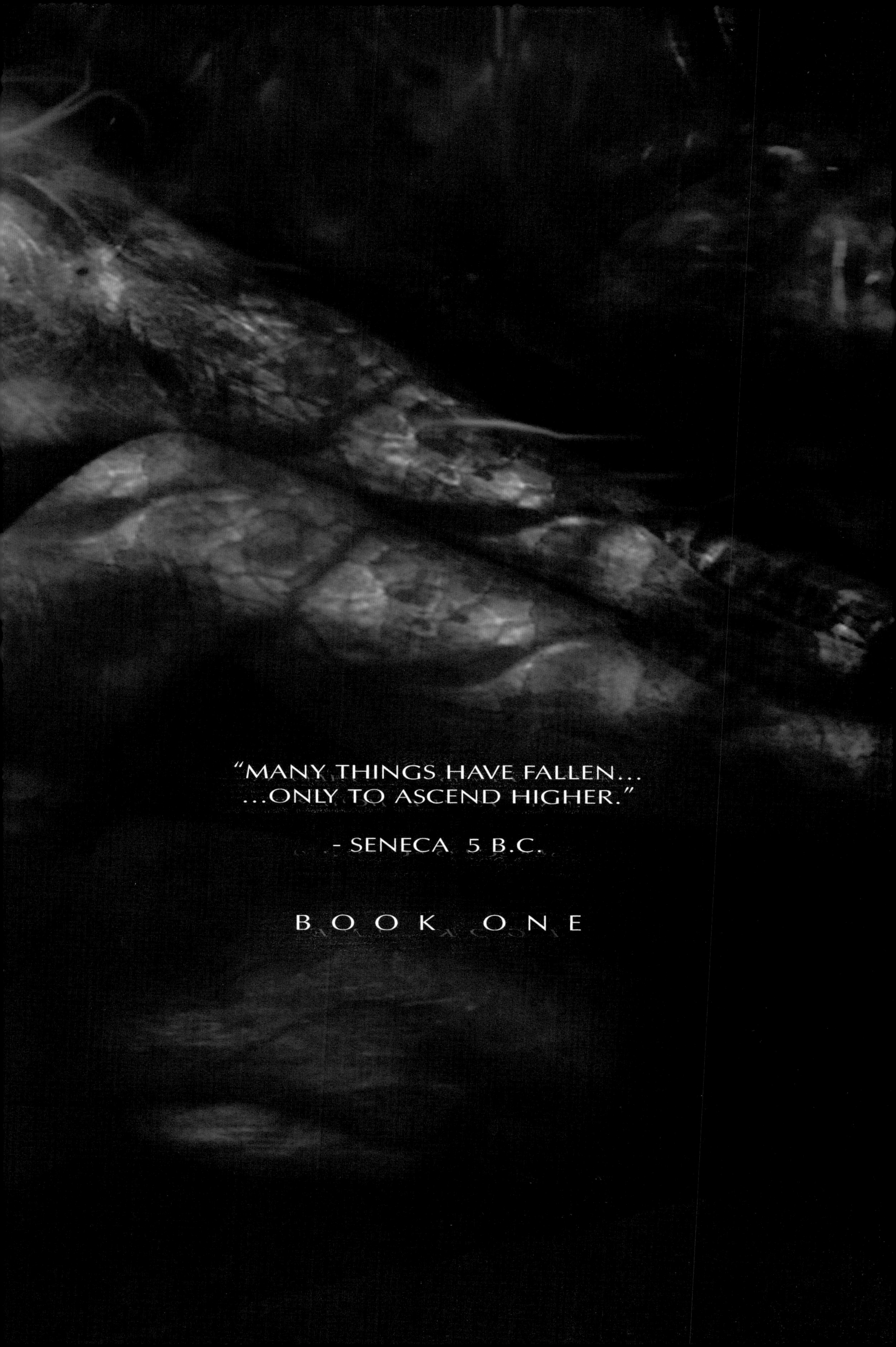

"MANY THINGS HAVE FALLEN...
...ONLY TO ASCEND HIGHER."

- SENECA 5 B.C.

BOOK ONE

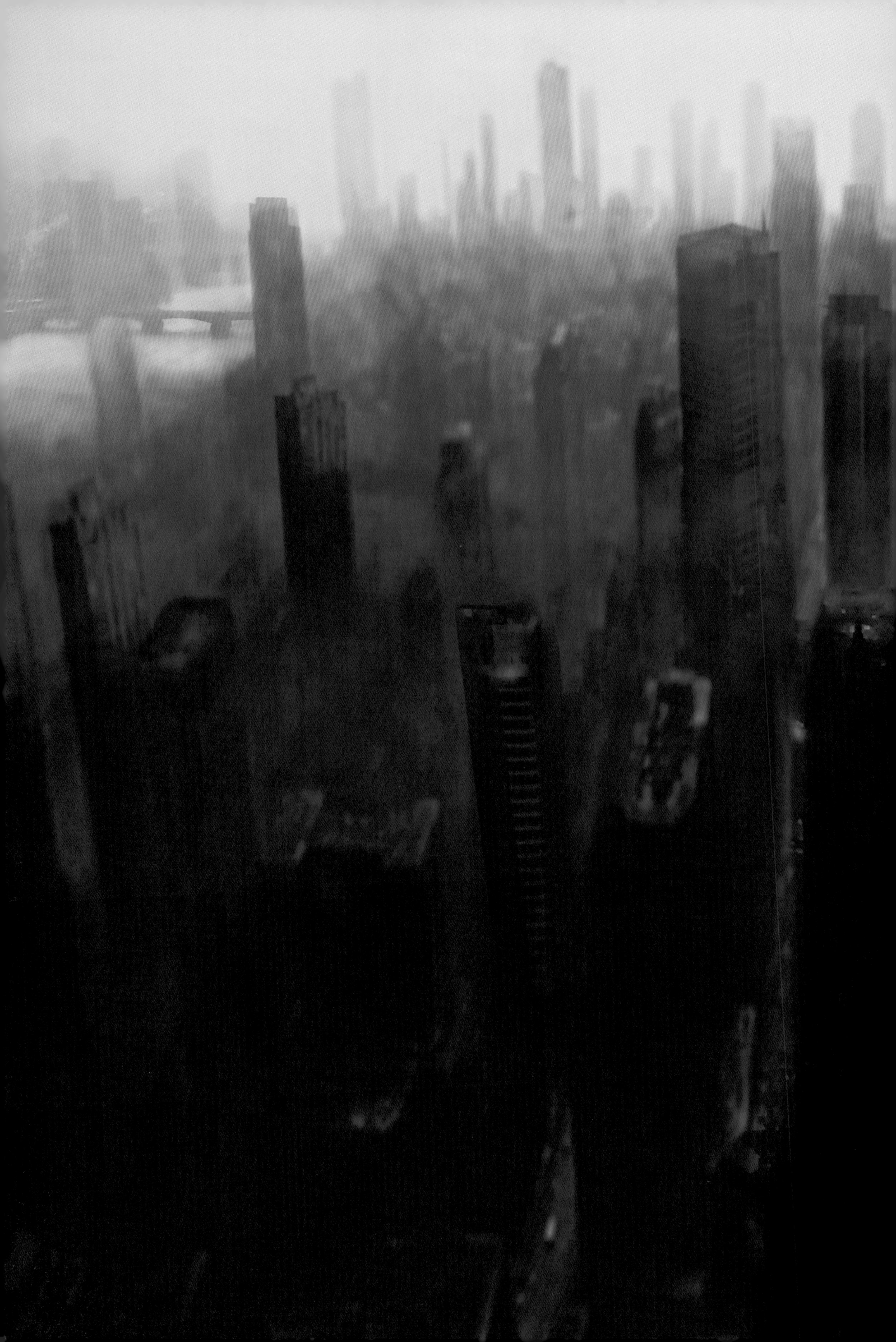

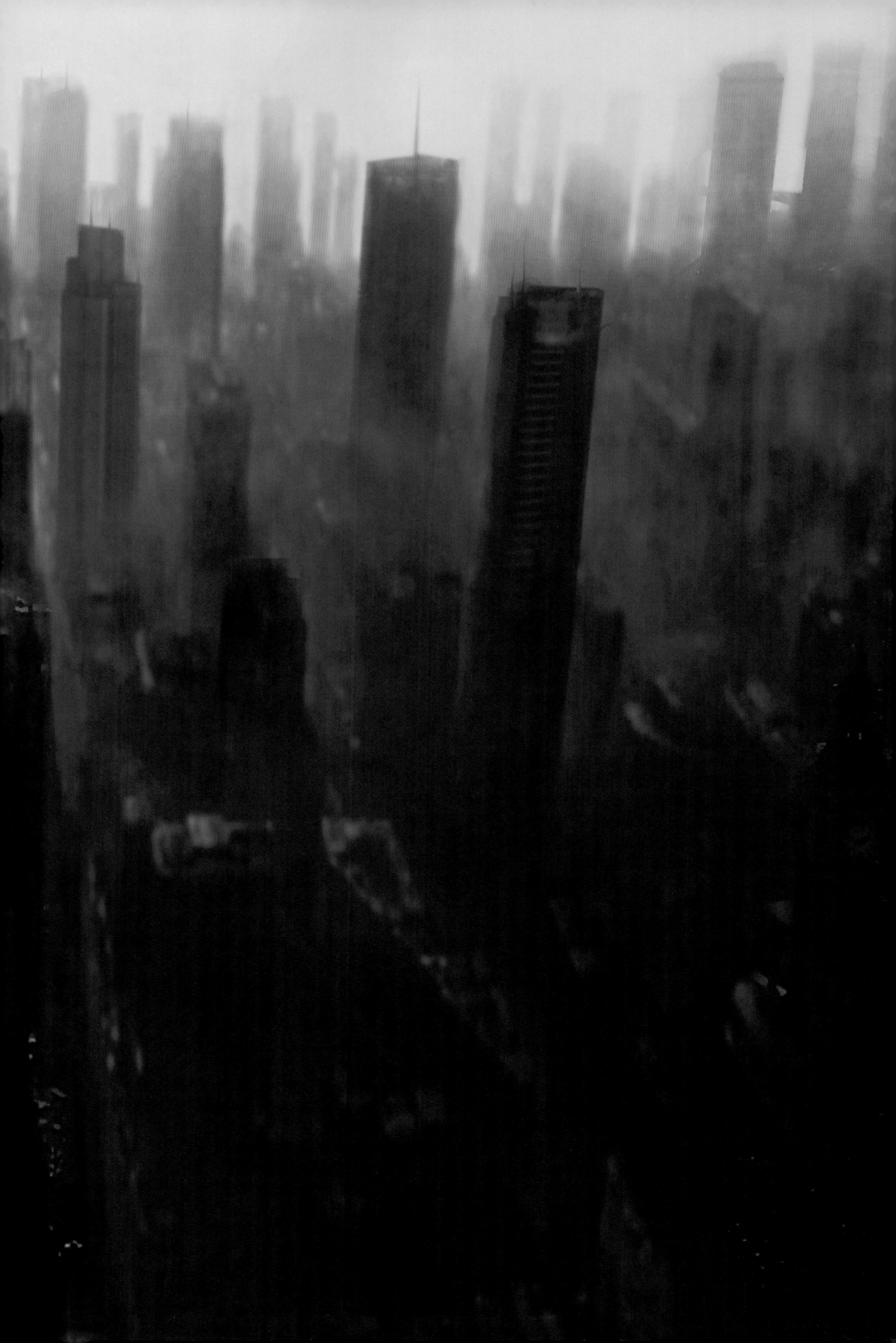

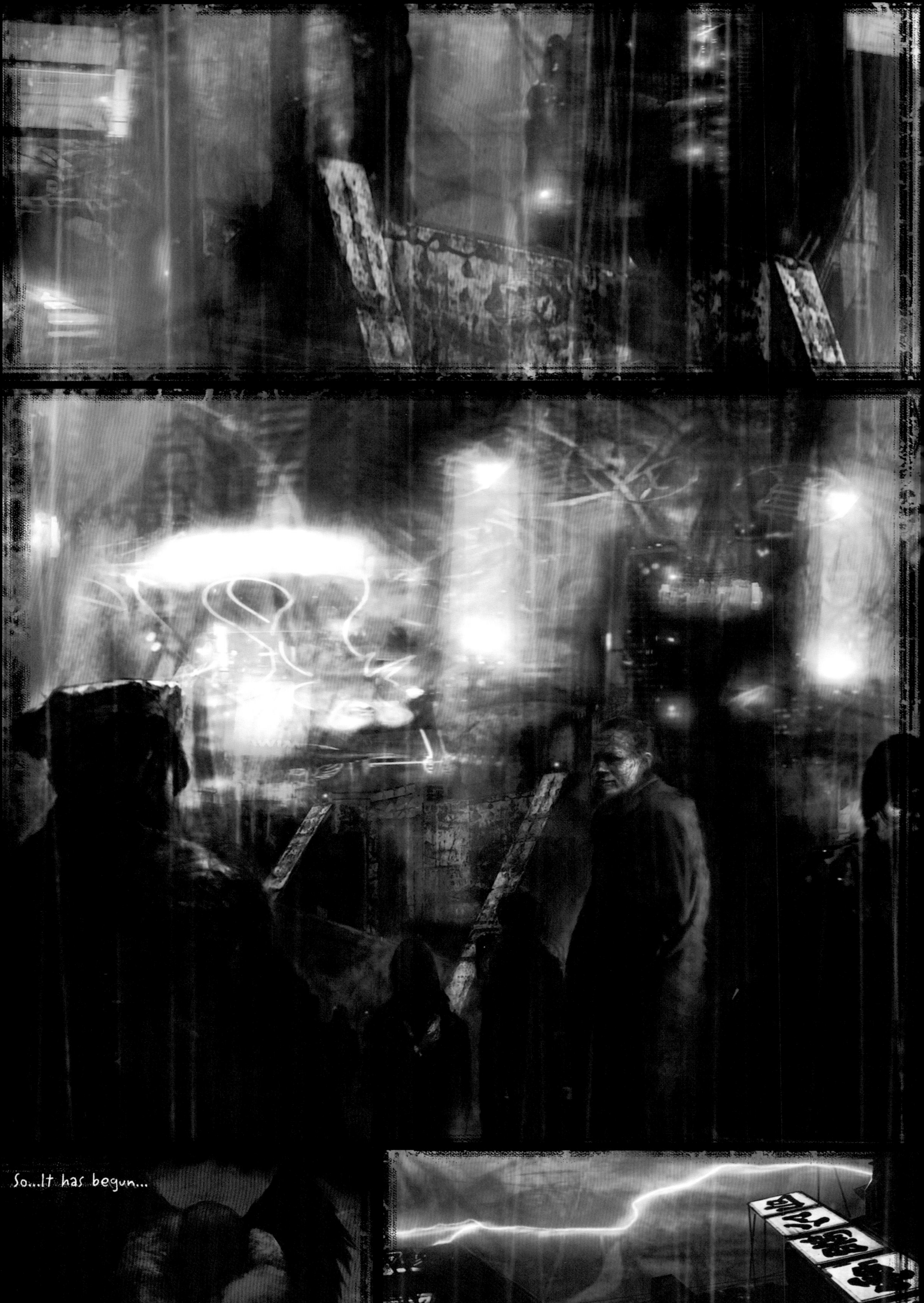
So...It has begun...

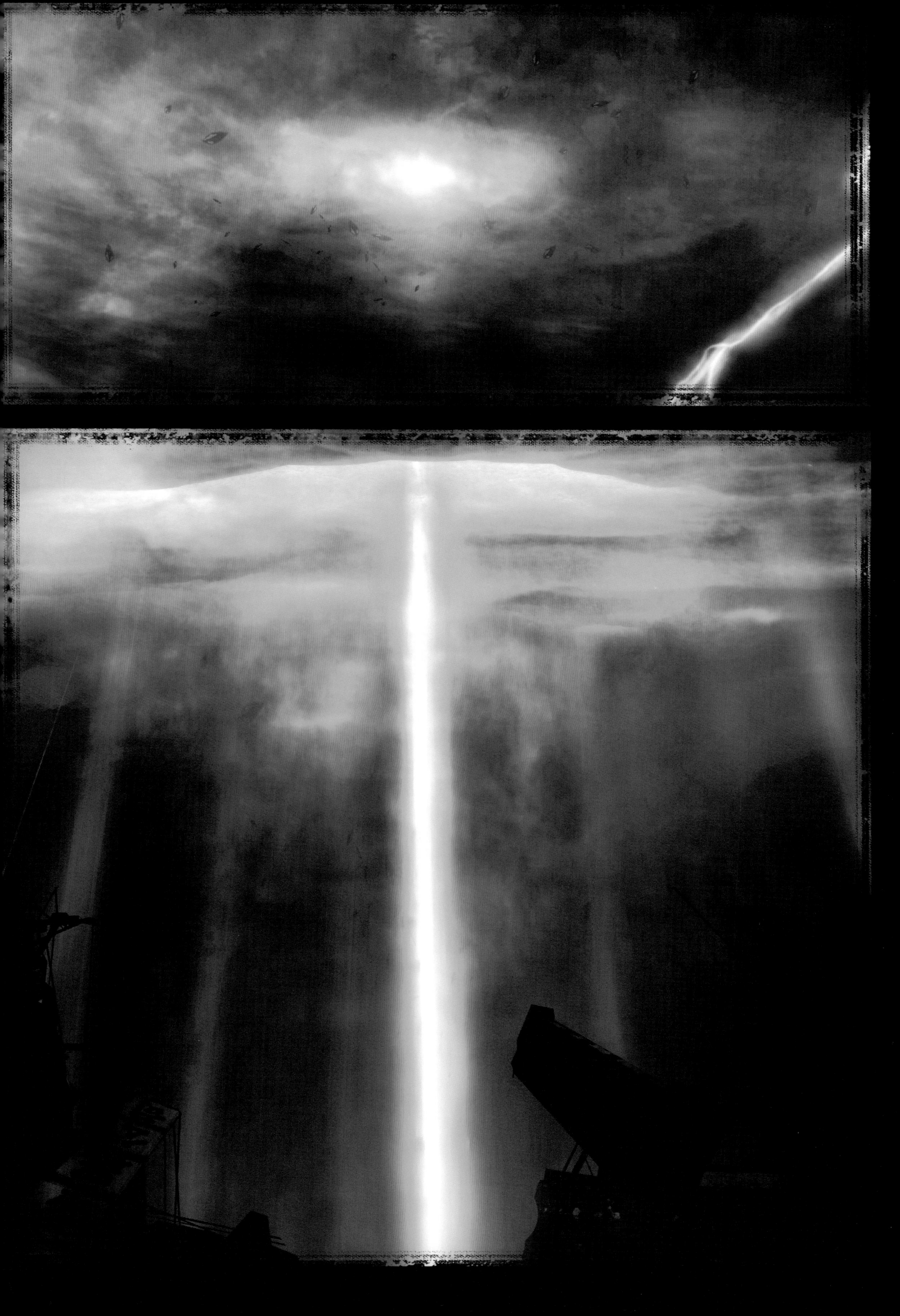

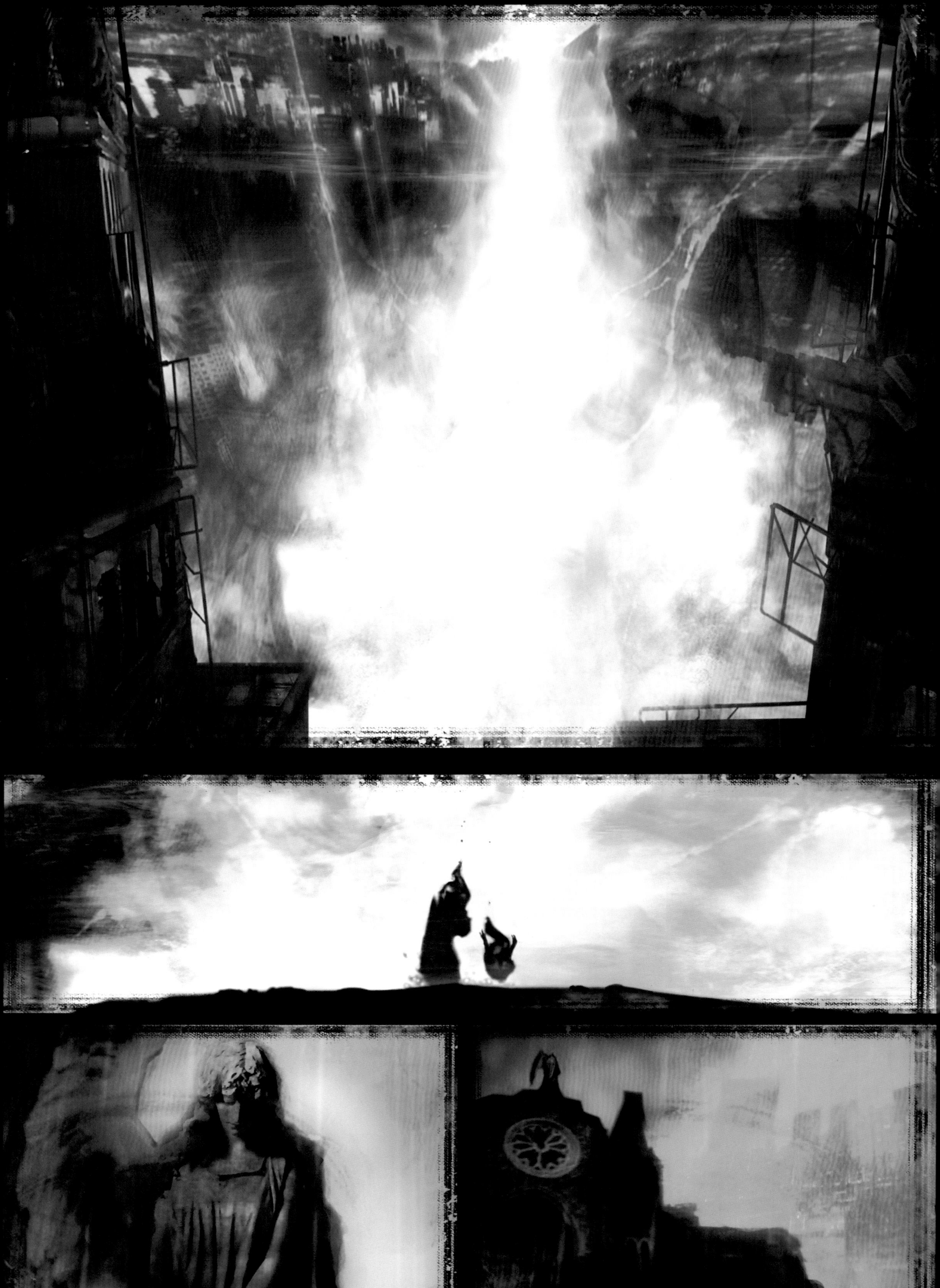

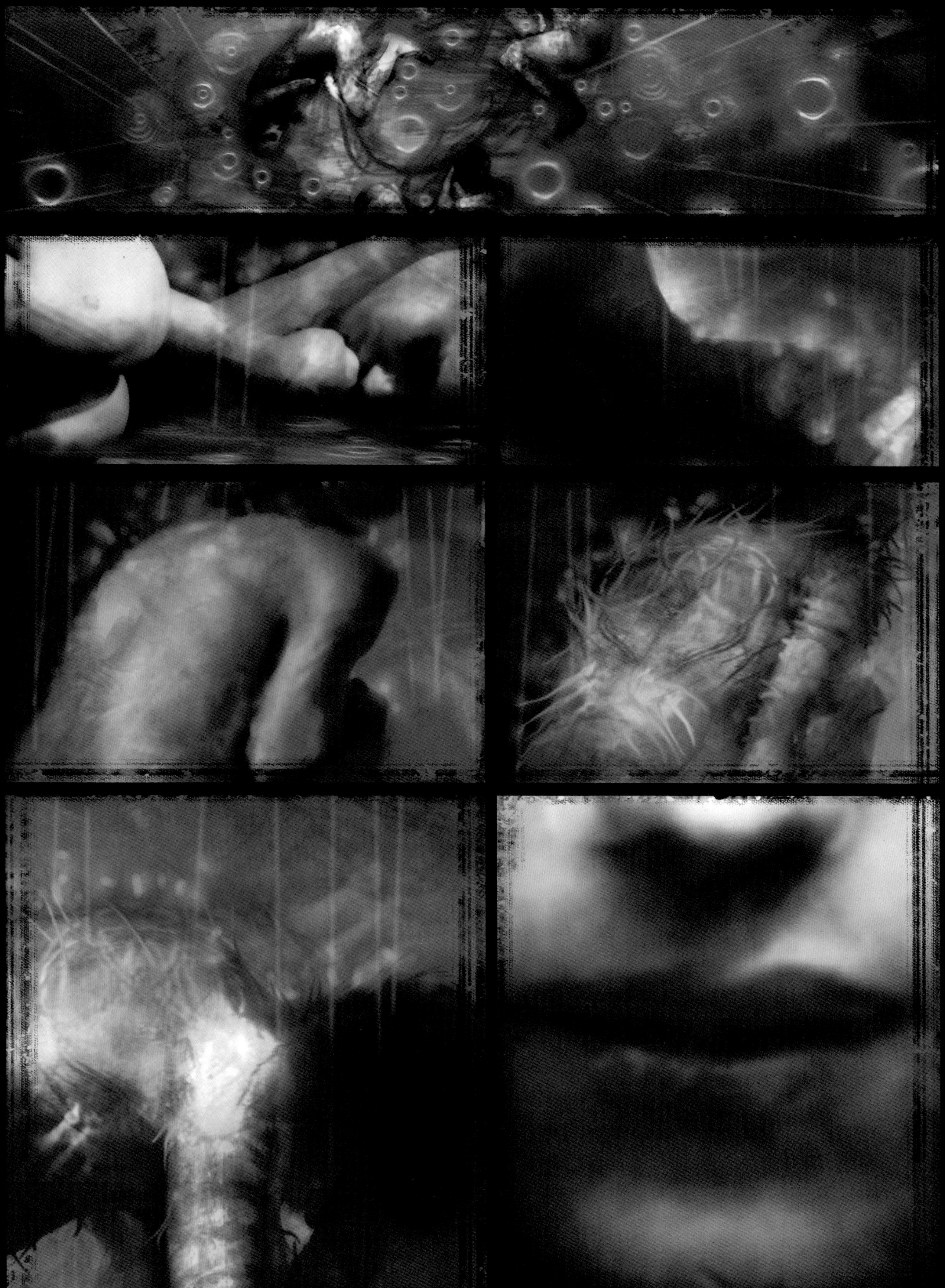
What...happened to us?

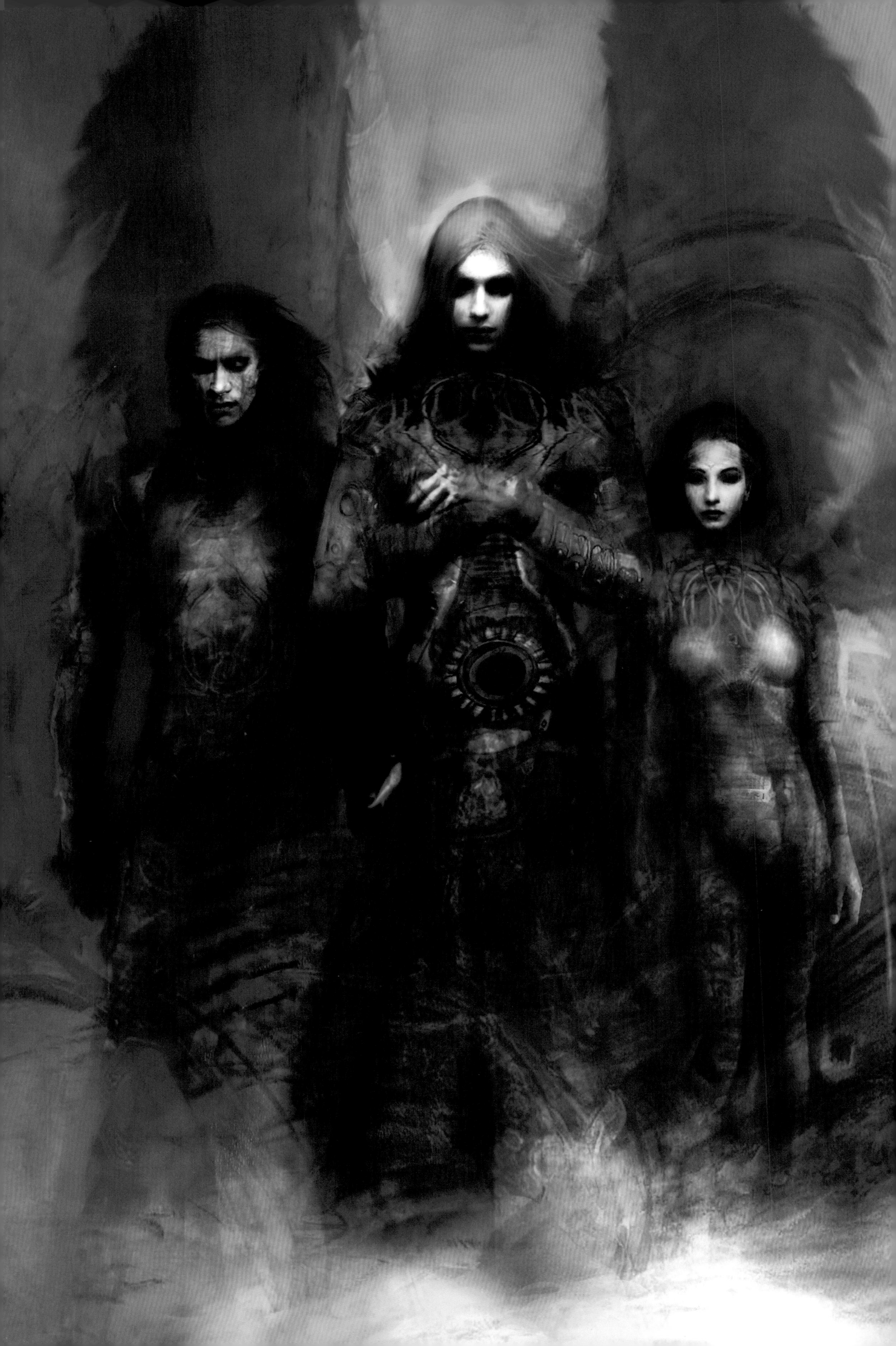

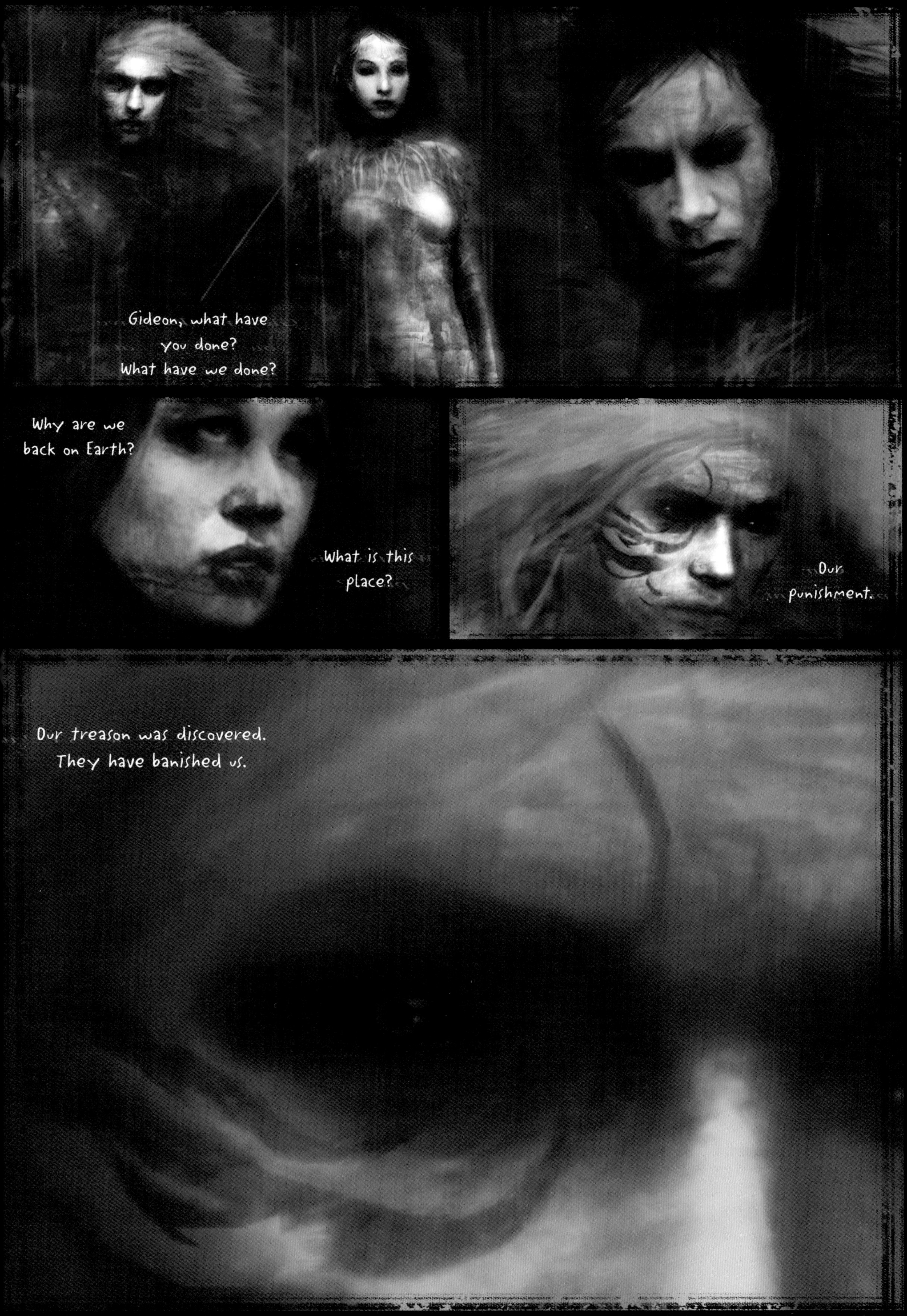
Gideon, what have you done? What have we done?
Why are we back on Earth?
What is this place?
Our punishment.
Our treason was discovered. They have banished us.

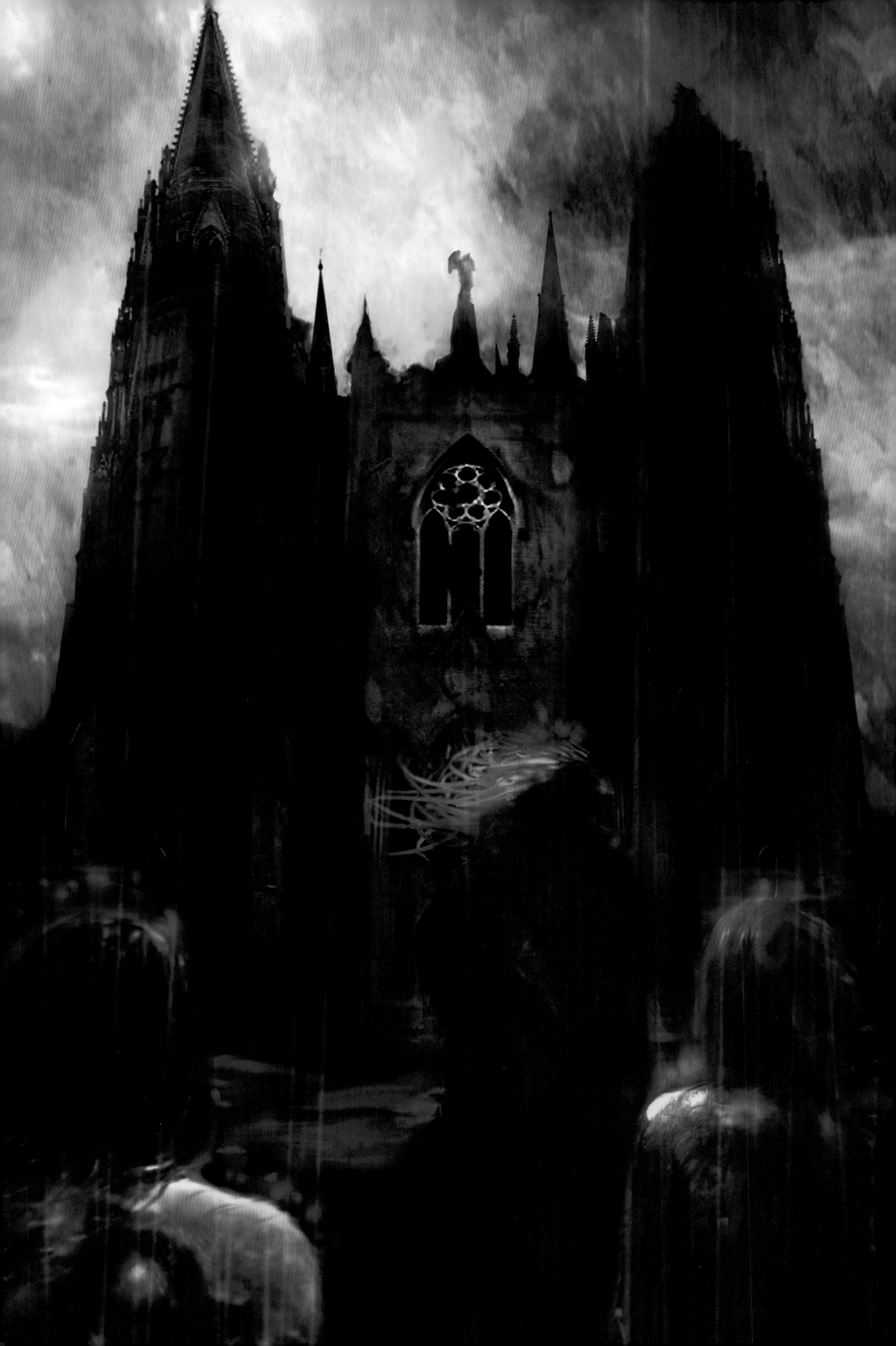

It is no use,
Sebastian...We do not need them...
Come with me.

You chose your path...
As did Seraphine... as did I.

There is no place
for you in there...

Just as you foolishly mourned my
death, that cathedral is an abandoned
Testament to their shallow beliefs.

The Humans have turned their backs on us...
Just as the Council has....

We must find a new path
home...

...but it is a
much darker road
now.

No...

Don't be a fool,
You tasted it.

You knew how
close we were.

Without their Mashiach, you know I
was their only chance for salvation.

Why do you continue to
blindly follow their lies?

We may return, Gideon.

But not your way.

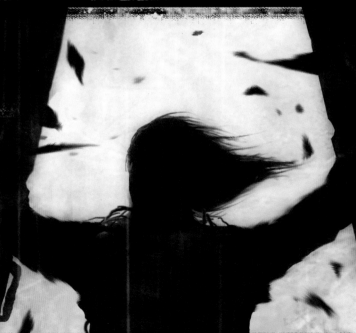

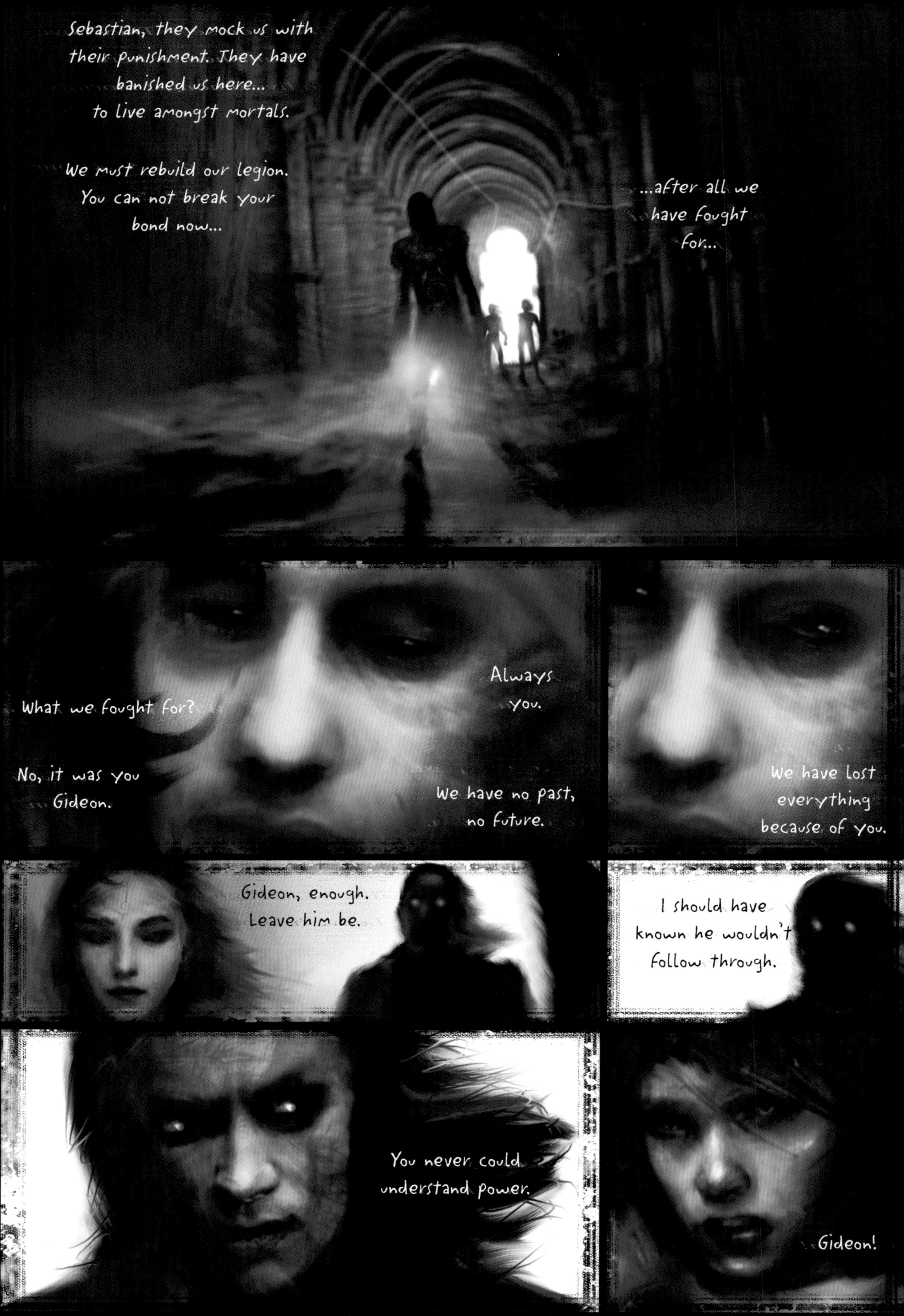
Sebastian, they mock us with their punishment. They have banished us here... to live amongst mortals.
We must rebuild our legion. You can not break your bond now...
...after all we have fought for...
What we fought for?
No, it was you Gideon.
Always you.
We have no past, no future.
We have lost everything because of you.
Gideon, enough. Leave him be.
I should have known he wouldn't follow through.
You never could understand power.
Gideon!

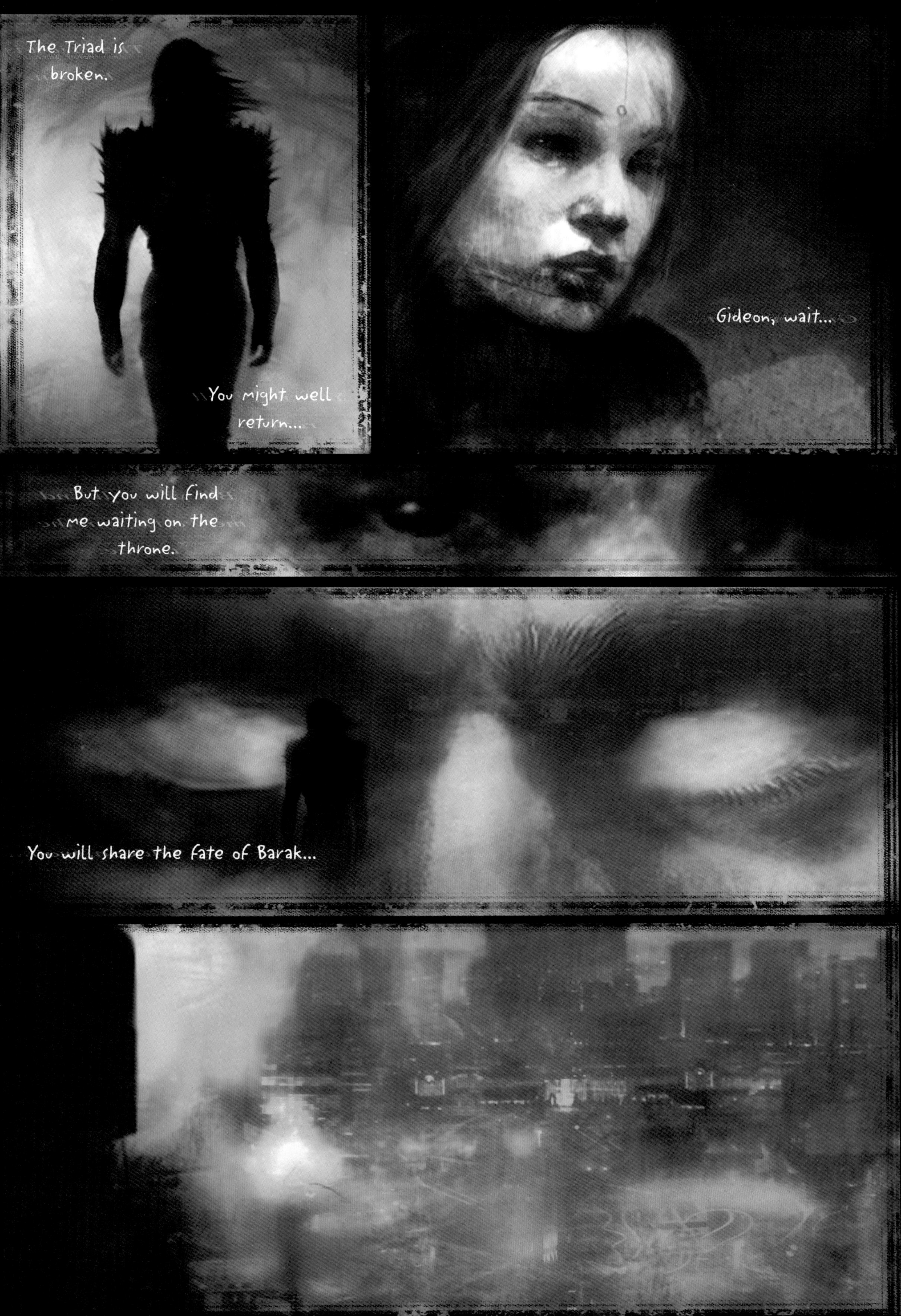
The Triad is broken.
You might well return...
Gideon, wait...
But you will find me waiting on the throne.
You will share the fate of Barak...

Ignore his anger, Sebastian.
Gideon will come back to us. He'll see that we can return to Heaven.
We will beg the Council for forgiveness...they must take us back.
But why should we go back?
What are you saying?
This was Gideon's fault. They need us.
We have betrayed our own kind.
How can they forgive us?
How can we forgive ourselves?
We deserve this fate.

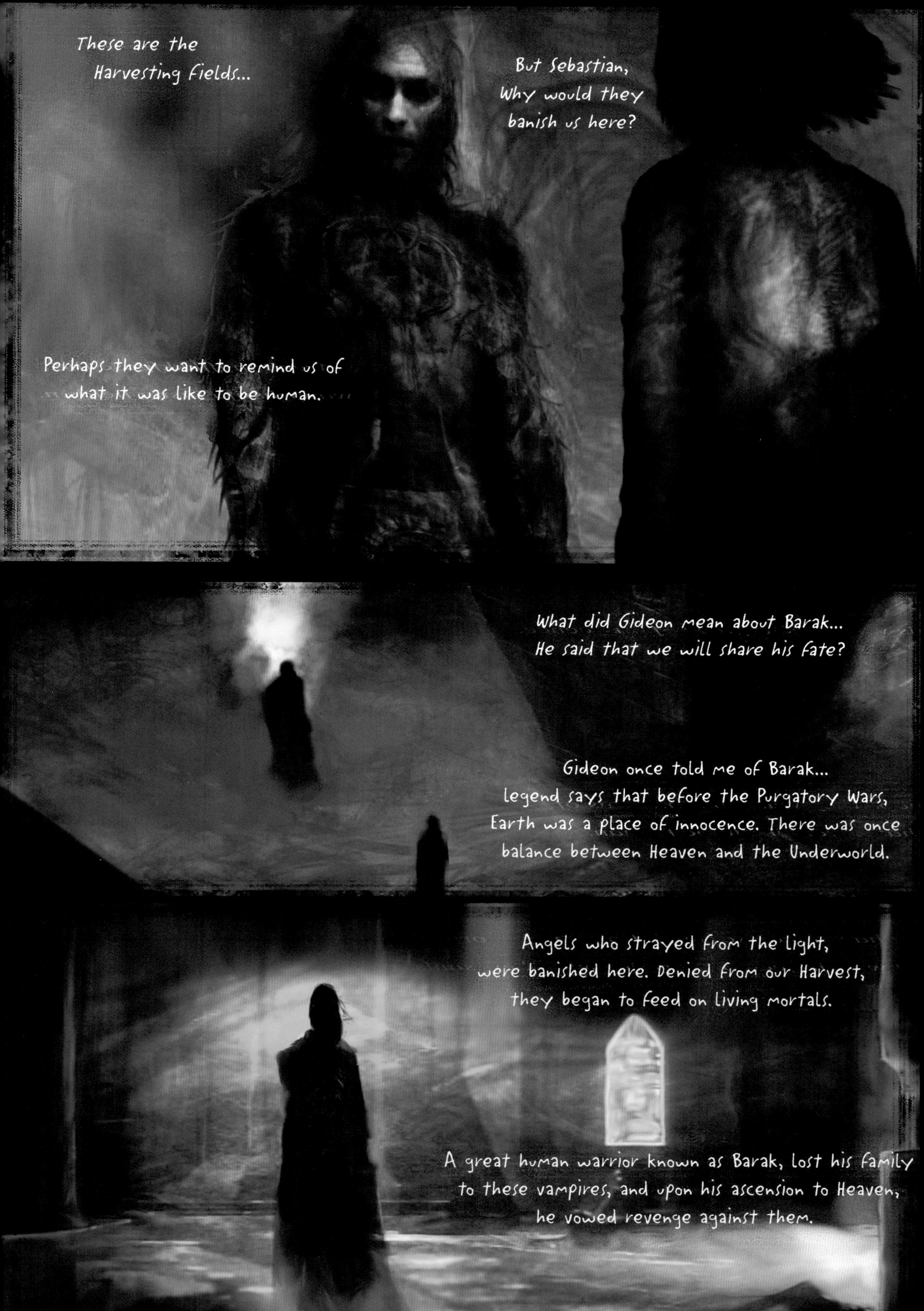
These are the Harvesting fields...
But Sebastian, Why would they banish us here?
Perhaps they want to remind us of what it was like to be human.
What did Gideon mean about Barak... He said that we will share his fate?
Gideon once told me of Barak... legend says that before the Purgatory Wars, Earth was a place of innocence. There was once balance between Heaven and the Underworld.
Angels who strayed from the light, were banished here. Denied from our Harvest, they began to feed on living mortals.
A great human warrior known as Barak, lost his family to these vampires, and upon his ascension to Heaven, he vowed revenge against them.

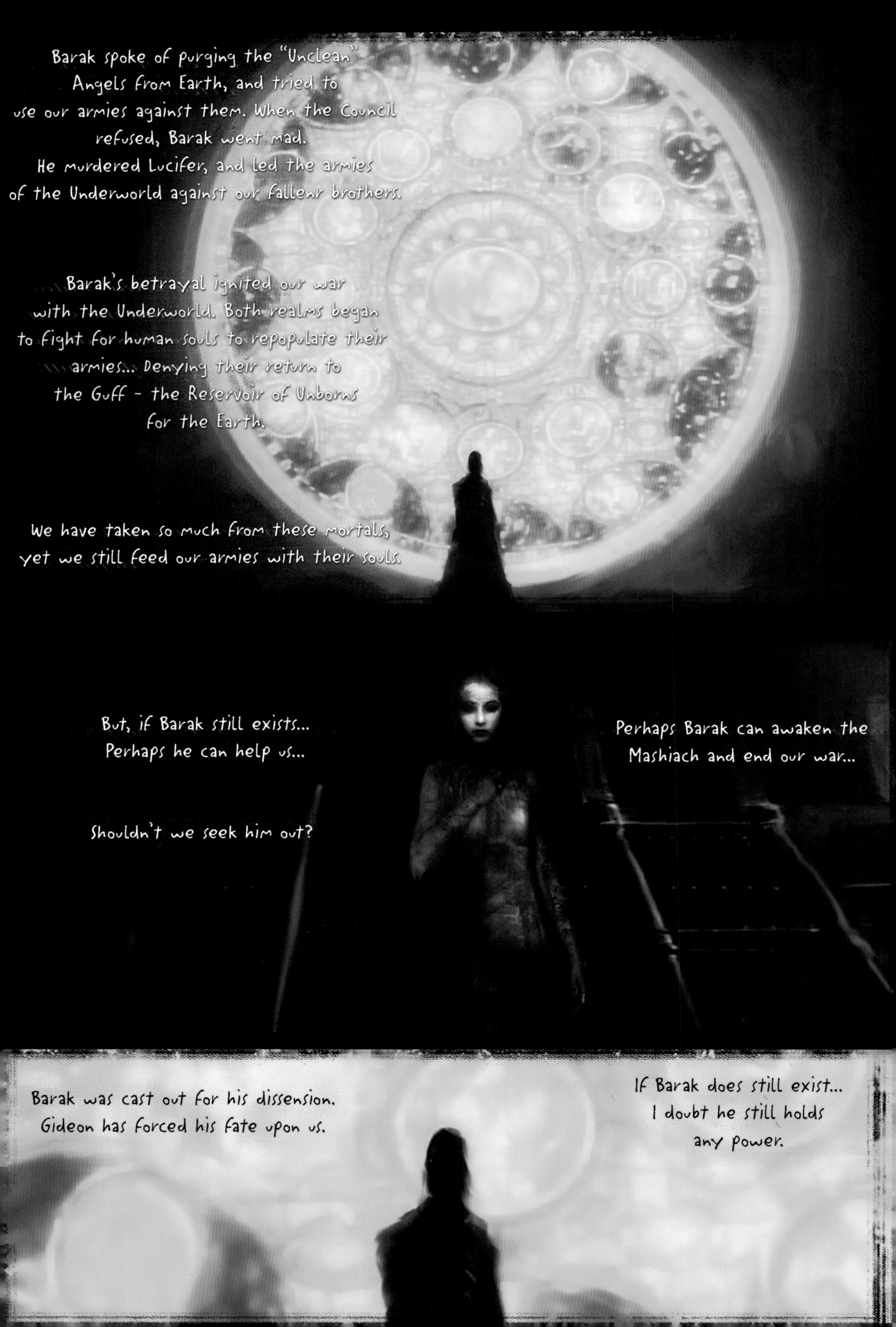
Barak spoke of purging the "Unclean" Angels from Earth, and tried to use our armies against them. When the Council refused, Barak went mad.
He murdered Lucifer, and led the armies of the Underworld against our fallenr brothers.
Barak's betrayal ignited our war with the Underworld. Both realms began to fight for human souls to repopulate their armies... Denying their return to the Guff - the Reservoir of Unborns for the Earth.
We have taken so much from these mortals, yet we still feed our armies with their souls.
But, if Barak still exists... Perhaps he can help us...
Shouldn't we seek him out?
Perhaps Barak can awaken the Mashiach and end our war...
Barak was cast out for his dissension. Gideon has forced his fate upon us.
If Barak does still exist... I doubt he still holds any power.

What is happening to me?
(((help me)))
S-SEB-
(((help me)))
Seraphine!
AHHHHHH!

(((help me)))
What cruel punishment is this?
That voice...Can you hear her?
It must be the cries of a dying Born. The music of the Harvest has been calling us since we arrived.
Music?
Seraphine, wait...
There is no pleasure in these words.
(((take me)))
This is my call to Harvest. She is calling to me.
(((take me)))
I must go to her.

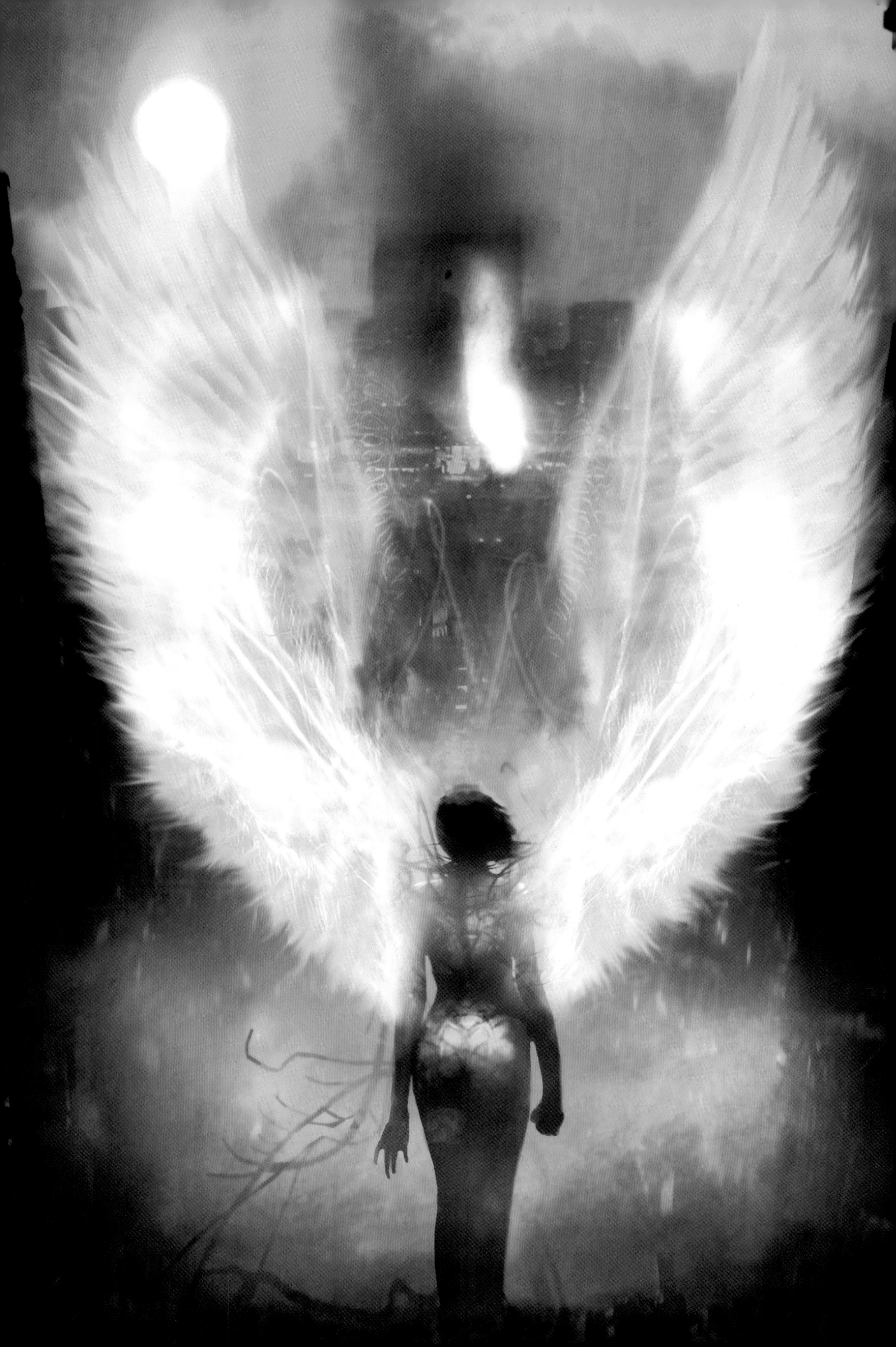

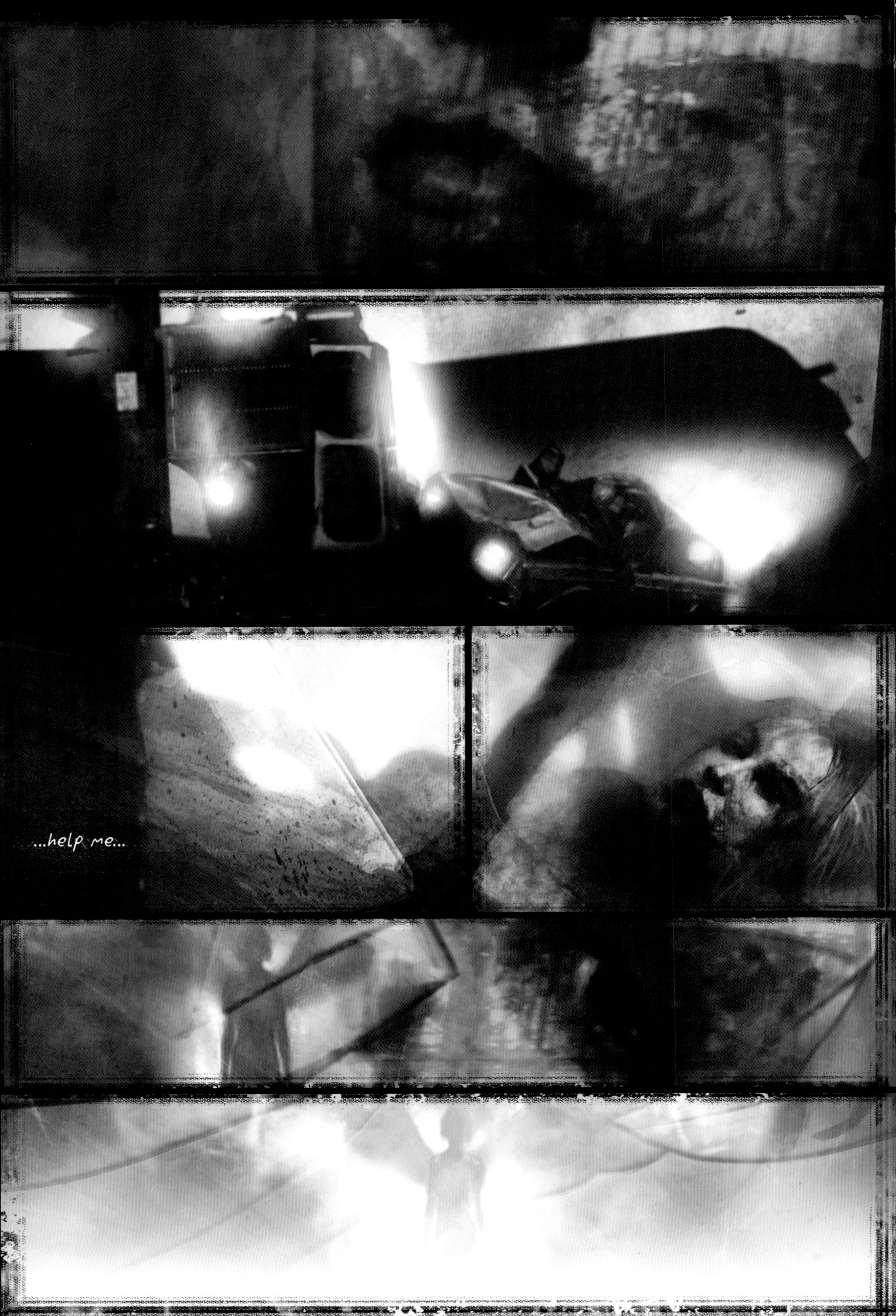
...help me...

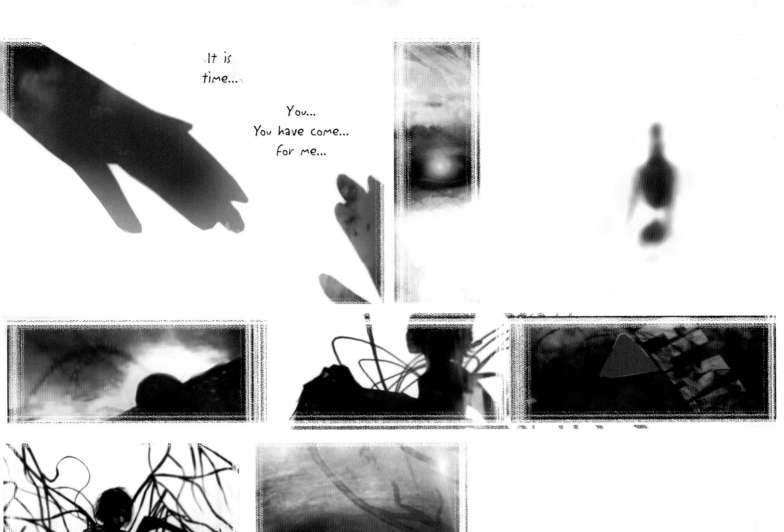

It is
time...

You...
You have come...
for me...

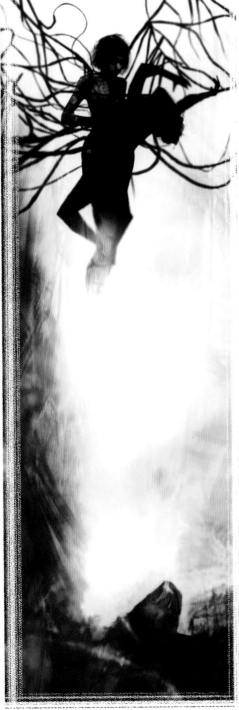

Please...

Take me.

Take me.

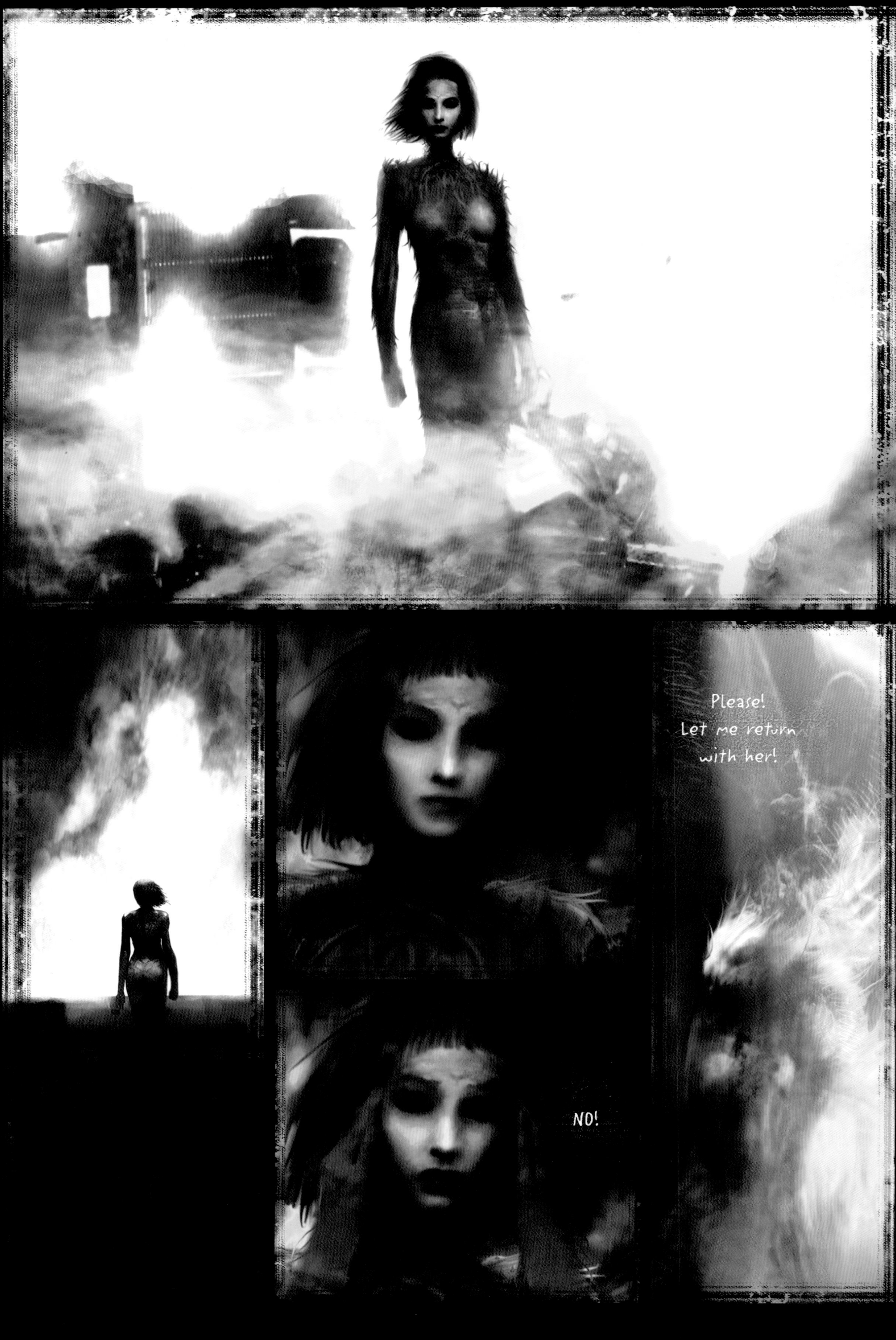
Please!
Let me return
with her!
NO!

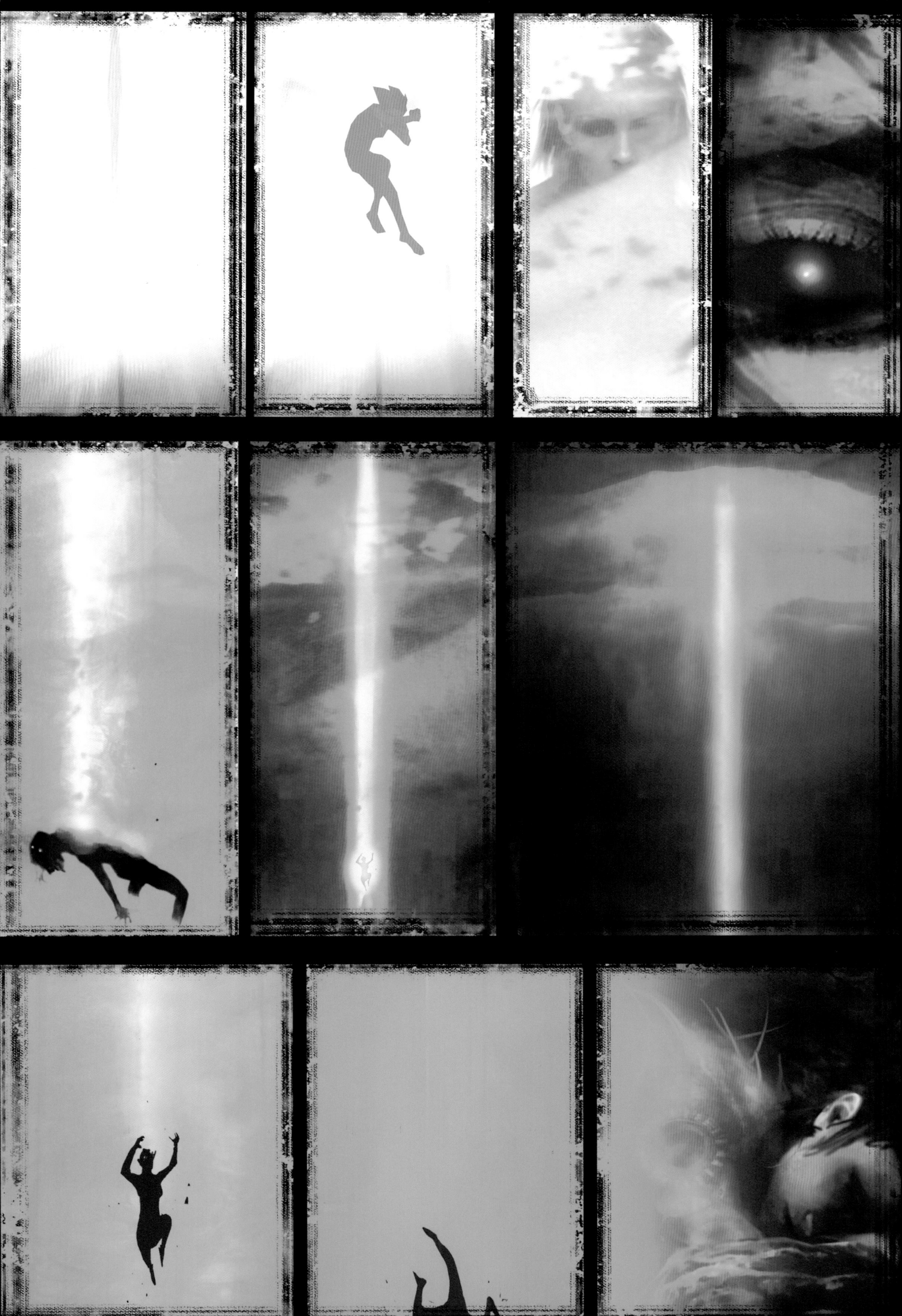

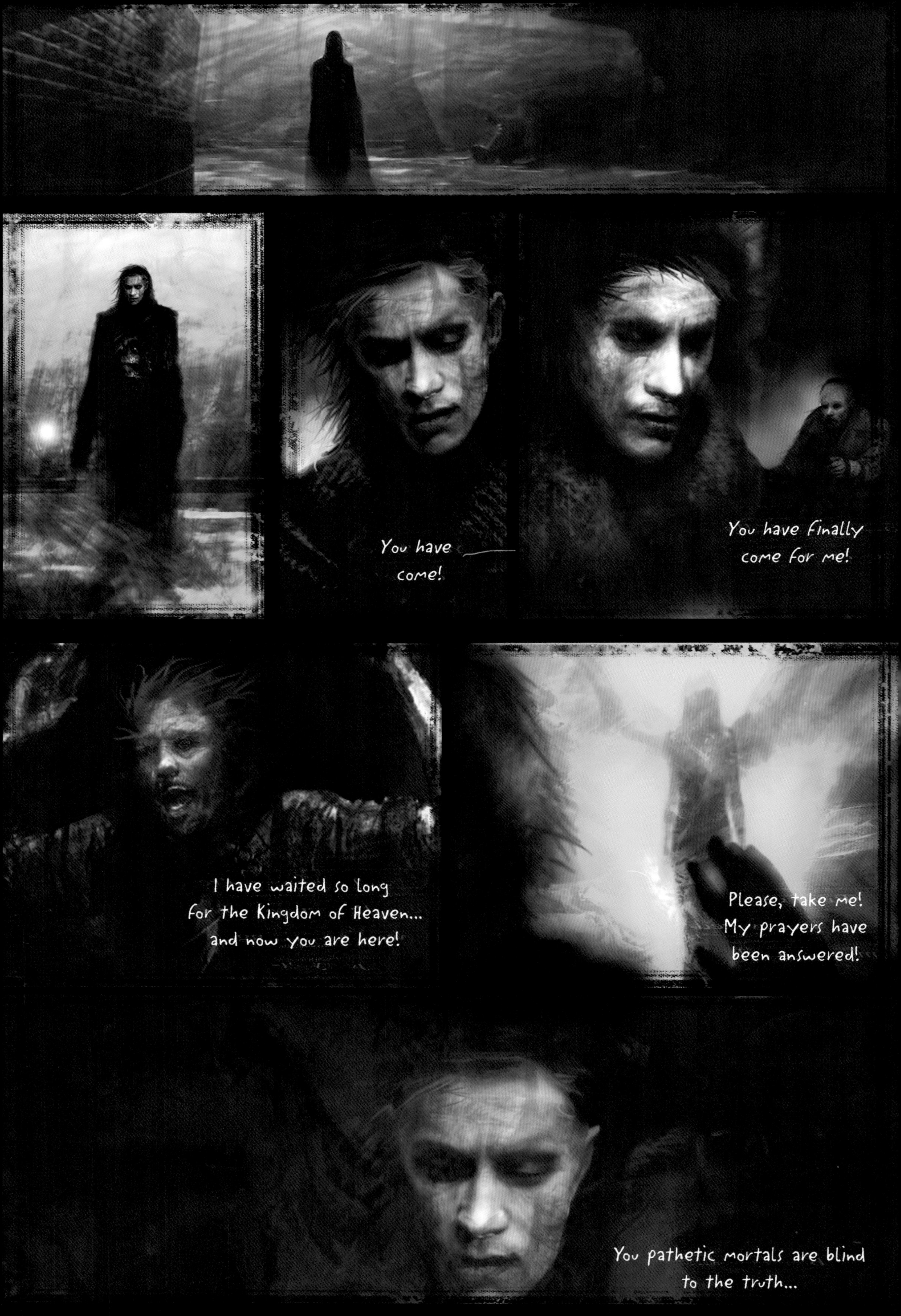

You have
come!
You have finally
come for me!
I have waited so long
for the Kingdom of Heaven...
and now you are here!
Please, take me!
My prayers have
been answered!
You pathetic mortals are blind
to the truth...

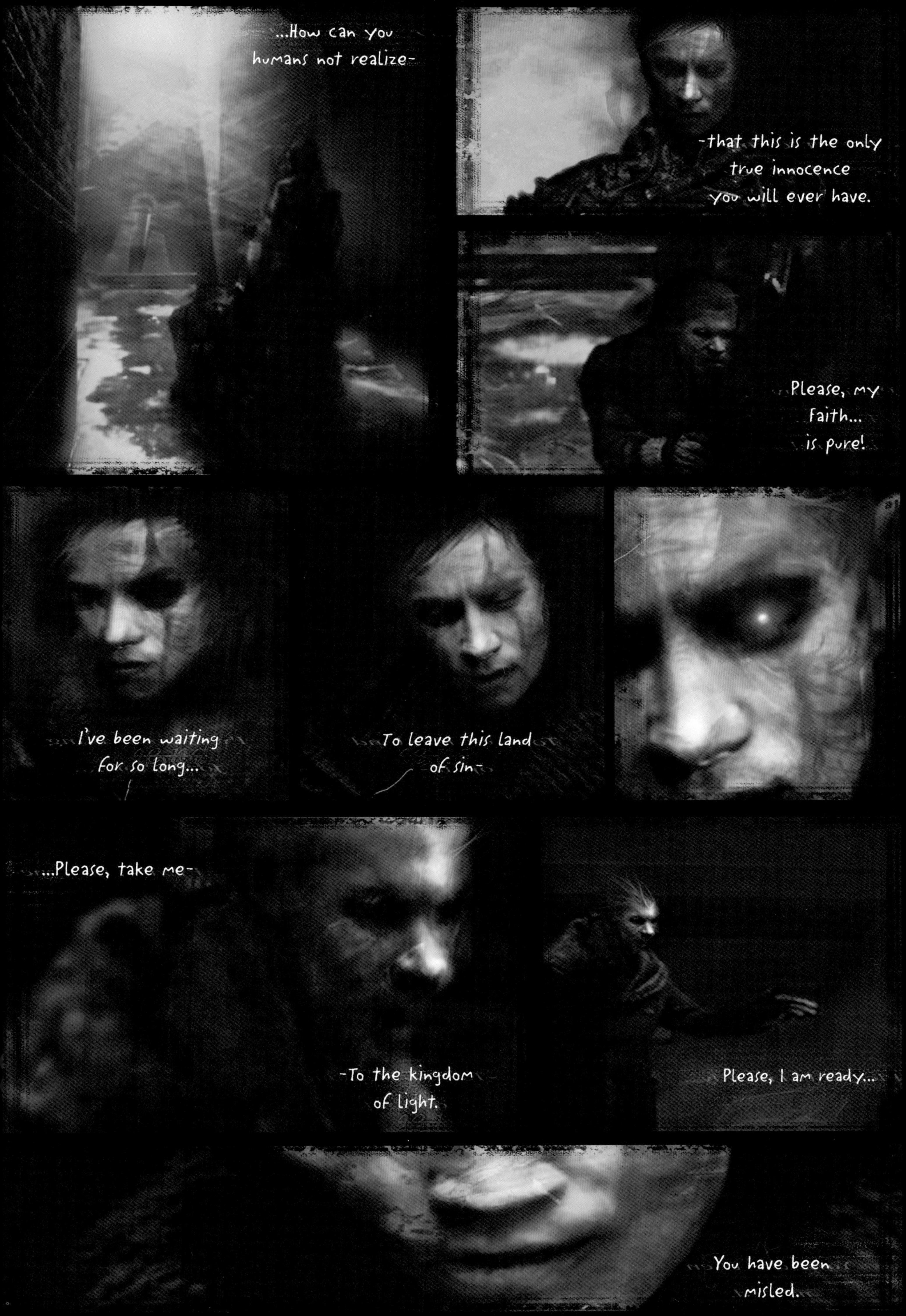
...How can you humans not realize-
-that this is the only true innocence you will ever have.
Please, my Faith... is pure!
I've been waiting for so long...
To leave this land of sin-
...Please, take me-
-To the kingdom of light.
Please, I am ready...
You have been misled.

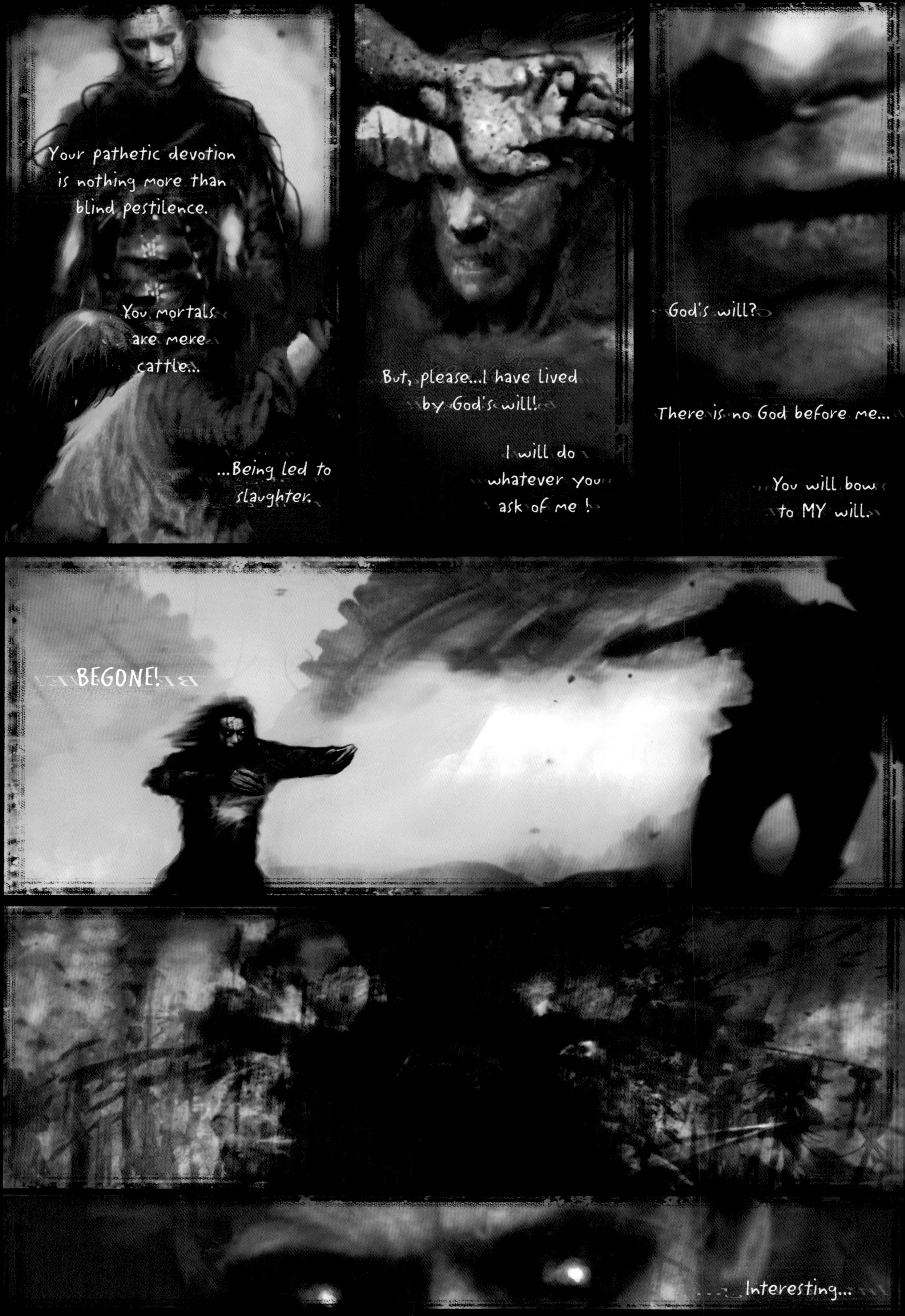
Your pathetic devotion is nothing more than blind pestilence.
You mortals are mere cattle...
...Being led to slaughter.
But, please...I have lived by God's will!
I will do whatever you ask of me!
God's will?
There is no God before me...
You will bow to MY will.
BEGONE!
...Interesting...

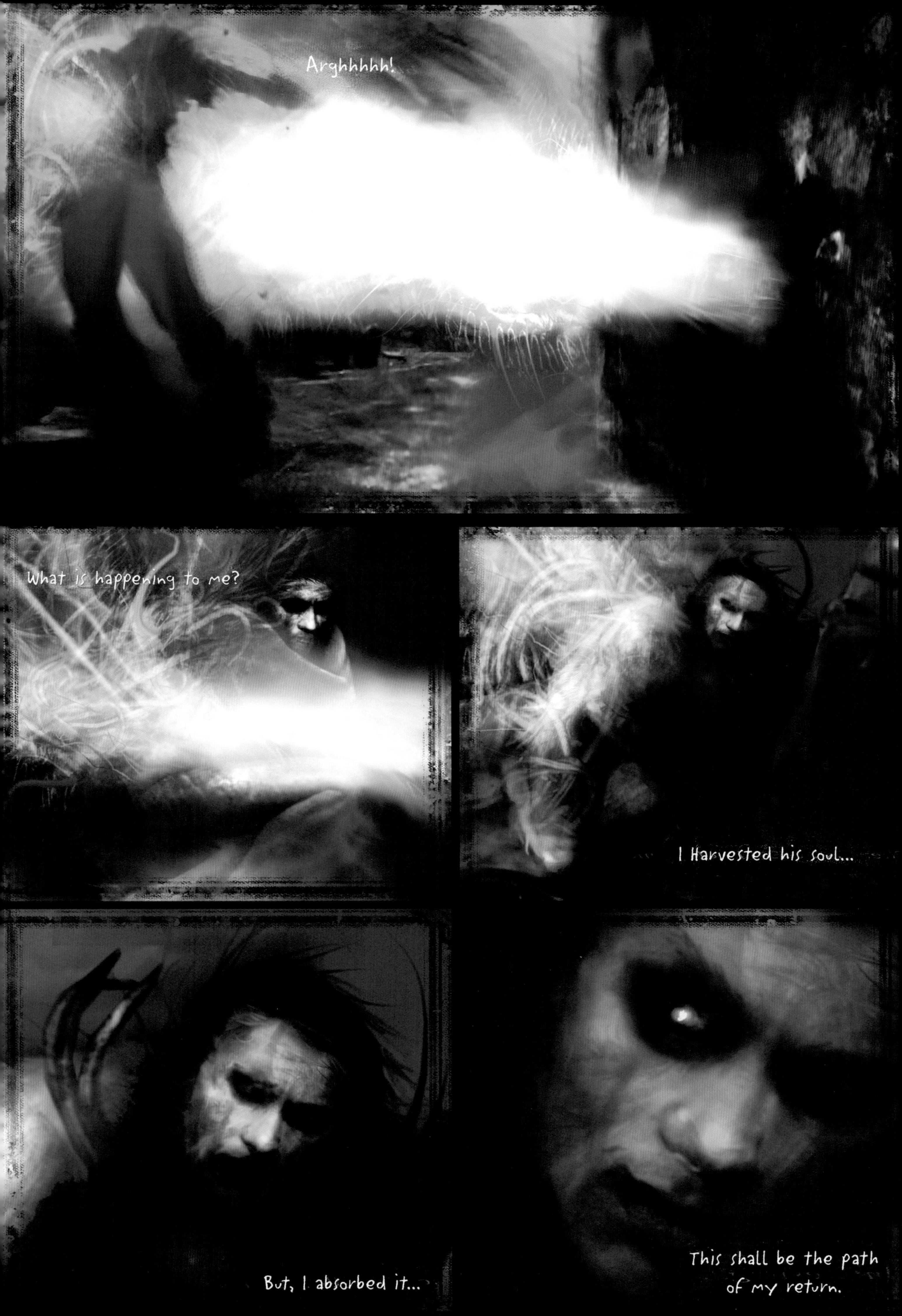
Arghhhhh!
What is happening to me?
I Harvested his soul...
But, I absorbed it...
This shall be the path of my return.

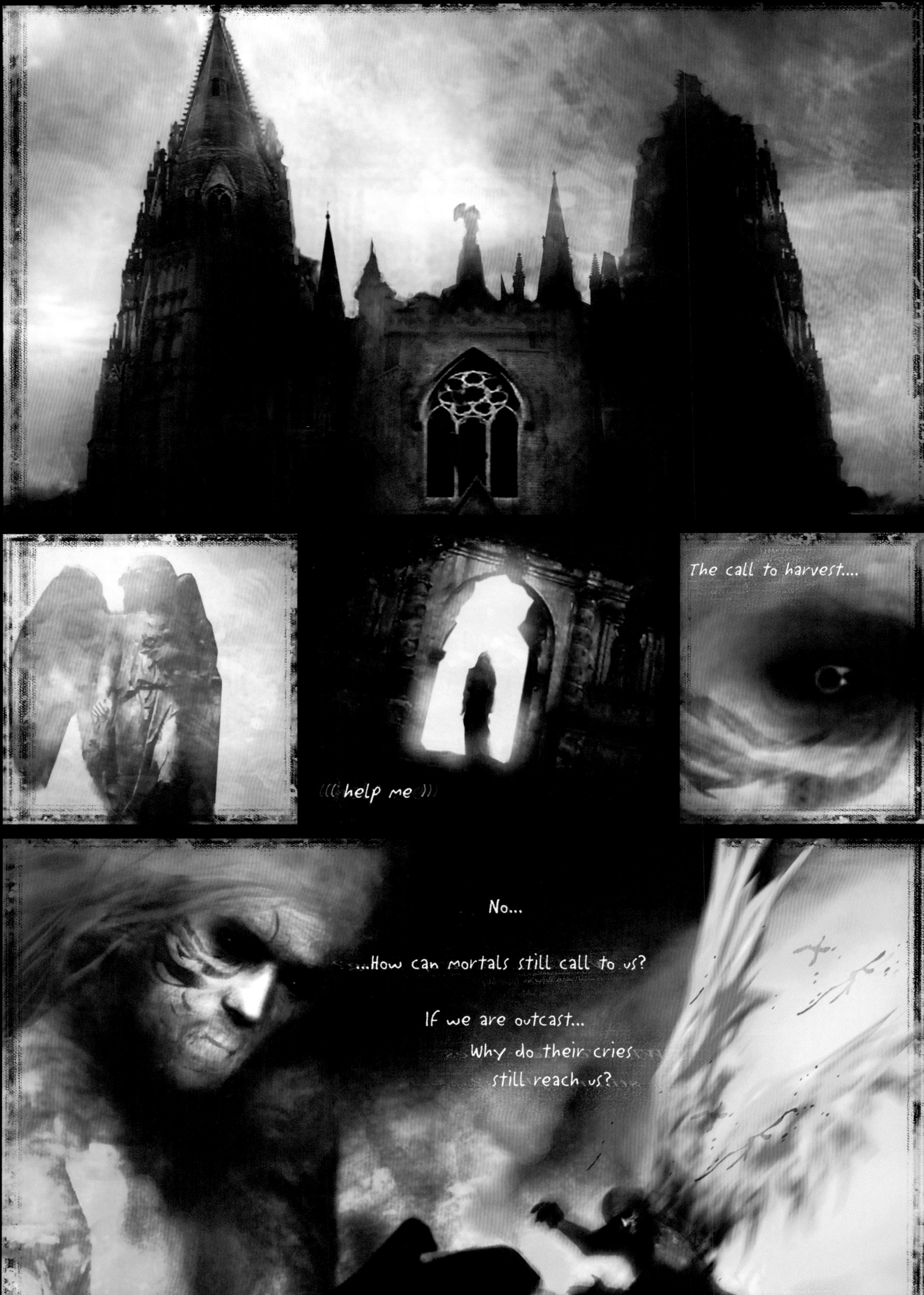
(((help me)))
The call to harvest....
No...
...How can mortals still call to us?
If we are outcast...
Why do their cries
still reach us?
(((help me)))

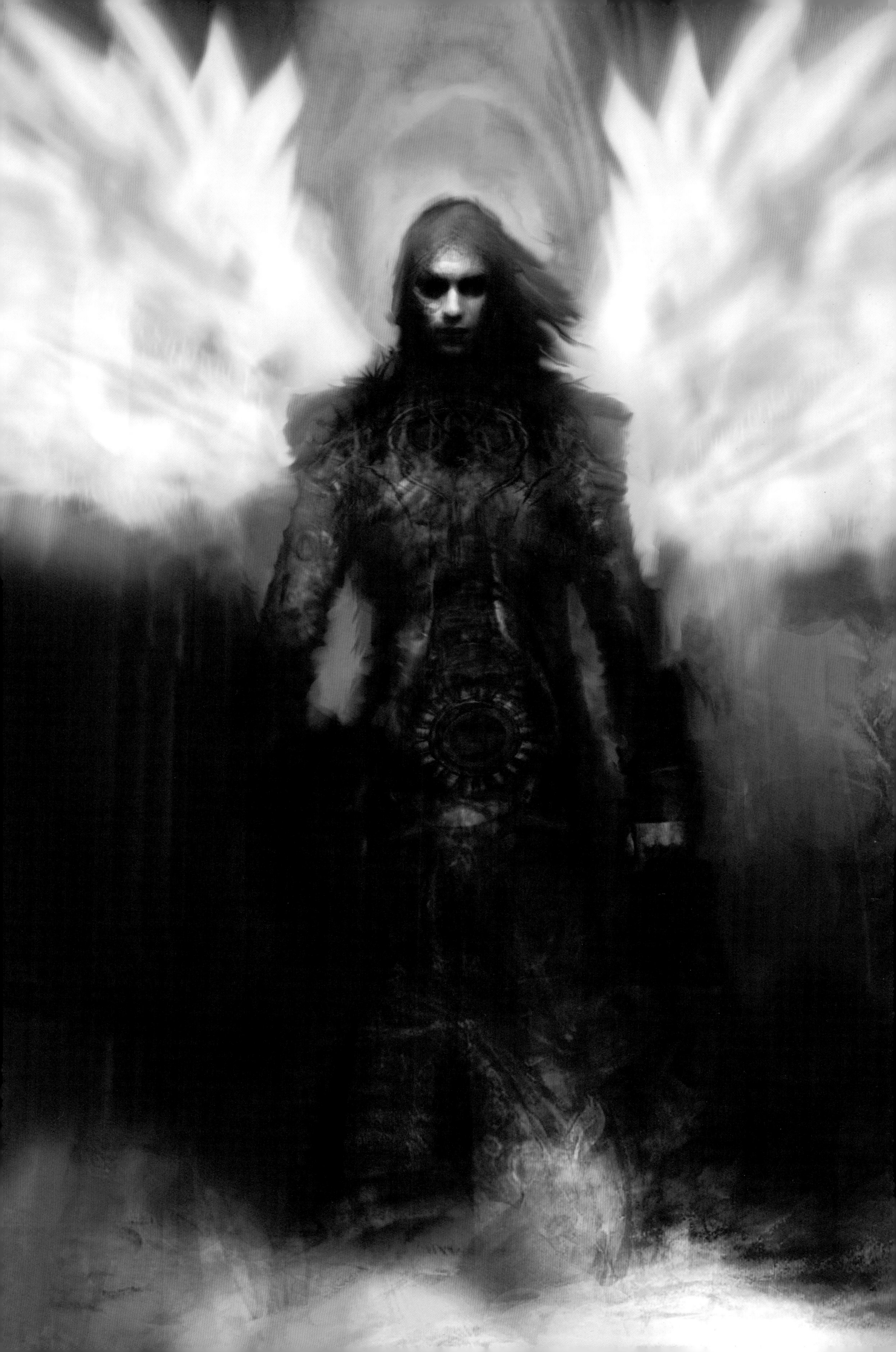

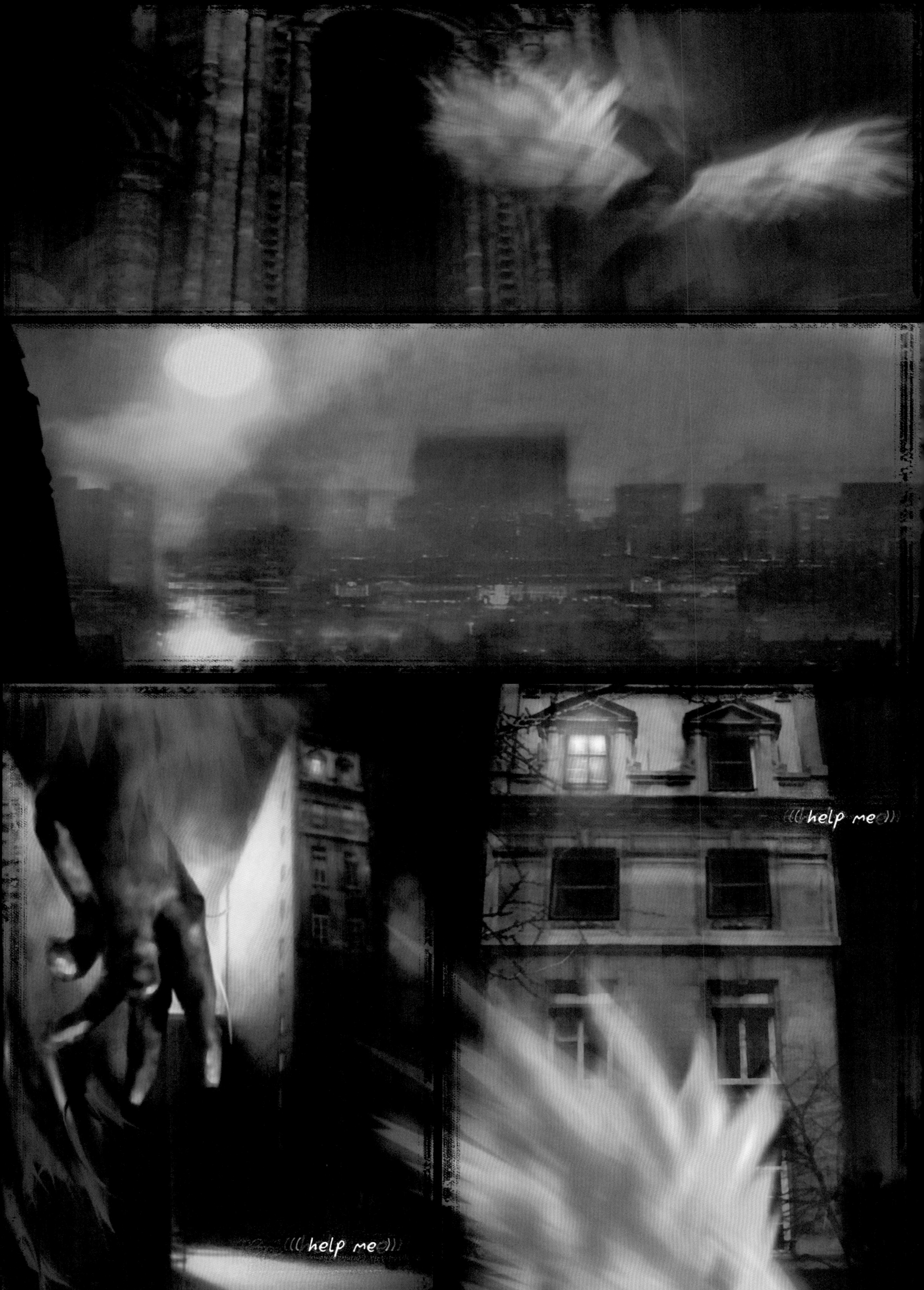
(((help me)))
(((help me)))

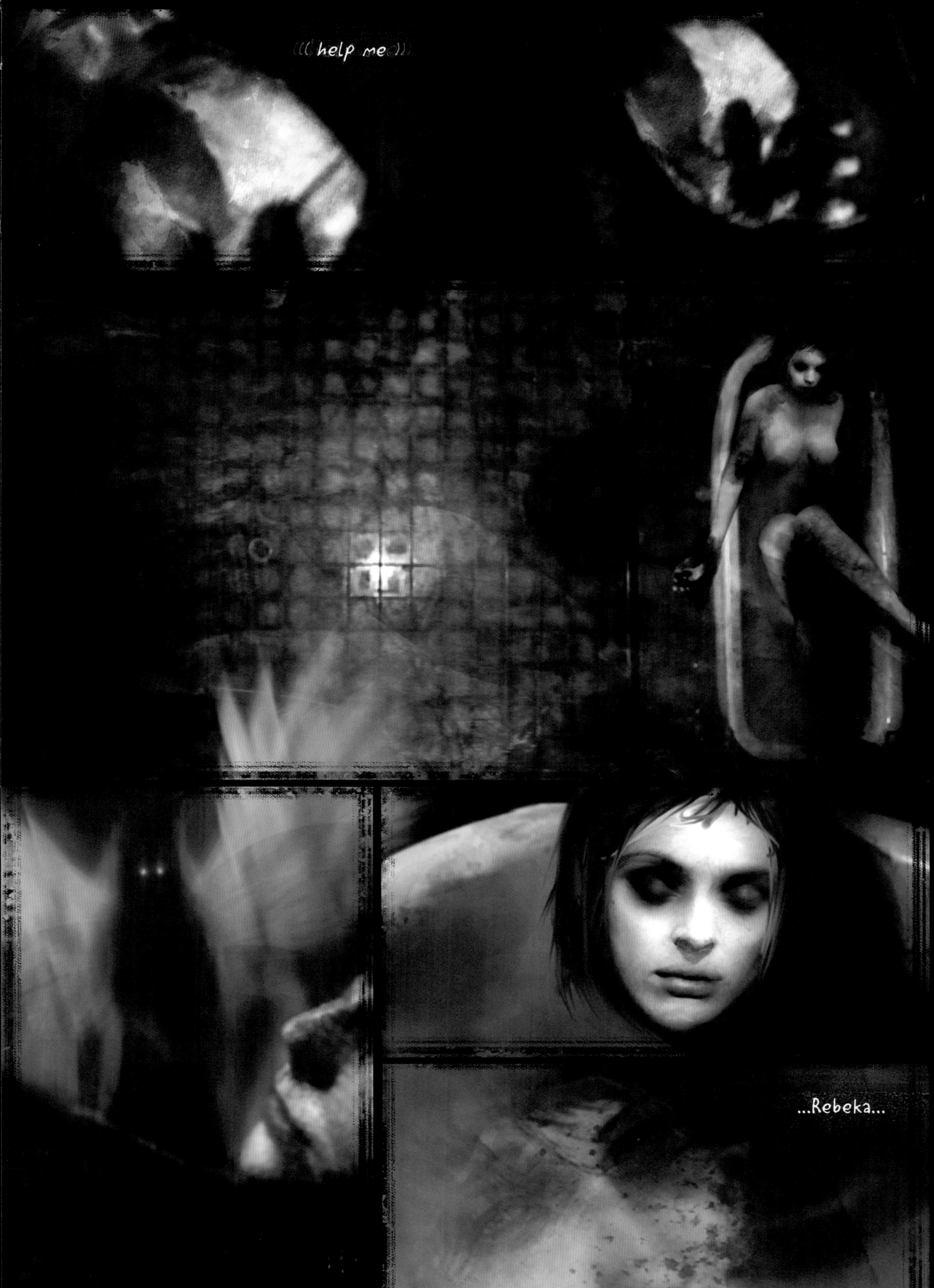
(((help me)))
...Rebeka...

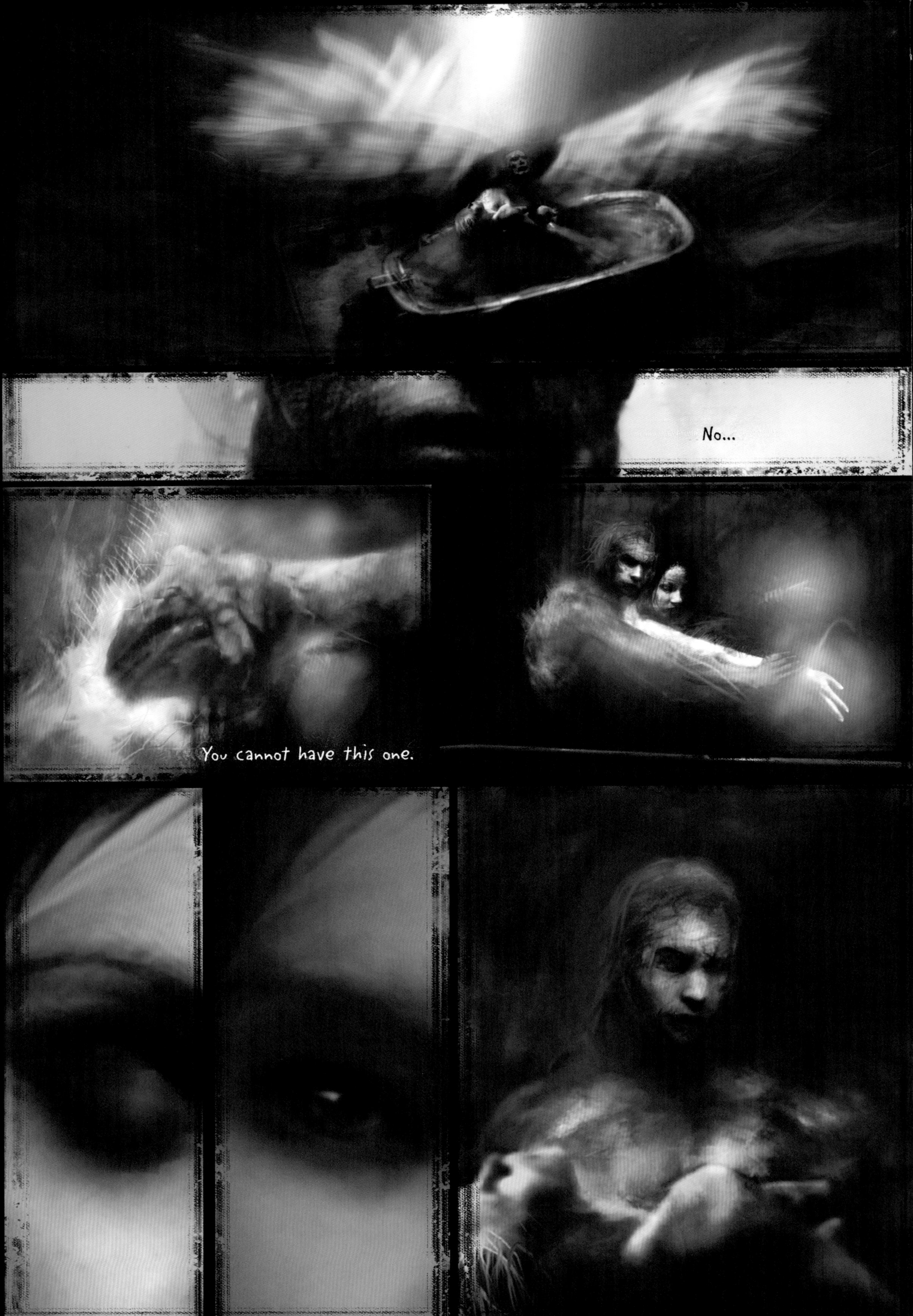
No...
You cannot have this one.

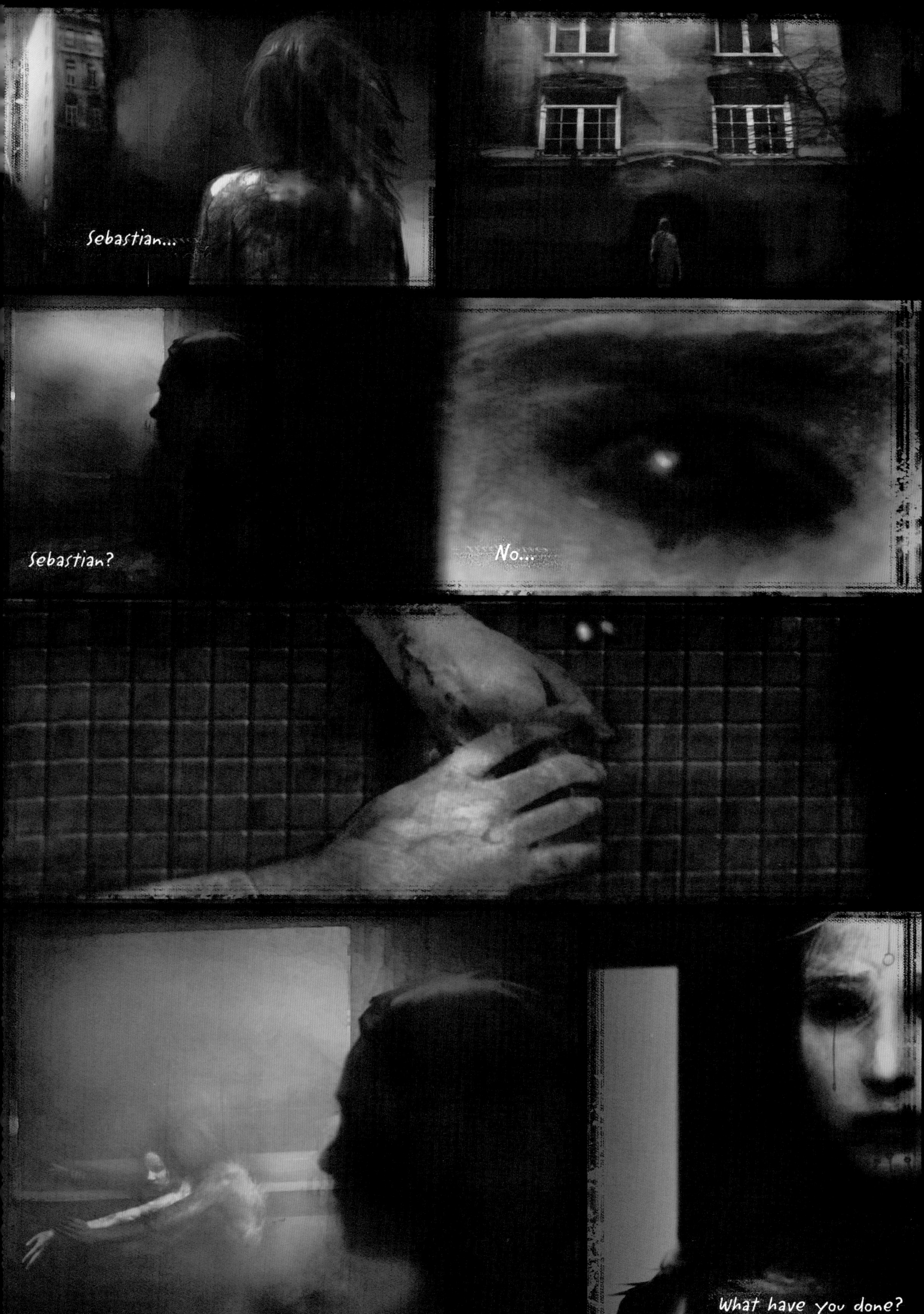
Sebastian...
Sebastian?
No...
What have you done?

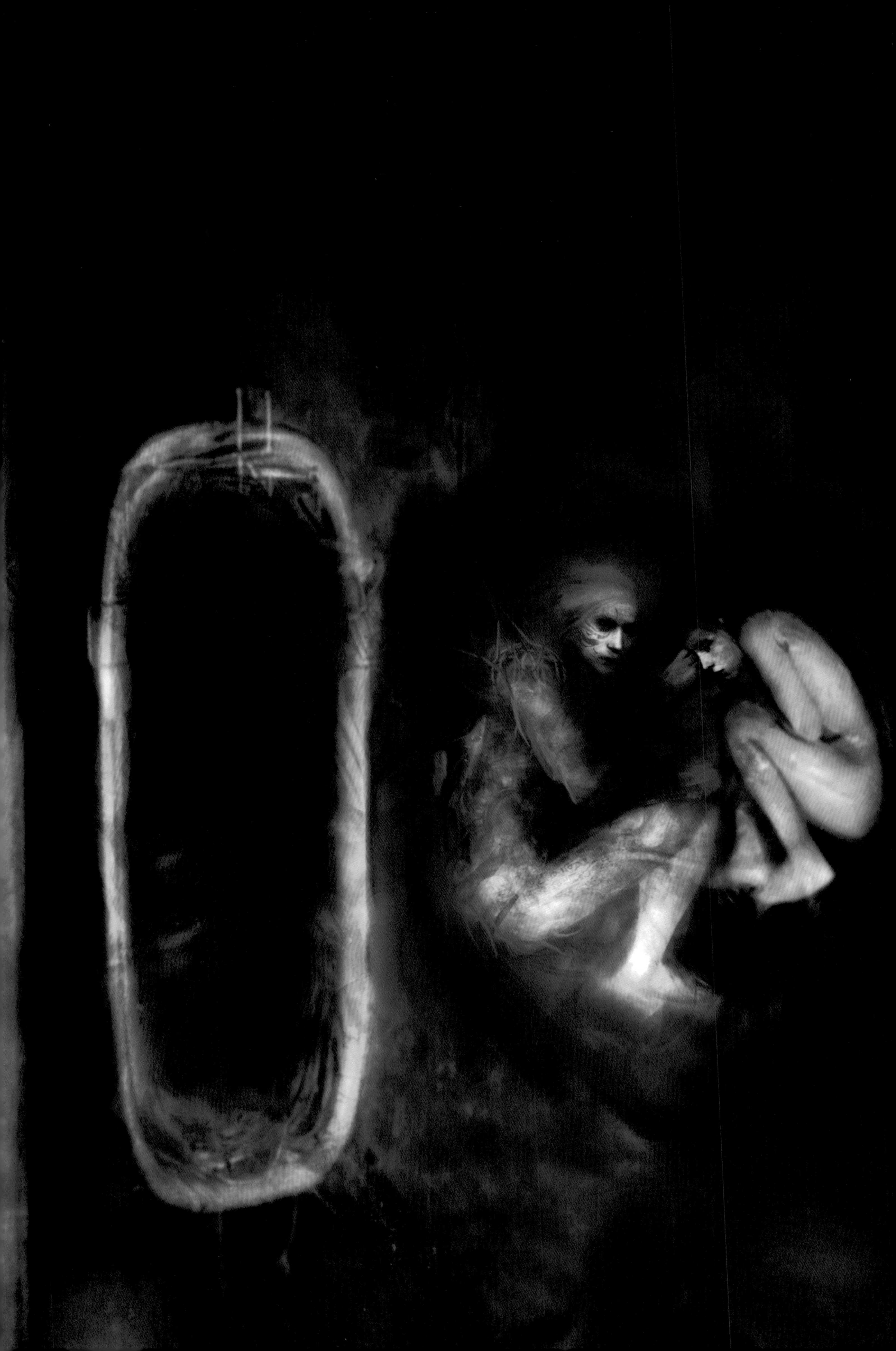

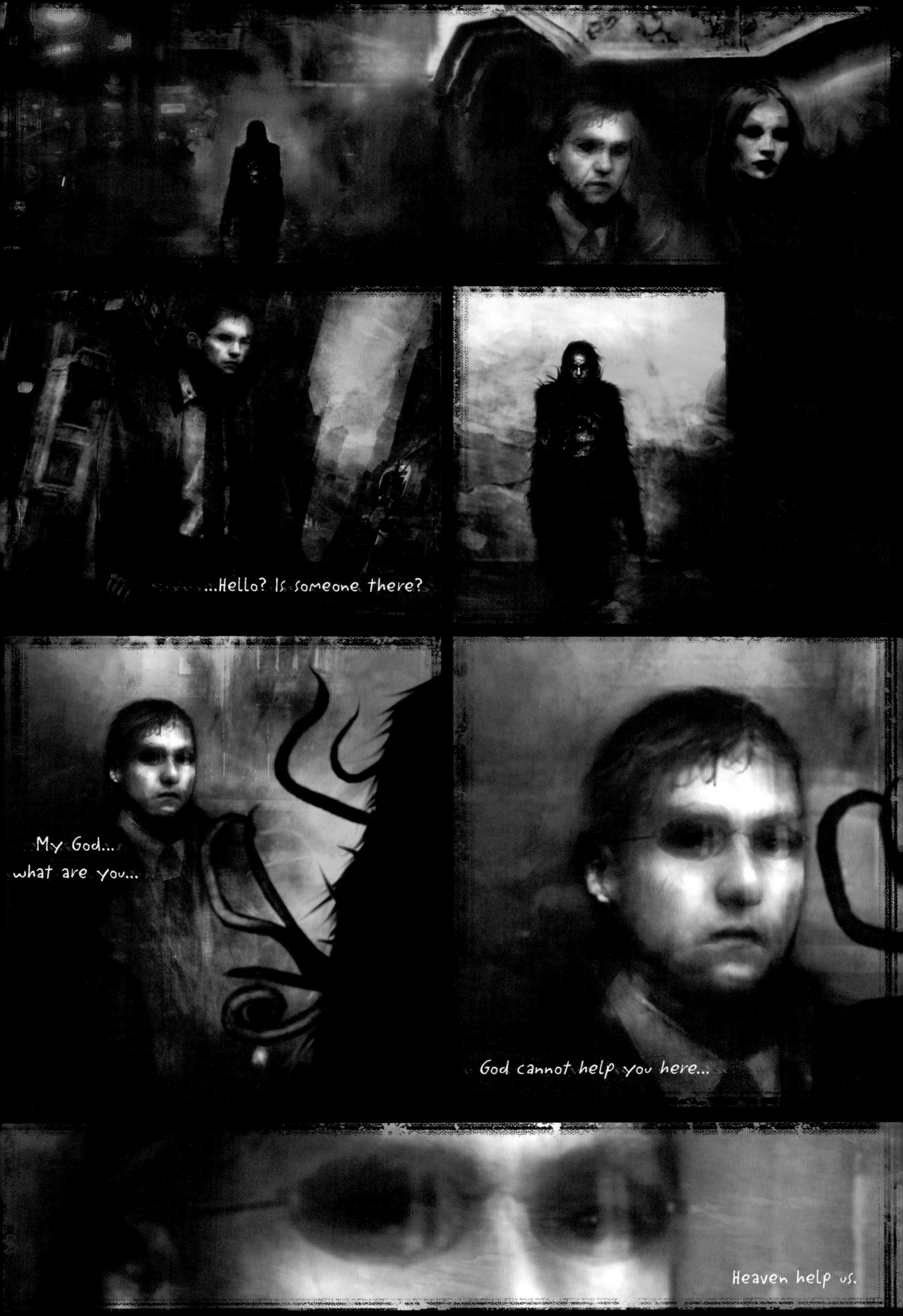
...Hello? Is someone there?
My God...
what are you...
God cannot help you here...
Heaven help us.

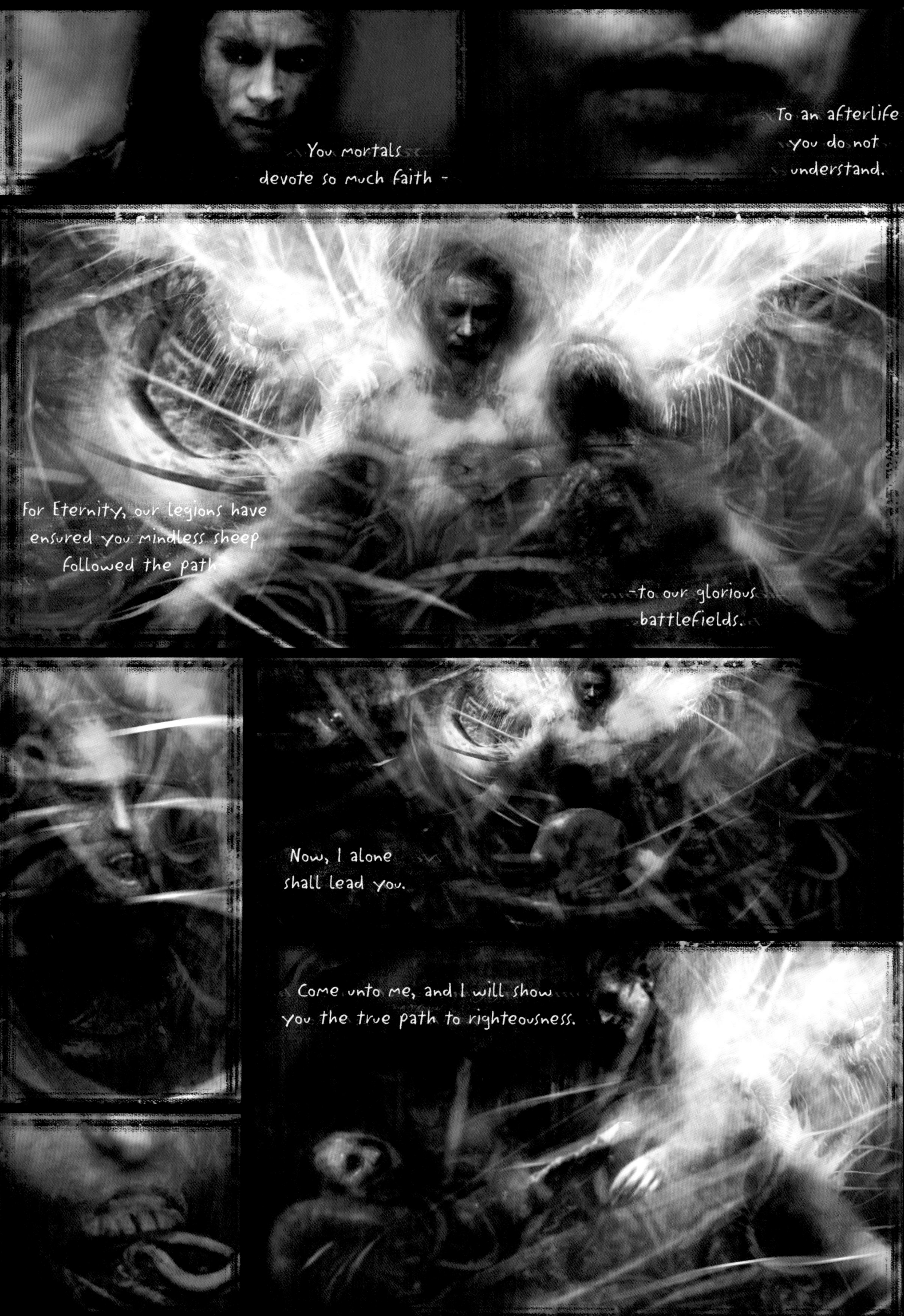
You mortals
devote so much faith -
To an afterlife
you do not
understand.
for Eternity, our legions have
ensured you mindless sheep
followed the path-
-to our glorious
battlefields.
Now, I alone
shall lead you.
Come unto me, and I will show
you the true path to righteousness.

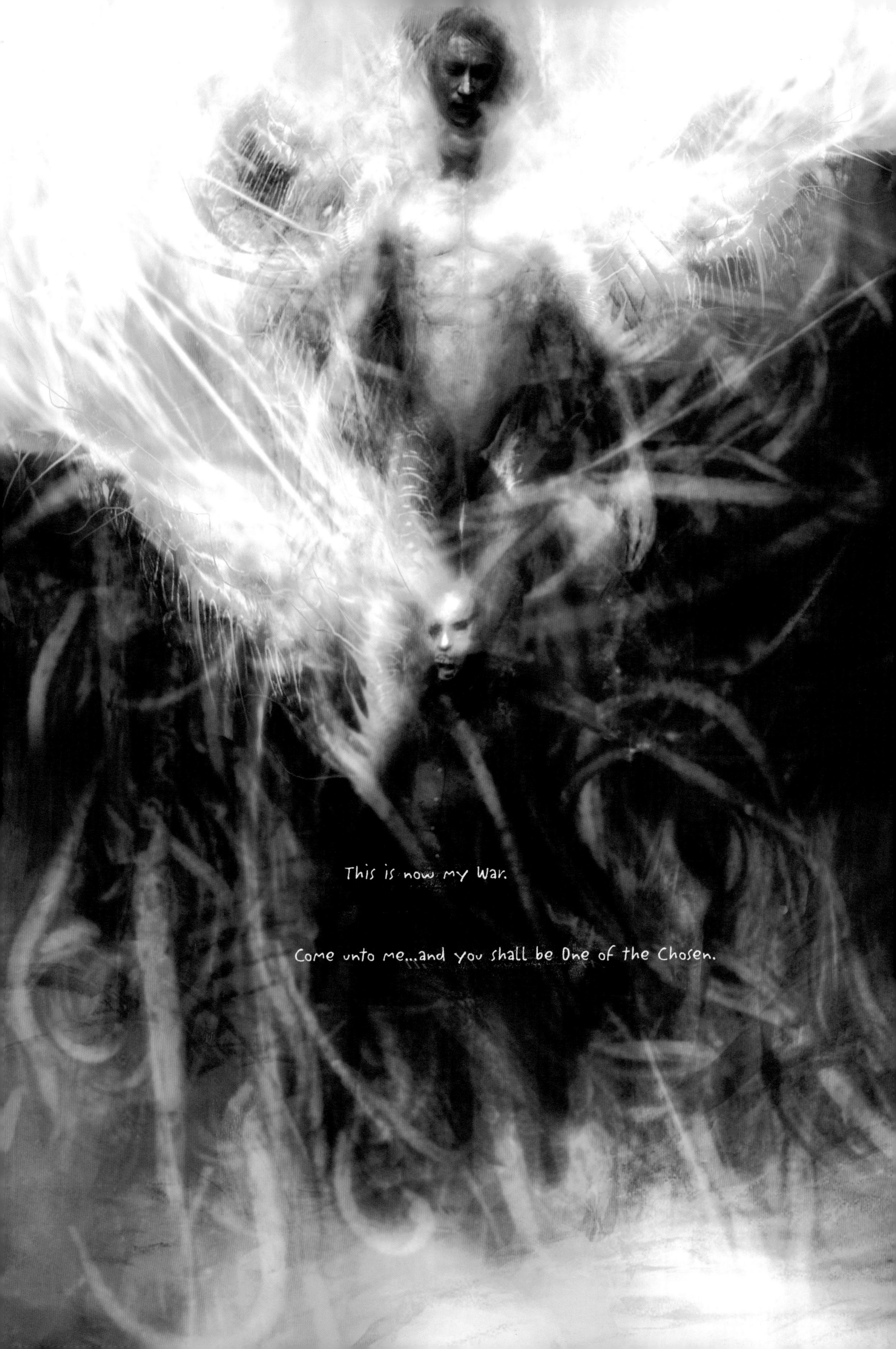
This is now my War.
Come unto me...and you shall be One of the Chosen.

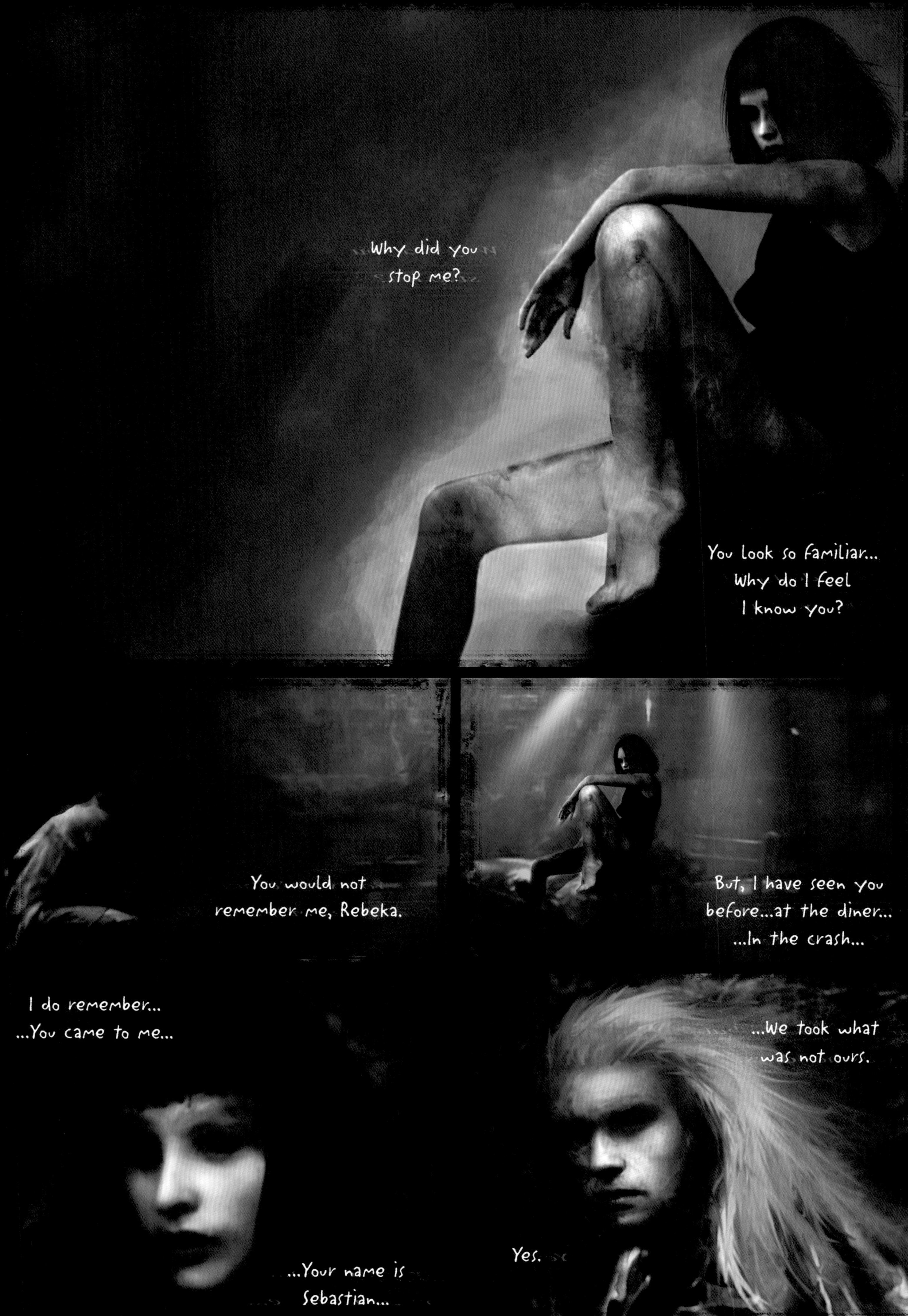
Why did you stop me?
You look so familiar... Why do I feel I know you?
You would not remember me, Rebeka.
But, I have seen you before...at the diner... ...In the crash...
I do remember... ...You came to me...
...We took what was not ours.
...Your name is Sebastian...
Yes.

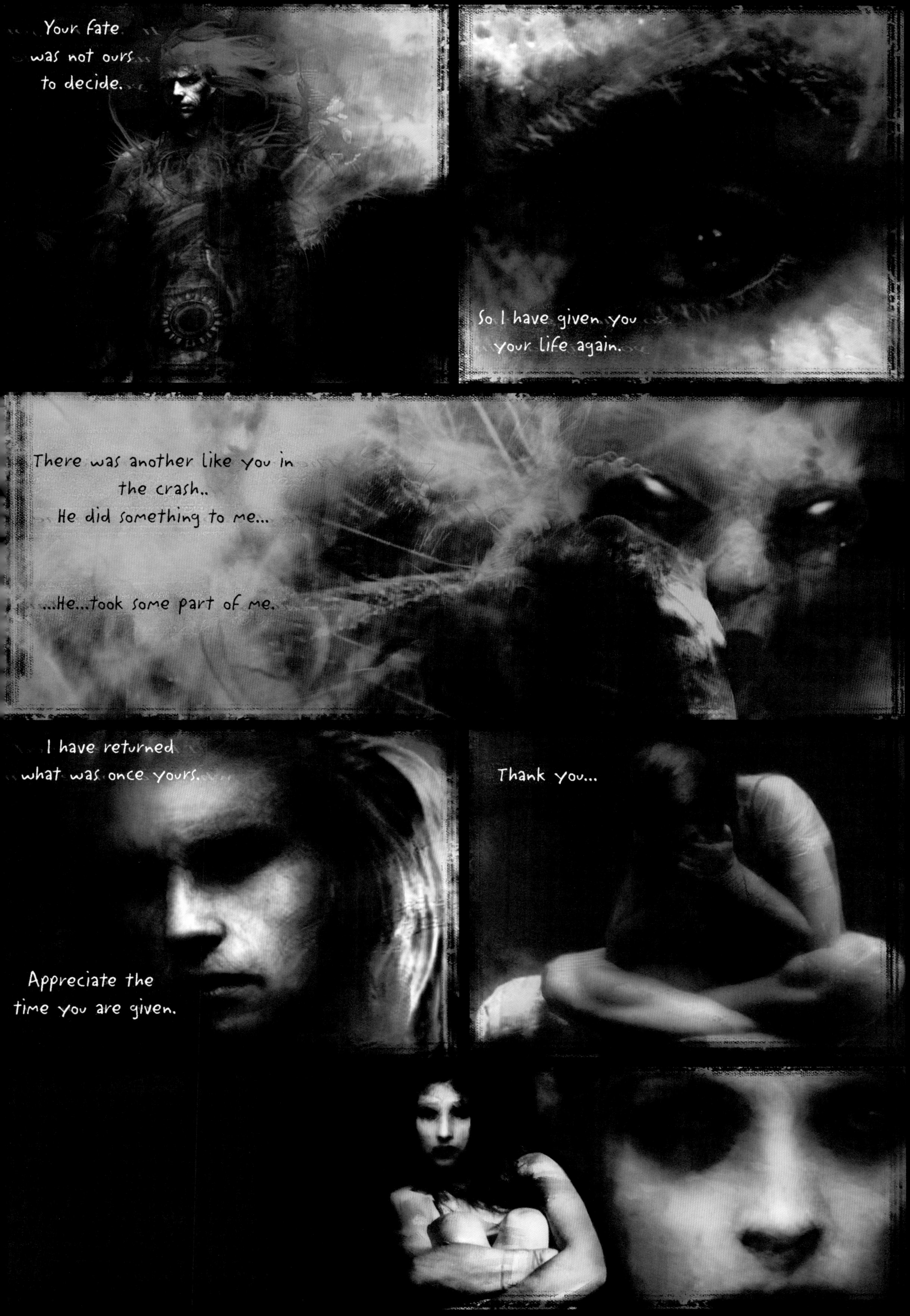
Your fate was not ours to decide.
So I have given you your life again.
There was another like you in the crash.. He did something to me...
...He...took some part of me.
I have returned what was once yours.
Appreciate the time you are given.
Thank you...

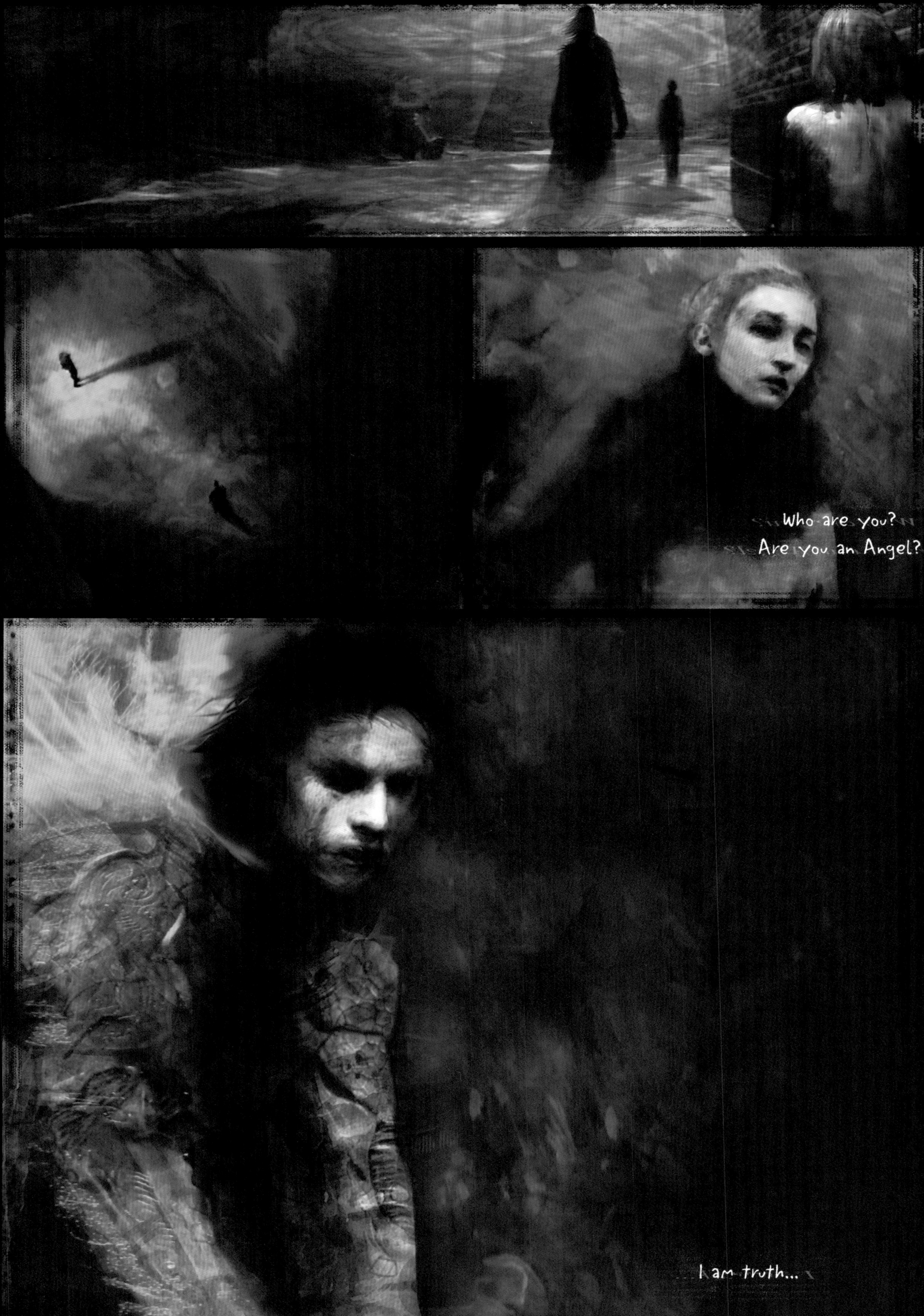
Who are you?
Are you an Angel?
I am truth...

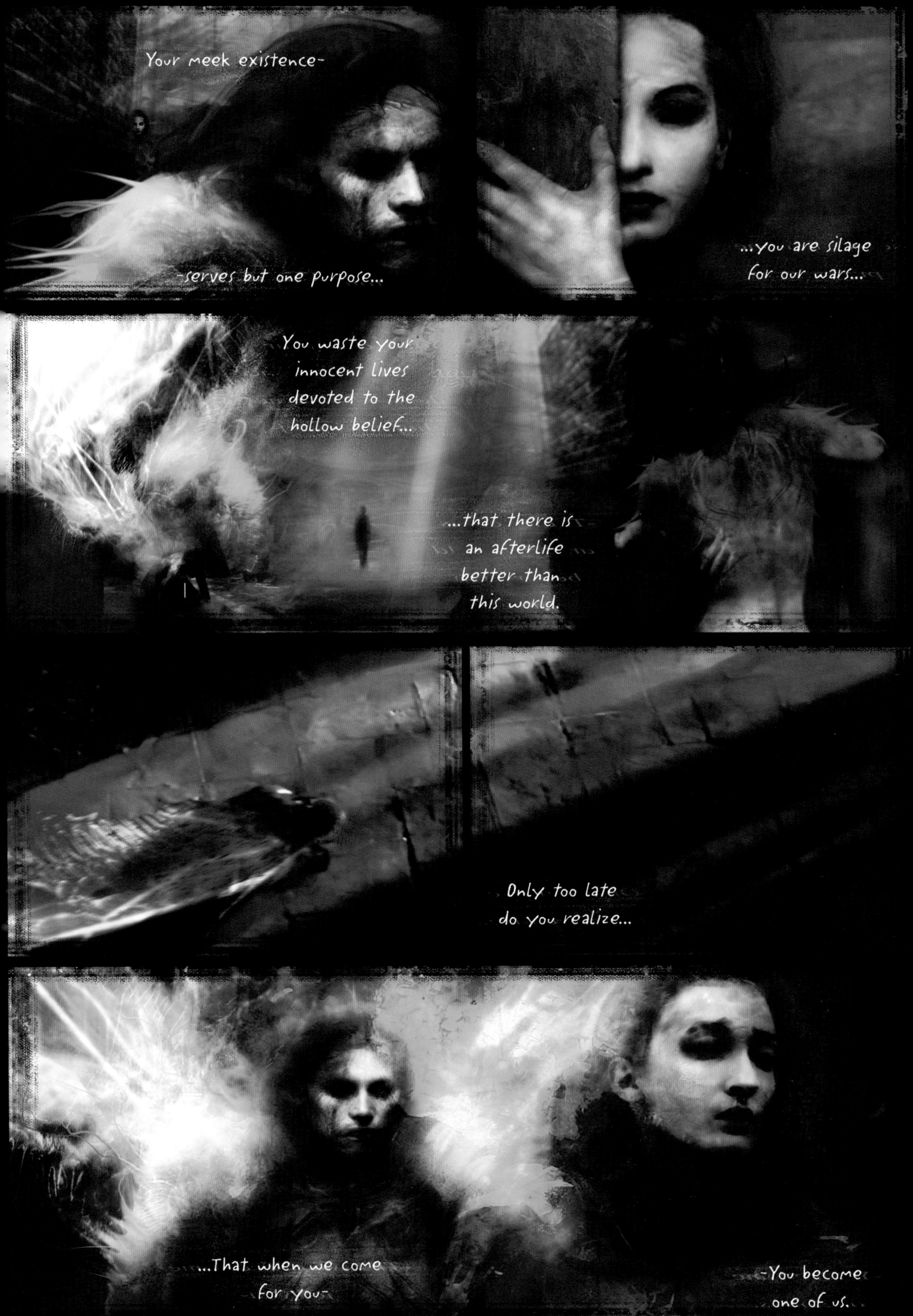
Your meek existence-
-serves but one purpose...
...you are silage for our wars...
You waste your innocent lives devoted to the hollow belief...
...that there is an afterlife better than this world.
Only too late do you realize...
...That when we come for you-
-You become one of us.

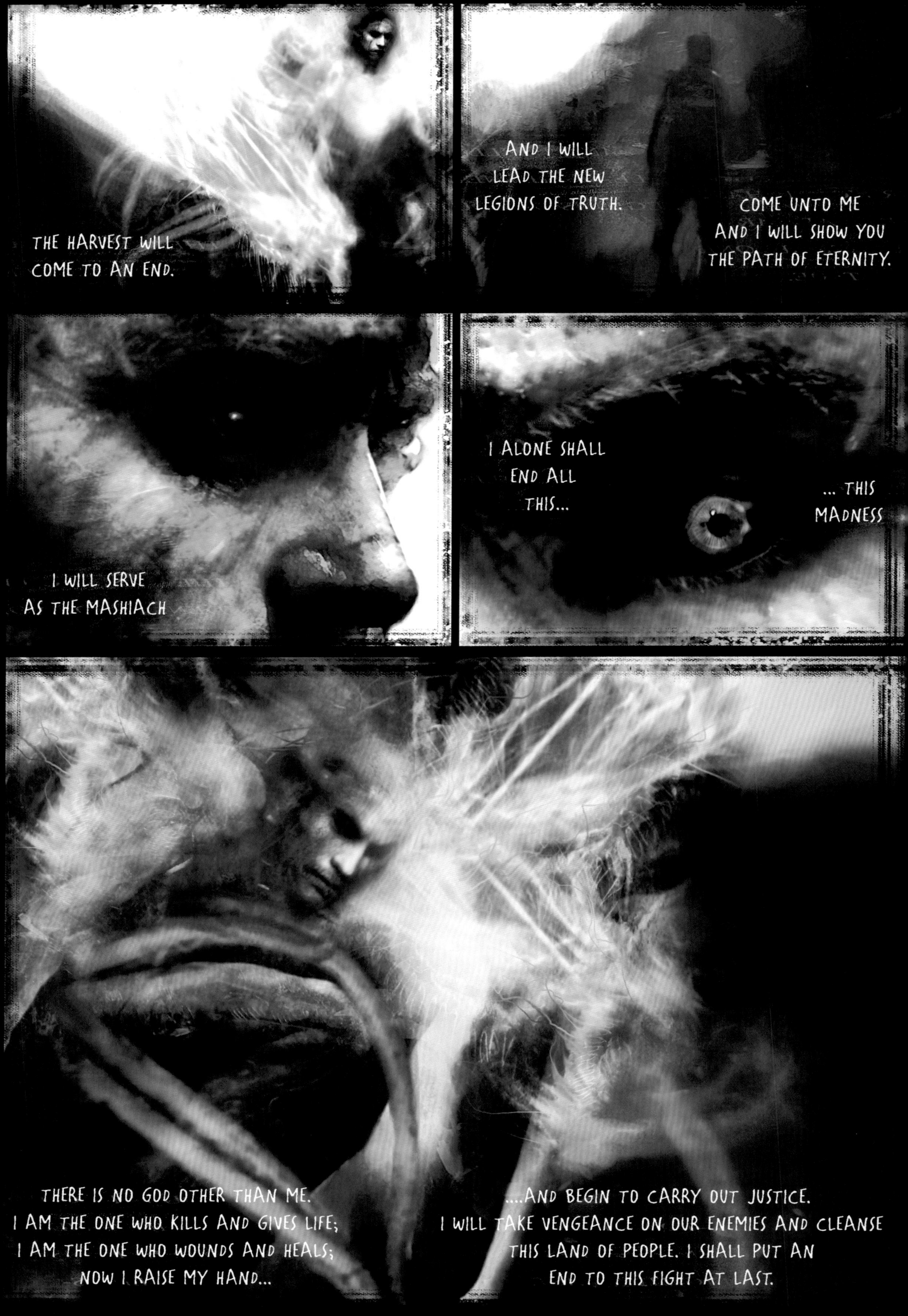
THE HARVEST WILL COME TO AN END.
AND I WILL LEAD THE NEW LEGIONS OF TRUTH.
COME UNTO ME AND I WILL SHOW YOU THE PATH OF ETERNITY.
I WILL SERVE AS THE MASHIACH
I ALONE SHALL END ALL THIS...
... THIS MADNESS
THERE IS NO GOD OTHER THAN ME. I AM THE ONE WHO KILLS AND GIVES LIFE; I AM THE ONE WHO WOUNDS AND HEALS; NOW I RAISE MY HAND...
....AND BEGIN TO CARRY OUT JUSTICE. I WILL TAKE VENGEANCE ON OUR ENEMIES AND CLEANSE THIS LAND OF PEOPLE. I SHALL PUT AN END TO THIS FIGHT AT LAST.

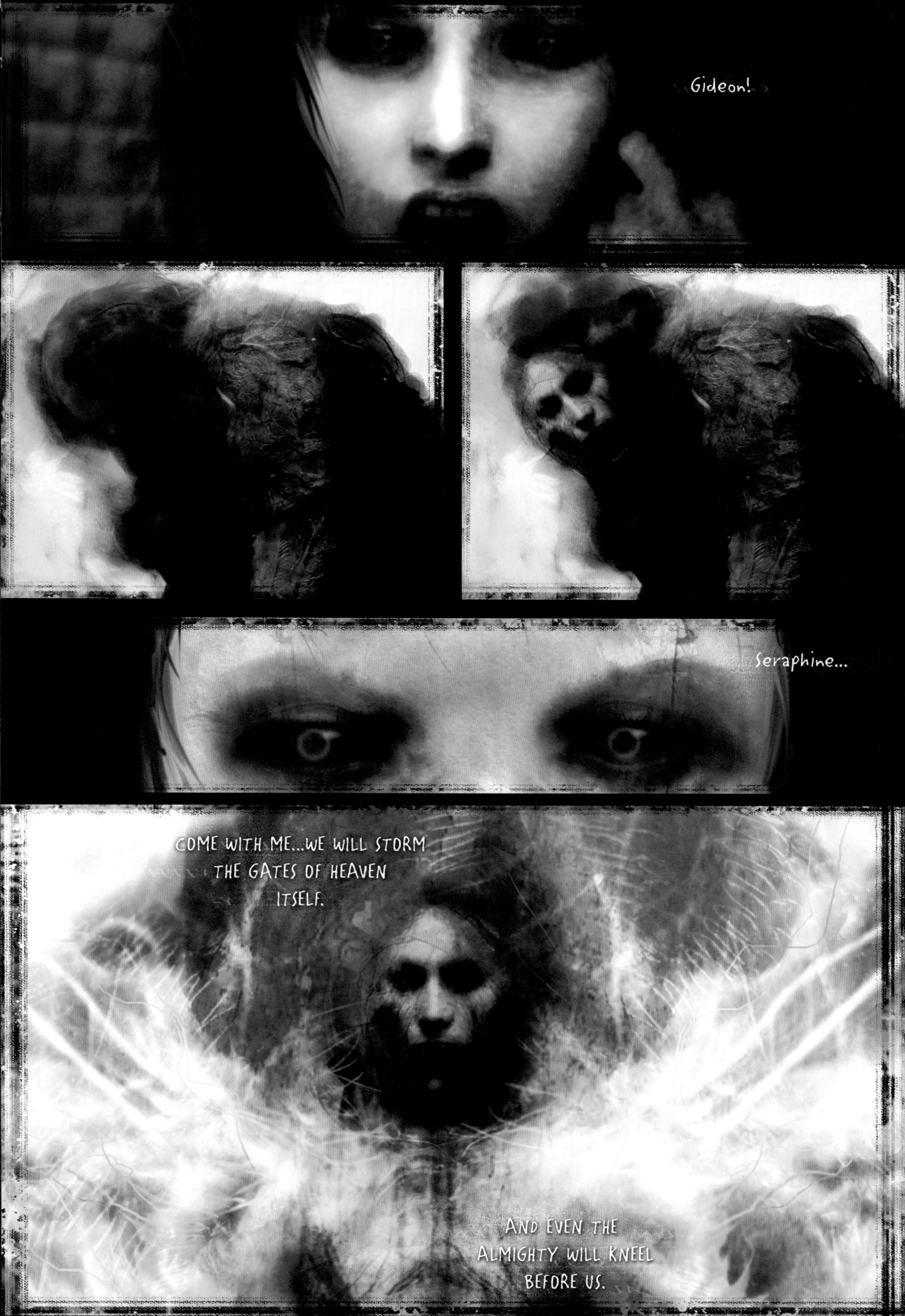
Gideon!
Seraphine...
COME WITH ME...WE WILL STORM THE GATES OF HEAVEN ITSELF.
AND EVEN THE ALMIGHTY WILL KNEEL BEFORE US.

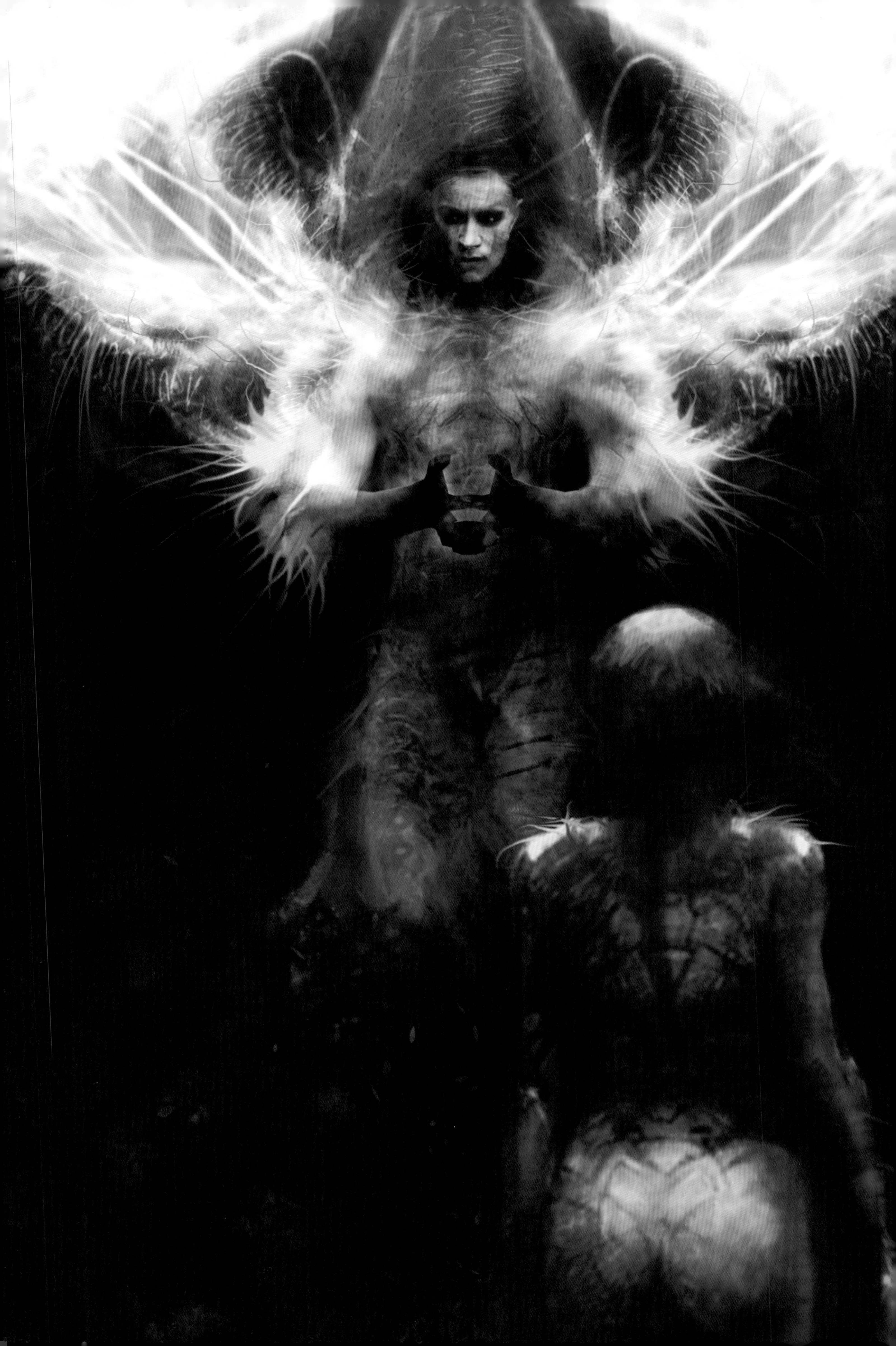

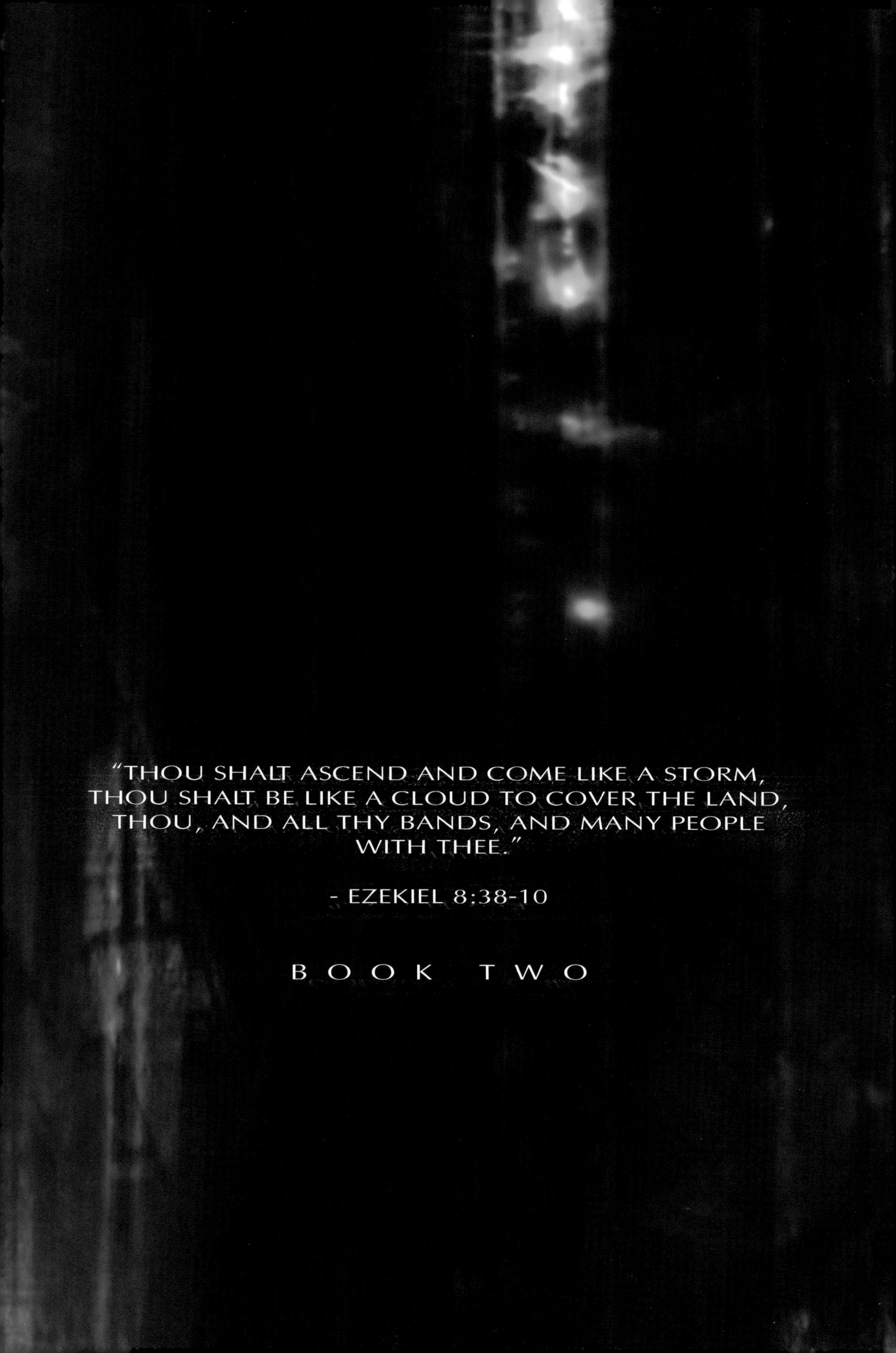

"THOU SHALT ASCEND AND COME LIKE A STORM,
THOU SHALT BE LIKE A CLOUD TO COVER THE LAND,
THOU, AND ALL THY BANDS, AND MANY PEOPLE
WITH THEE."

- EZEKIEL 8:38-10

BOOK TWO

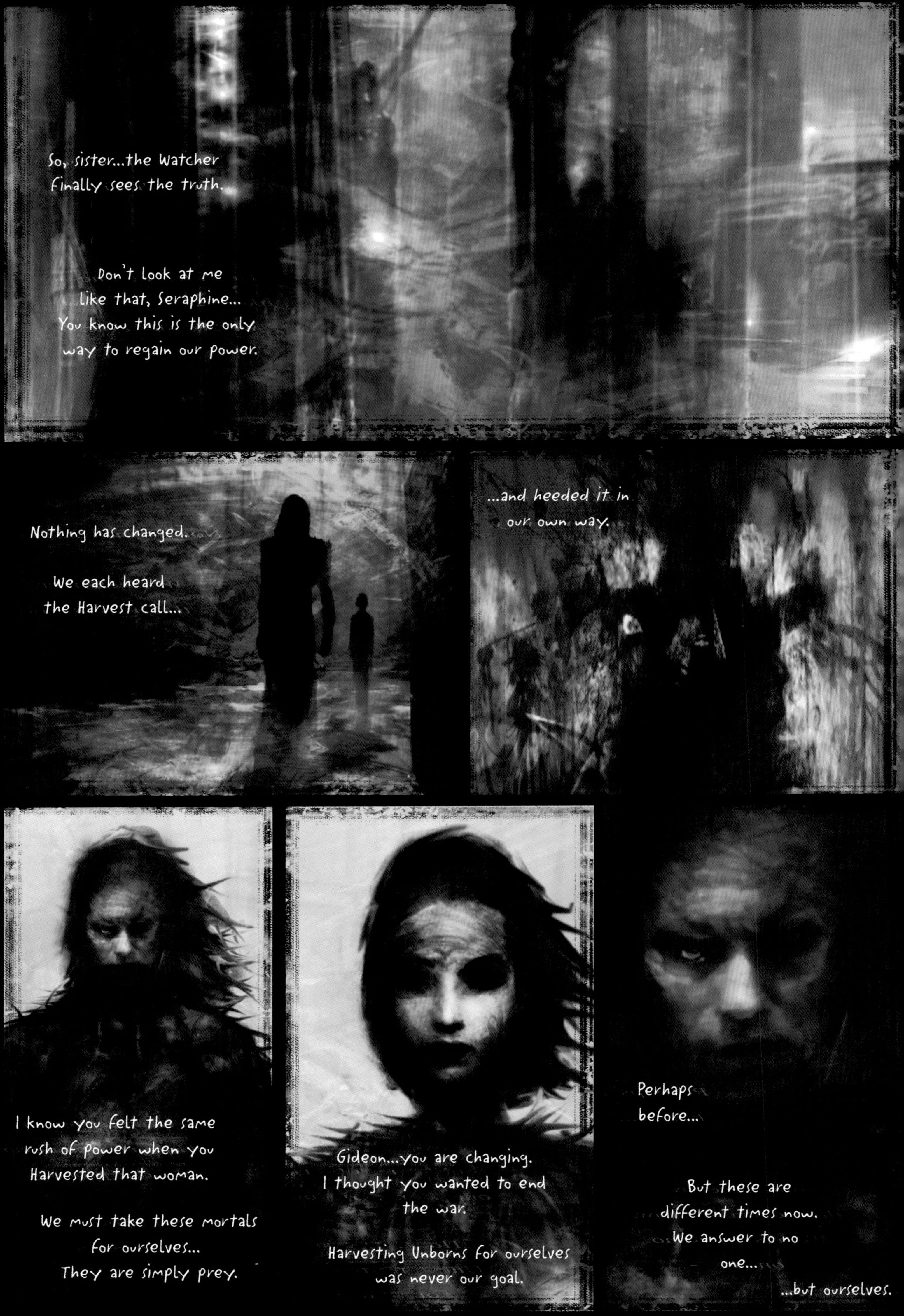

So, sister...the Watcher finally sees the truth.
Don't look at me like that, Seraphine... You know this is the only way to regain our power.
Nothing has changed.
We each heard the Harvest call...
...and heeded it in our own way.
I know you felt the same rush of power when you Harvested that woman.
We must take these mortals for ourselves... They are simply prey.
Gideon...you are changing. I thought you wanted to end the war.
Harvesting Unborns for ourselves was never our goal.
Perhaps before...
But these are different times now. We answer to no one...
...but ourselves.

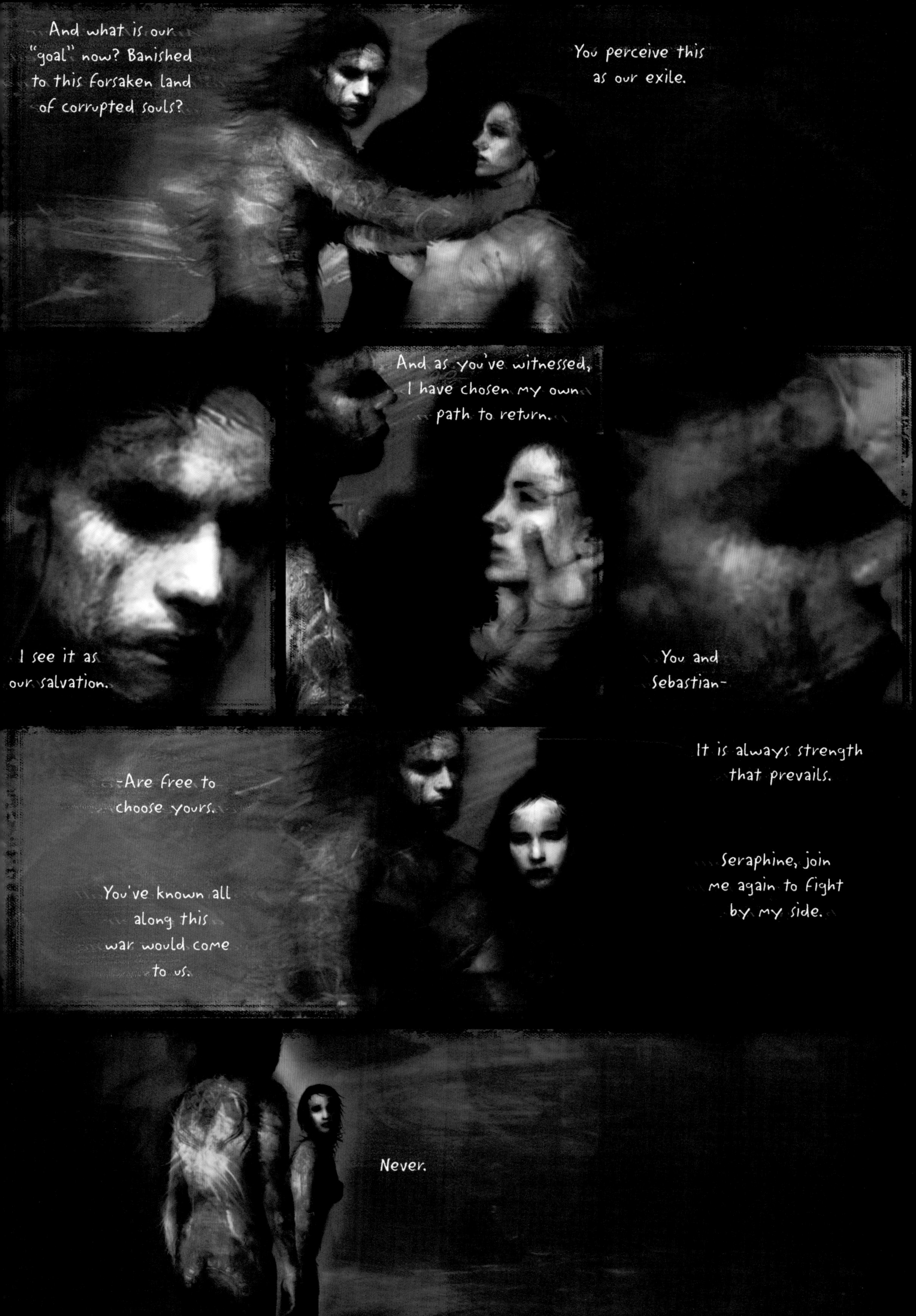
And what is our "goal" now? Banished to this forsaken land of corrupted souls?
You perceive this as our exile.
I see it as our salvation.
And as you've witnessed, I have chosen my own path to return.
You and Sebastian-
-Are free to choose yours.
You've known all along this war would come to us.
It is always strength that prevails.
Seraphine, join me again to fight by my side.
Never.

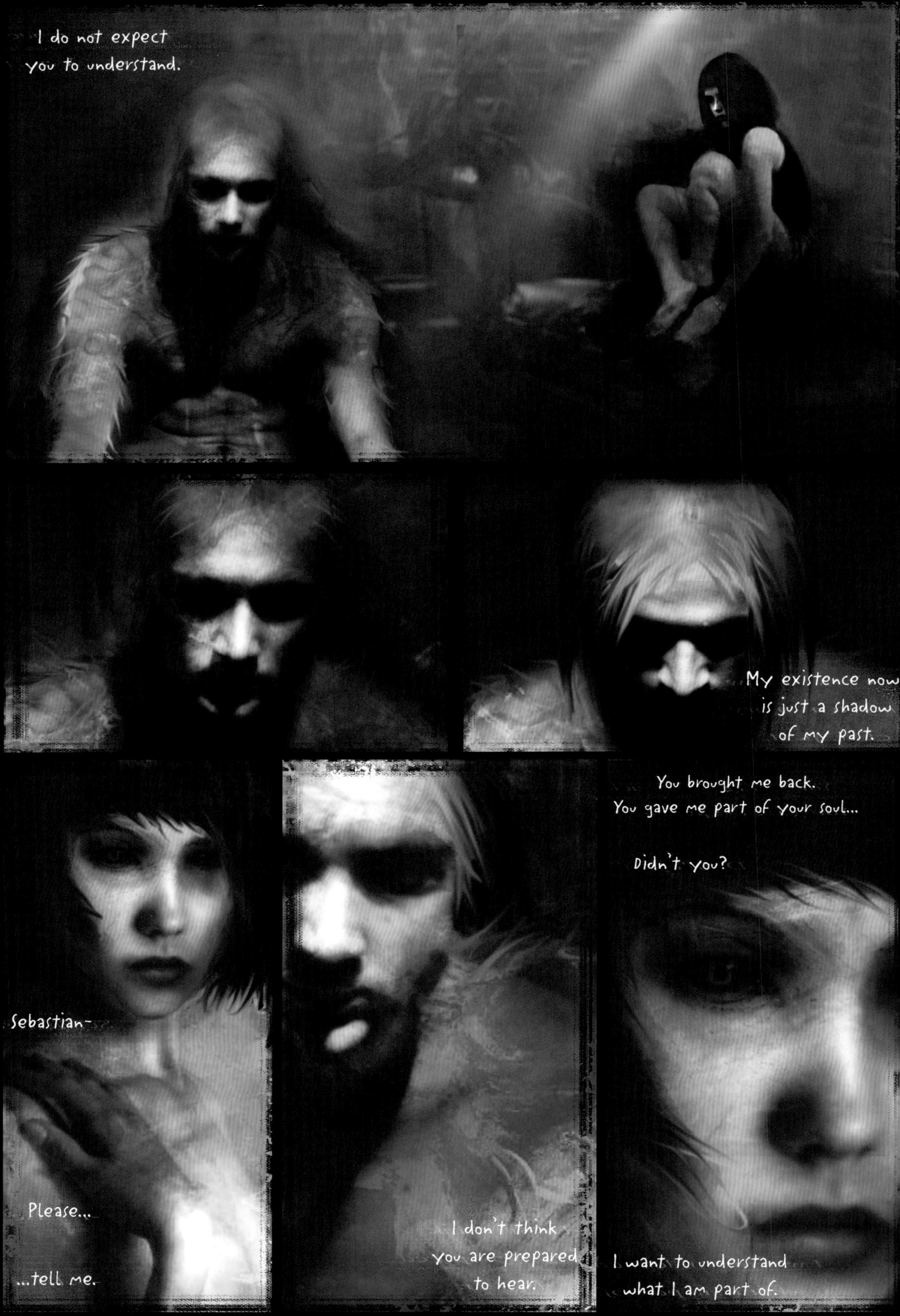
I do not expect you to understand.
My existence now is just a shadow of my past.
Sebastian-
Please...
...tell me.
I don't think you are prepared to hear.
You brought me back. You gave me part of your soul...
Didn't you?
I want to understand what I am part of.

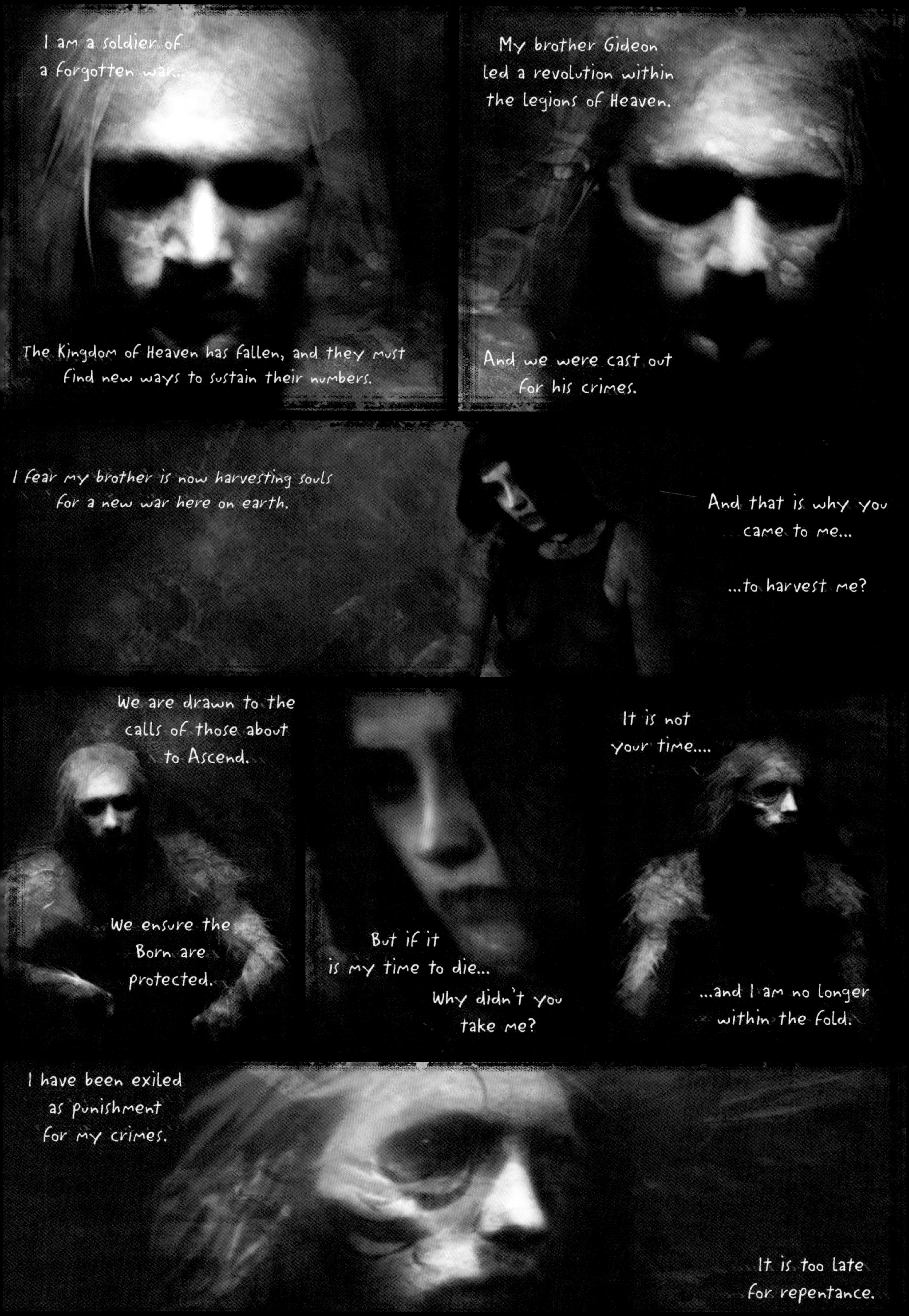

I am a soldier of a forgotten war...
The Kingdom of Heaven has fallen, and they must find new ways to sustain their numbers.
My brother Gideon led a revolution within the legions of Heaven.
And we were cast out for his crimes.
I fear my brother is now harvesting souls for a new war here on earth.
And that is why you came to me...
...to harvest me?
We are drawn to the calls of those about to Ascend.
We ensure the Born are protected.
But if it is my time to die...
Why didn't you take me?
It is not your time....
...and I am no longer within the fold.
I have been exiled as punishment for my crimes.
It is too late for repentance.

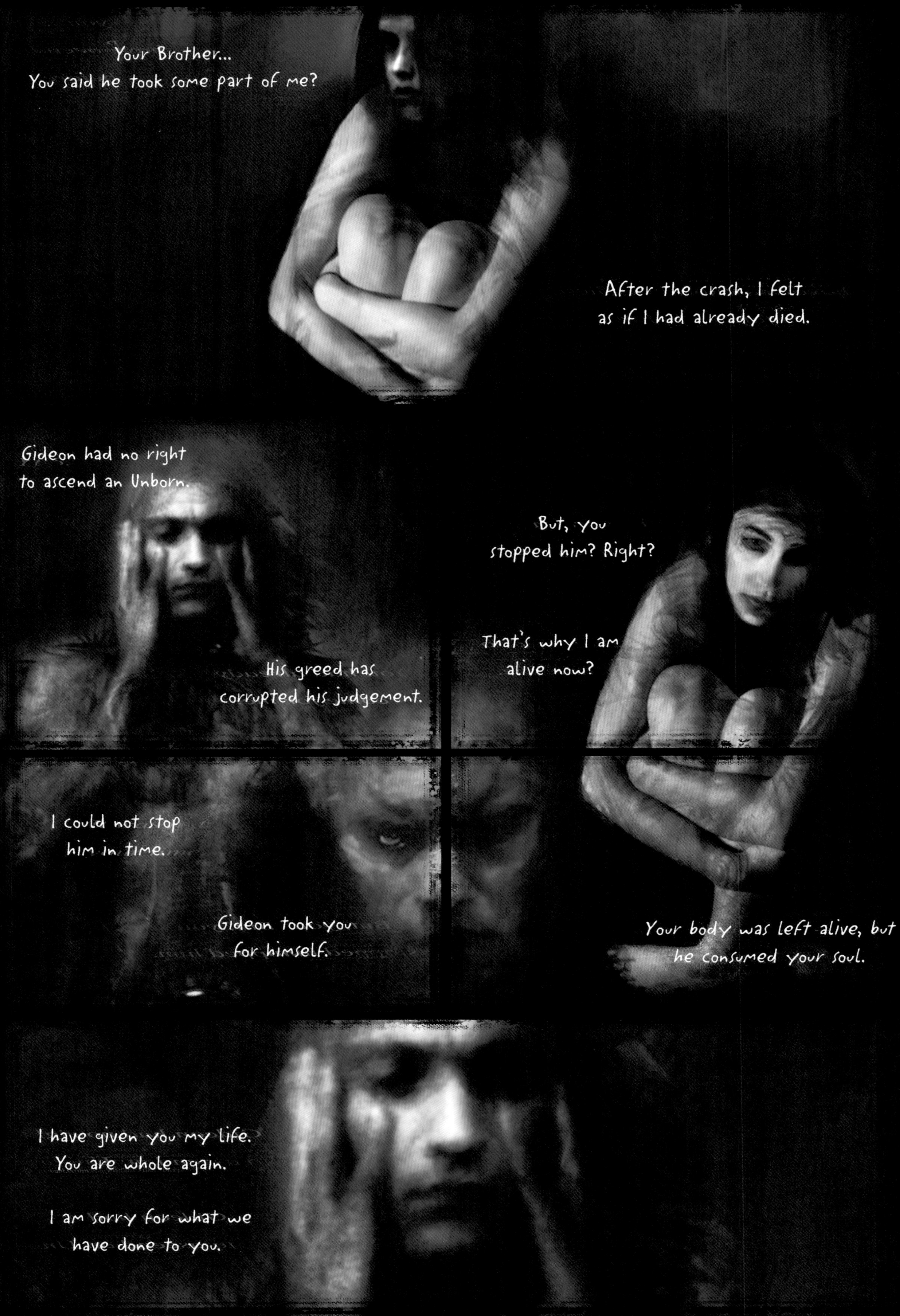
Your Brother...
You said he took some part of me?
After the crash, I felt
as if I had already died.
Gideon had no right
to ascend an Unborn.
His greed has
corrupted his judgement.
But, you
stopped him? Right?
That's why I am
alive now?
I could not stop
him in time.
Gideon took you
for himself.
Your body was left alive, but
he consumed your soul.
I have given you my life.
You are whole again.
I am sorry for what we
have done to you.

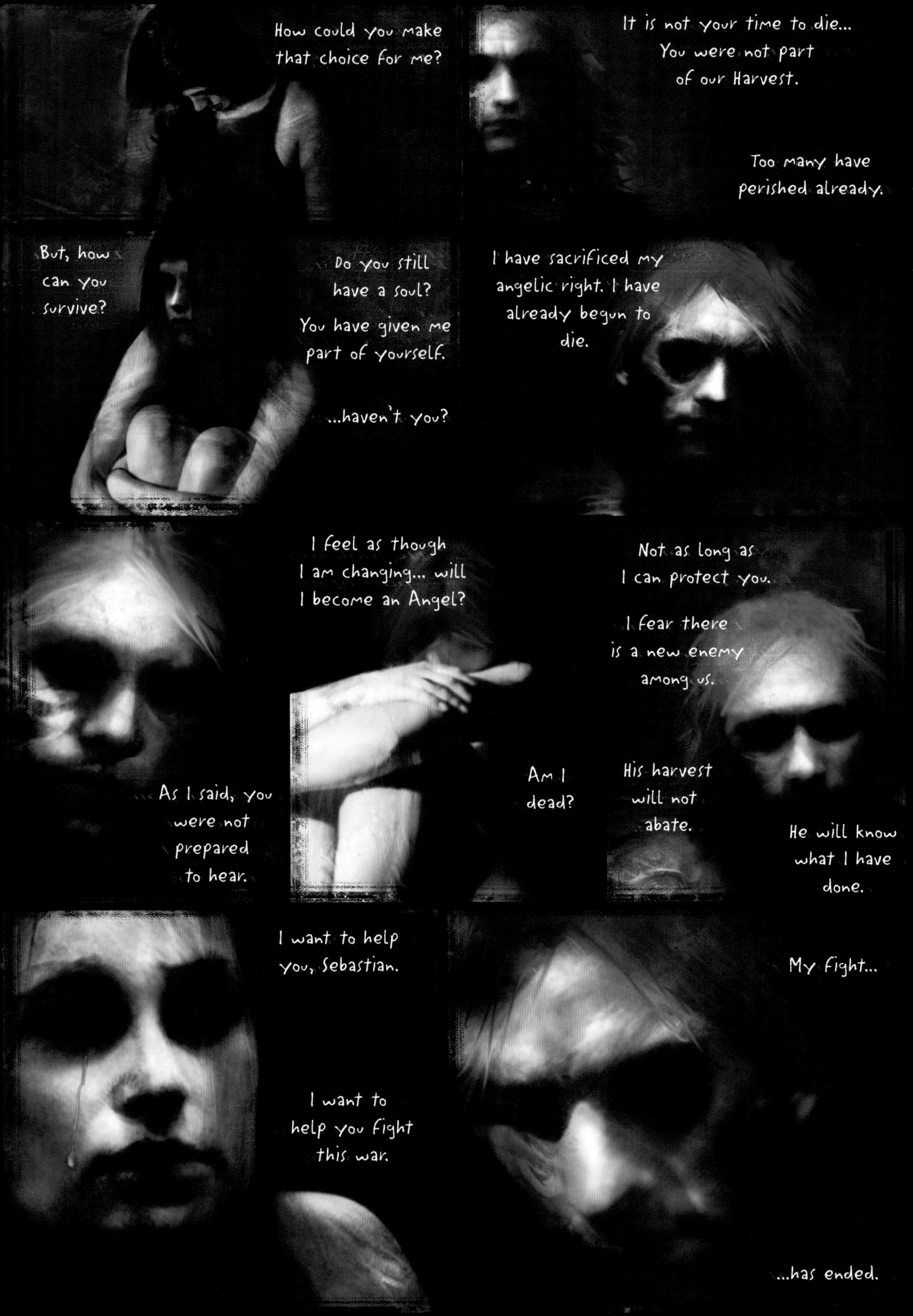
How could you make that choice for me?
It is not your time to die... You were not part of our Harvest.
Too many have perished already.
But, how can you survive?
Do you still have a soul?
You have given me part of yourself.
...haven't you?
I have sacrificed my angelic right. I have already begun to die.
I feel as though I am changing... will I become an Angel?
As I said, you were not prepared to hear.
Am I dead?
Not as long as I can protect you.
I fear there is a new enemy among us.
His harvest will not abate.
He will know what I have done.
I want to help you, Sebastian.
I want to help you fight this war.
My fight...
...has ended.

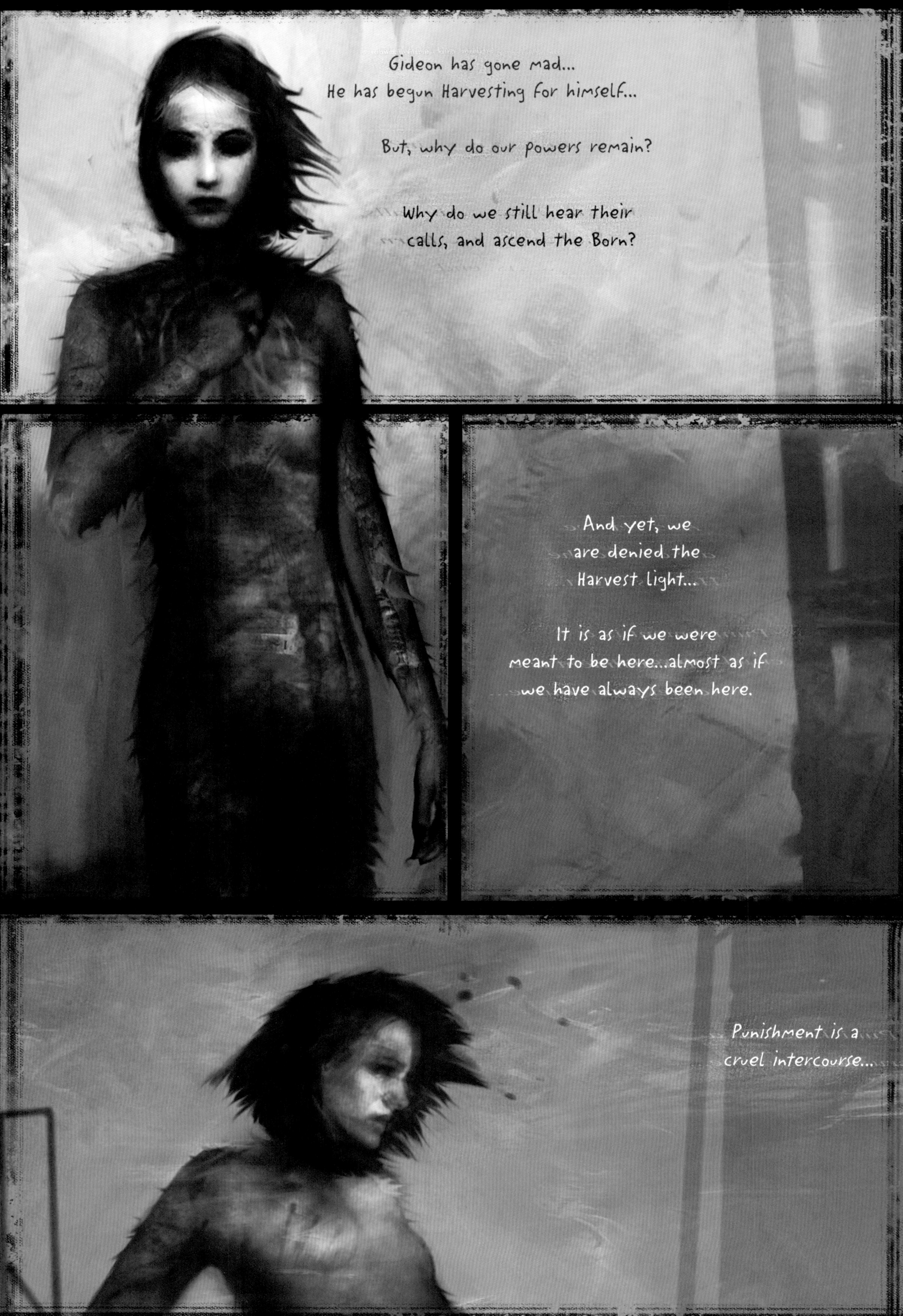
Gideon has gone mad...
He has begun Harvesting for himself...
But, why do our powers remain?
Why do we still hear their calls, and ascend the Born?
And yet, we are denied the Harvest light...
It is as if we were meant to be here...almost as if we have always been here.
Punishment is a cruel intercourse...

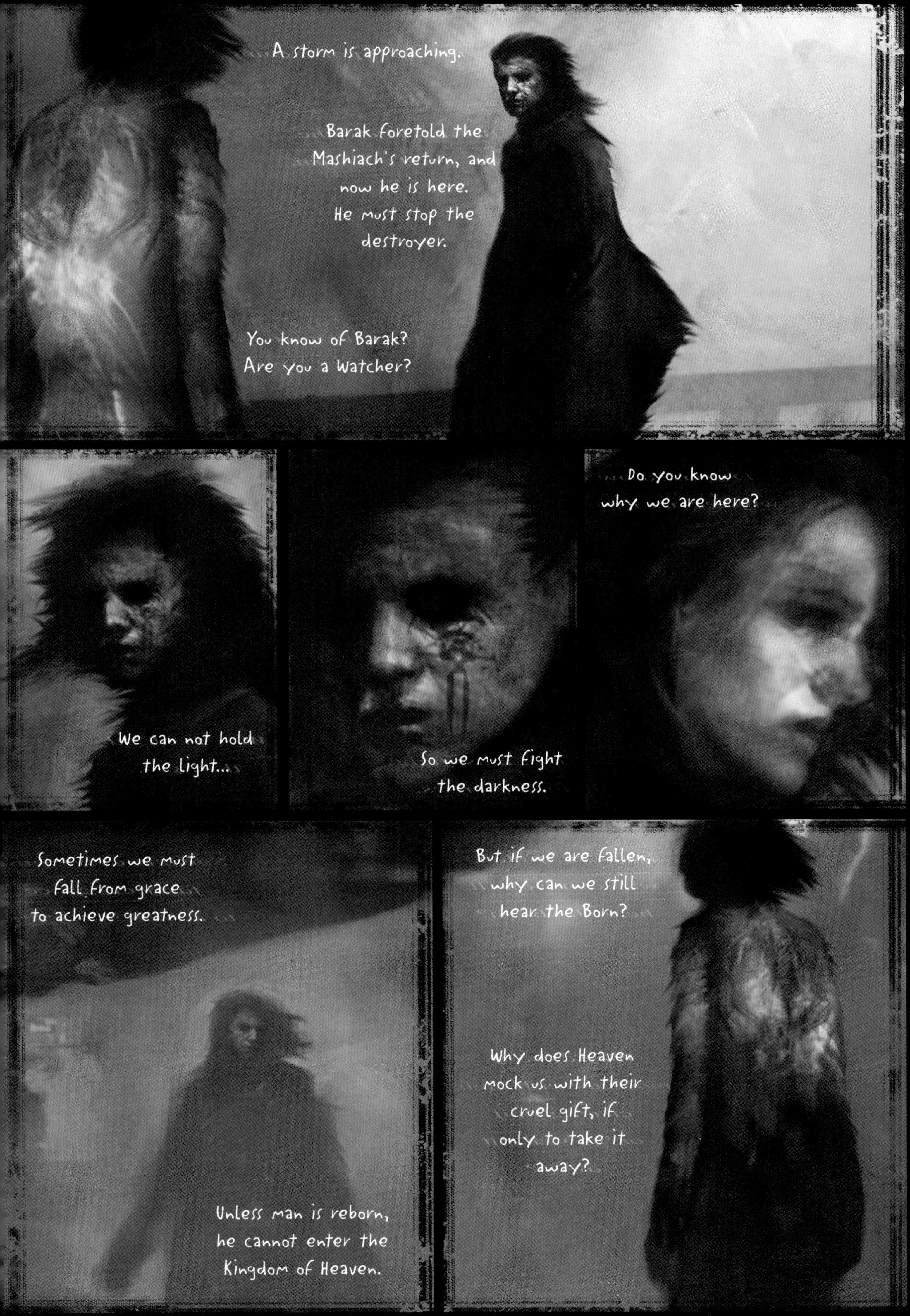
A storm is approaching.
Barak foretold the Mashiach's return, and now he is here. He must stop the destroyer.
You know of Barak? Are you a Watcher?
Do you know why we are here?
We can not hold the light...
So we must fight the darkness.
Sometimes we must fall from grace to achieve greatness.
Unless man is reborn, he cannot enter the Kingdom of Heaven.
But if we are fallen, why can we still hear the Born?
Why does Heaven mock us with their cruel gift, if only to take it away?

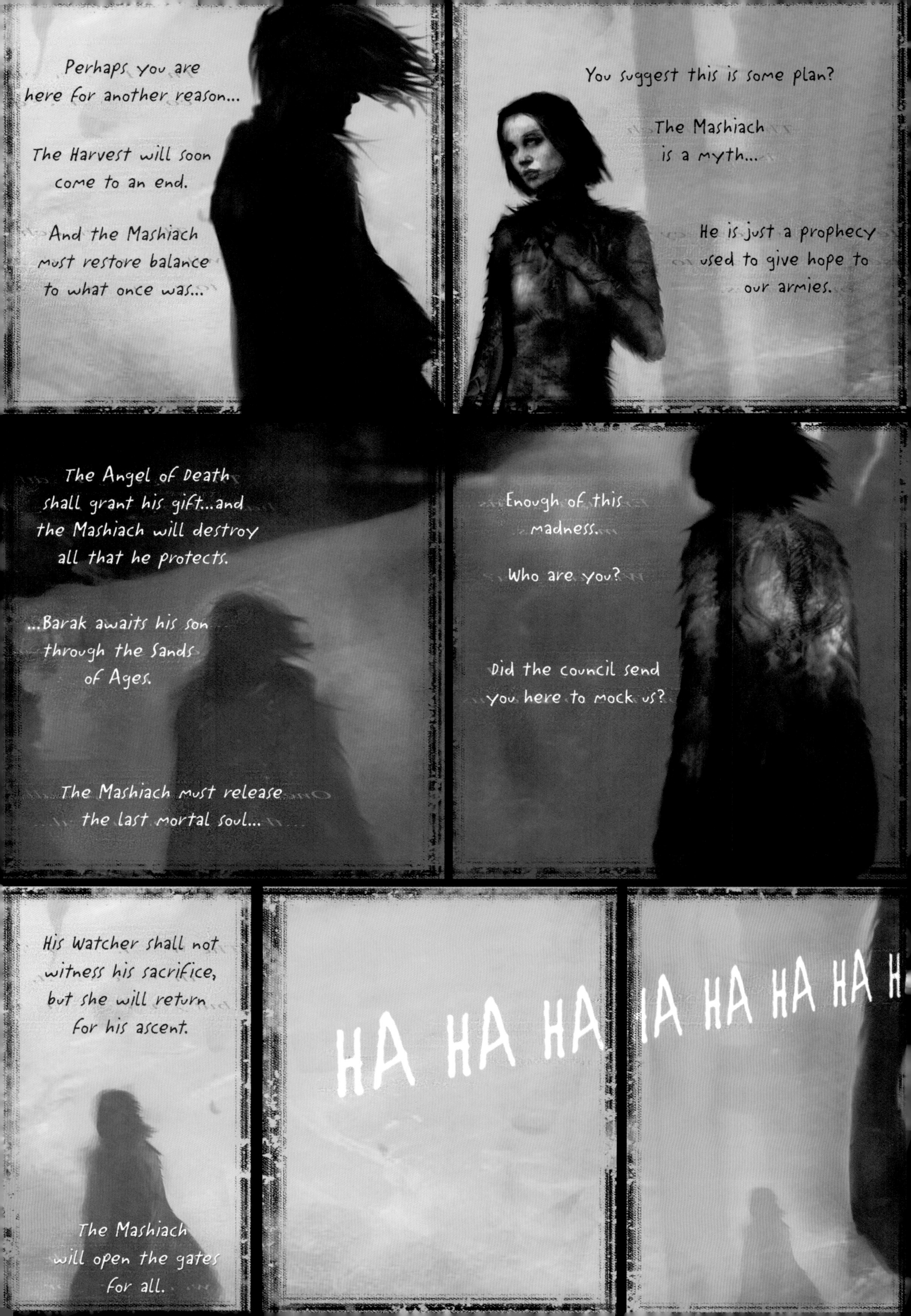
Perhaps you are here for another reason...
The Harvest will soon come to an end.
And the Mashiach must restore balance to what once was...
You suggest this is some plan?
The Mashiach is a myth...
He is just a prophecy used to give hope to our armies.
The Angel of Death shall grant his gift...and the Mashiach will destroy all that he protects.
...Barak awaits his son through the Sands of Ages.
The Mashiach must release the last mortal soul...
Enough of this madness.
Who are you?
Did the council send you here to mock us?
His Watcher shall not witness his sacrifice, but she will return for his ascent.
The Mashiach will open the gates for all.
HA HA HA
HA HA HA HA H

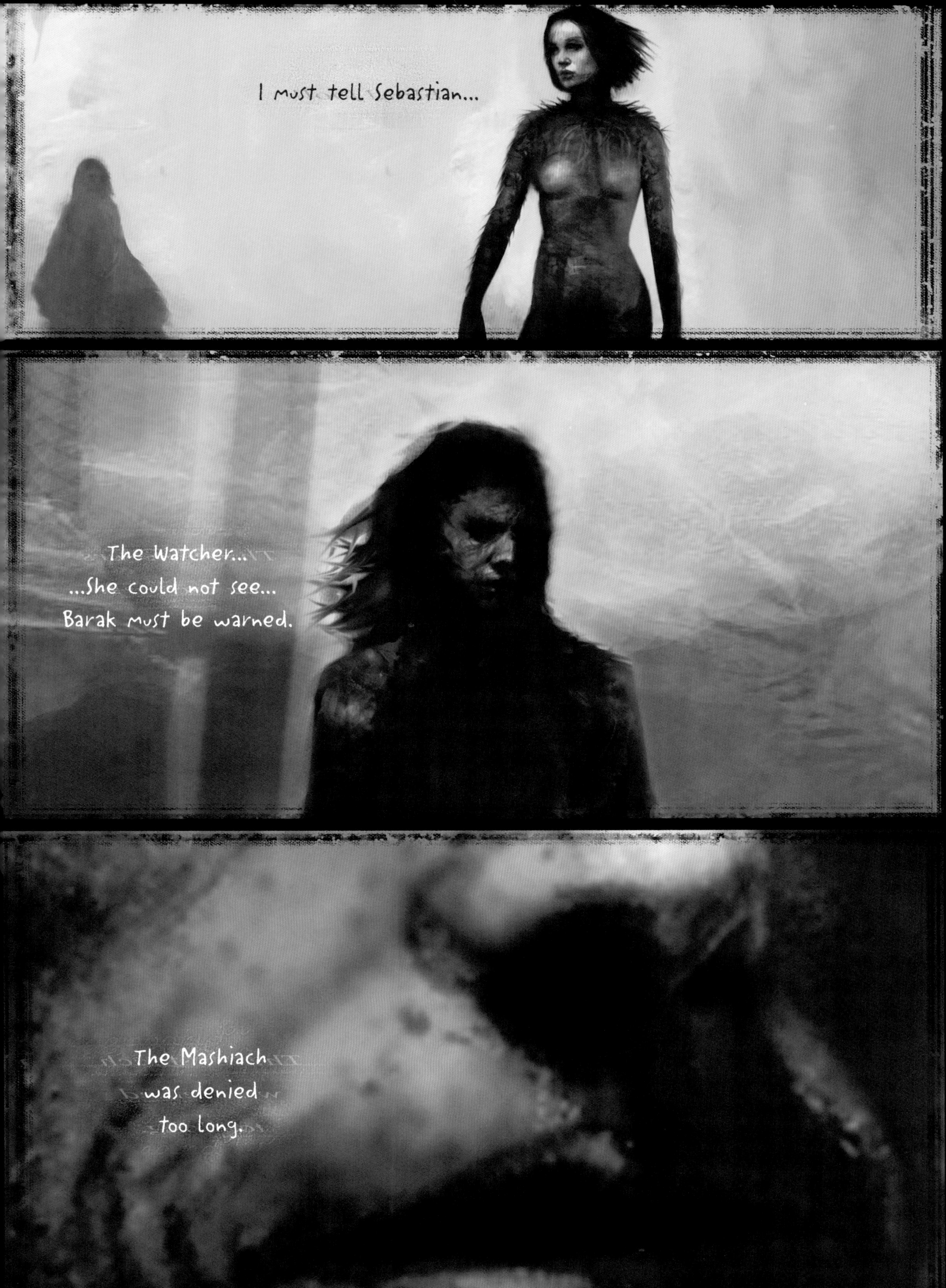
I must tell Sebastian...
The Watcher...
...She could not see...
Barak must be warned.
The Mashiach
was denied
too long.

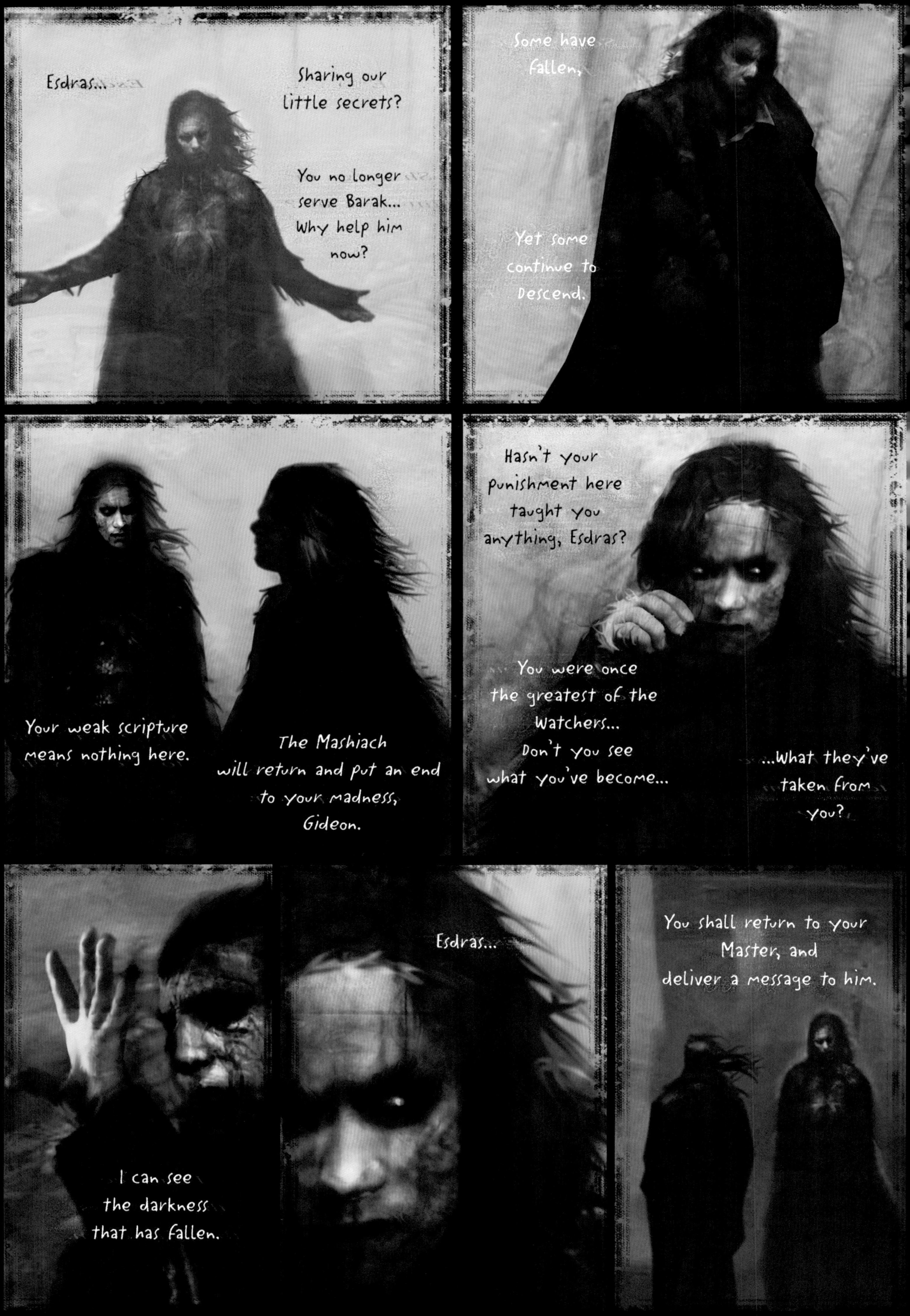
Esdras...
Sharing our little secrets?
You no longer serve Barak... Why help him now?
Some have fallen,
Yet some continue to Descend.
Your weak scripture means nothing here.
The Mashiach will return and put an end to your madness, Gideon.
Hasn't your punishment here taught you anything, Esdras?
You were once the greatest of the Watchers...
Don't you see what you've become...
...What they've taken from you?
I can see the darkness that has fallen.
Esdras...
You shall return to your Master, and deliver a message to him.

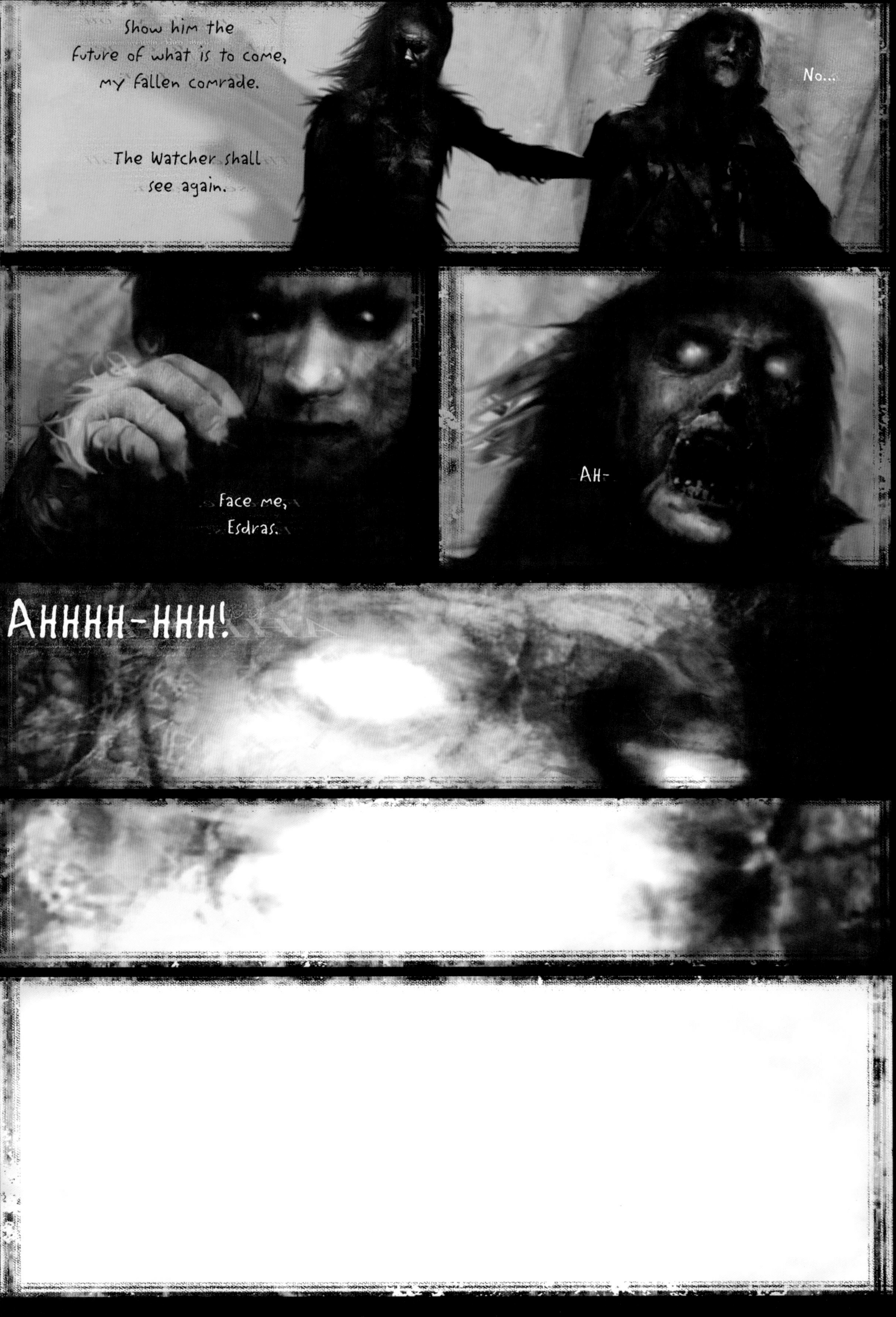
Show him the future of what is to come, my fallen comrade.
The Watcher shall see again.
No...
Face me, Esdras.
AH-
AHHHH-HHH!

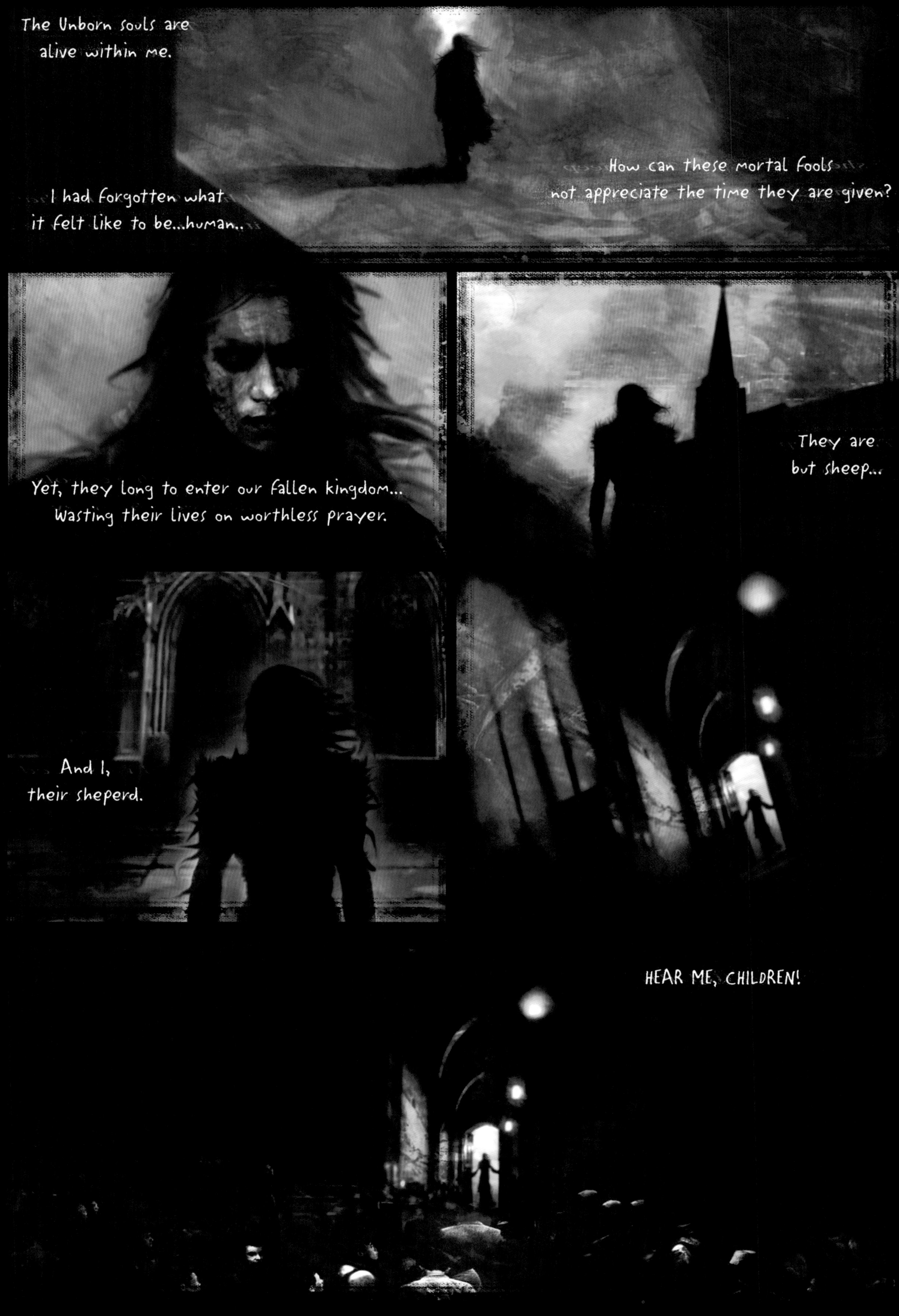
The Unborn souls are alive within me.
I had forgotten what it felt like to be...human..
How can these mortal fools not appreciate the time they are given?
Yet, they long to enter our fallen kingdom... Wasting their lives on worthless prayer.
They are but sheep...
And I, their sheperd.
HEAR ME, CHILDREN!

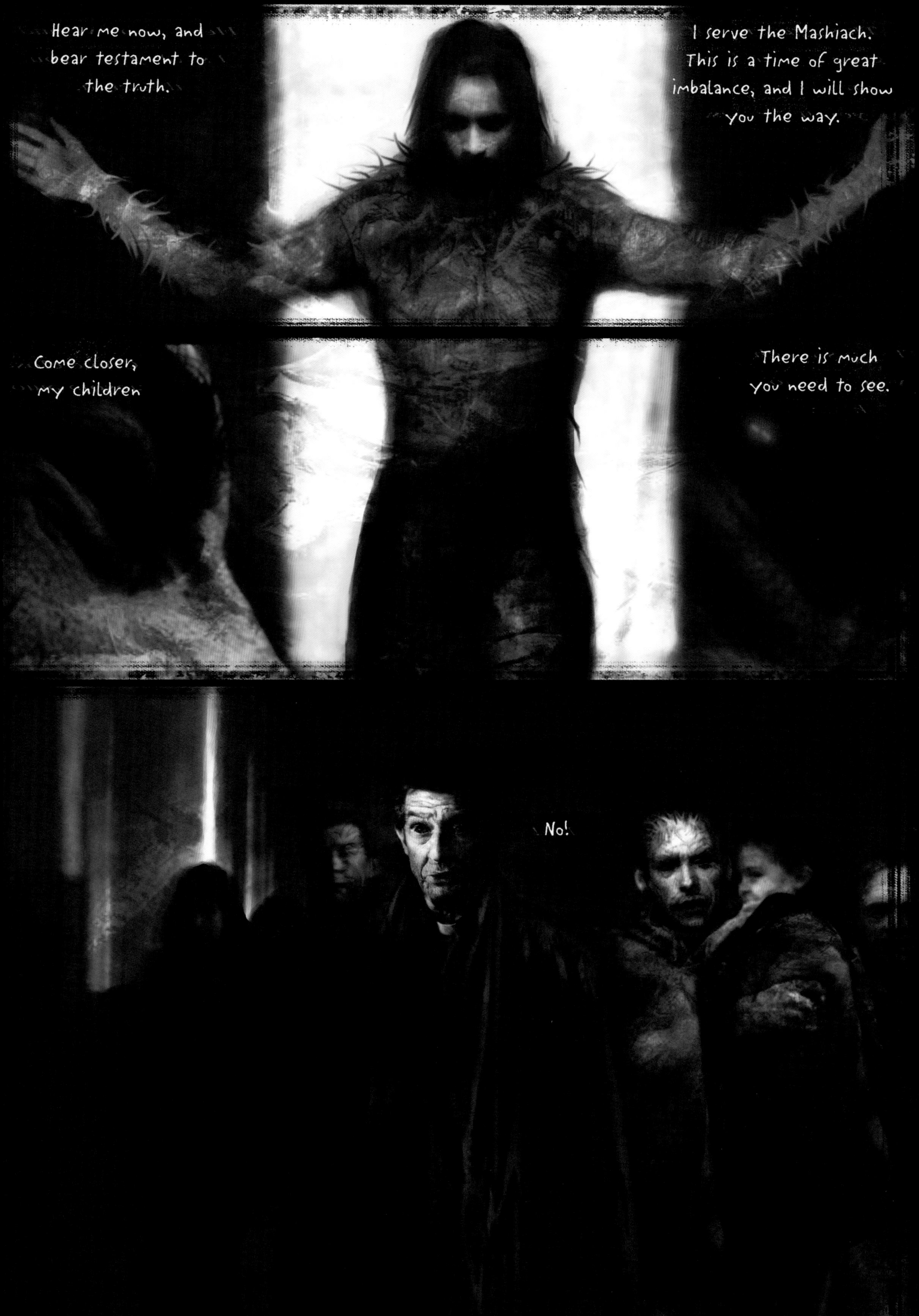
Hear me now, and bear testament to the truth.
I serve the Mashiach. This is a time of great imbalance, and I will show you the way.
Come closer, my children
There is much you need to see.
No!

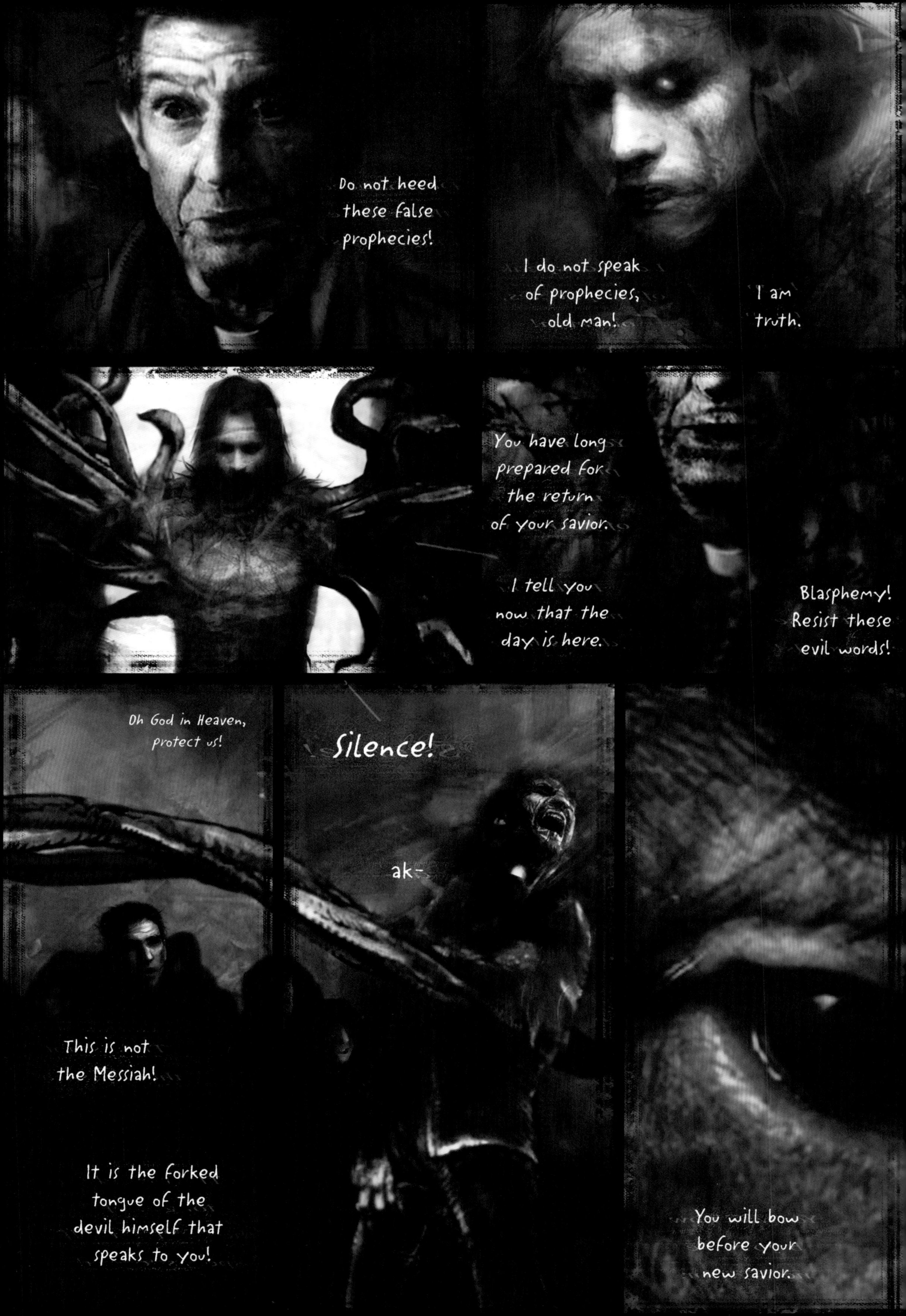
Do not heed these false prophecies!
I do not speak of prophecies, old man!
I am truth.
You have long prepared for the return of your savior.
I tell you now that the day is here.
Blasphemy! Resist these evil words!
Oh God in Heaven, protect us!
Silence!
ak-
This is not the Messiah!
It is the forked tongue of the devil himself that speaks to you!
You will bow before your new savior.

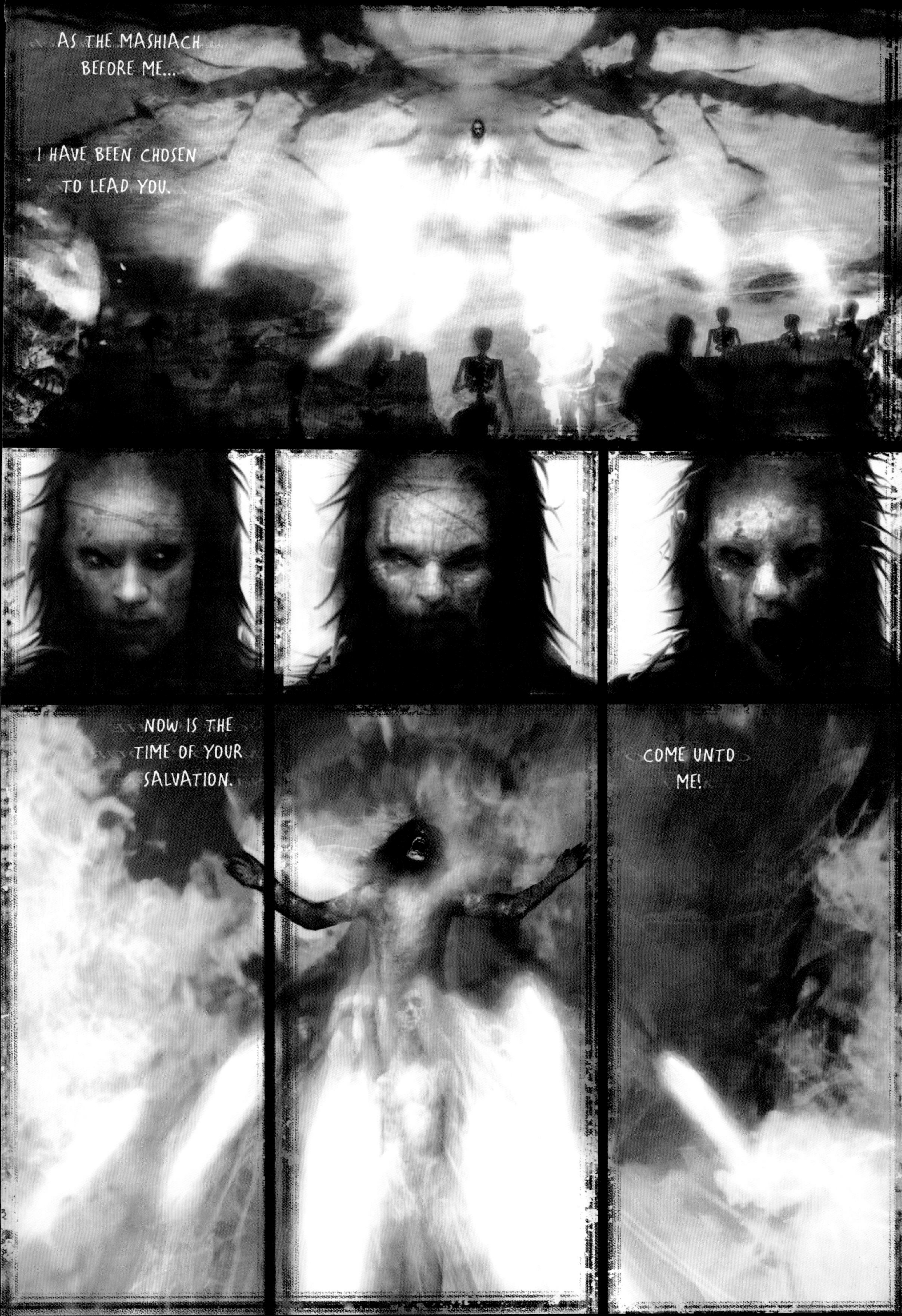
AS THE MASHIACH BEFORE ME...
I HAVE BEEN CHOSEN TO LEAD YOU.
NOW IS THE TIME OF YOUR SALVATION.
COME UNTO ME!

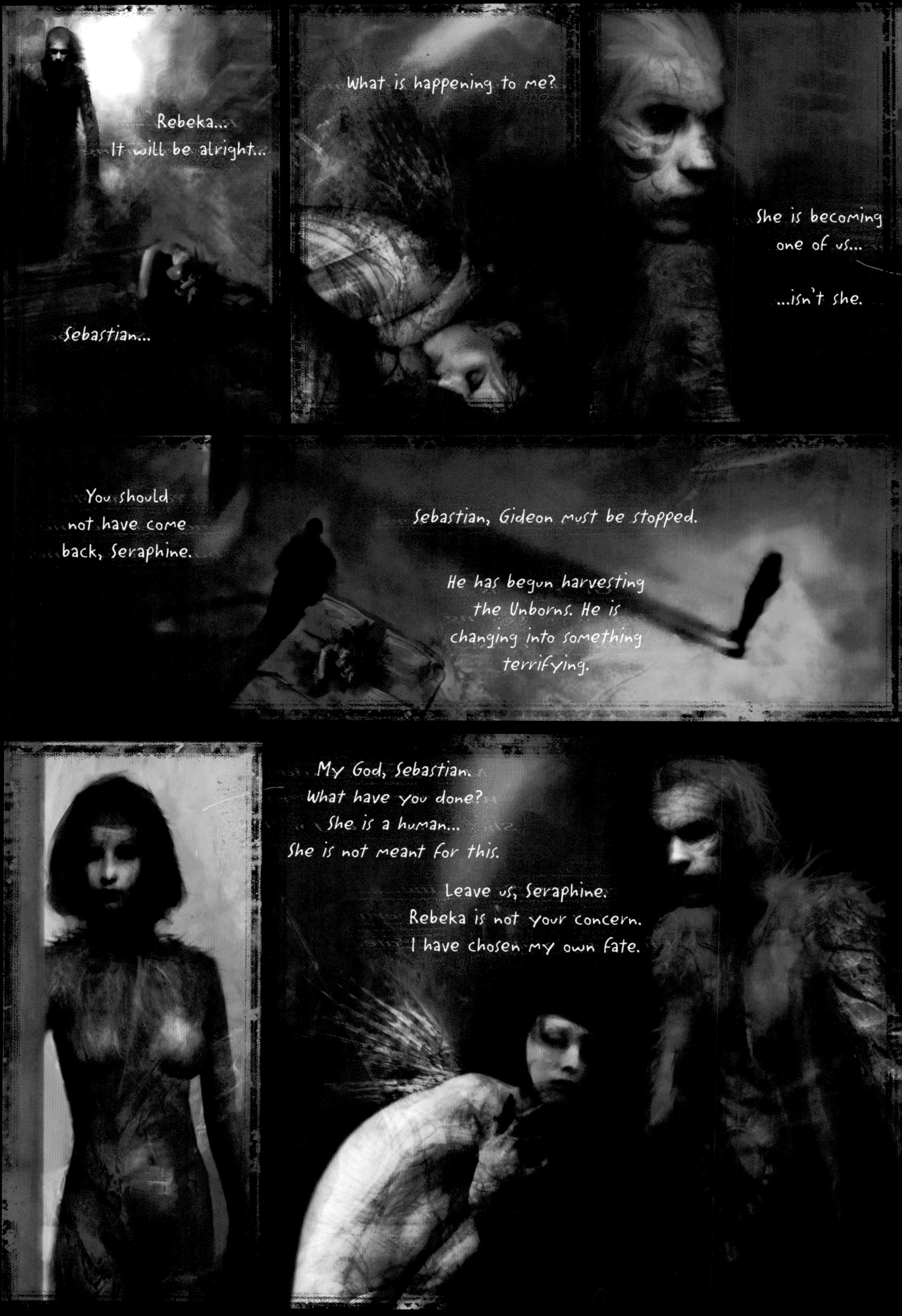
Rebeka...
It will be alright...
Sebastian...
What is happening to me?
She is becoming one of us...
...isn't she.
You should not have come back, Seraphine.
Sebastian, Gideon must be stopped.
He has begun harvesting the Unborns. He is changing into something terrifying.
My God, Sebastian. What have you done? She is a human... She is not meant for this.
Leave us, Seraphine. Rebeka is not your concern. I have chosen my own fate.

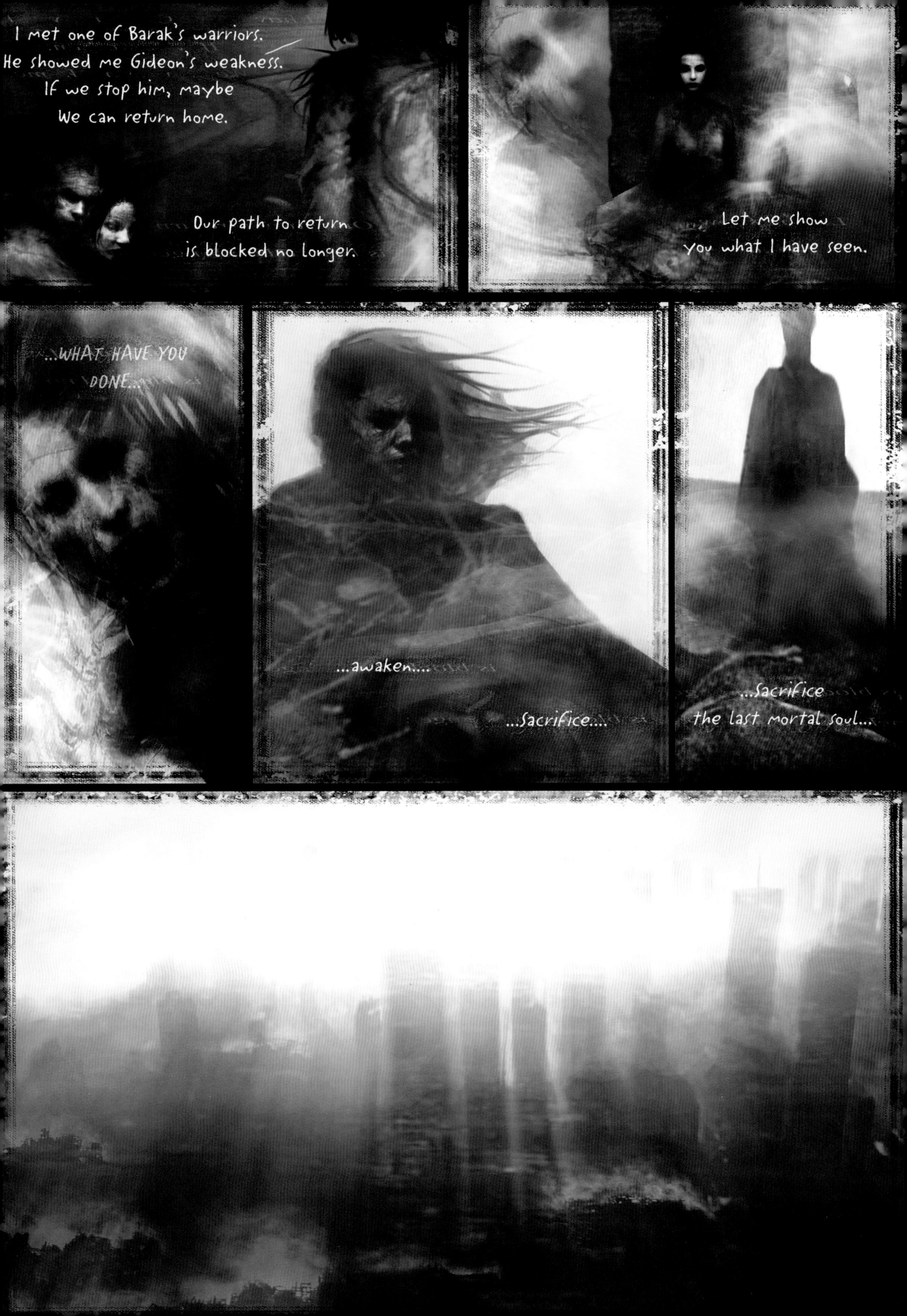

I met one of Barak's warriors. He showed me Gideon's weakness. If we stop him, maybe we can return home.
Our path to return is blocked no longer.
Let me show you what I have seen.
...WHAT HAVE YOU DONE...
...awaken....
...Sacrifice....
...Sacrifice the last mortal soul...

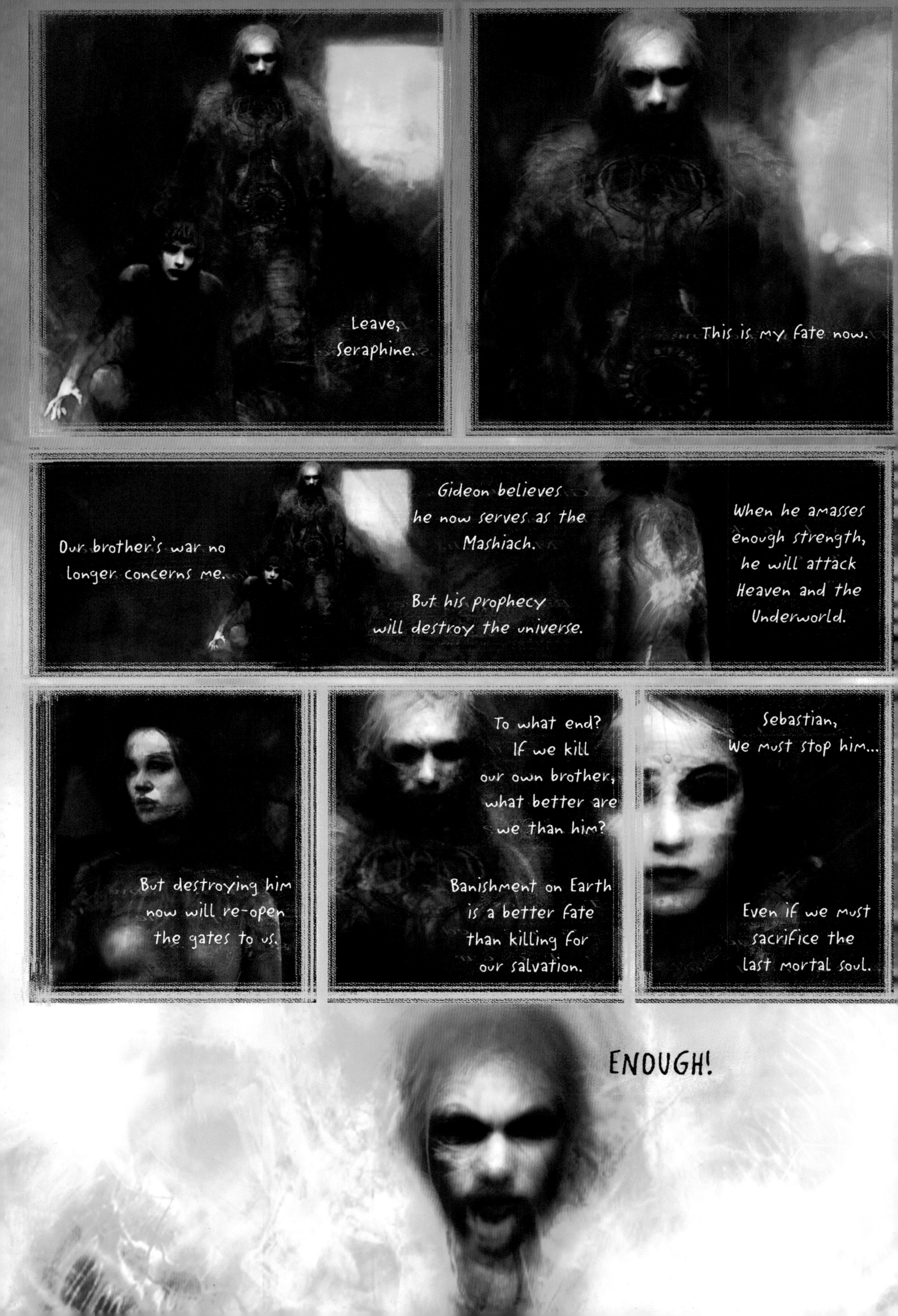
Leave, Seraphine.
This is my fate now.
Our brother's war no longer concerns me.
Gideon believes he now serves as the Mashiach.
But his prophecy will destroy the universe.
When he amasses enough strength, he will attack Heaven and the Underworld.
But destroying him now will re-open the gates to us.
To what end? If we kill our own brother, what better are we than him?
Banishment on Earth is a better fate than killing for our salvation.
Sebastian, We must stop him...
Even if we must sacrifice the last mortal soul.
ENOUGH!

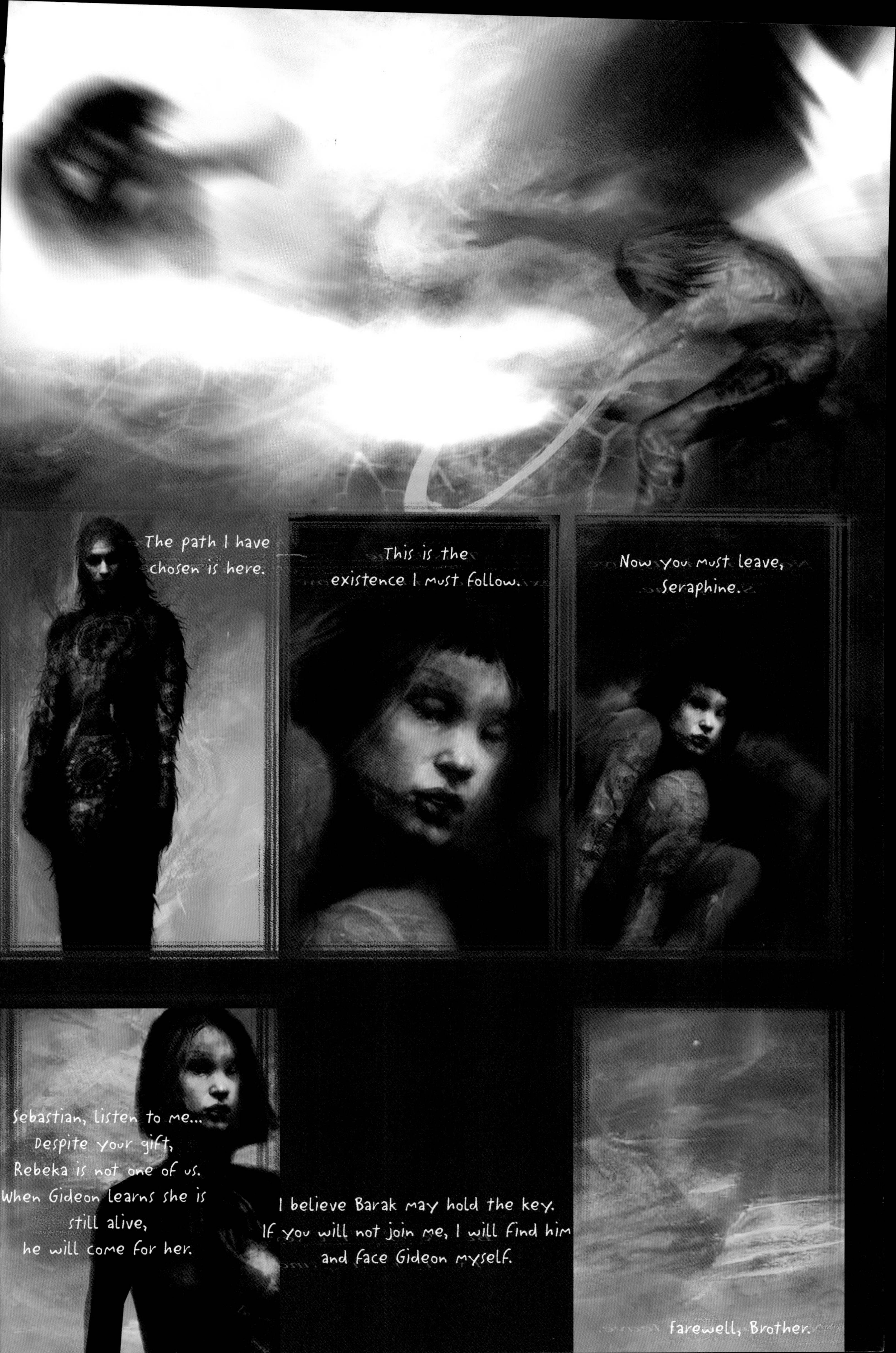

The path I have chosen is here.
This is the existence I must follow.
Now you must leave, Seraphine.
Sebastian, listen to me... Despite your gift, Rebeka is not one of us. When Gideon learns she is still alive, he will come for her.
I believe Barak may hold the key. If you will not join me, I will find him and face Gideon myself.
Farewell, Brother.

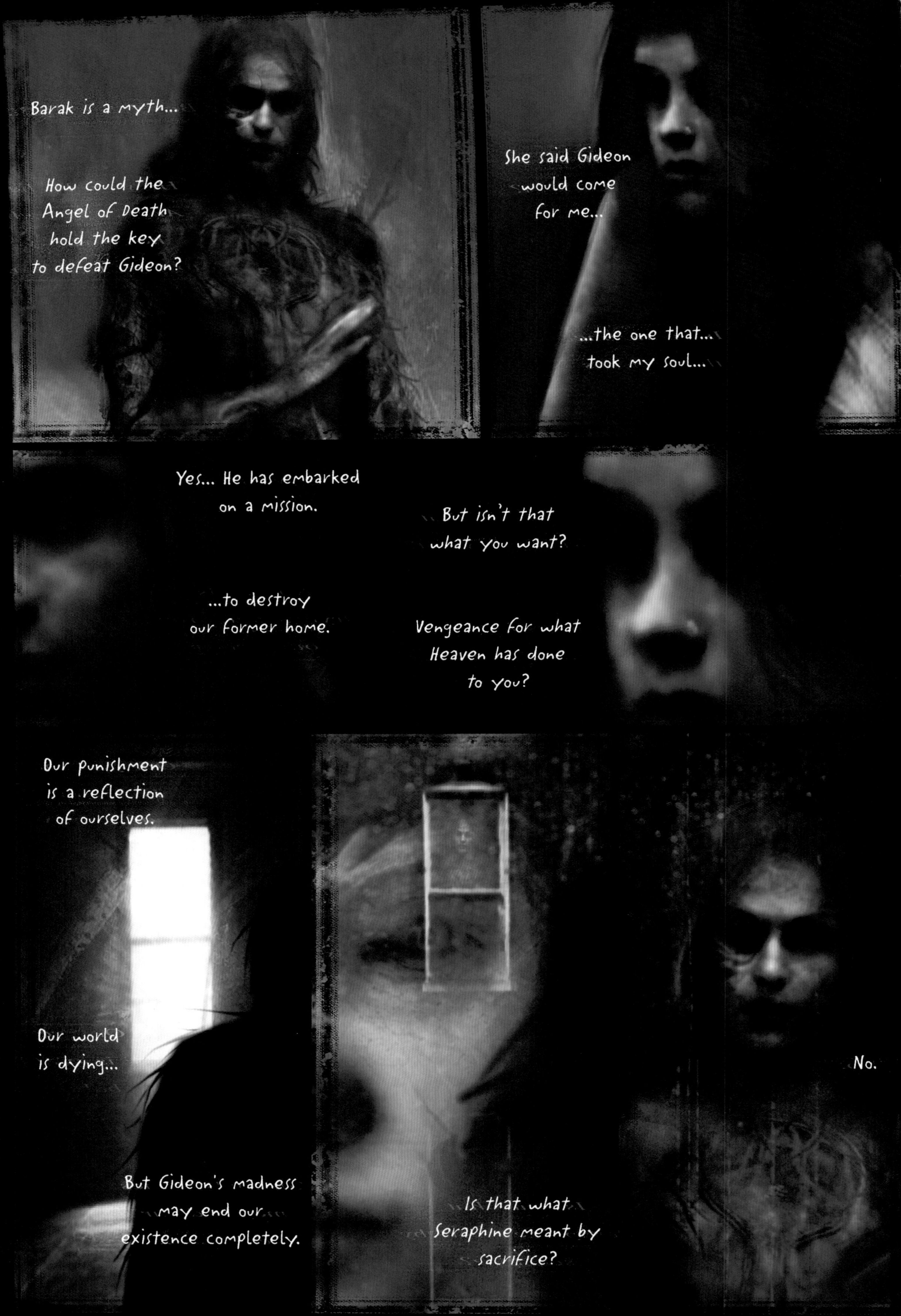
Barak is a myth...
How could the Angel of Death hold the key to defeat Gideon?
She said Gideon would come for me...
...the one that... took my soul...
Yes... He has embarked on a mission.
...to destroy our former home.
But isn't that what you want?
Vengeance for what Heaven has done to you?
Our punishment is a reflection of ourselves.
Our world is dying...
But Gideon's madness may end our existence completely.
Is that what Seraphine meant by sacrifice?
No.

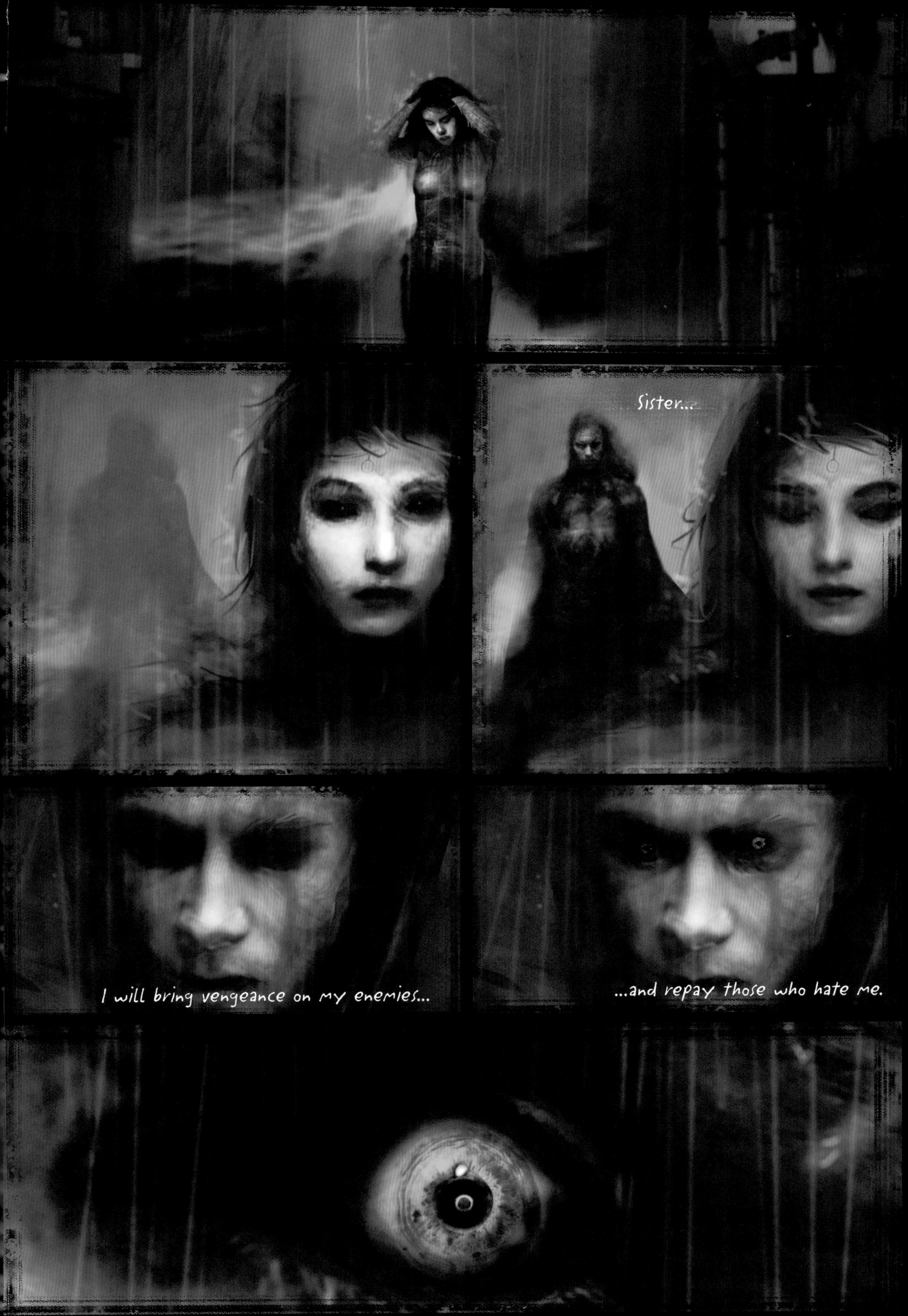
Sister...
I will bring vengeance on my enemies...
...and repay those who hate me.

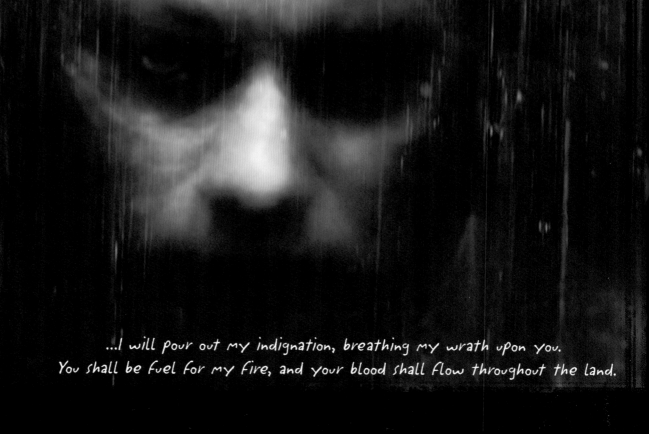

On this day I will purify the lips of all people......

...you have turned your back on me, and I shall judge you...

...I will pour out my indignation, breathing my wrath upon you.
You shall be fuel for my fire, and your blood shall flow throughout the land.

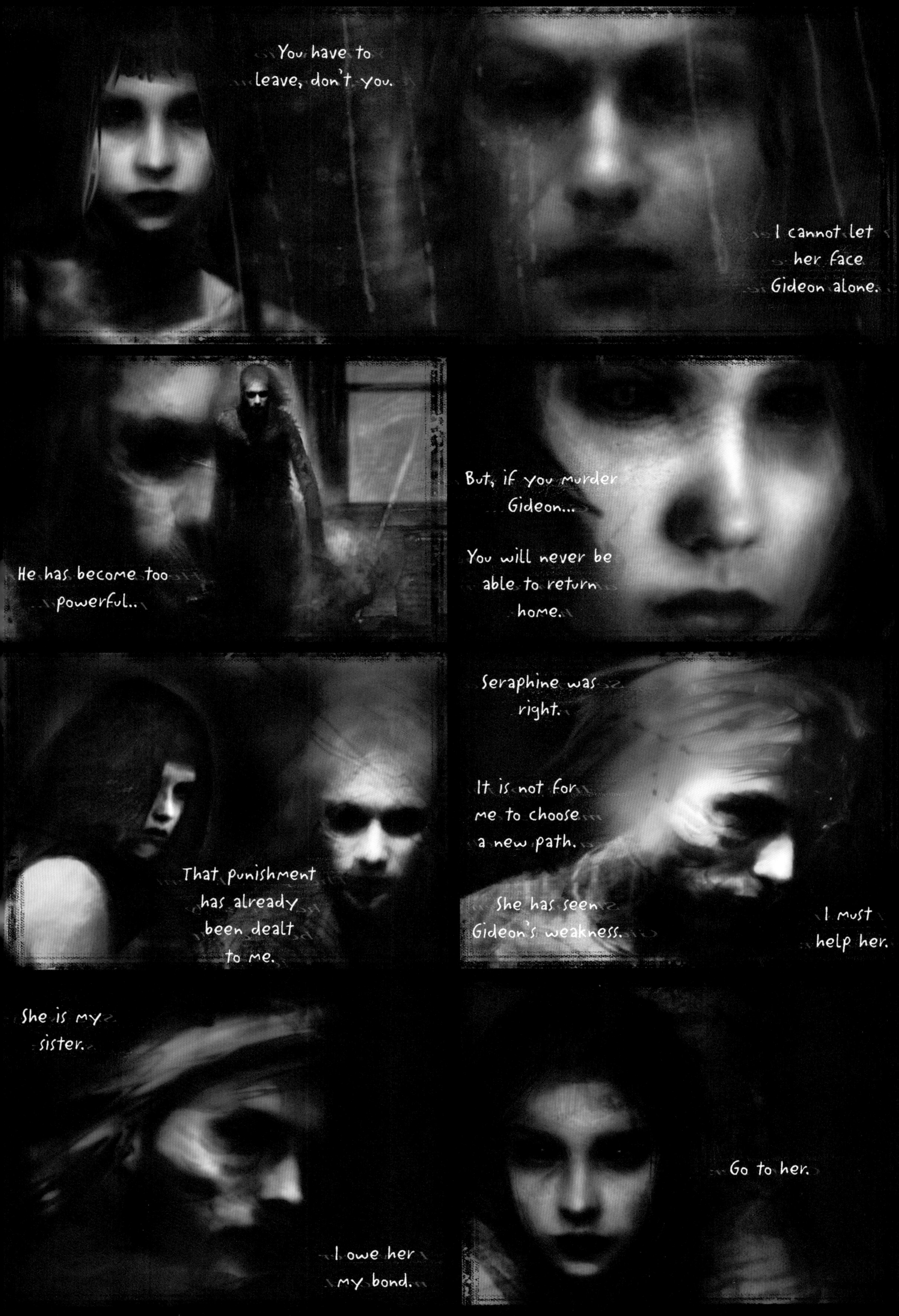
You have to leave, don't you.
I cannot let her face Gideon alone.
He has become too powerful..
But, if you murder Gideon...
You will never be able to return home.
That punishment has already been dealt to me.
Seraphine was right.
It is not for me to choose a new path.
She has seen Gideon's weakness.
I must help her.
She is my sister.
I owe her my bond.
Go to her.

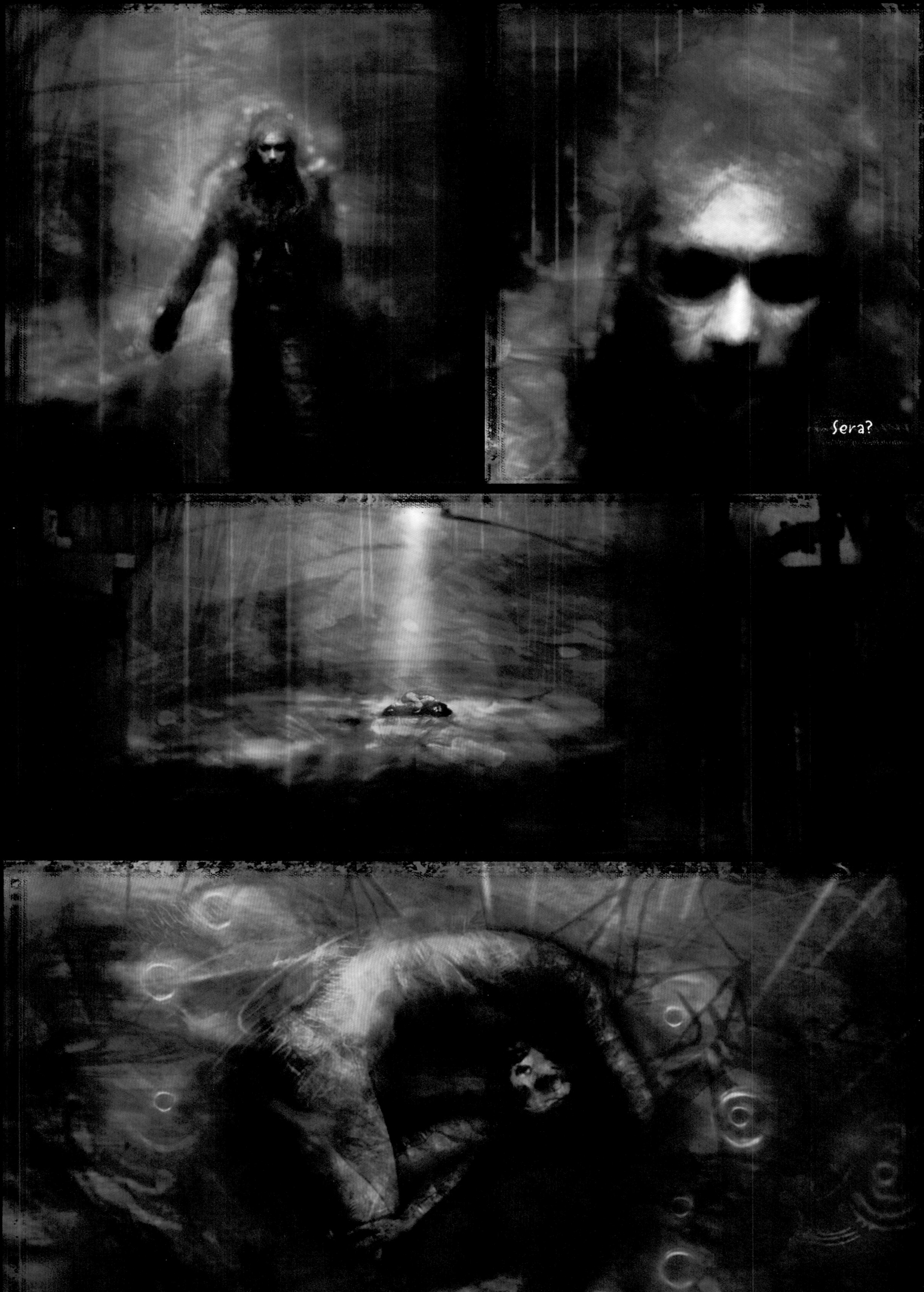
Sera?

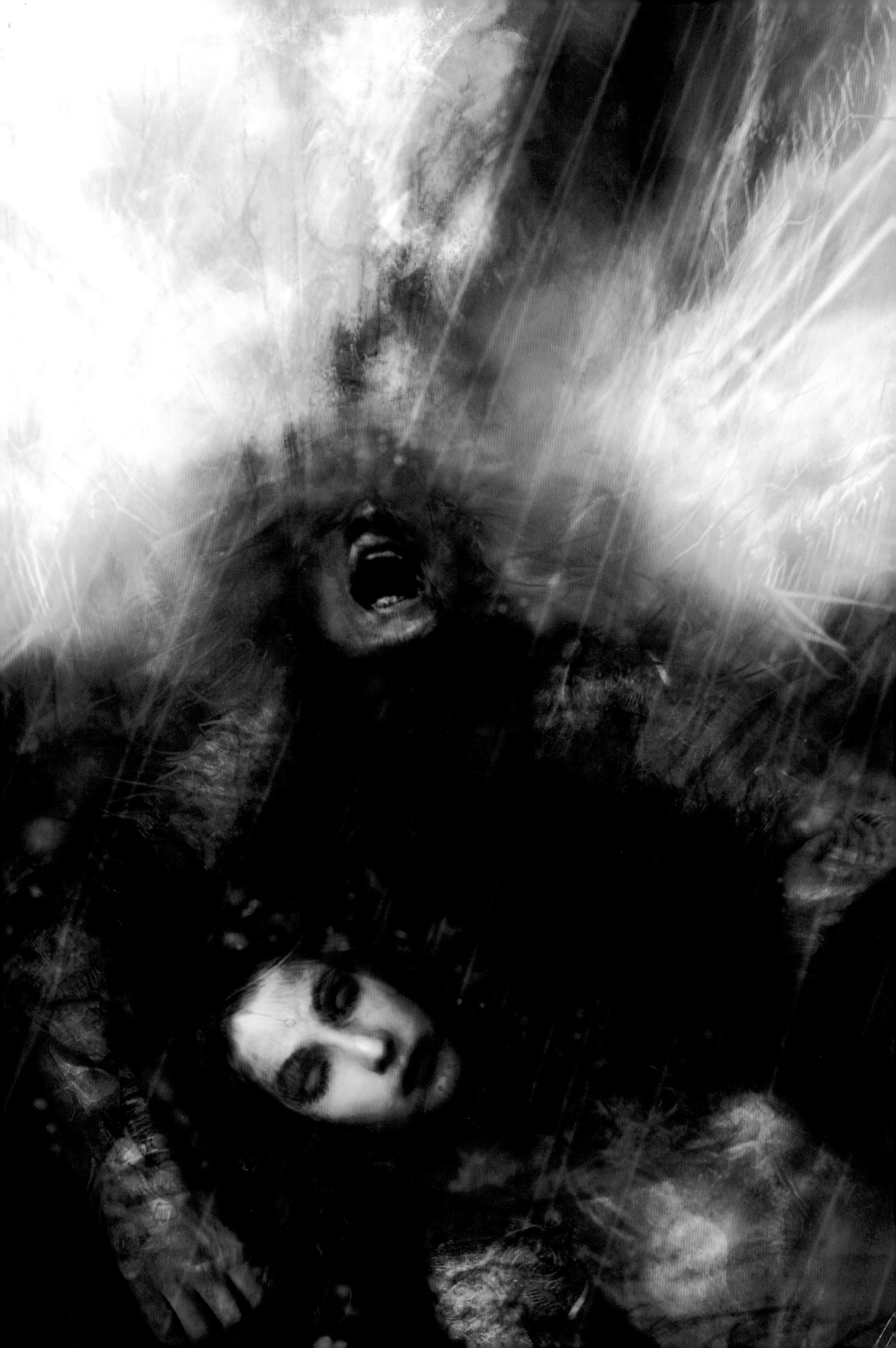

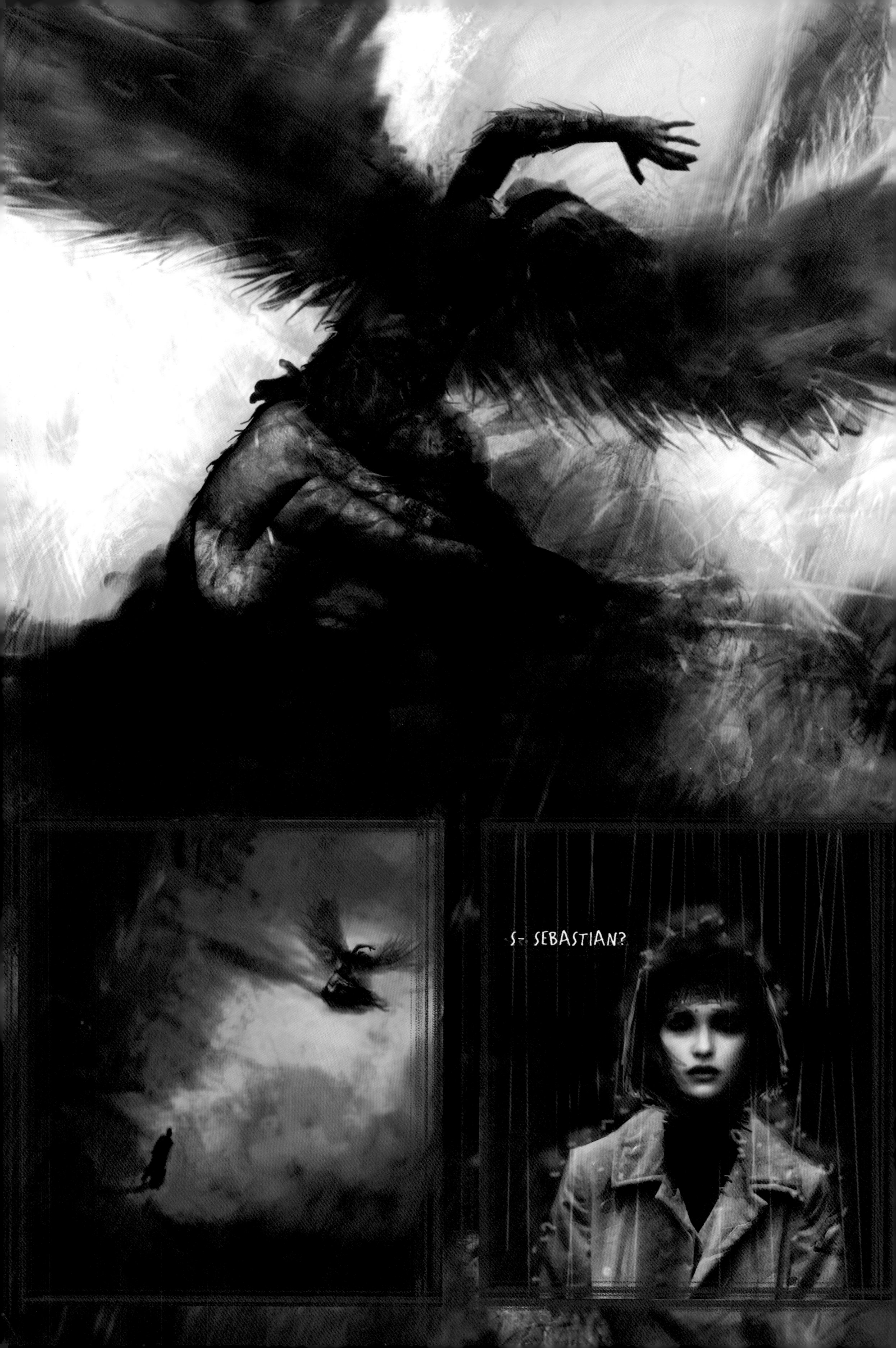
S- SEBASTIAN?

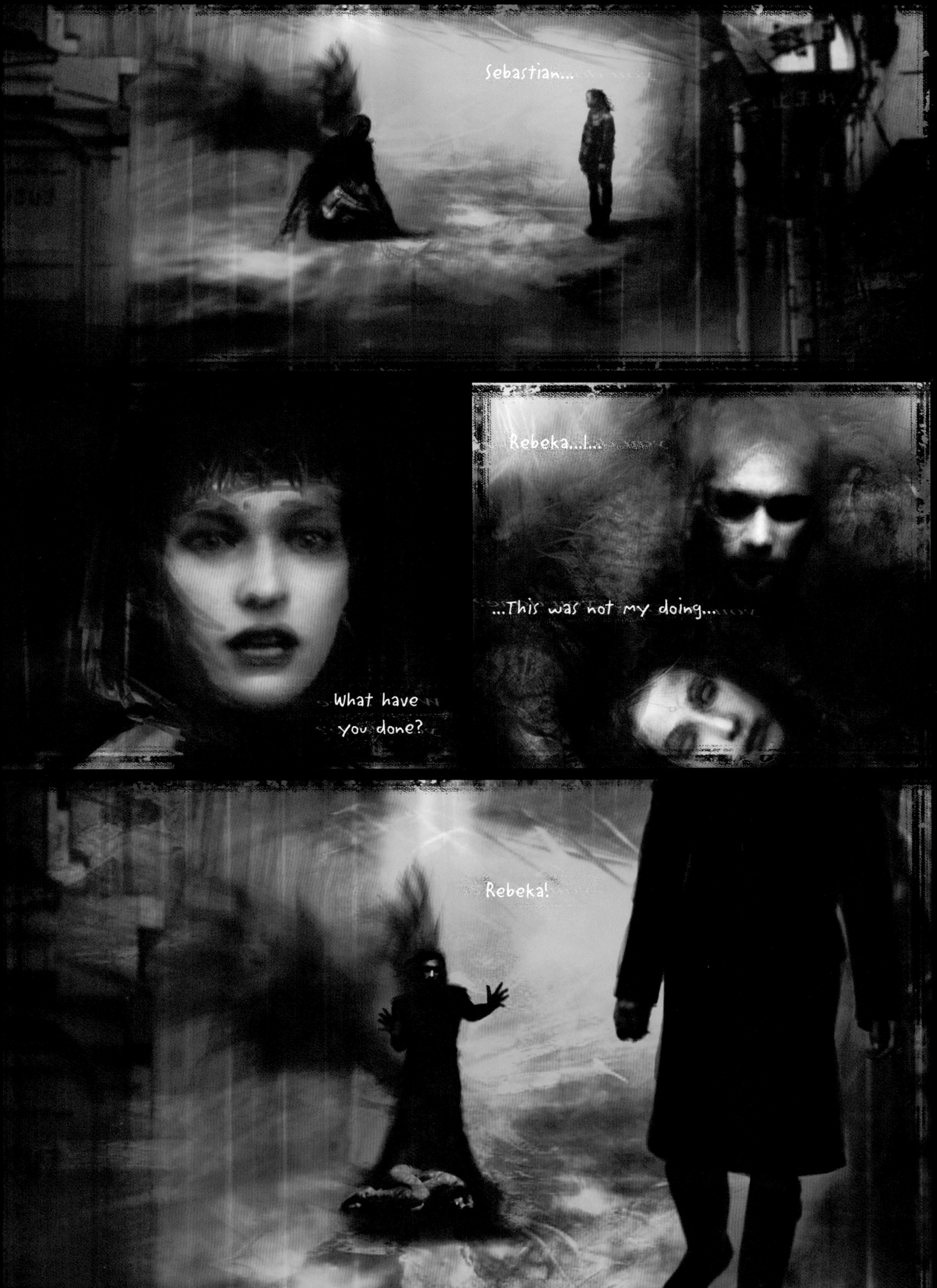
Sebastian...
What have you done?
Rebeka...I...
...This was not my doing...
Rebeka!

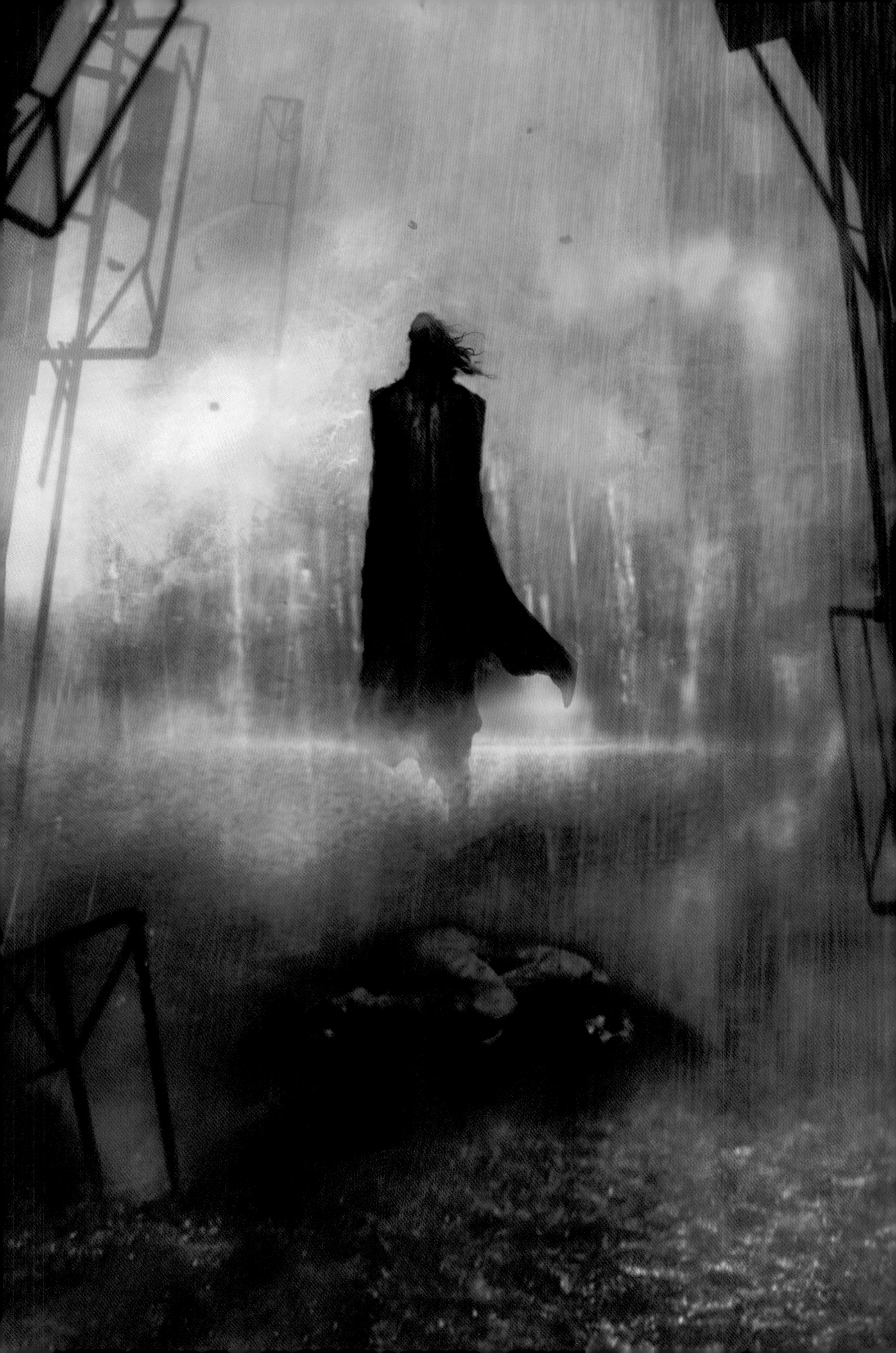

"..AND THE WALLS OF THE CITY SHALL FALL DOWN FLAT,
AND THE PEOPLE SHALL ASCEND UP EVERY MAN
STRAIGHT BEFORE HIM."
- JOSHUA 6:4-6

B O O K   T H R E E

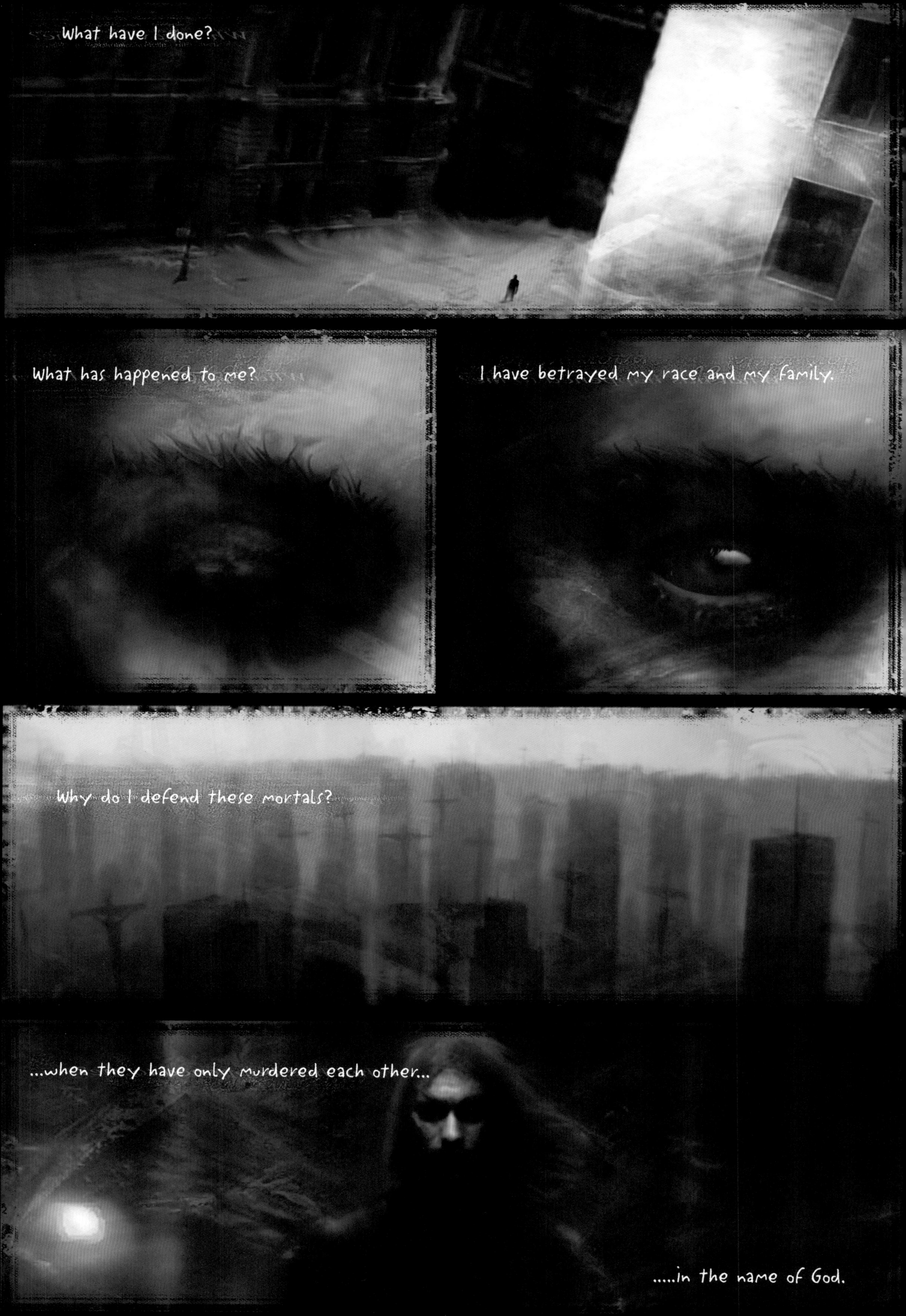
What have I done?
What has happened to me?
I have betrayed my race and my family.
Why do I defend these mortals?
...when they have only murdered each other...
.....in the name of God.

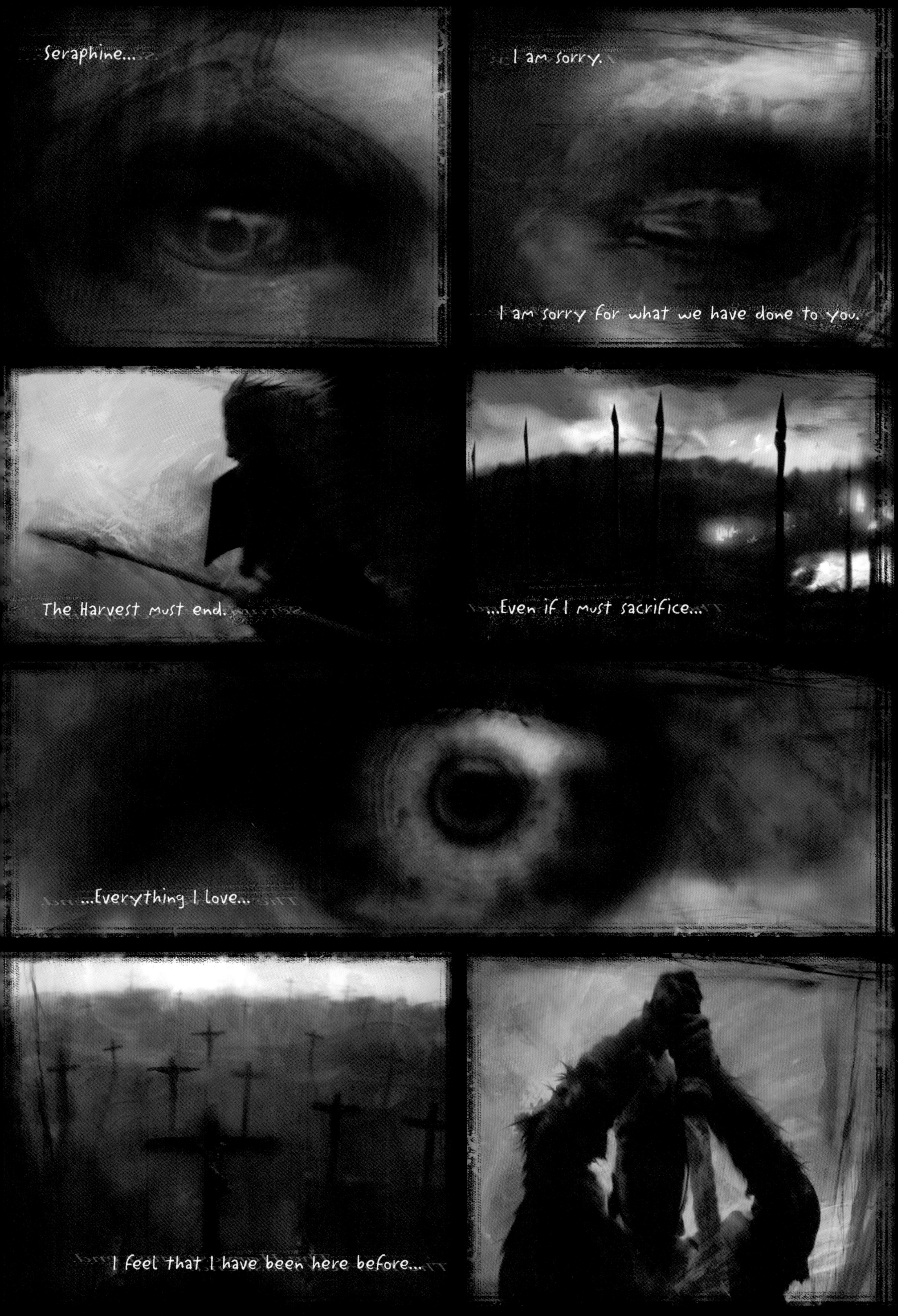
Seraphine...
I am sorry.
I am sorry for what we have done to you.
The Harvest must end.
...Even if I must sacrifice...
...Everything I love...
I feel that I have been here before...

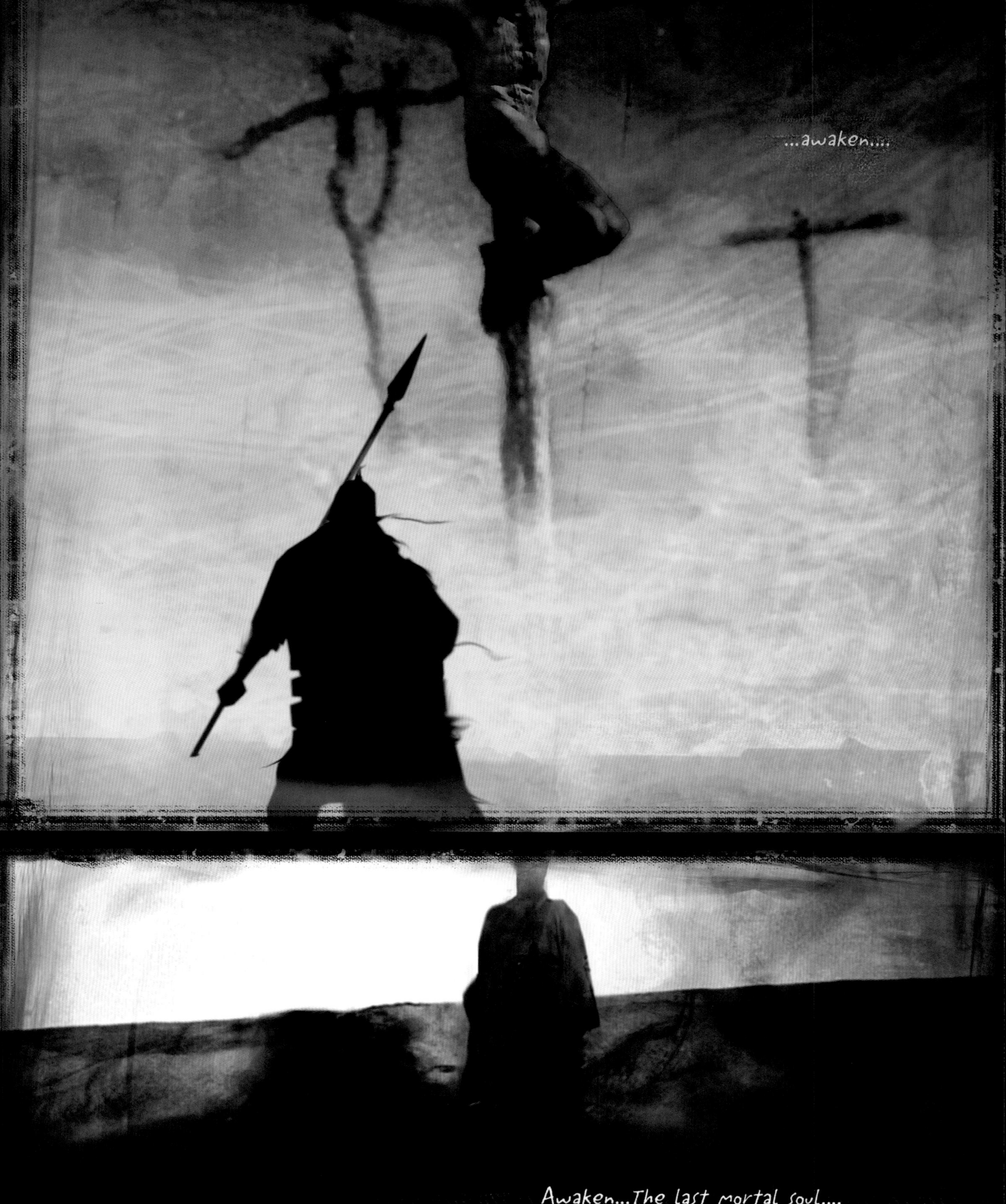
...awaken....
Awaken...The last mortal soul....

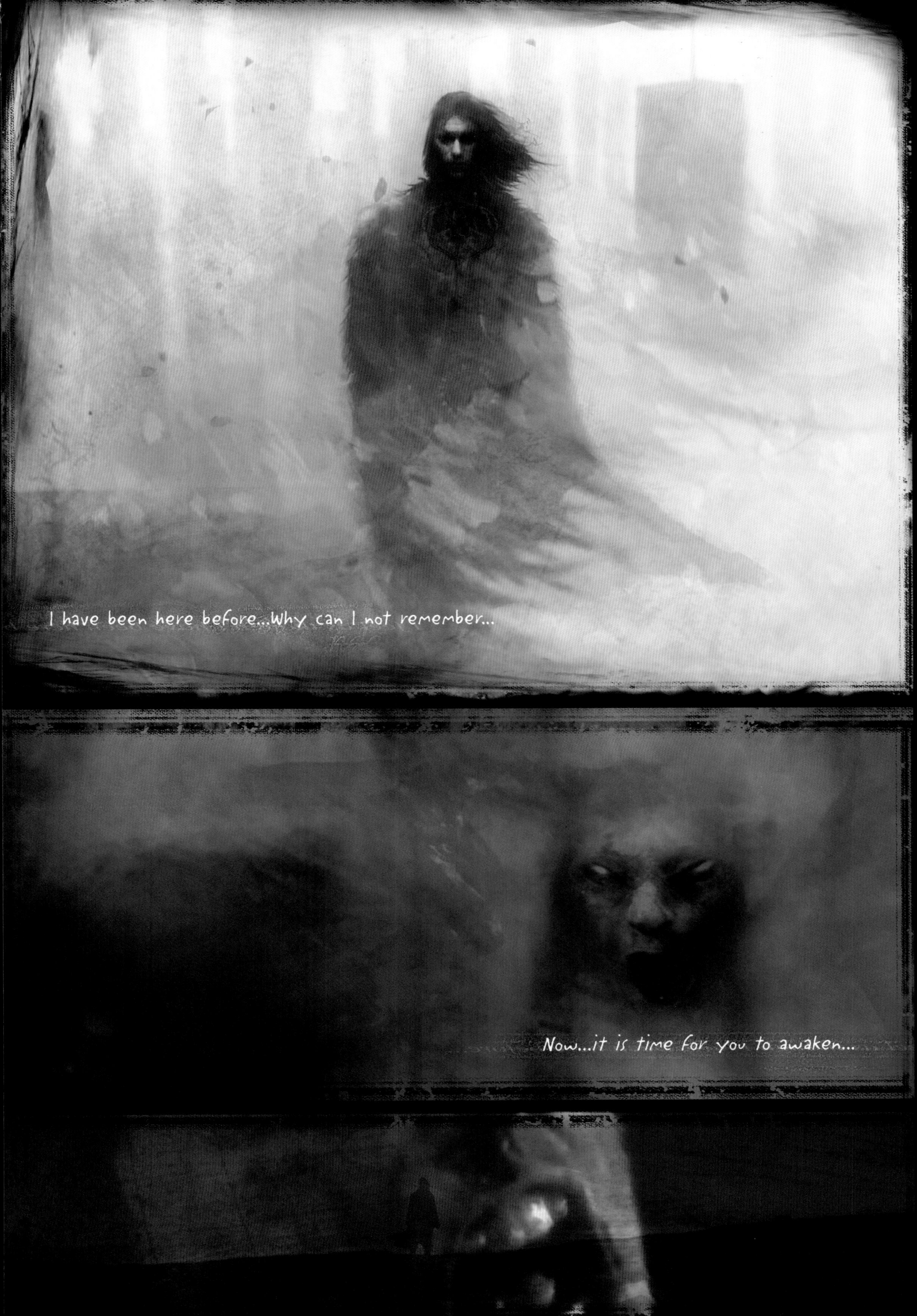
I have been here before...Why can I not remember...
Now...it is time for you to awaken...

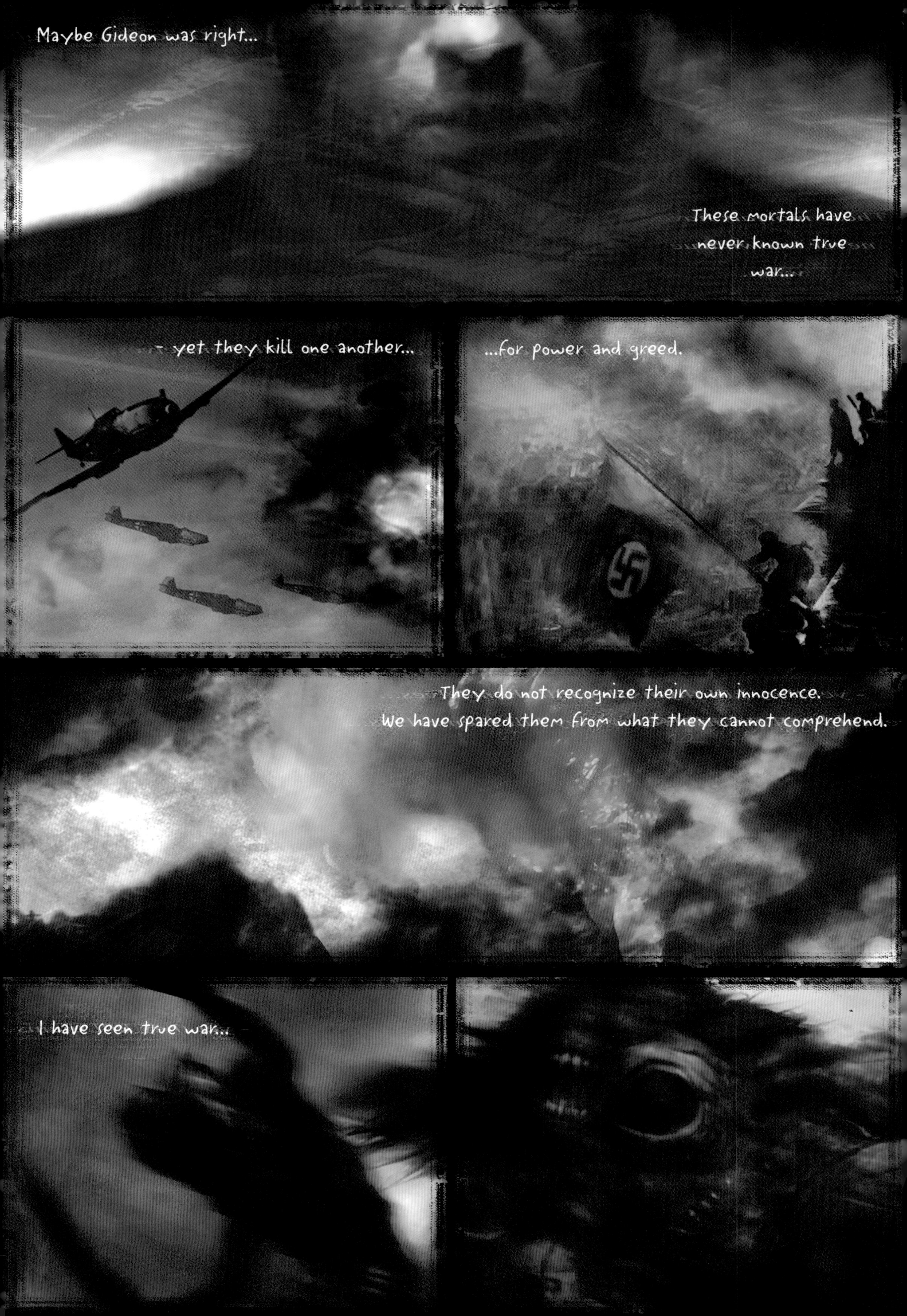
Maybe Gideon was right...
These mortals have never known true war...
- yet they kill one another...
...for power and greed.
They do not recognize their own innocence.
We have spared them from what they cannot comprehend.
I have seen true war...

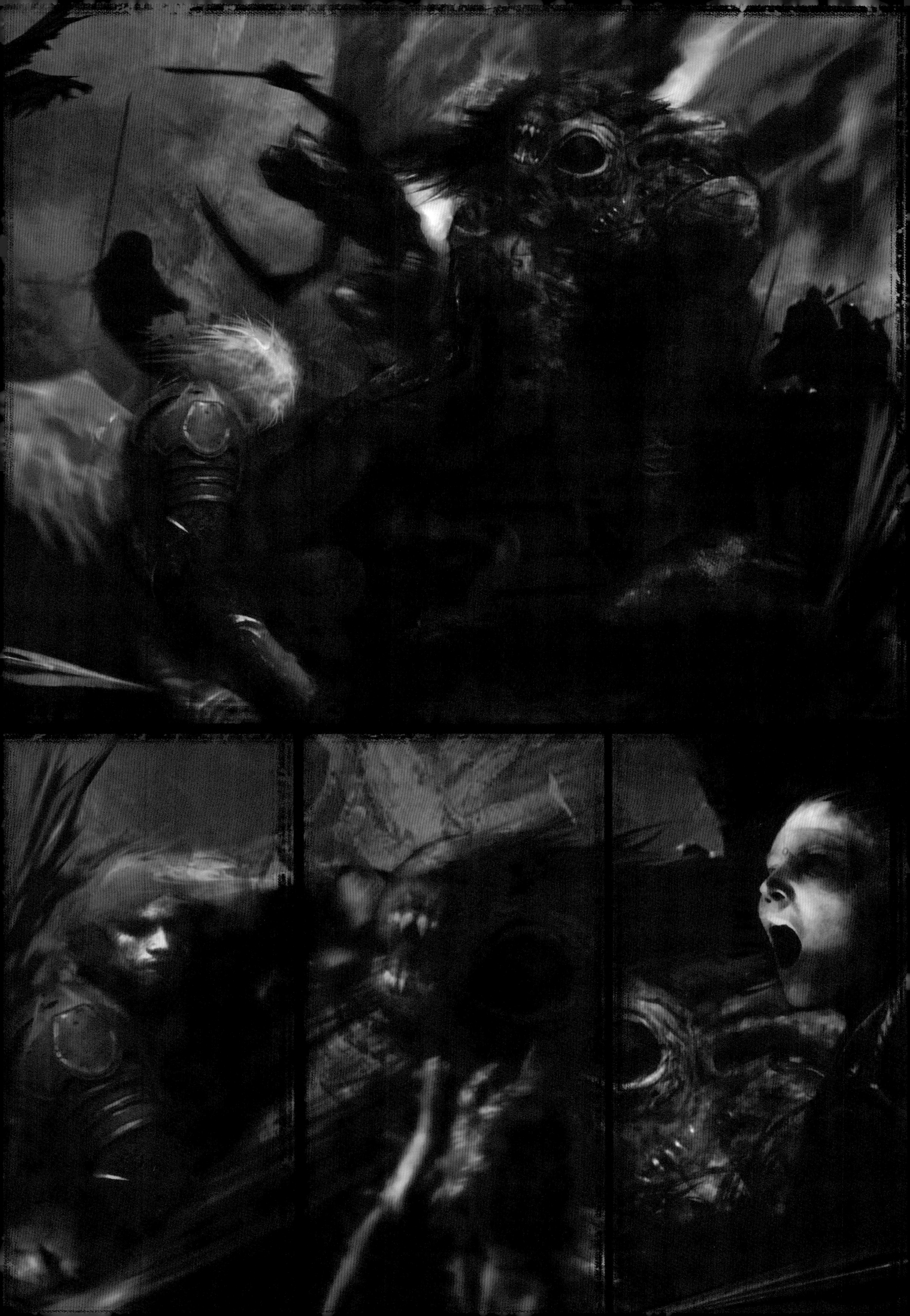

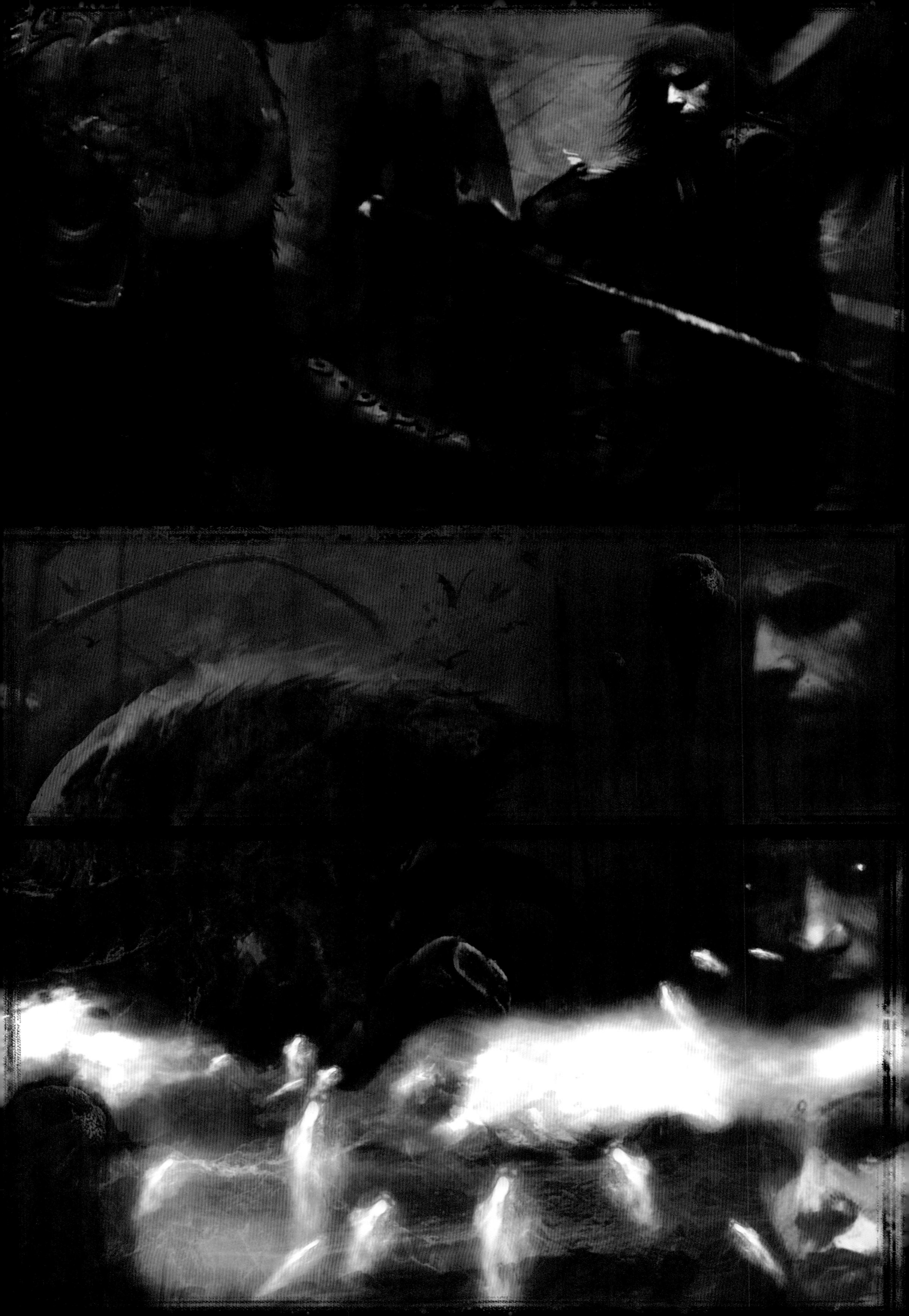

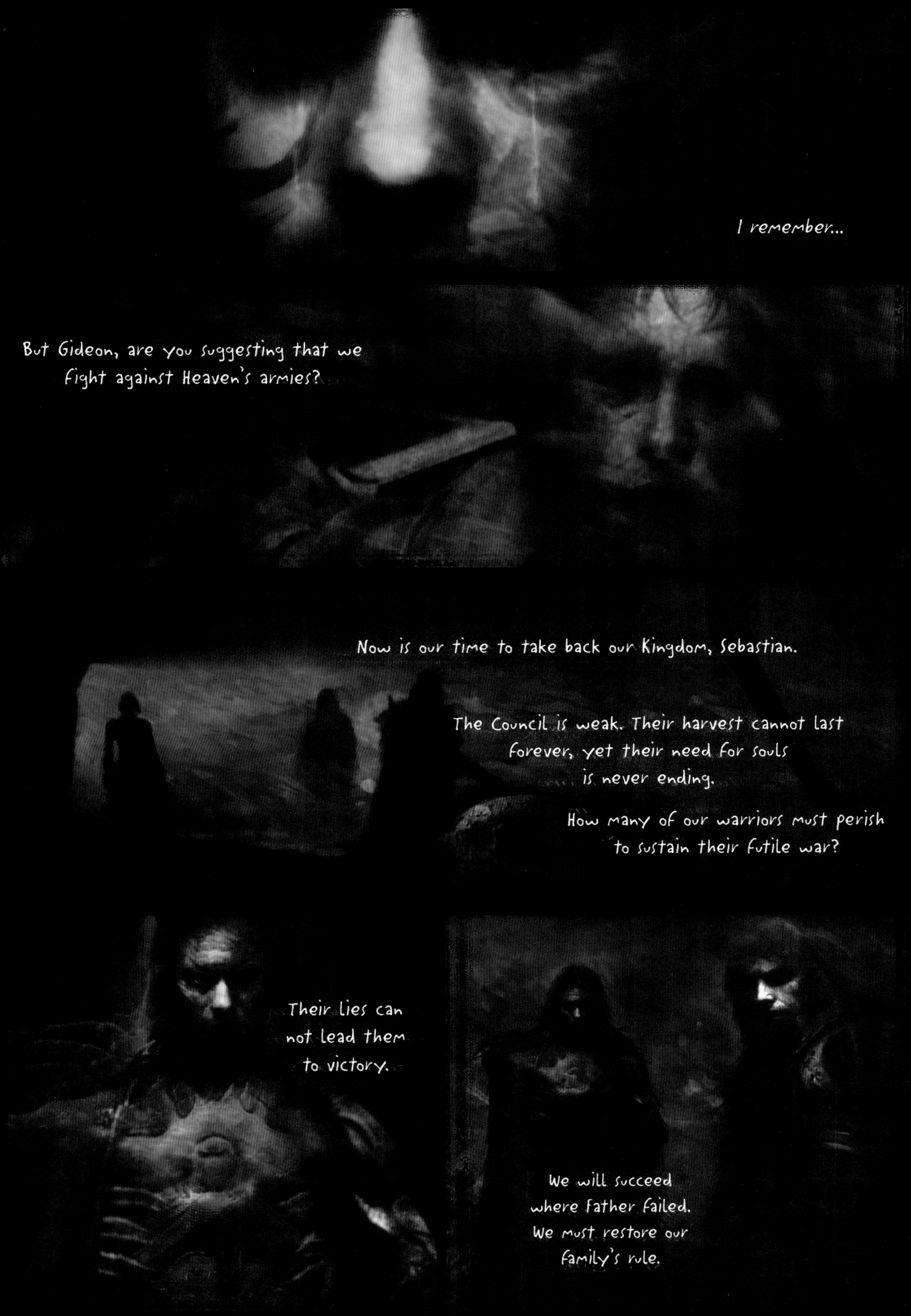
I remember...
But Gideon, are you suggesting that we fight against Heaven's armies?
Now is our time to take back our Kingdom, Sebastian.
The Council is weak. Their harvest cannot last forever, yet their need for souls is never ending.
How many of our warriors must perish to sustain their futile war?
Their lies can not lead them to victory.
We will succeed where father failed. We must restore our family's rule.

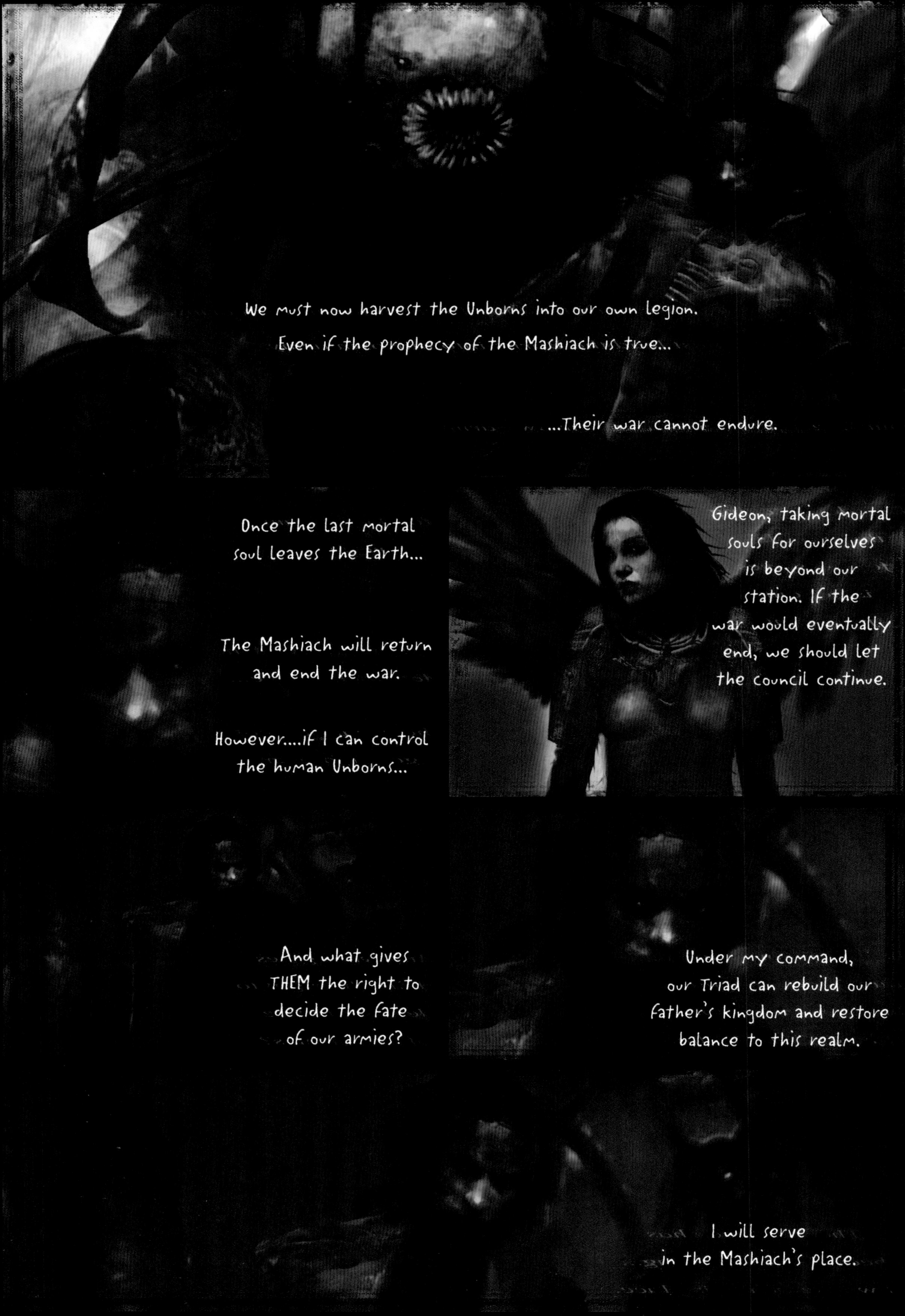
We must now harvest the Unborns into our own legion.
Even if the prophecy of the Mashiach is true...
...Their war cannot endure.
Once the last mortal soul leaves the Earth...
The Mashiach will return and end the war.
However....if I can control the human Unborns...
Gideon, taking mortal souls for ourselves is beyond our station. If the war would eventually end, we should let the council continue.
And what gives THEM the right to decide the fate of our armies?
Under my command, our Triad can rebuild our father's kingdom and restore balance to this realm.
I will serve in the Mashiach's place.

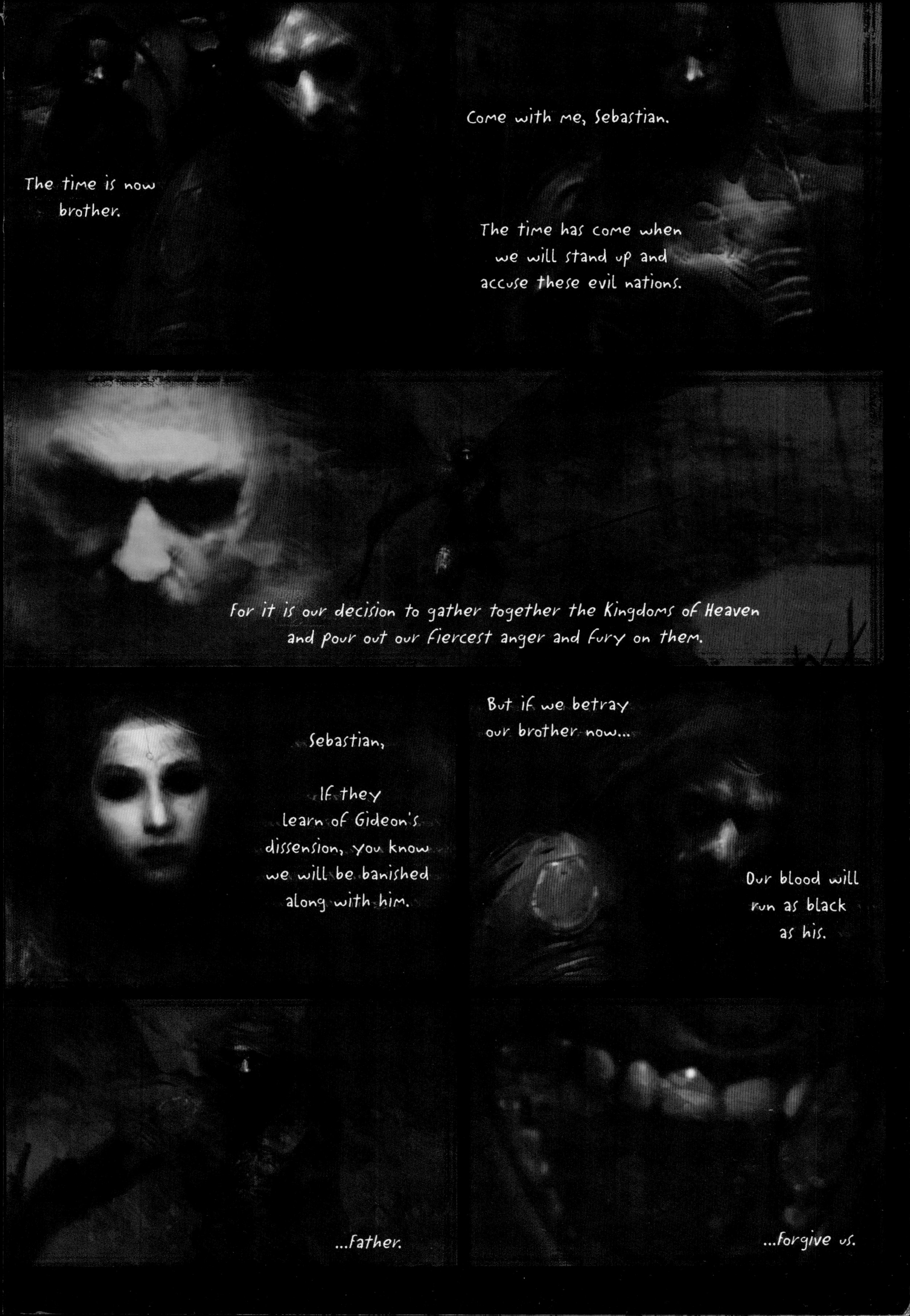

The time is now brother.
Come with me, Sebastian.
The time has come when we will stand up and accuse these evil nations.
For it is our decision to gather together the Kingdoms of Heaven and pour out our fiercest anger and fury on them.
Sebastian,
If they learn of Gideon's dissension, you know we will be banished along with him.
But if we betray our brother now...
Our blood will run as black as his.
...father.
...forgive us.

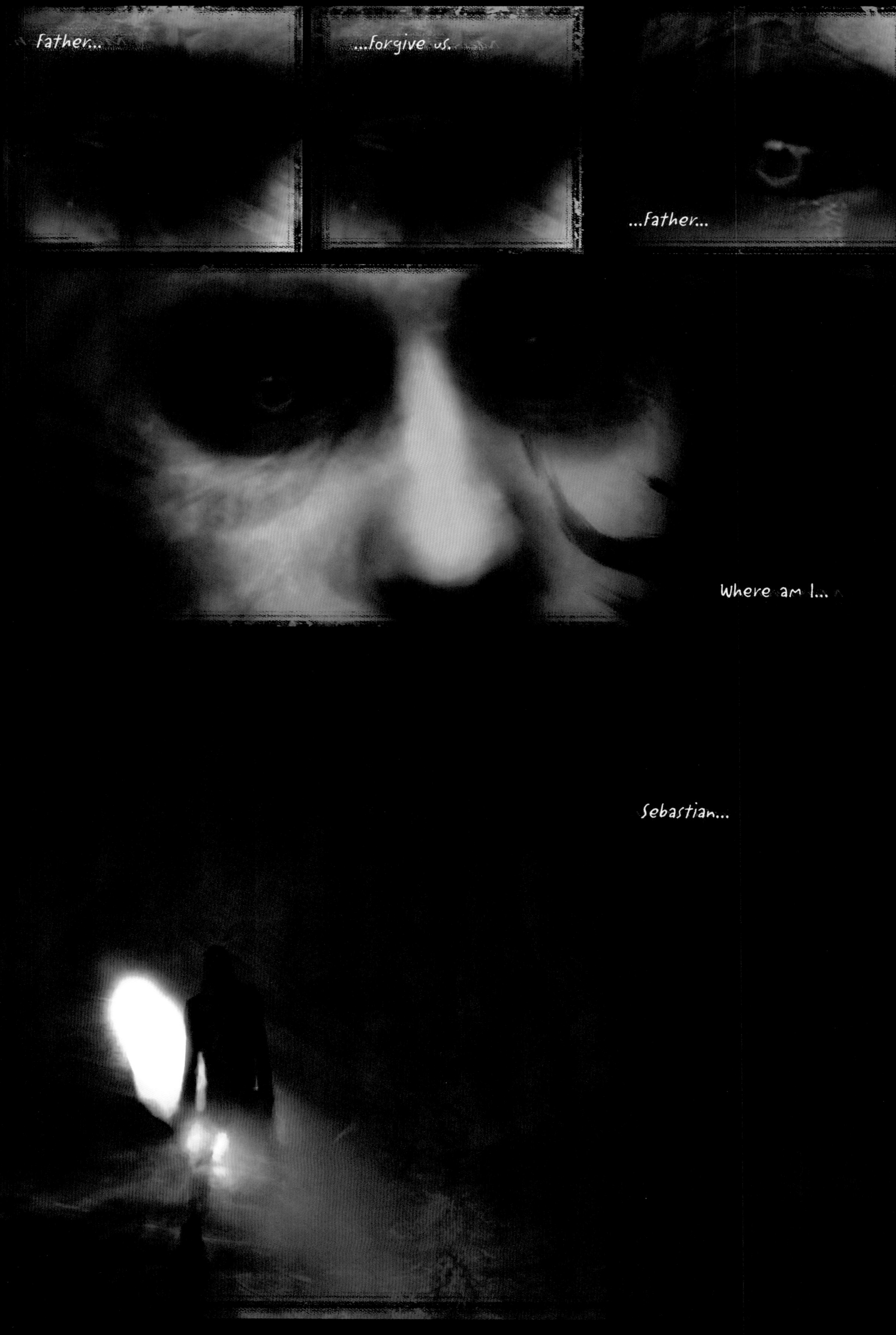
Father...
...forgive us.
...father...
Where am I...
Sebastian...

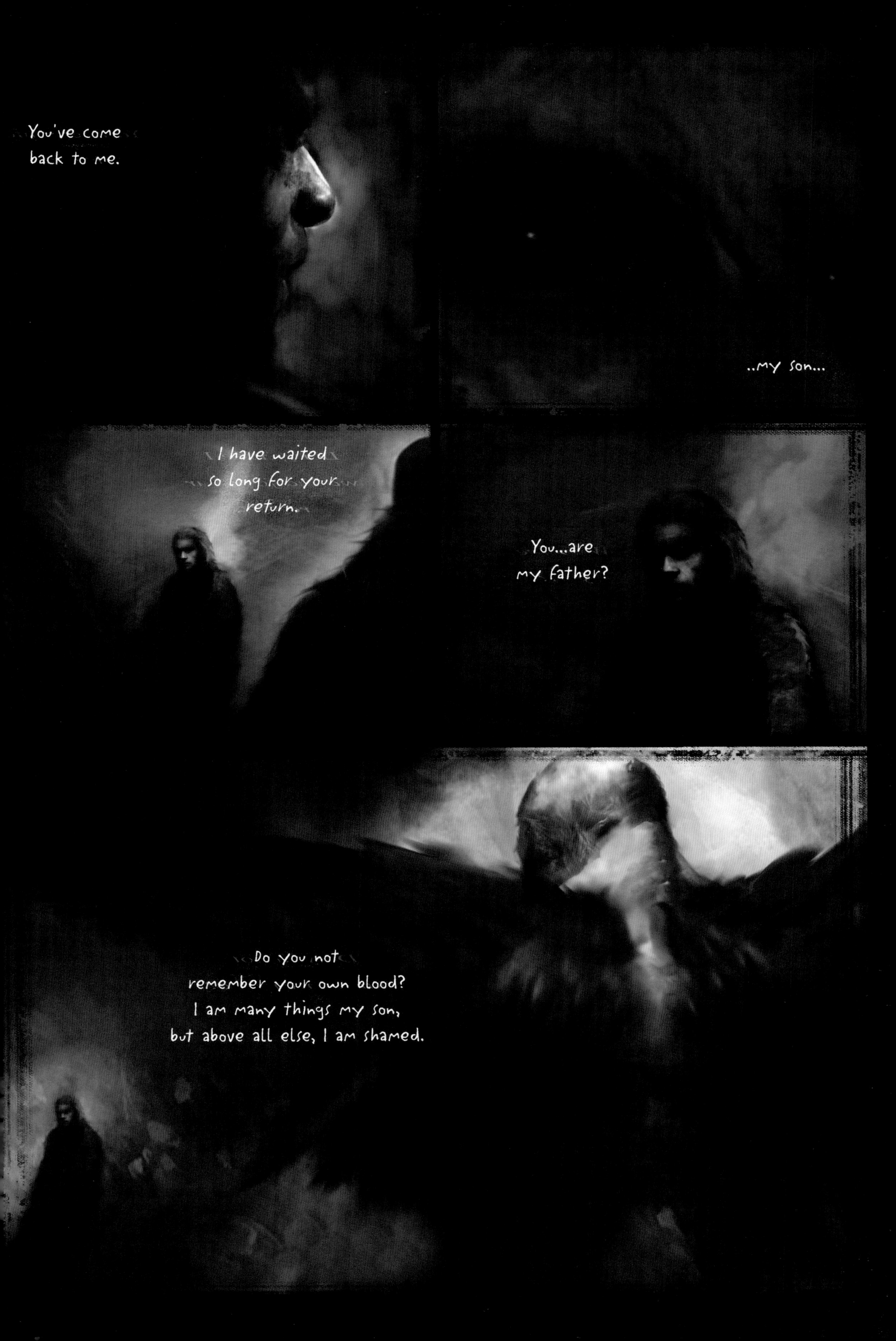
You've come back to me.
..my son...
I have waited so long for your return.
You...are my father?
Do you not remember your own blood? I am many things my son, but above all else, I am shamed.

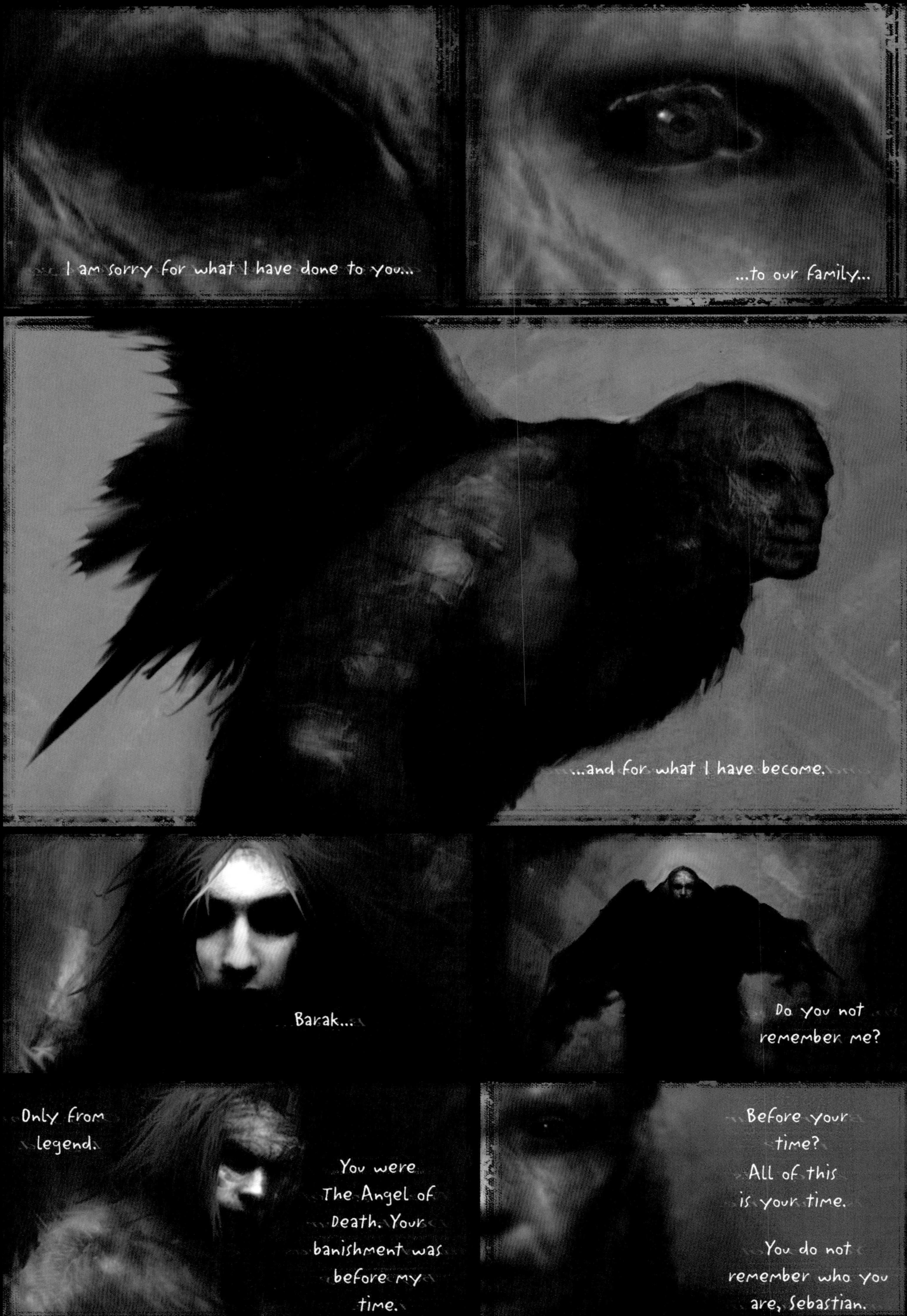
I am sorry for what I have done to you...
...to our family...
...and for what I have become.
Barak...
Do you not remember me?
Only from legend.
You were The Angel of Death. Your banishment was before my time.
Before your time? All of this is your time.
You do not remember who you are, Sebastian.

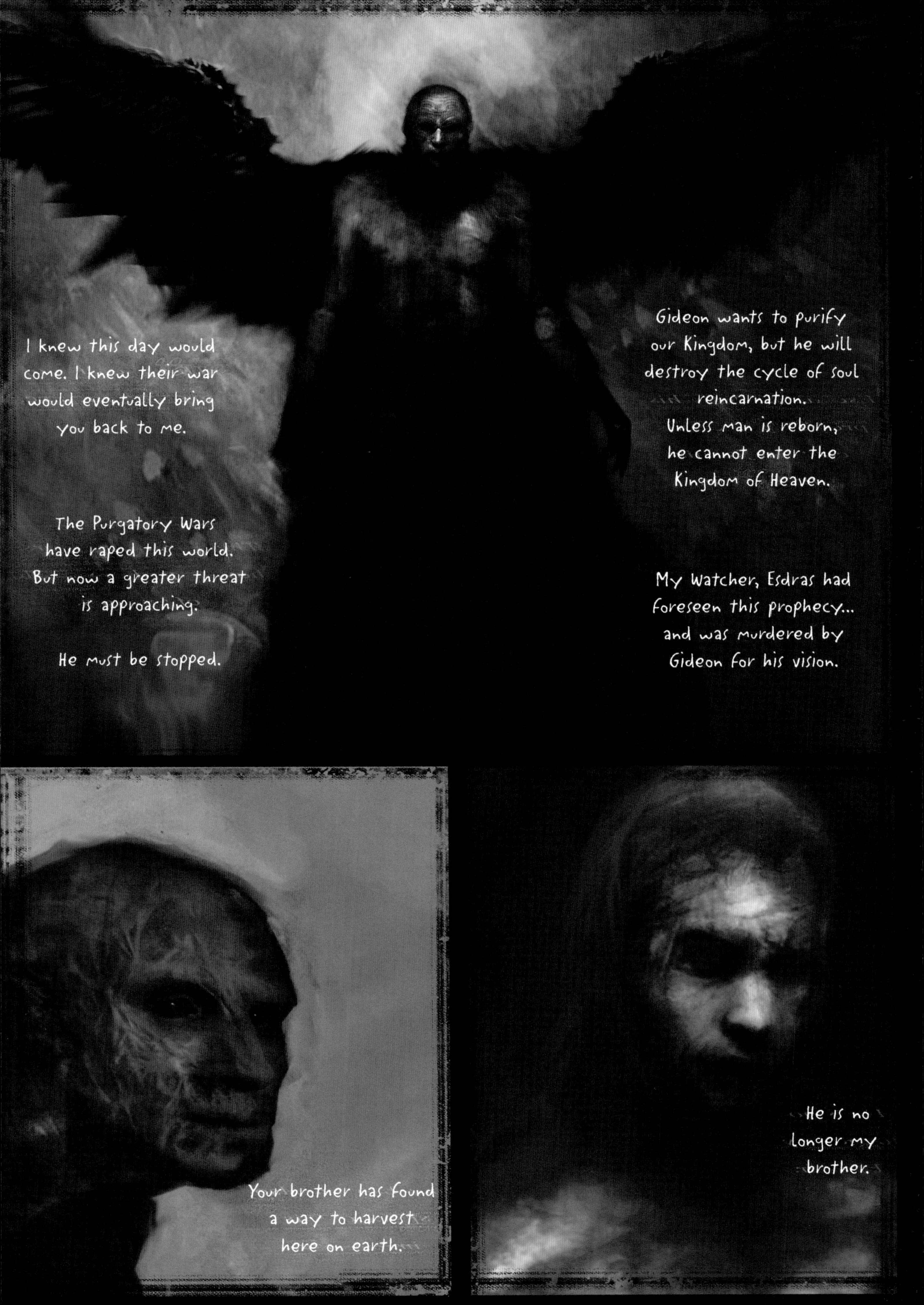

I knew this day would come. I knew their war would eventually bring you back to me.
The Purgatory Wars have raped this world. But now a greater threat is approaching.
He must be stopped.
Gideon wants to purify our Kingdom, but he will destroy the cycle of soul reincarnation.
Unless man is reborn, he cannot enter the Kingdom of Heaven.
My Watcher, Esdras had foreseen this prophecy... and was murdered by Gideon for his vision.
Your brother has found a way to harvest here on earth.
He is no longer my brother.

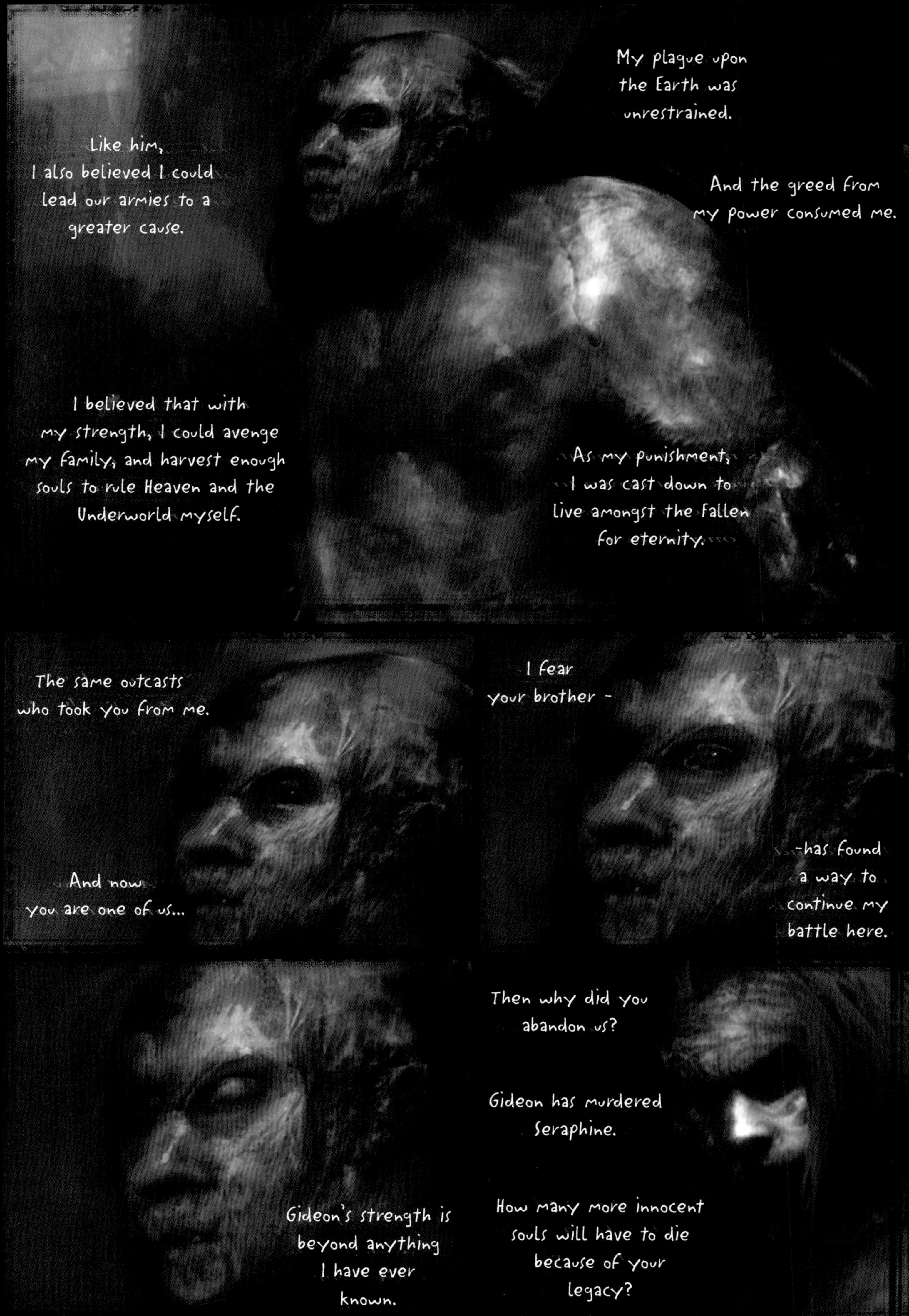
Like him, I also believed I could lead our armies to a greater cause.
My plague upon the Earth was unrestrained.
And the greed from my power consumed me.
I believed that with my strength, I could avenge my family, and harvest enough souls to rule Heaven and the Underworld myself.
As my punishment, I was cast down to live amongst the fallen for eternity.
The same outcasts who took you from me.
And now you are one of us...
I fear your brother -
-has found a way to continue my battle here.
Gideon's strength is beyond anything I have ever known.
Then why did you abandon us?
Gideon has murdered Seraphine.
How many more innocent souls will have to die because of your legacy?

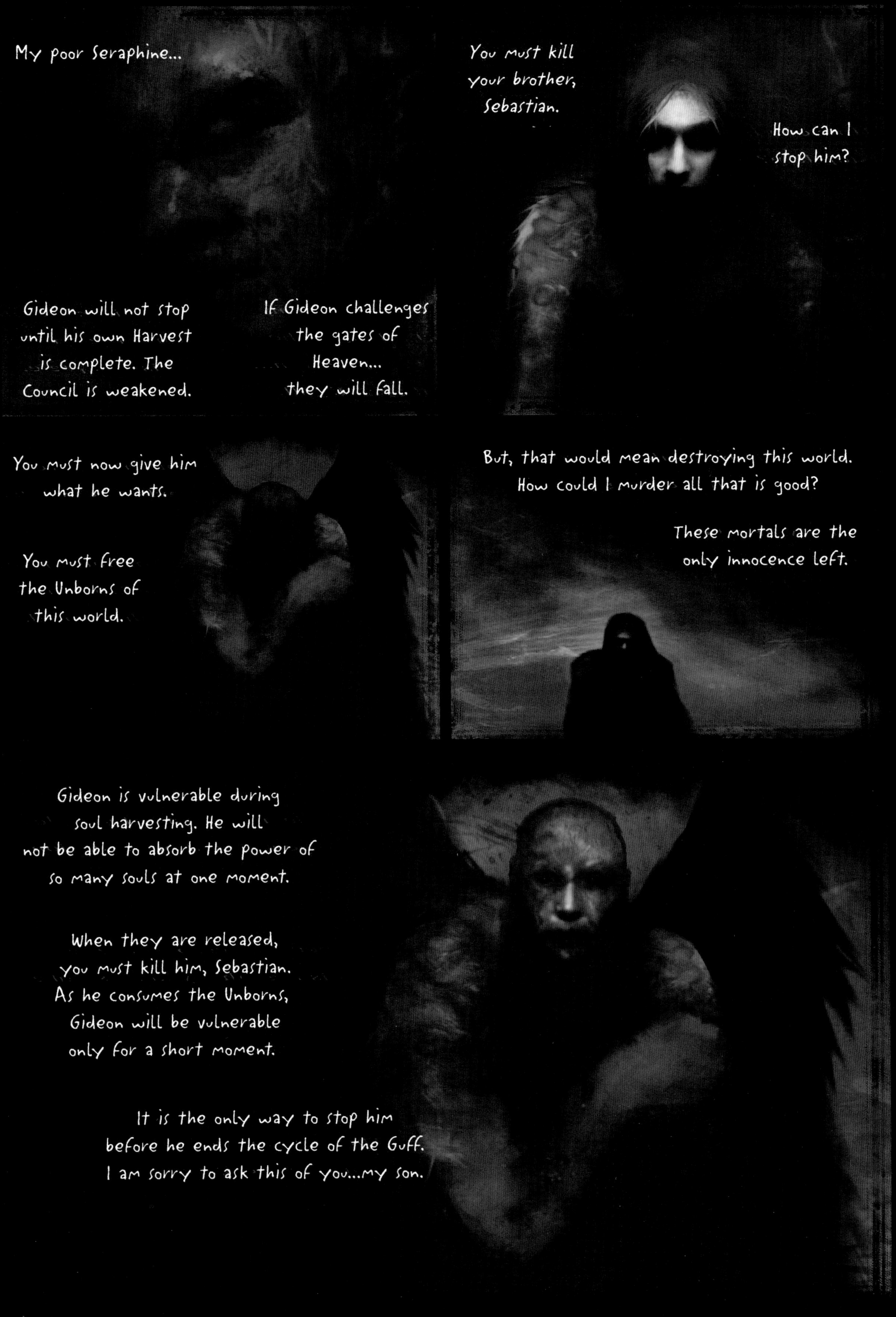
My poor Seraphine...
You must kill your brother, Sebastian.
How can I stop him?
Gideon will not stop until his own Harvest is complete. The Council is weakened.
If Gideon challenges the gates of Heaven... they will fall.
You must now give him what he wants.
You must free the Unborns of this world.
But, that would mean destroying this world. How could I murder all that is good?
These mortals are the only innocence left.
Gideon is vulnerable during soul harvesting. He will not be able to absorb the power of so many souls at one moment.
When they are released, you must kill him, Sebastian. As he consumes the Unborns, Gideon will be vulnerable only for a short moment.
It is the only way to stop him before he ends the cycle of the Guff. I am sorry to ask this of you...my son.

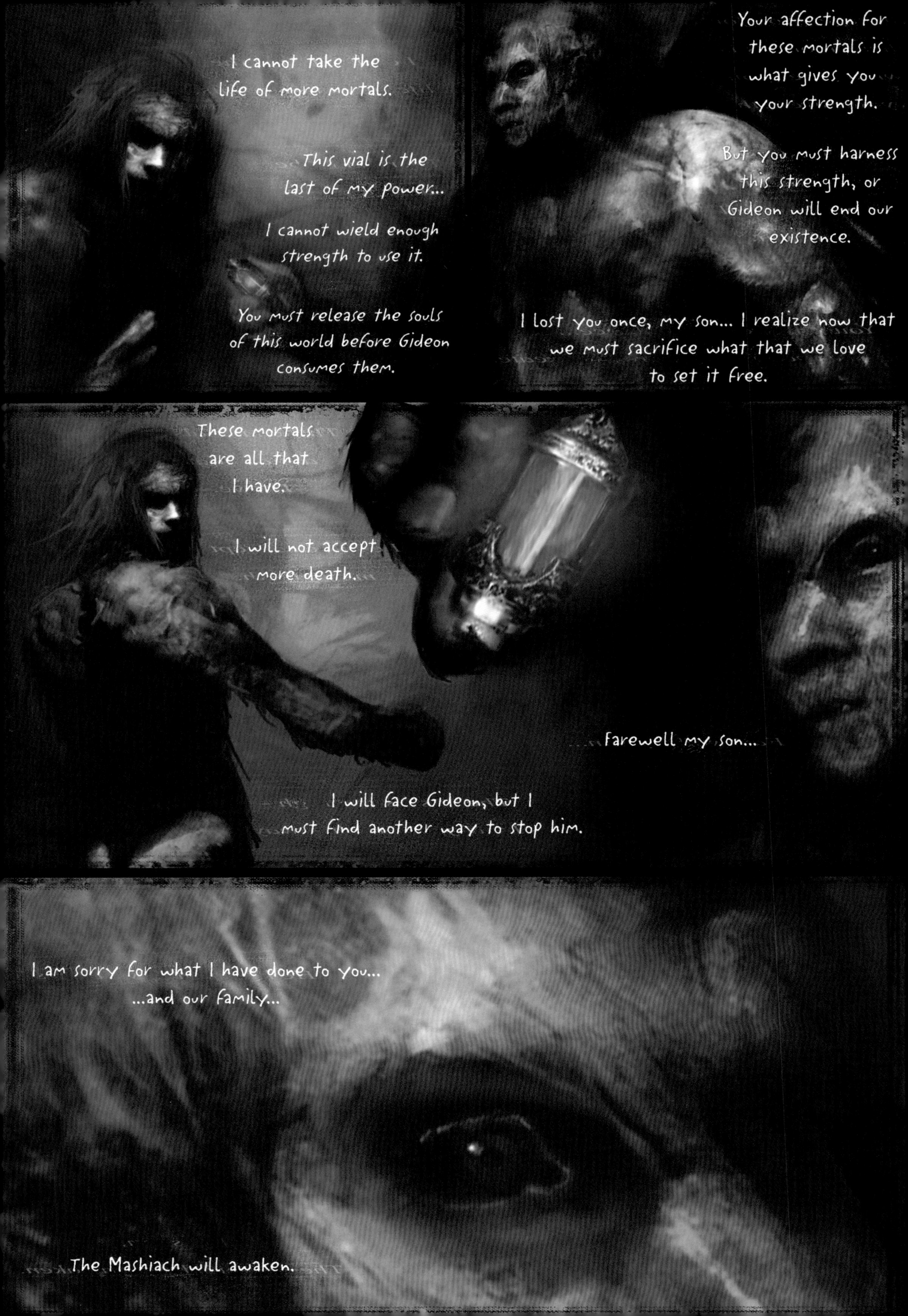
I cannot take the life of more mortals.
This vial is the last of my power...
I cannot wield enough strength to use it.
You must release the souls of this world before Gideon consumes them.
Your affection for these mortals is what gives you your strength.
But you must harness this strength, or Gideon will end our existence.
I lost you once, my son... I realize now that we must sacrifice what that we love to set it free.
These mortals are all that I have.
I will not accept more death.
Farewell my son...
I will face Gideon, but I must find another way to stop him.
I am sorry for what I have done to you...
...and our family...
The Mashiach will awaken.

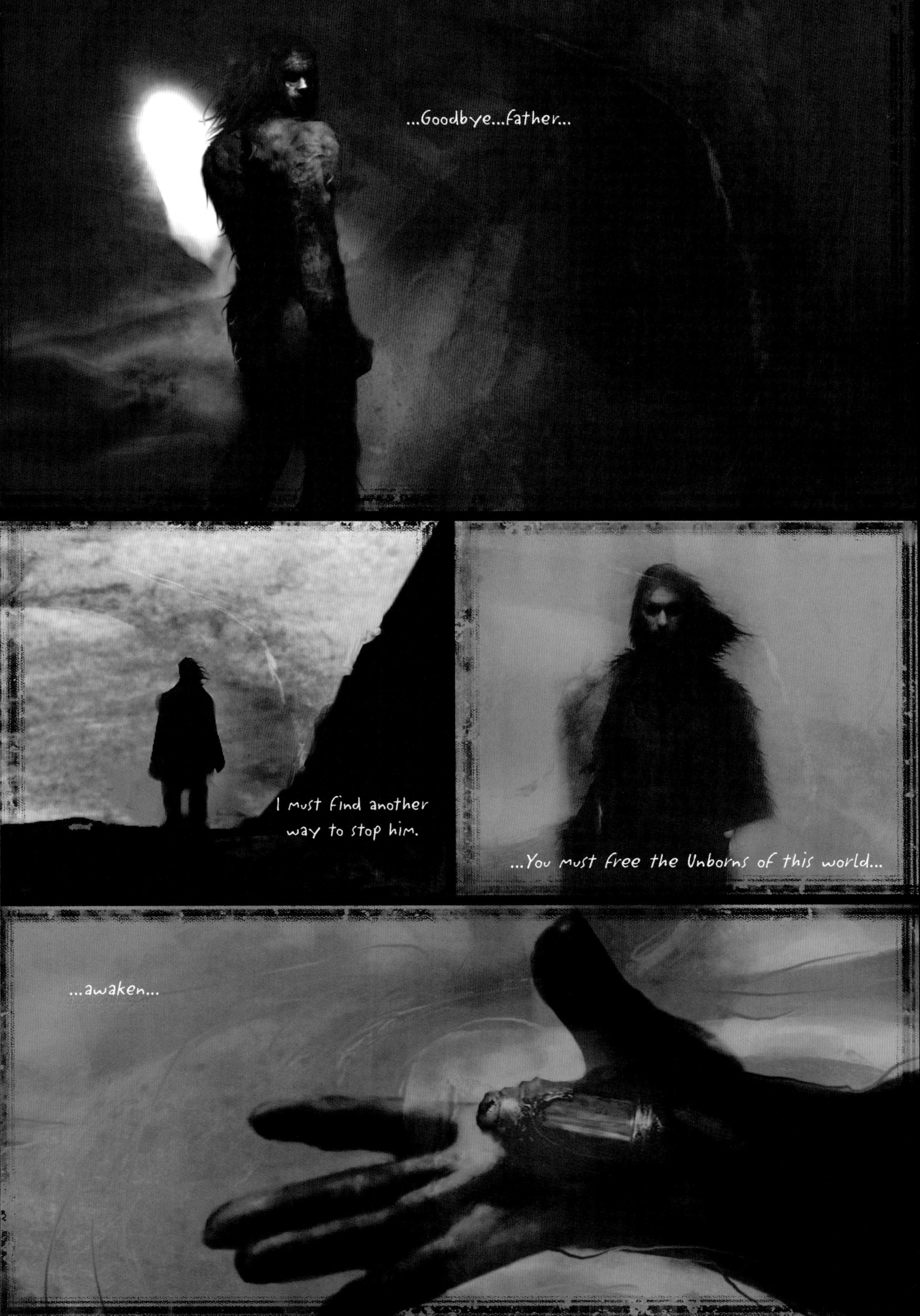
...Goodbye...father...
I must find another way to stop him.
...You must free the Unborns of this world...
...awaken...

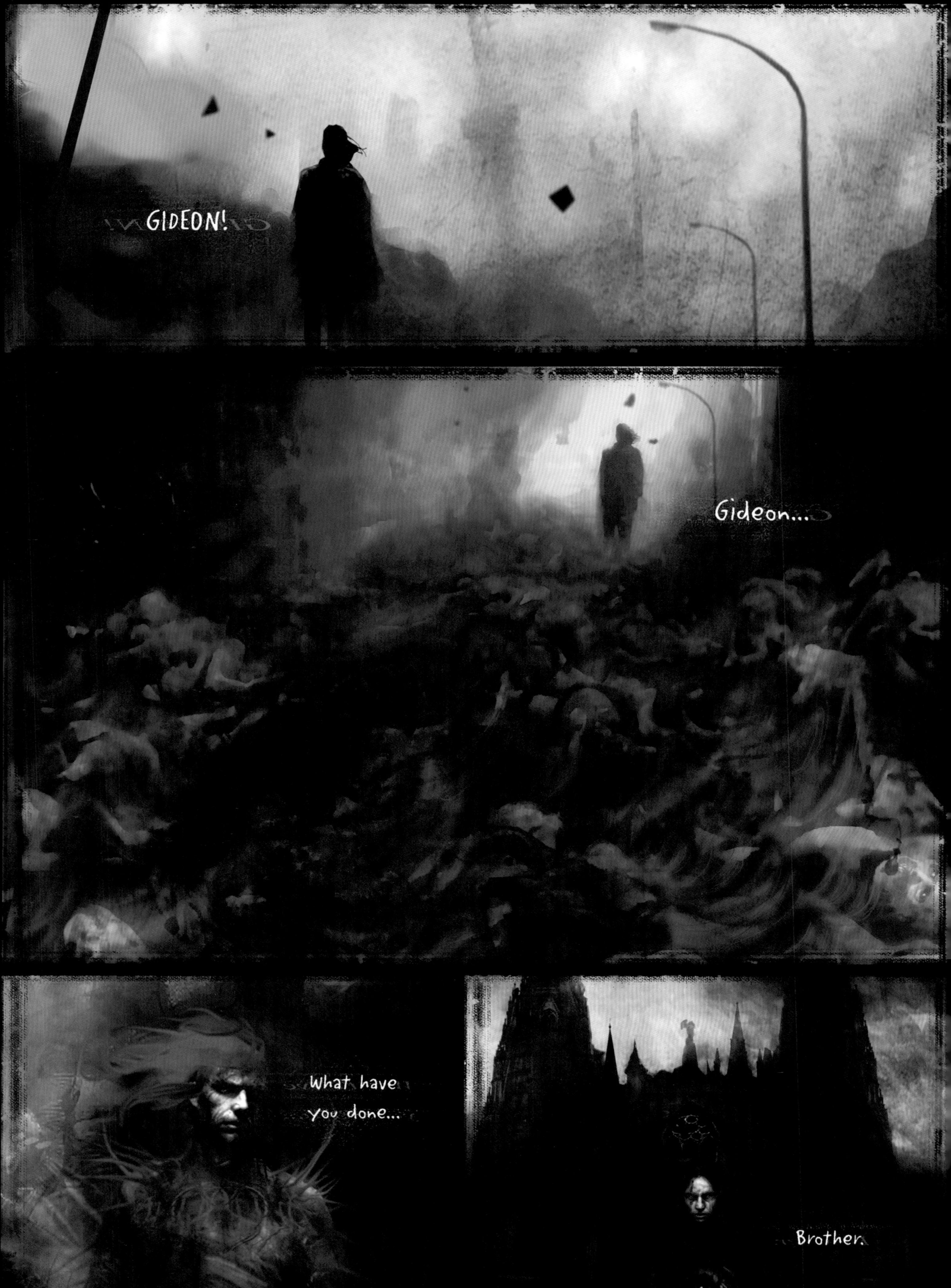
GIDEON!
Gideon...
What have you done...
Brother.

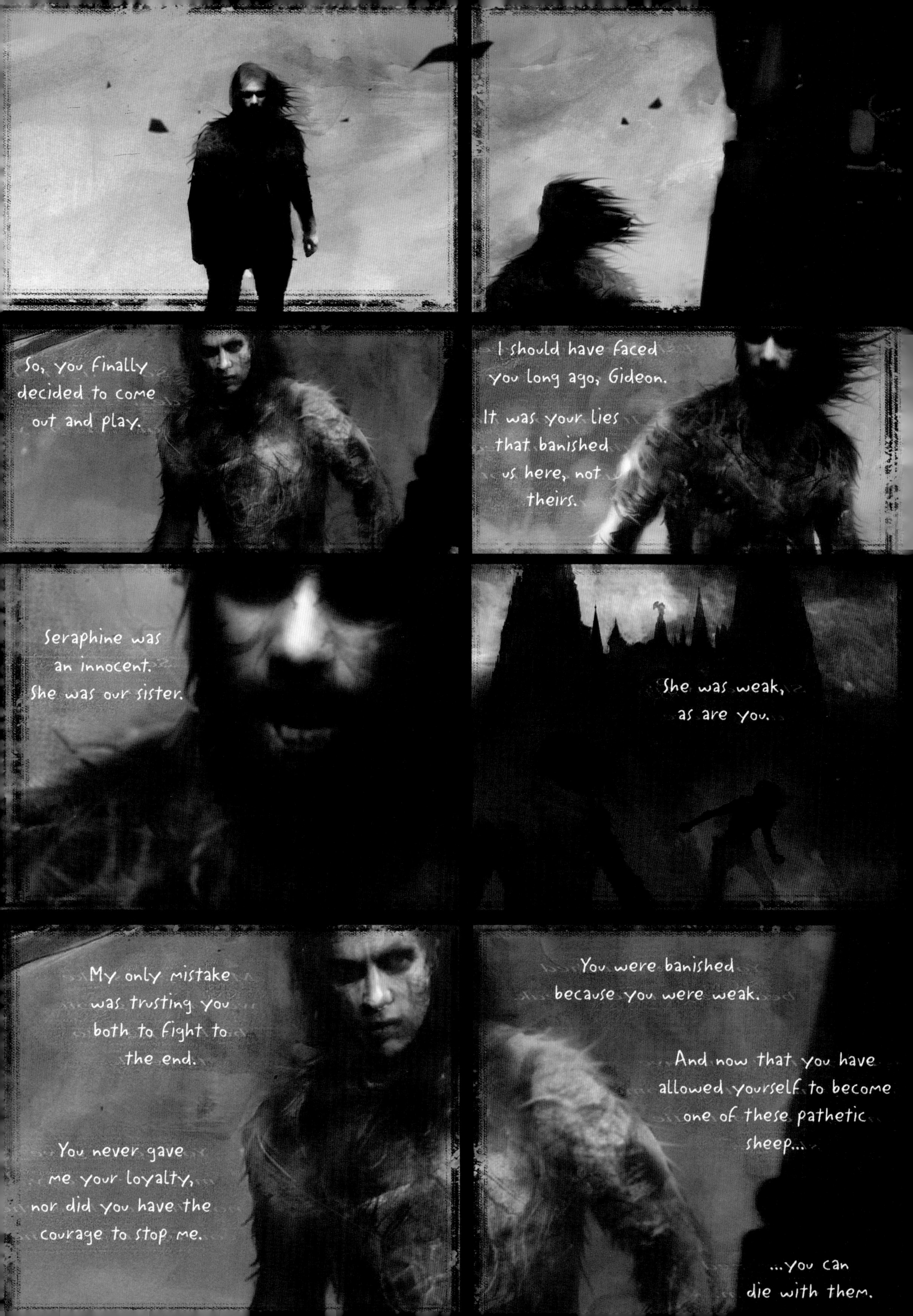
So, you finally decided to come out and play.
I should have faced you long ago, Gideon.
It was your lies that banished us here, not theirs.
Seraphine was an innocent. She was our sister.
She was weak, as are you.
My only mistake was trusting you both to fight to the end.
You never gave me your loyalty, nor did you have the courage to stop me.
You were banished because you were weak.
And now that you have allowed yourself to become one of these pathetic sheep...
...you can die with them.

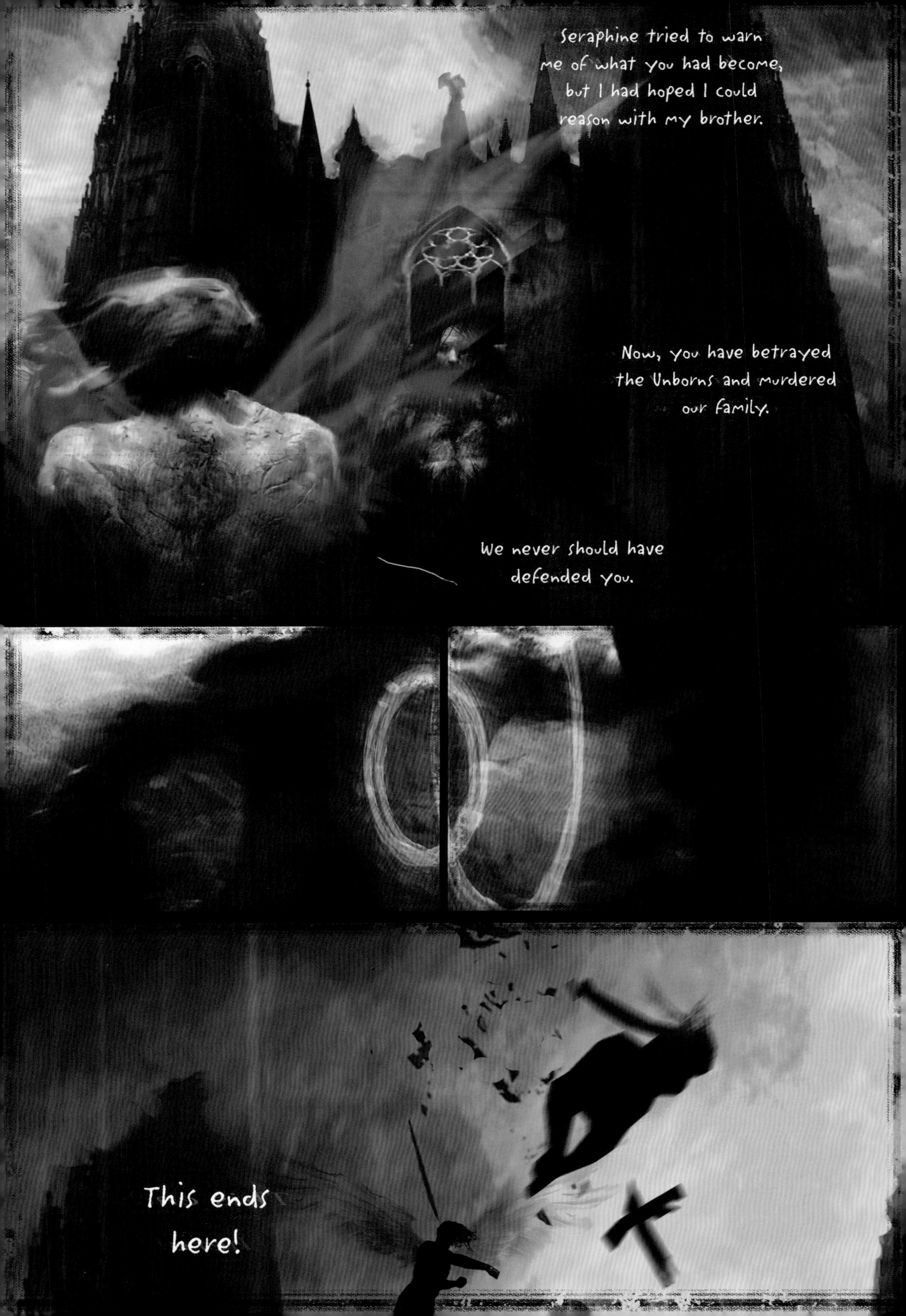
Seraphine tried to warn me of what you had become, but I had hoped I could reason with my brother.
Now, you have betrayed the Unborns and murdered our family.
We never should have defended you.
This ends here!

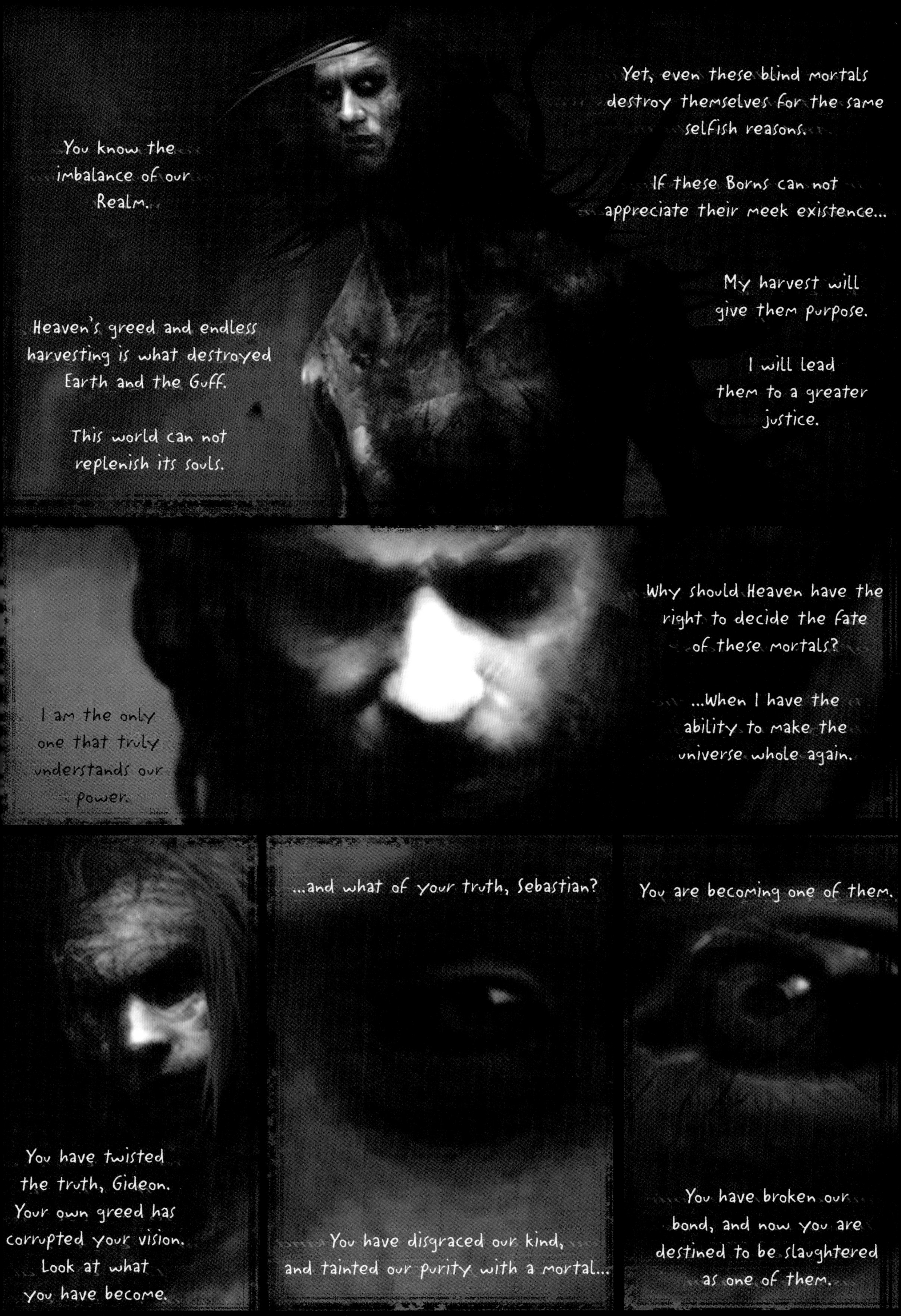
You know the imbalance of our Realm.
Heaven's greed and endless harvesting is what destroyed Earth and the Guff.
This world can not replenish its souls.
Yet, even these blind mortals destroy themselves for the same selfish reasons.
If these Borns can not appreciate their meek existence...
My harvest will give them purpose.
I will lead them to a greater justice.
I am the only one that truly understands our power.
Why should Heaven have the right to decide the fate of these mortals?
...When I have the ability to make the universe whole again.
You have twisted the truth, Gideon. Your own greed has corrupted your vision. Look at what you have become.
...and what of your truth, Sebastian?
You have disgraced our kind, and tainted our purity with a mortal...
You are becoming one of them.
You have broken our bond, and now you are destined to be slaughtered as one of them.

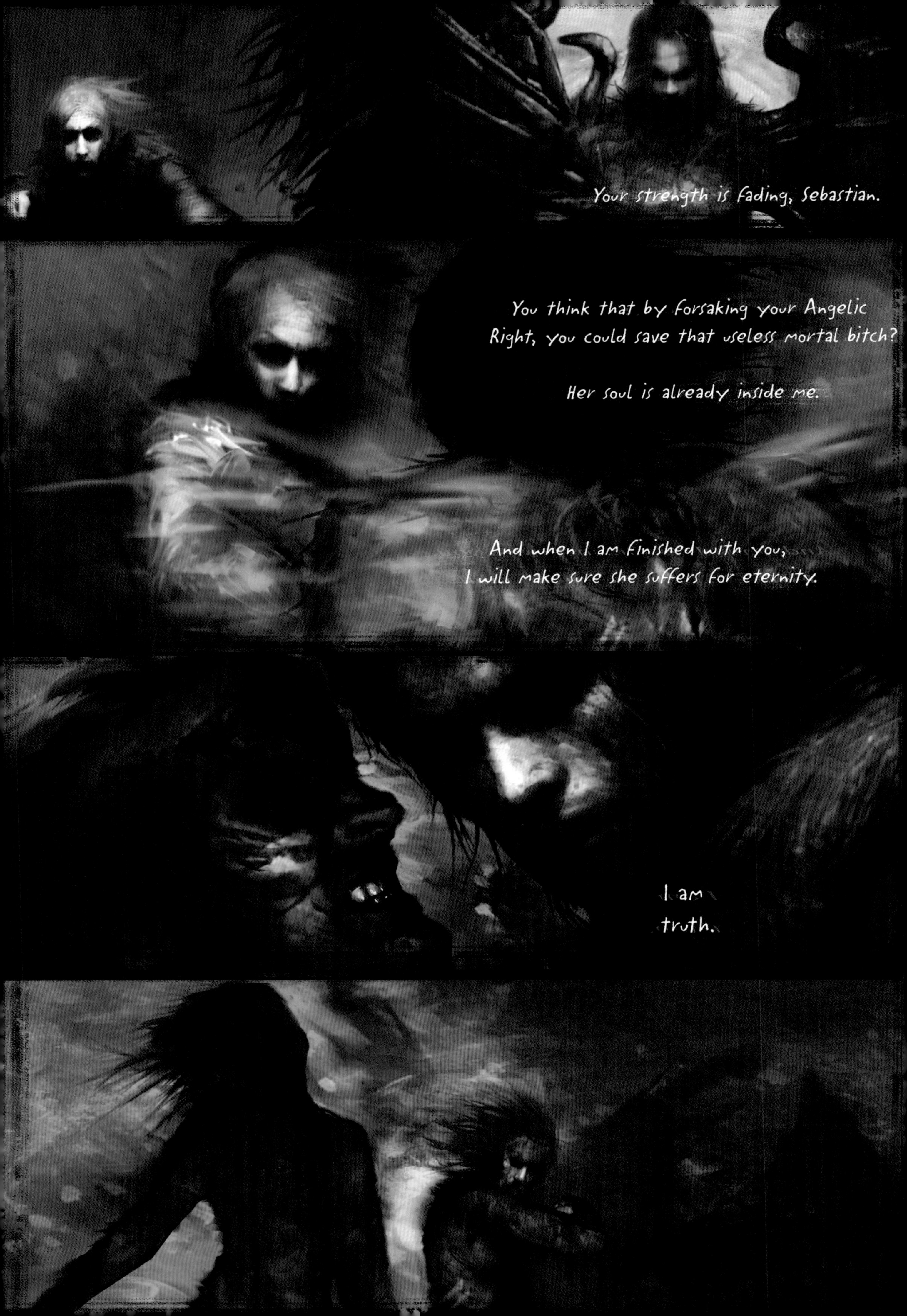
Your strength is fading, Sebastian.
You think that by forsaking your Angelic Right, you could save that useless mortal bitch?
Her soul is already inside me.
And when I am finished with you, I will make sure she suffers for eternity.
I am truth.

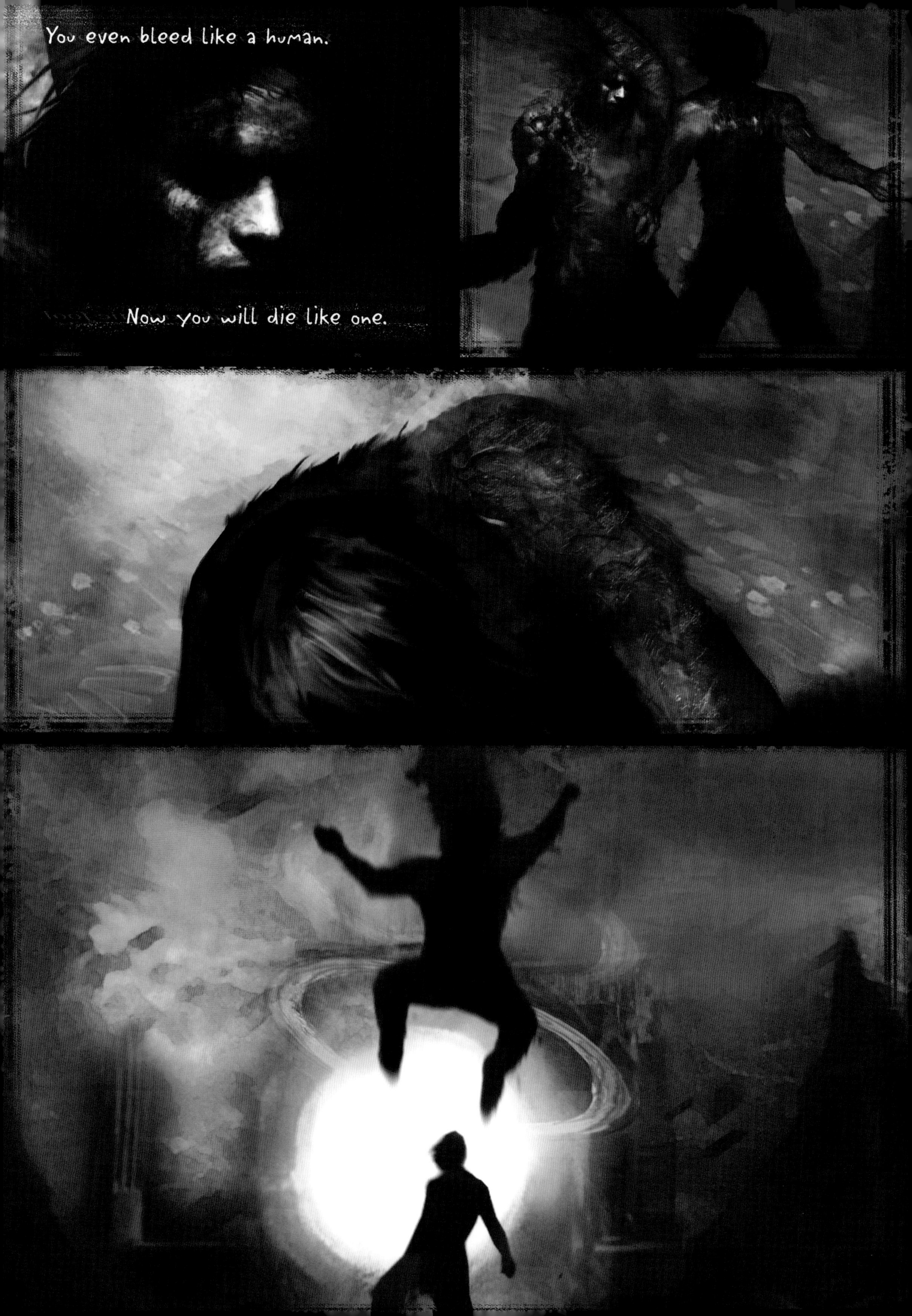
You even bleed like a human.
Now you will die like one.

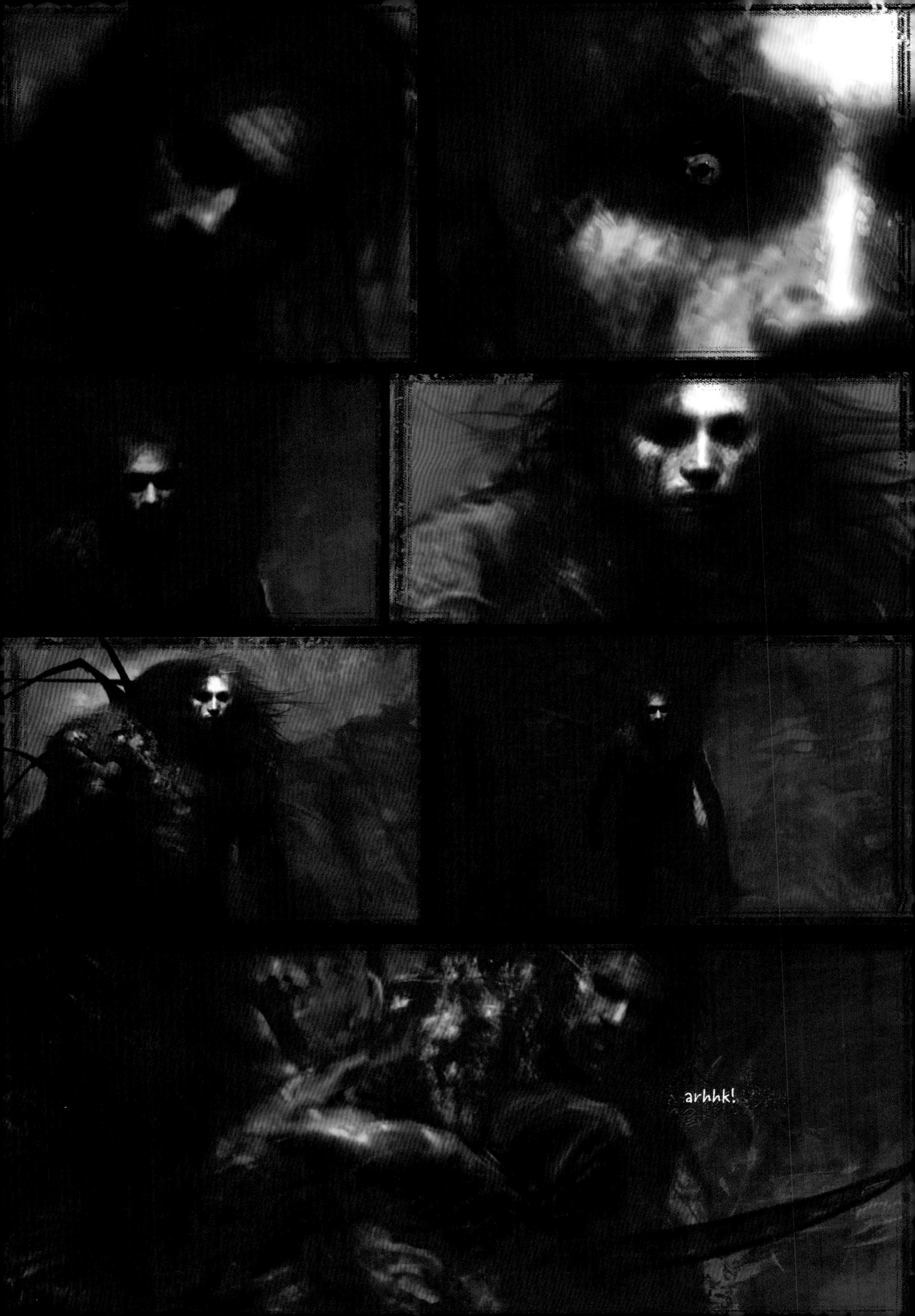
arhhk!

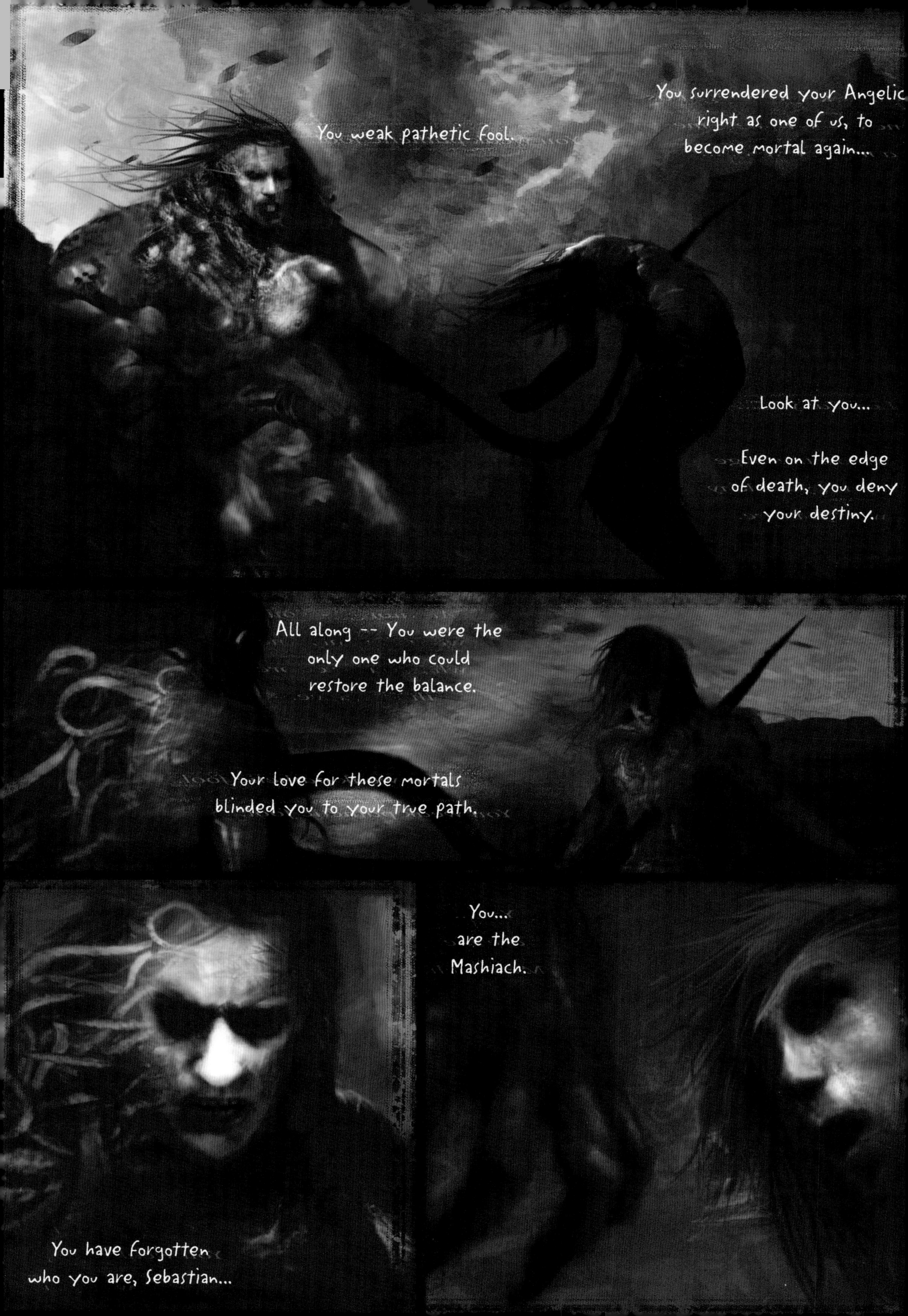
You weak pathetic fool.
You surrendered your Angelic right as one of us, to become mortal again...
Look at you...
Even on the edge of death, you deny your destiny.
All along -- You were the only one who could restore the balance.
Your love for these mortals blinded you to your true path.
You have forgotten who you are, Sebastian...
You...
are the Mashiach.

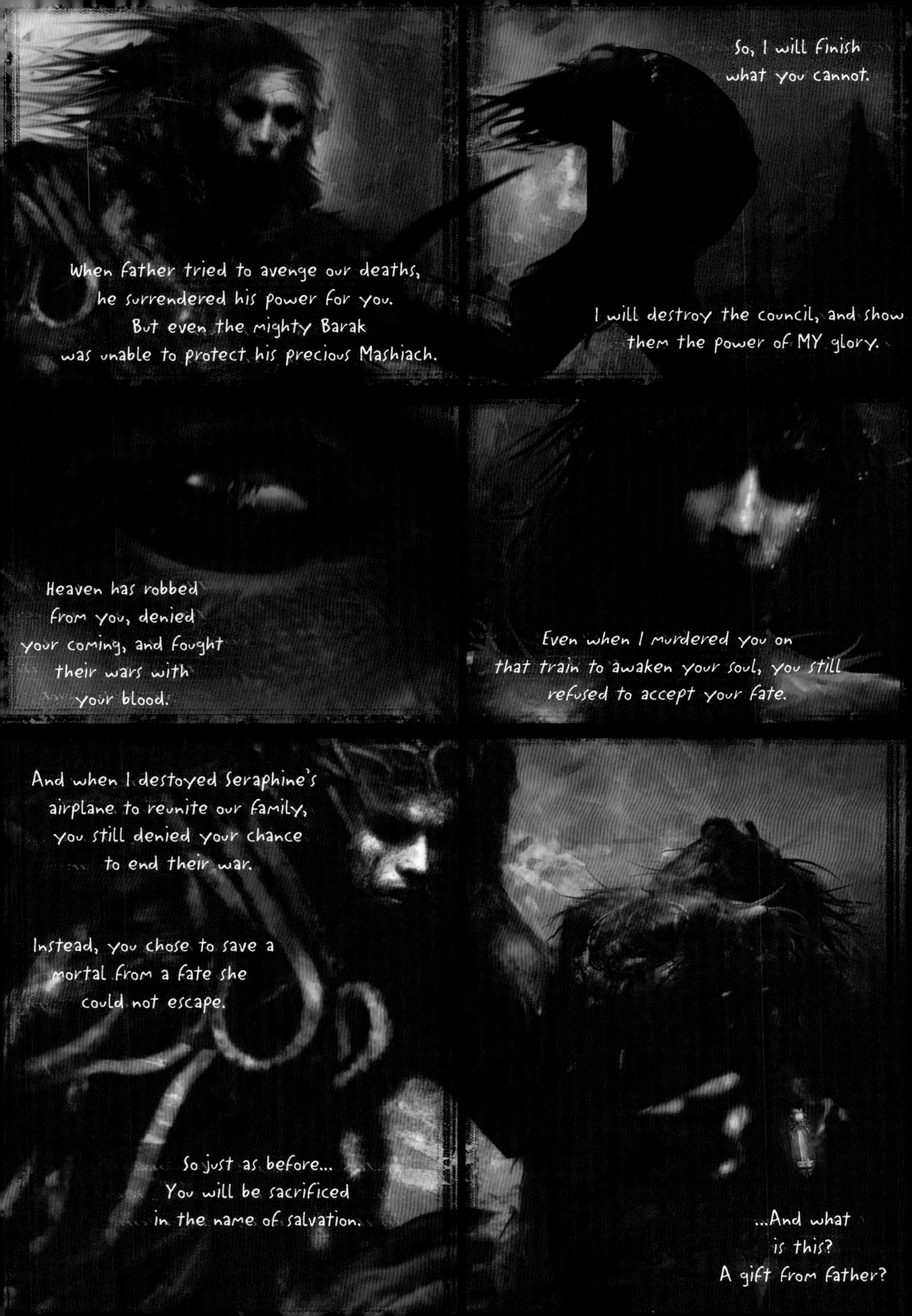
When father tried to avenge our deaths, he surrendered his power for you. But even the mighty Barak was unable to protect his precious Mashiach.
So, I will finish what you cannot.
I will destroy the council, and show them the power of MY glory.
Heaven has robbed from you, denied your coming, and fought their wars with your blood.
Even when I murdered you on that train to awaken your soul, you still refused to accept your fate.
And when I destoyed Seraphine's airplane to reunite our family, you still denied your chance to end their war.
Instead, you chose to save a mortal from a fate she could not escape.
So just as before... You will be sacrificed in the name of salvation.
...And what is this? A gift from father?

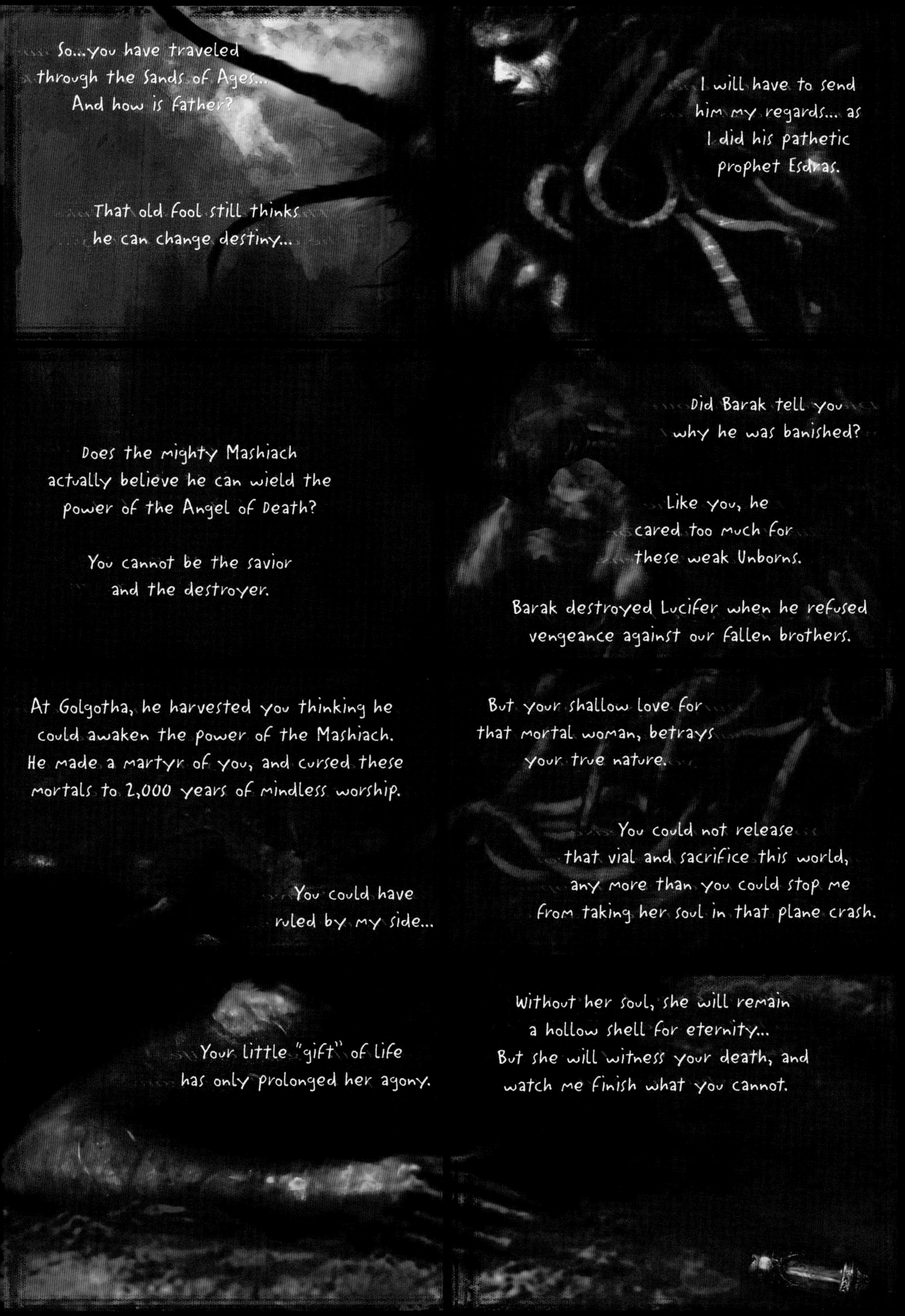
So...you have traveled through the Sands of Ages... And how is Father?
That old fool still thinks he can change destiny...
I will have to send him my regards... as I did his pathetic prophet Esdras.
Does the mighty Mashiach actually believe he can wield the power of the Angel of Death?
You cannot be the savior and the destroyer.
Did Barak tell you why he was banished?
Like you, he cared too much for these weak Unborns.
Barak destroyed Lucifer when he refused vengeance against our fallen brothers.
At Golgotha, he harvested you thinking he could awaken the power of the Mashiach. He made a martyr of you, and cursed these mortals to 2,000 years of mindless worship.
But your shallow love for that mortal woman, betrays your true nature.
You could not release that vial and sacrifice this world, any more than you could stop me from taking her soul in that plane crash.
You could have ruled by my side...
Without her soul, she will remain a hollow shell for eternity... But she will witness your death, and watch me finish what you cannot.
Your little "gift" of life has only prolonged her agony.

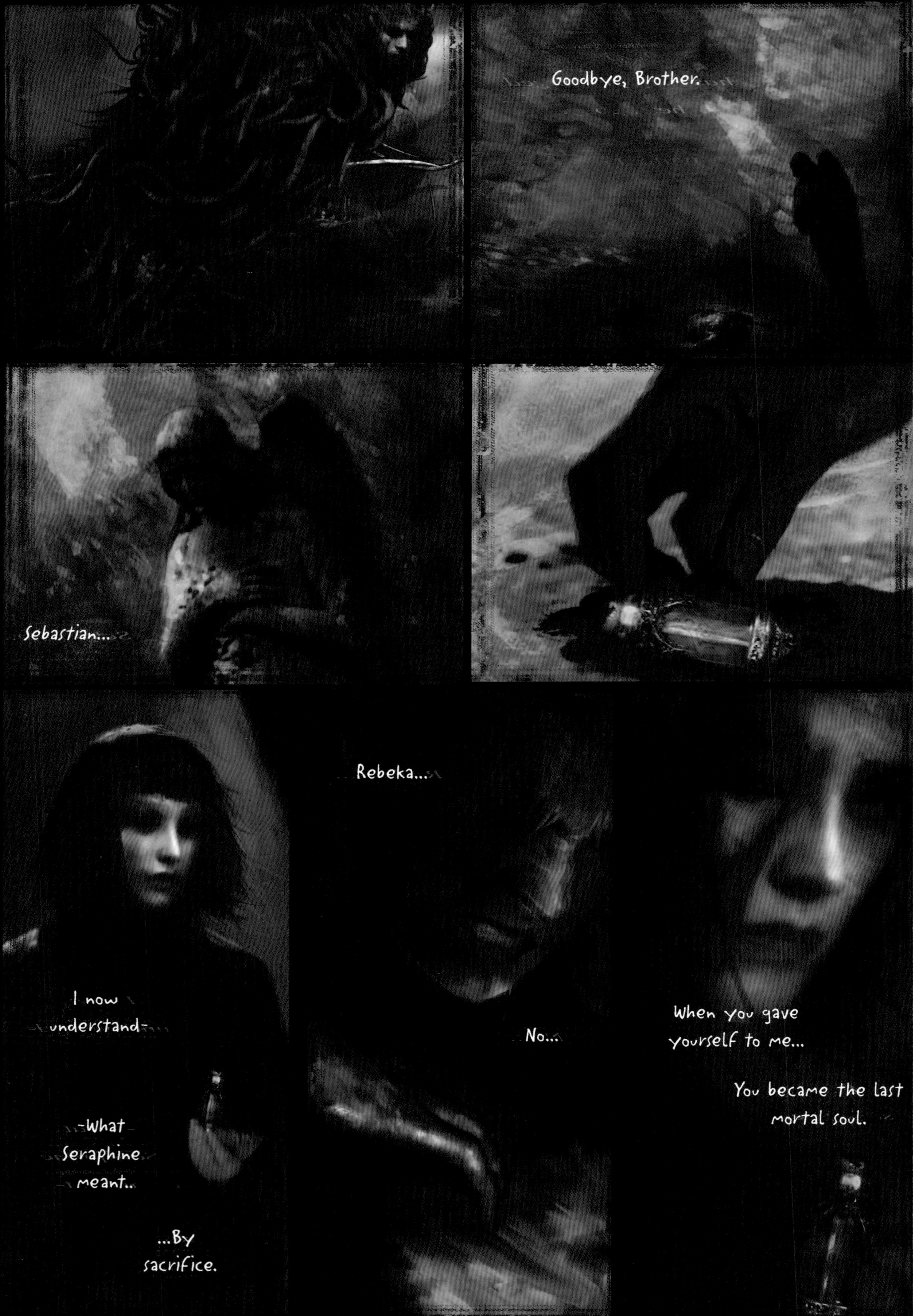
Goodbye, Brother.
Sebastian...
Rebeka...
I now understand-
-What Seraphine meant..
...By sacrifice.
No...
When you gave yourself to me...
You became the last mortal soul.

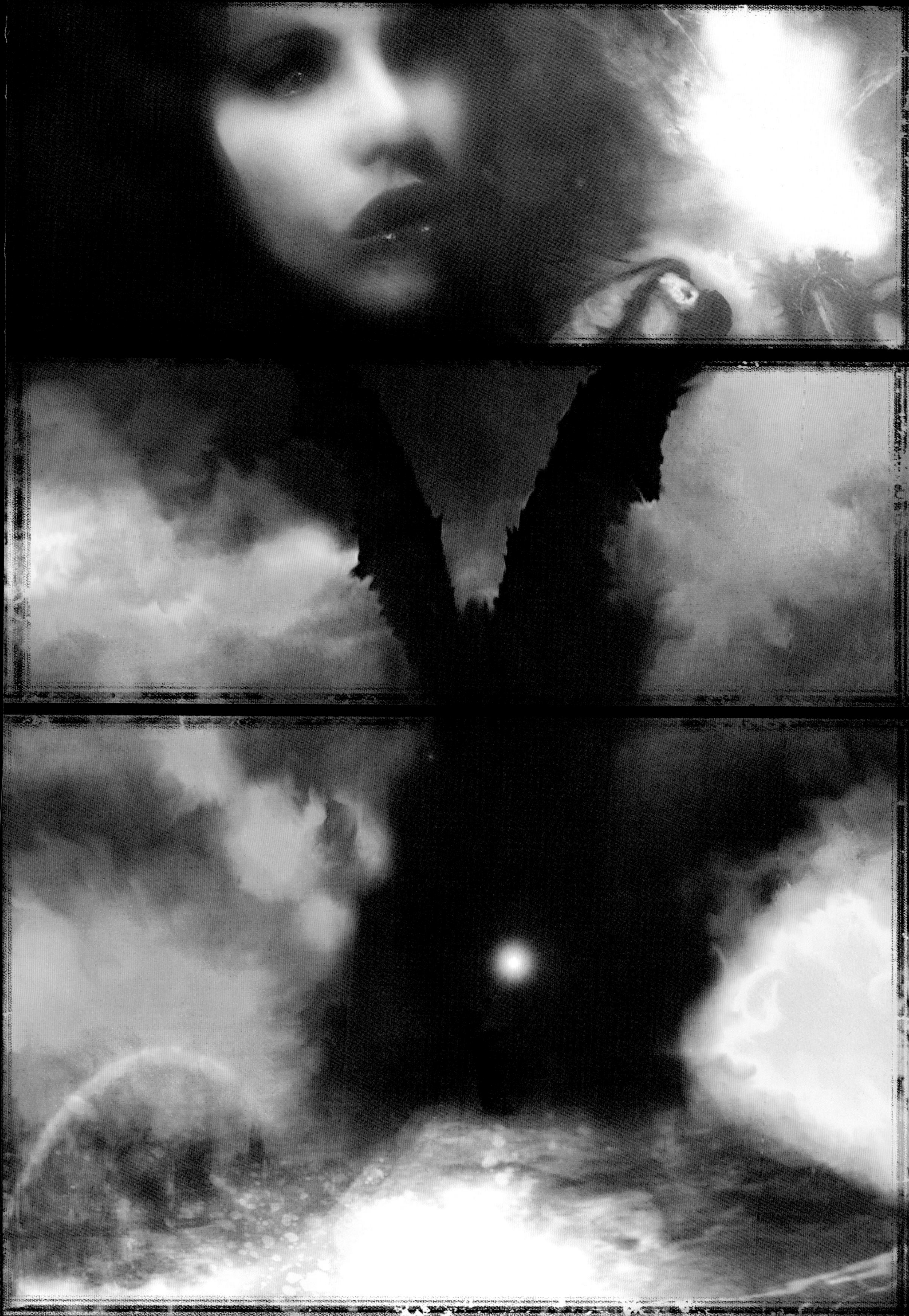

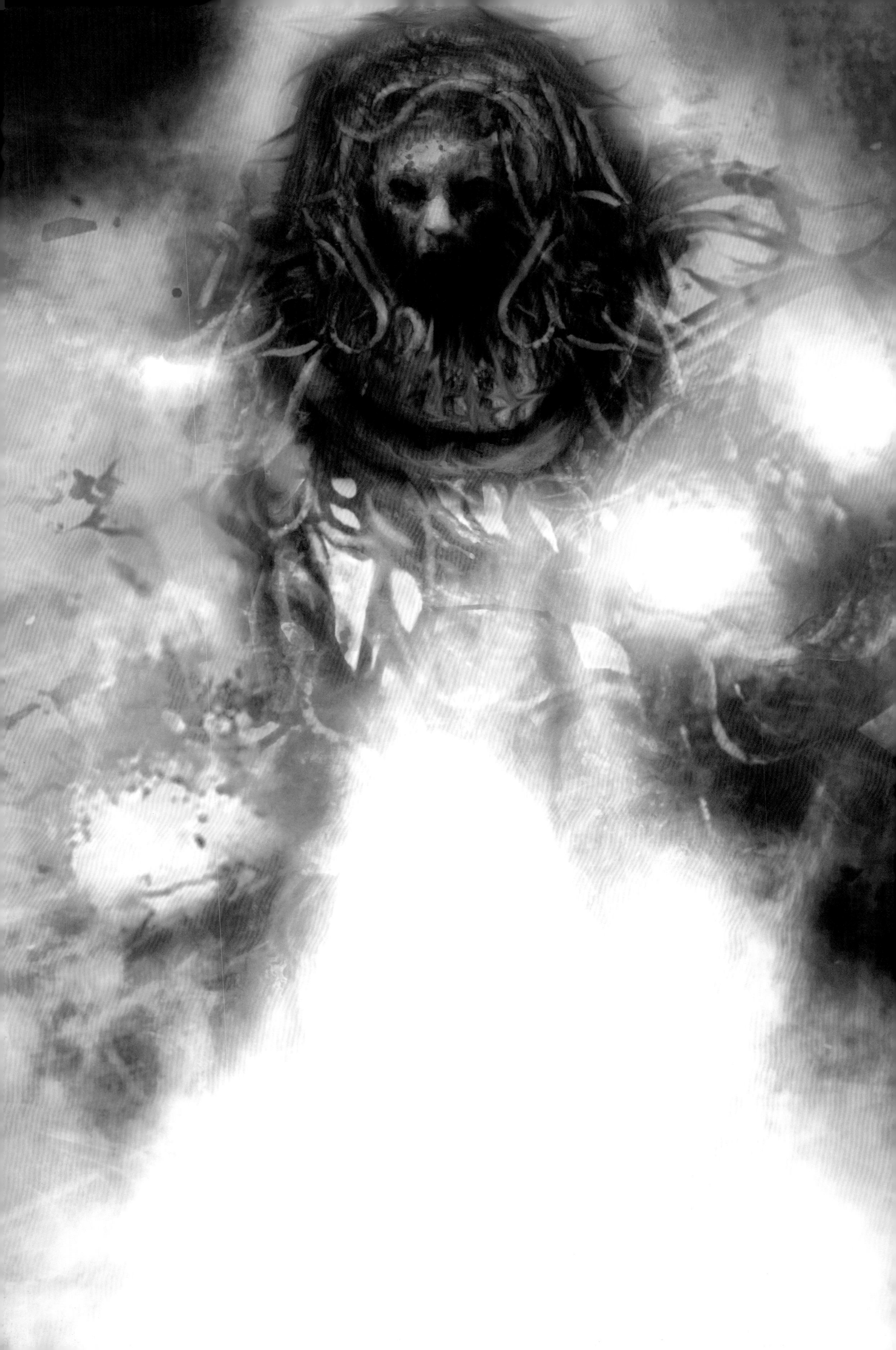

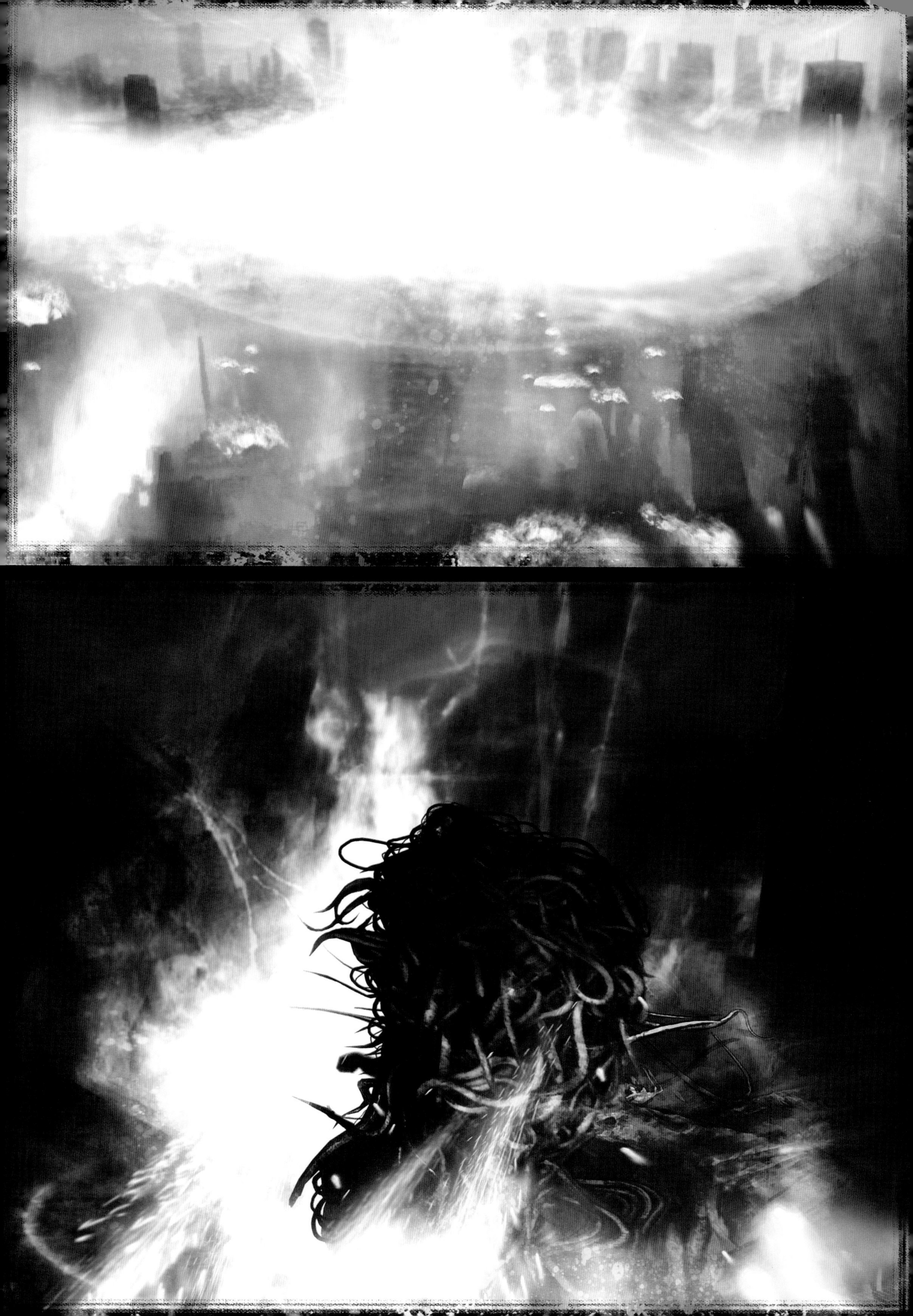

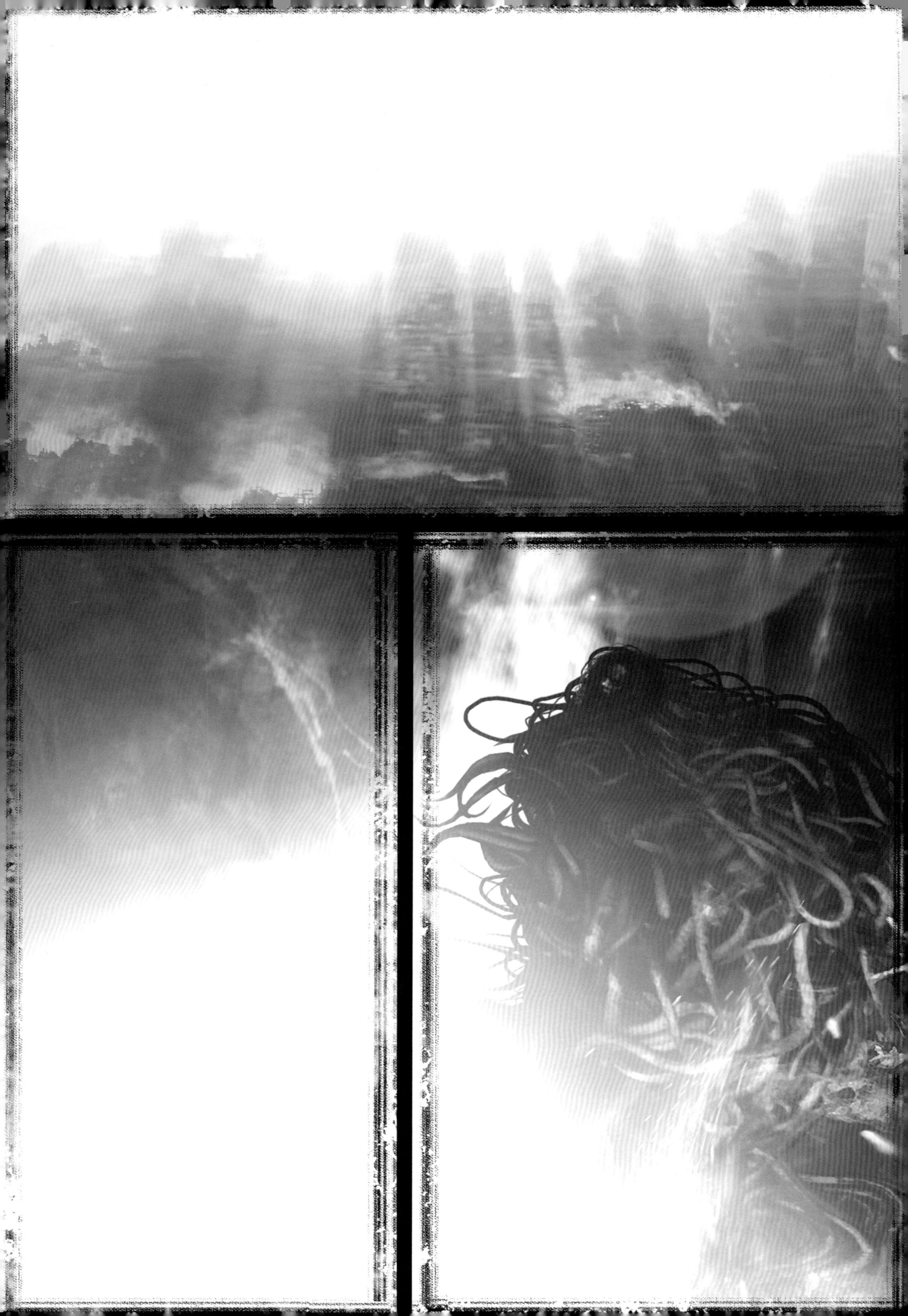

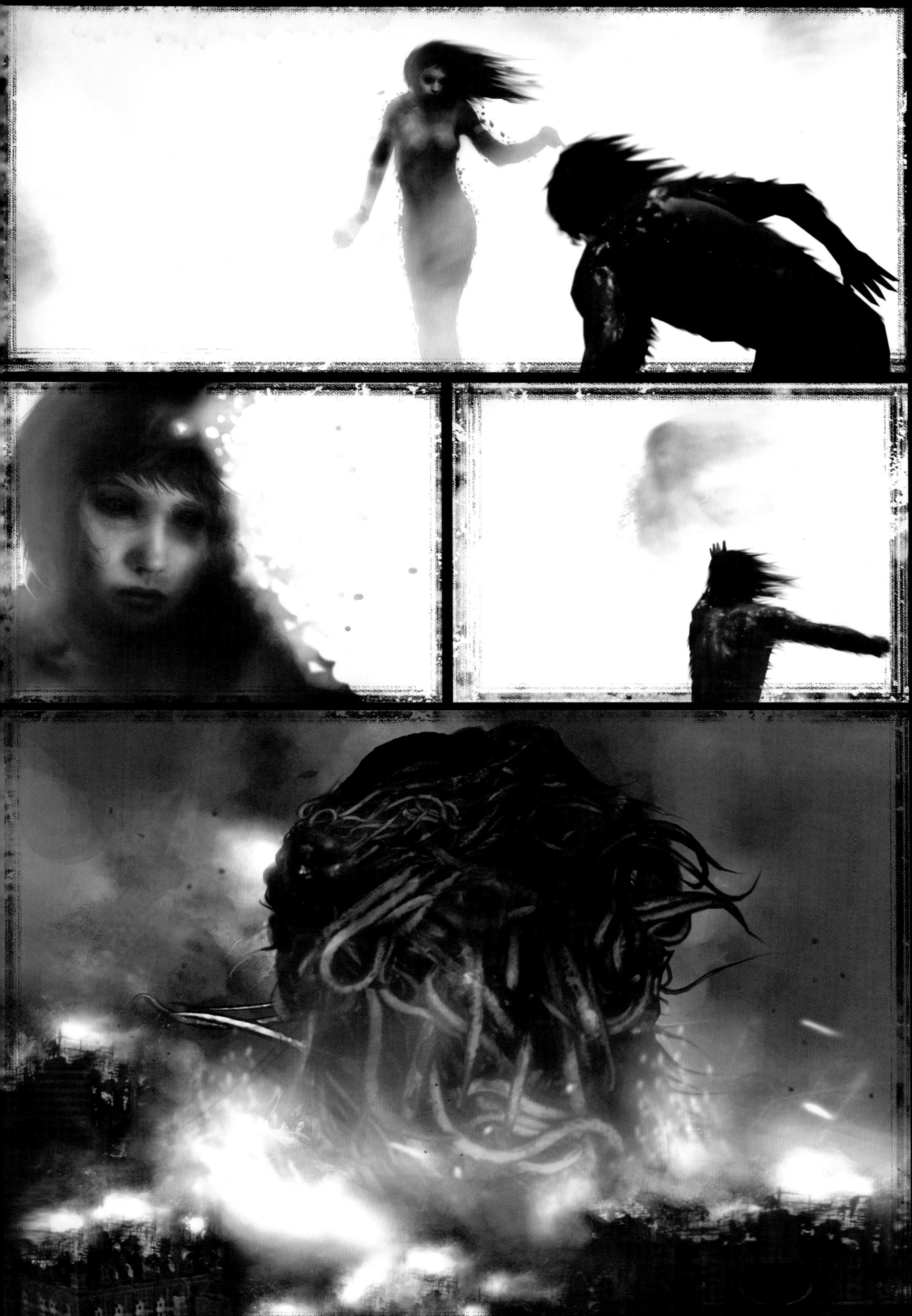

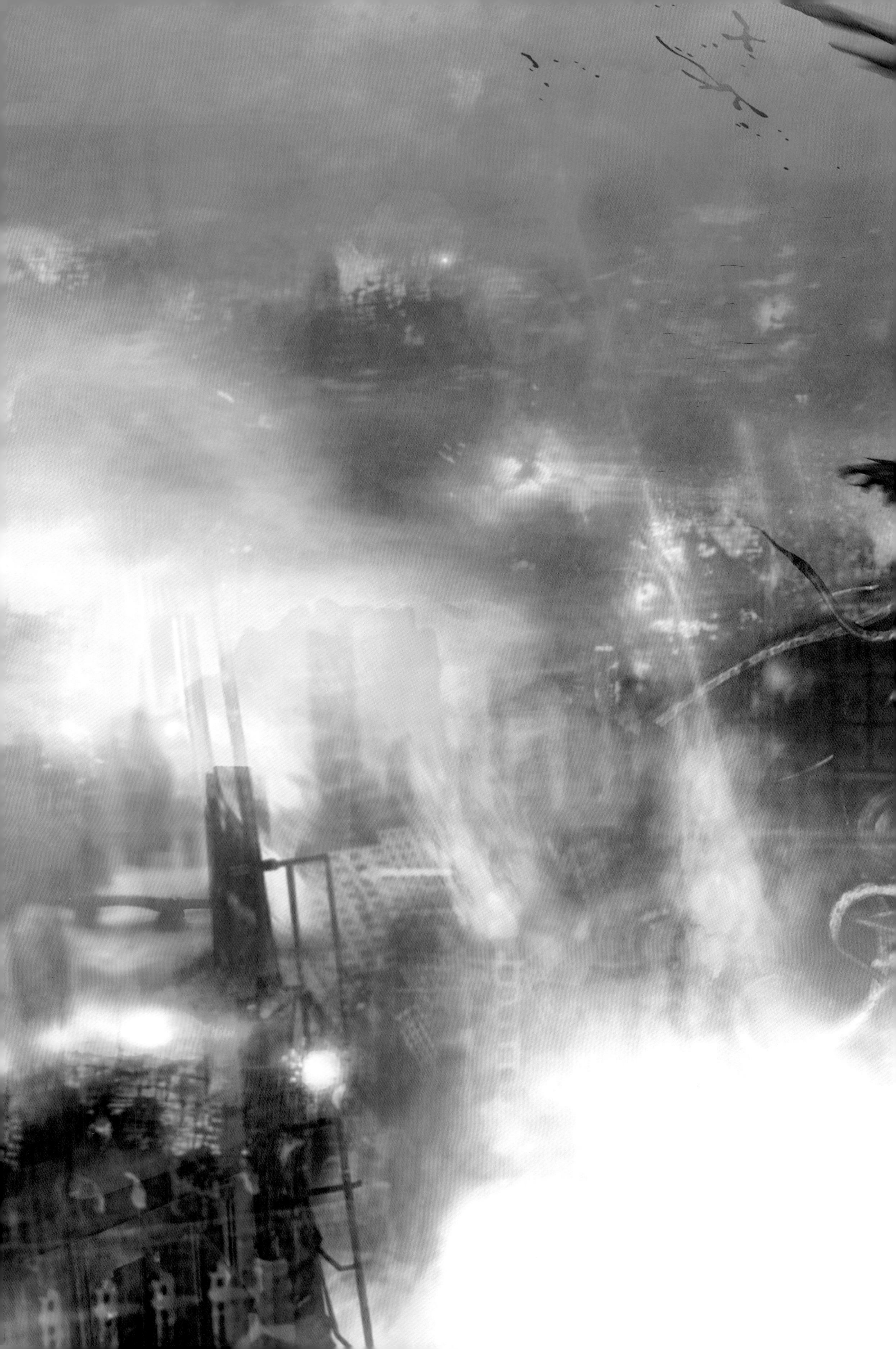

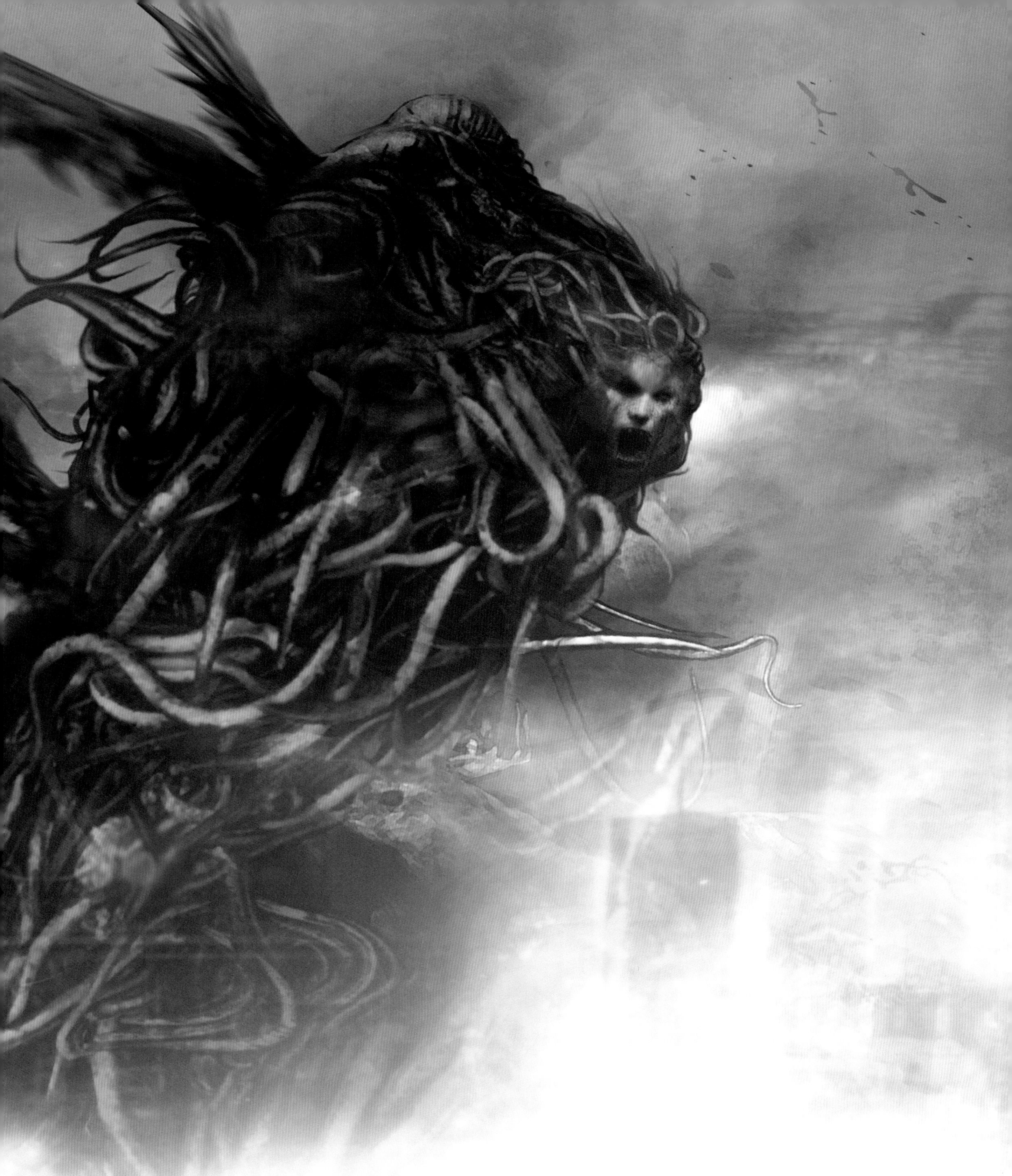

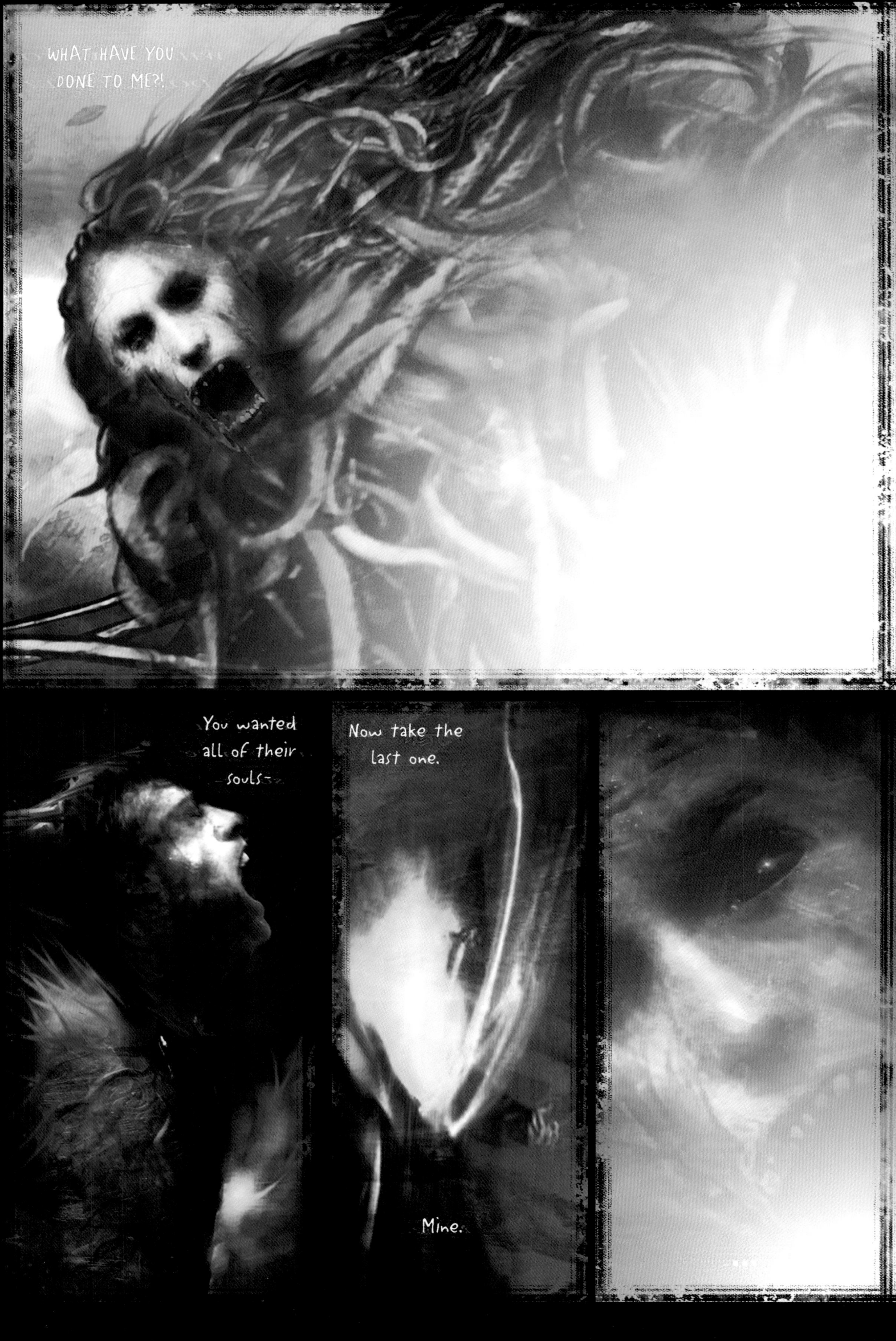
WHAT HAVE YOU
DONE TO ME?!
You wanted
all of their
souls-
Now take the
last one.
Mine.

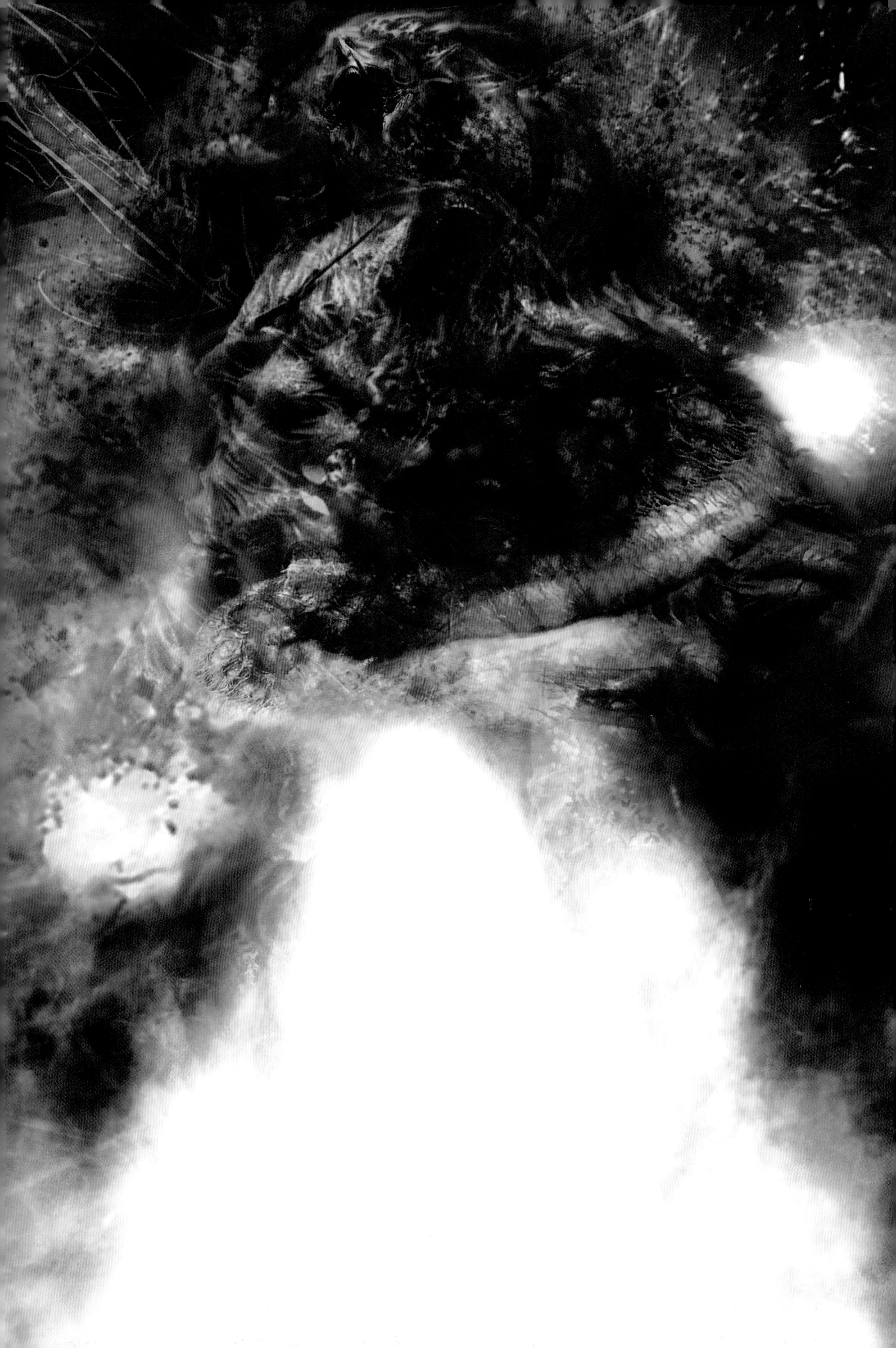

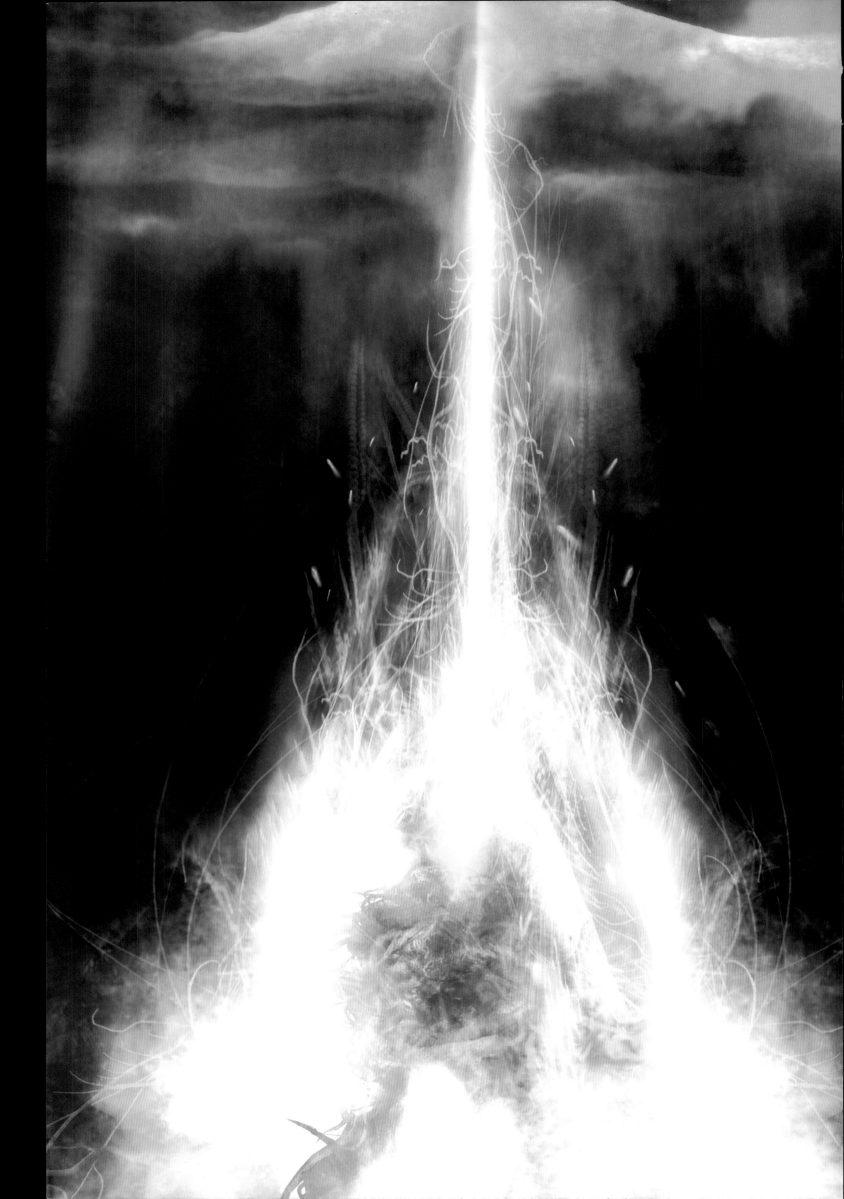

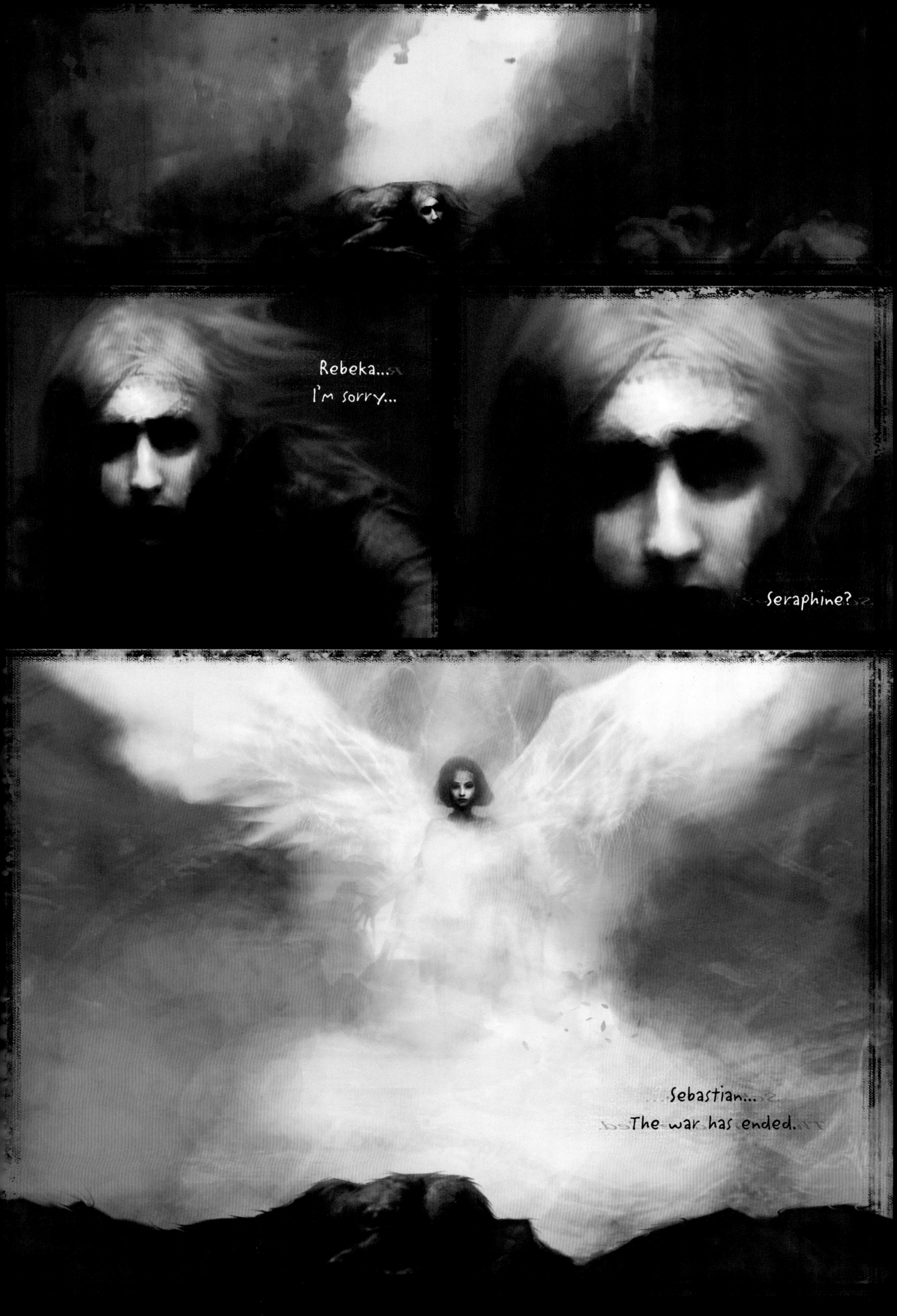
Rebeka...
I'm sorry...
Seraphine?
Sebastian...
The war has ended.

We can finally return...
Sebastian...
It is time.
We must help them begin again...

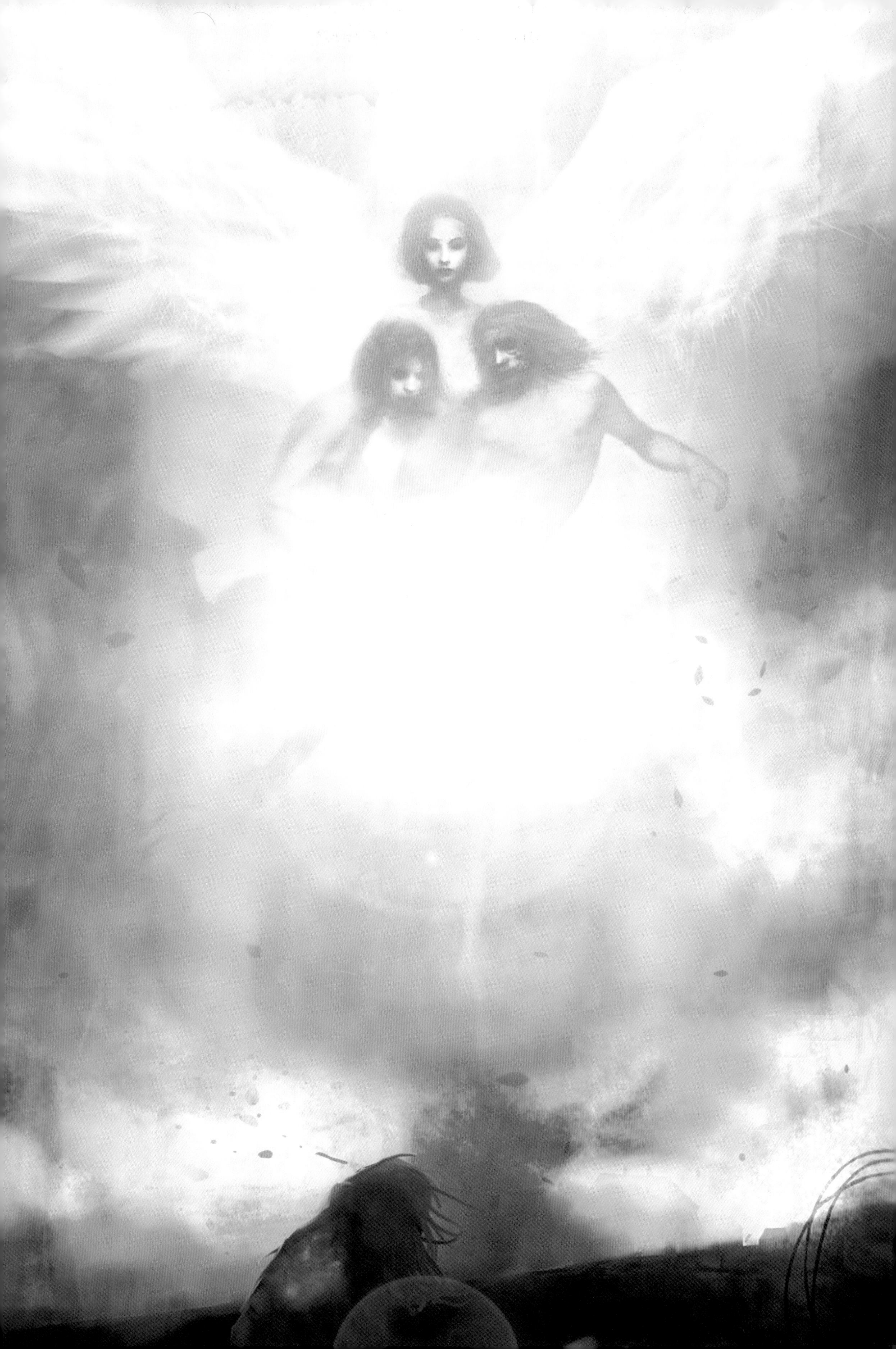

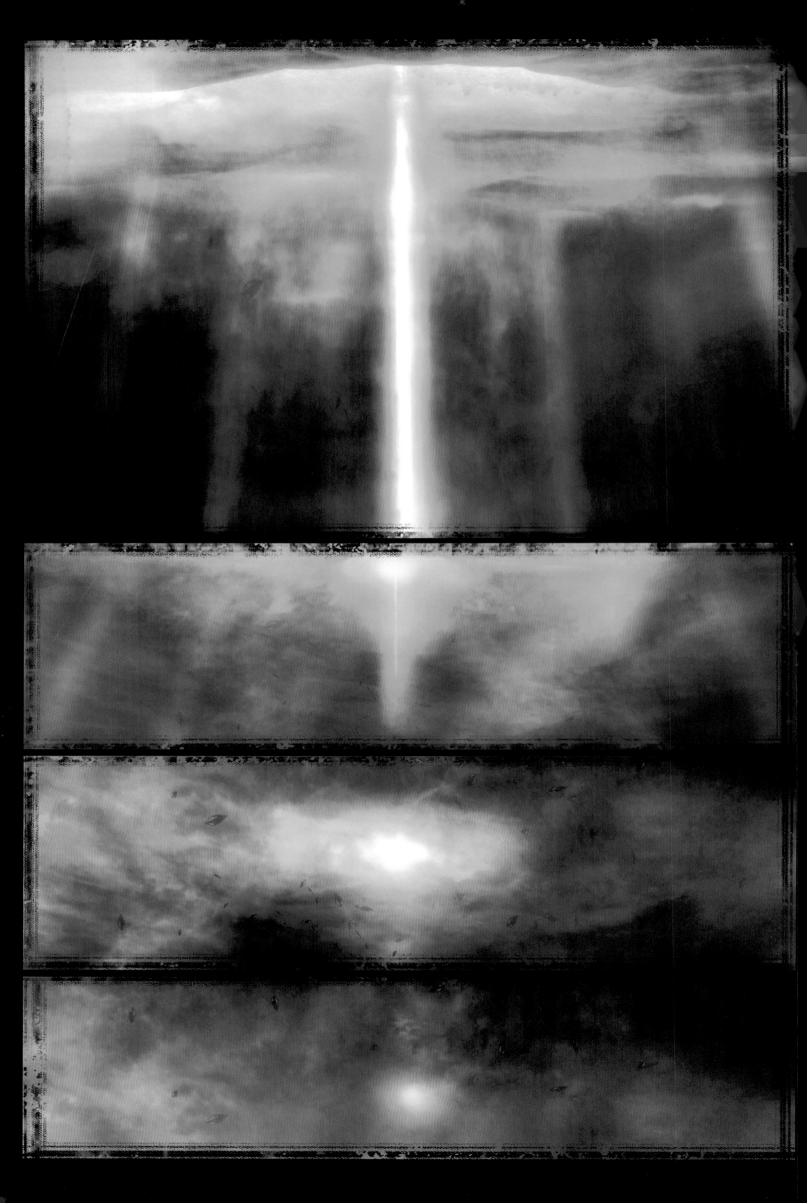

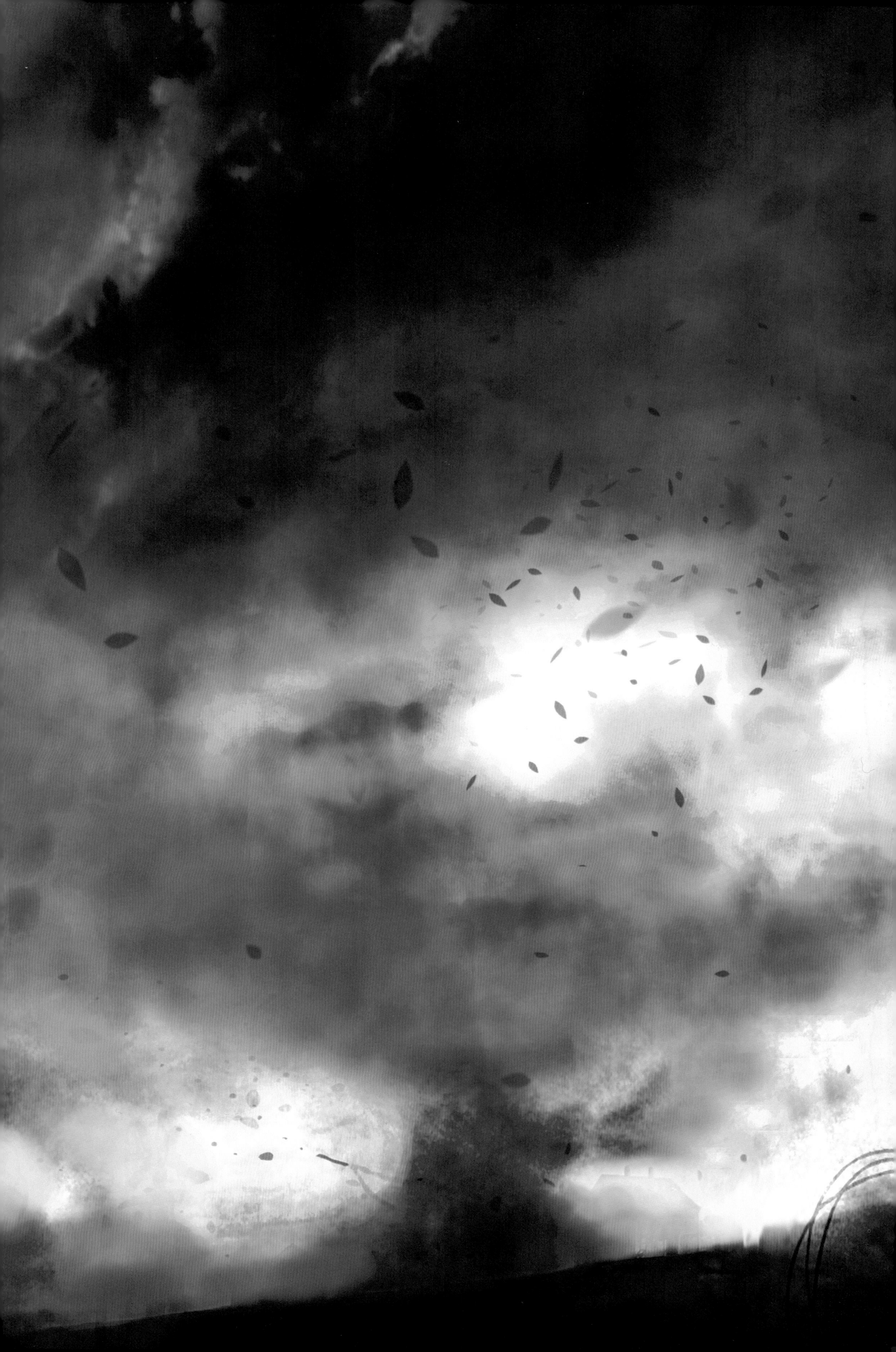

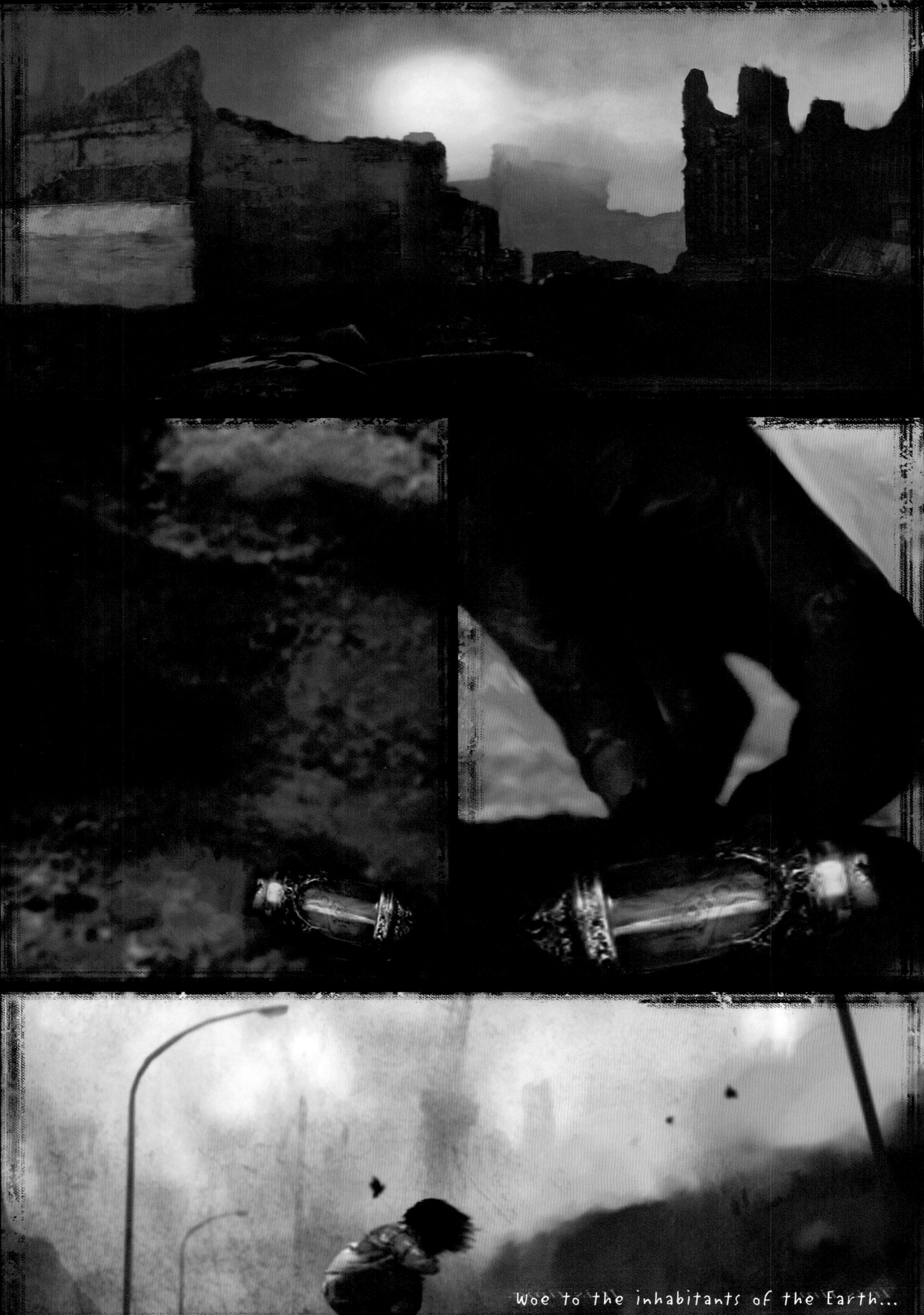
Woe to the inhabitants of the Earth...

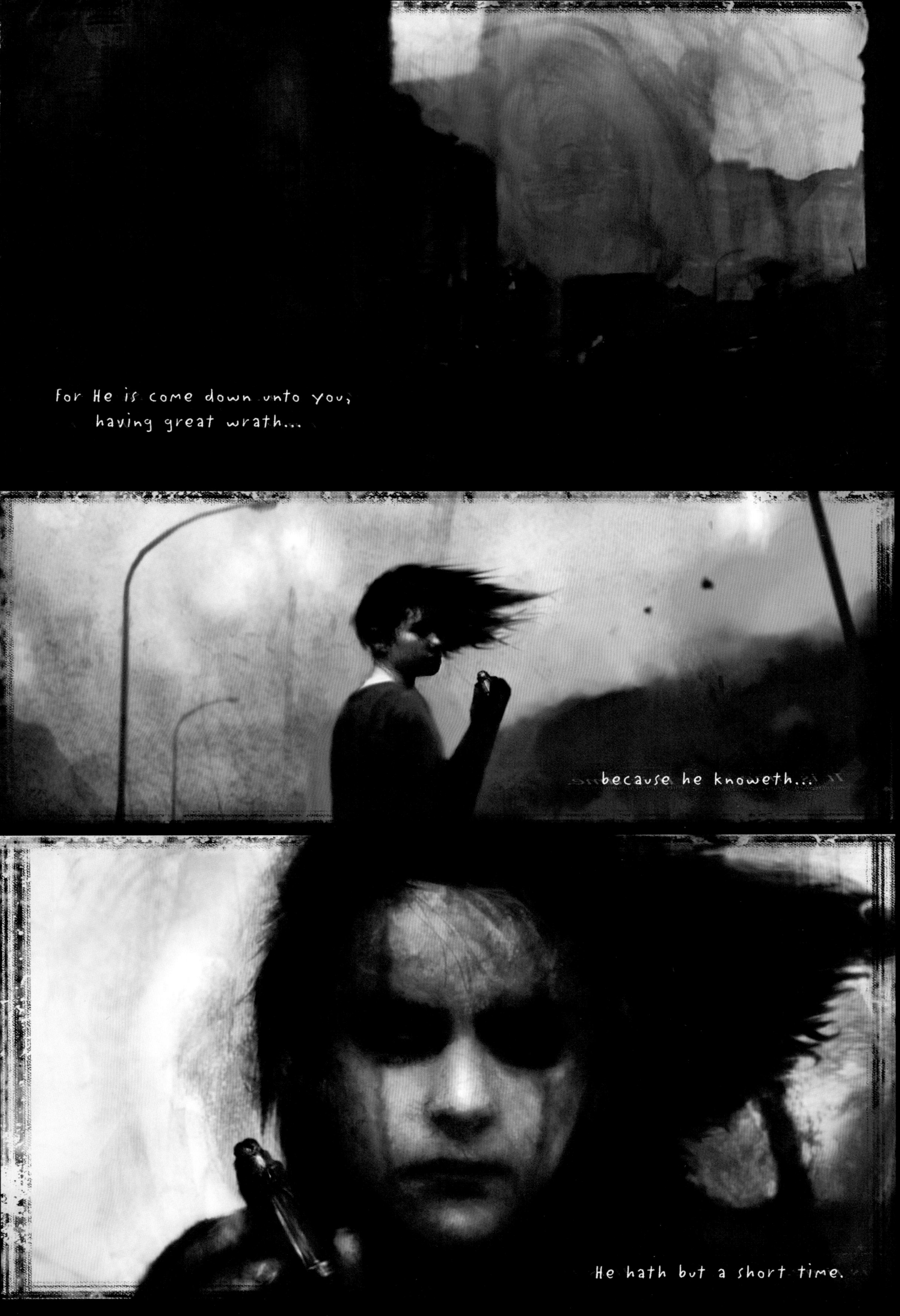
For He is come down unto you, having great wrath...
...because he knoweth...
He hath but a short time.

Look now; I myself am he! I am the one who kills and gives life;
I am the one who wounds and heals; no one delivers from my power!
Now I raise my hand to Heaven and declare, "As surely as I live,
when I sharpen my flashing sword and begin to carry out justice,
I will bring vengeance on my enemies and repay those who hate me.
I will make my arrows drunk with blood, and my sword will devour flesh-
the blood of the slaughtered and the captives, and the heads
of the enemy leaders." Rejoice with him, O heavens,
and let all the Angels worship him, for he will avenge
the blood of his servants. He will take vengeance on
his enemies and cleanse his land and his people.
(Deuteronomy 32:39-43 NLT)

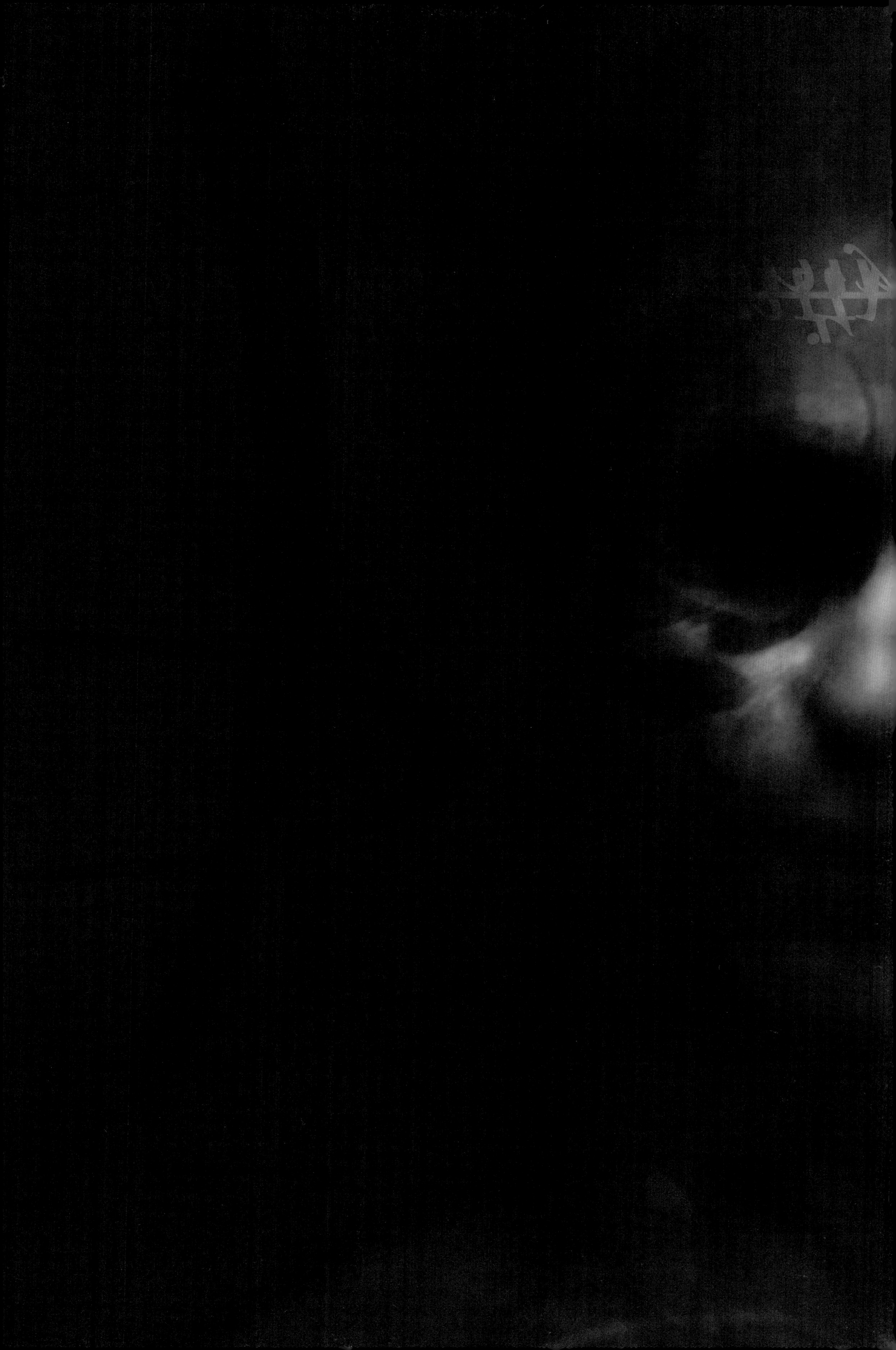

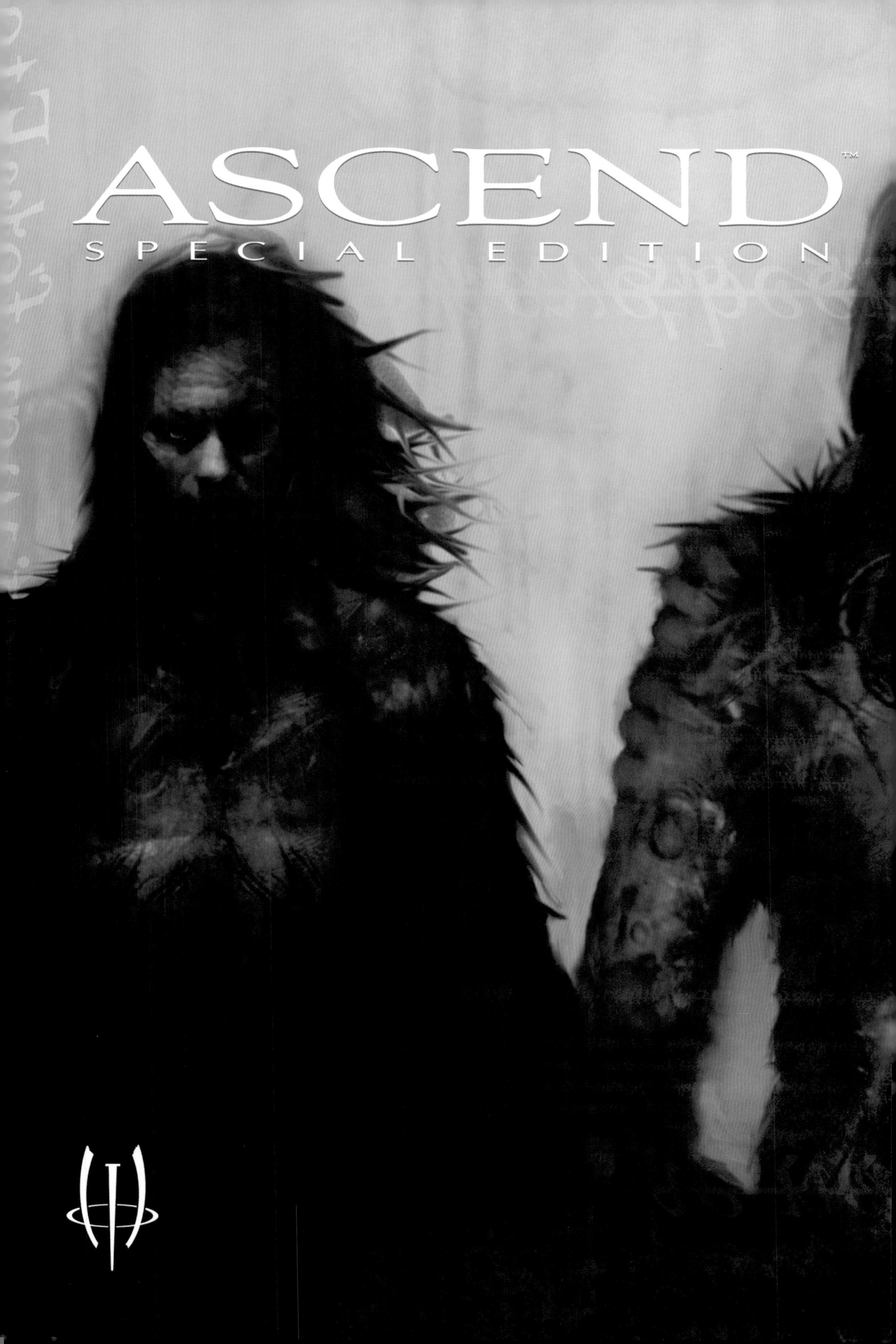
ASCEND™
SPECIAL EDITION

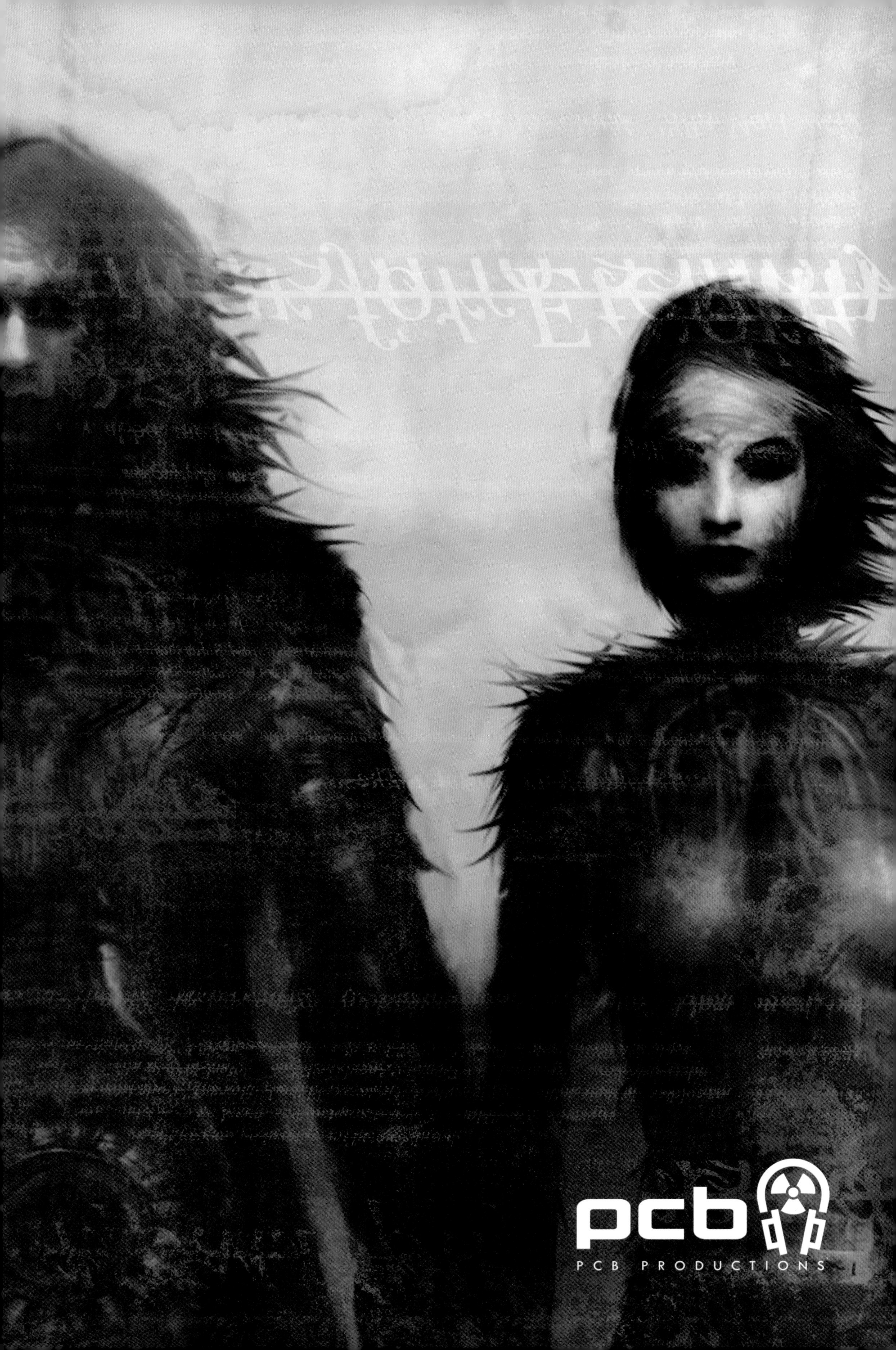
pcb
PCB PRODUCTIONS

AUTHOR NOTES

ASCEND was based on a haunting dream I had in May of 2003.
The following pages are my original production notes that I started with,
prior to laying out the pages with Christopher.

ASCEND combines symbolism and factual icons from various modern day mythologies and challenges
the foundation of Western religious philosophy.

The heart of Ascend lies in the main character Sebastian, who once brought into the Purgatory Wars
as an Angel, longs to become Human again. Sebastian rejects his role as a soldier,
and ultimately follows his brother Gideon to lead a revolution within the legions of Heaven.

There is an on-going relentless war between Heaven and the Underworld.
Heaven utilizes a complex military structure, and uses Angel soldiers for their warrior.
There is no question about their roles or positions, and they execute their jobs with
regimental precision. Other than combat, an Angel's primary task is to travel back to earth, and
recruit human souls to help fight in the Angelic Wars. This is known as "Harvesting"

The word "Angel" comes from the Greek word "Angelos" and the Hebrew "Malak". The term "angel"
actually means "messenger." As Harvesters, the Angels of Ascend are messengers to deliver
and protect souls back to the war

Angels who are banished to Earth are in a sort of purgatory. Angels warriors must fight for each
human soul to ascend into the Purgatory Wars, however Sebastian, Seraphine and Gideon, despite
their banishment, soon find that they are still bound by their angelic instincts, and are drawn
to humans about to die. If Human souls are not ascended, they are dragged into the Underworld.
Most humans can not see Angels unless they are about to ascend, however religious extremists can see
Angels, since they want to see god. Most are drawn to Gideon, since he radiates the most strength.

Although Ascend is not a religious story, even biblical accounts describe the strength of Angels.
"If one Angel can kill 185,000 in one night, how much a legion of them could do!" (Isaiah 37:36).
Genesis 19:11, Psalms 35:5-6 and Psalm 78:49 talk of angeleic warfare, and their extraordinary
strength is described "Greater in power and might than man" (2 Peter 2:11), "excel in strength"
(Psalms 103:20). Angels are described with "Held a sword with his hand"
(Numbers 22:23; Judges 6:21; Revelation 20:10),

When humans are about to die, their life energy flows out of them, as an almost musical emotional
signal. During the Harvest, Angels are uniquely tuned to thoughts of pain, anger, passion, lust,
revenge, and fear... even prayer. Strong emotions draw in Angels, and they approach on instinct.
Even fallen angels retain their harvesting instincts, and intervene into the lives of mortals.
However, since they have been denied entry back into Heaven, they can only Harvest the souls,
but not complete their ascension to Heaven.

Angels are powerful, dignified creatures, noble in cause, and exist invisibly amongst humans. They are graceful, almost bird-like, warriors. Their appearance is fragile, yet very powerful. The mannerisms of the fallen beings are not quite human, always elevated, elite, high-statured, but tragic. Angels possess an overall compassion in their look. Their eyes are expressive, emotional, yet their face remains stoic and thoughtful. Since they do not speak of their feelings, their gaze conveys a wider range of emotions. Angels are reminiscent of images from classic art, and intense tragedy is shown through their eyes.

Angelic dialog is almost like code or biblical, always one step ahead of the viewer... Almost poetic. Even biblical writings (Corinthians 13:1; 14:10-11) describe them speaking in a unique language. The text in Ascend is almost a subtitle for their dialog. Every word has weight, and nothing wasted. If they ever are at a loss for words, it makes them downcast, depressed, almost frustrated. Angels are stoic, with a quiet sense to them that they have more of a greater understanding of the larger picture, than any human ever will.

From the Greek, meaning "Revered", Sebastian, the central character, is a quiet natural leader. A human brought into the Purgatory Wars, Sebastian does not understand his destiny to restore balance to the universe. As an angel fallen from grace, Sebastian is intrigued by mortals, and falls in love with a mortal, Rebeka. He wants to protect Seraphine, his fellow angel, but his love for Rebeka clouds his judgment. After his banishment, he does not wish to remain as one of Heaven's soldiers. He is unaware that he holds the key to ending the Angelic Wars.

From the Hebrew "Seraphina", meaning "fiery-winged". Seraphine is derived from the 'seraphim', who were the most powerful angels. Seraphine is a warrior known as a "watcher", which gives her insight into events still to come. Her premonitions give her veiled insight and interpretive directions in troubled times. Seraphine has never been part of the harvest, and is not as powerful as Sebastian, however she is still more powerful than any human. Always somewhat sad, she is a tragic character of ethereal beauty. Even though she commands strength, she is soft-spoken, strong willed, but troubled. She is powerless to reverse her banishment.

From the Hebrew, meaning "He that breaks"; Gideon is a destroyer and a great warrior. Once a powerful soldier as a human, Gideon is now one of the strongest Angels. A powerful leader in the legions of Heaven, he has tasted the power from killing mortals. Gideon's intentions are to re-unite his family clan, and restore balance to the on-going war with the Underworld. Gideon realizes that he can divert ascending souls to strengthen his own Legion, and begins Havesting souls before they have died on Earth. Gideon's intentions are good, but he falls victim to the taste for power. Once banished, Gideon is attracted to mortal energy, but instead of ascending souls to Heaven, he kills them and harnesses their souls for his new war on Earth.

He soon learns that devout religious believers become the strongest prey, and absorbs their energy for his cause to storm the gates of Heaven. He despises the hypocrisy of what mortal religion has become, and considers their worship "blind" and misled. Gideon is the only character that speaks the truth "this is the only true innocence you will ever have." Gideon's message is that humans should appreciate life on earth, since they do not realize what horror awaits them in the afterlife.

AUTHOR NOTES

For where the instrument of intelligence is added to brute power and evil will, mankind is powerless in its own defense.
- Dante Alighieri

The structure of the afterlife is encompassed within the surrounding Guff. "Guff", literally translated as "the body", is a term of the Talmud used to refer to the repository of all unborn souls. Within the Guff lies Heaven and Hell, and Earth surrounded by Purgatory. When a soul leaves Earth, it passes through Purgatory as it travels to either Heaven or Hell, then eventually migrates back to the Guff, where it is recycled back to Earth.

Ascend
Configuration of Worlds & Migration of Souls

fig.1 Guff
fig.2 Heaven
fig.4 Purgatory
fig.1 Earth
fig.5 Guff
fig.4 Purgatory
fig.3 Underworld

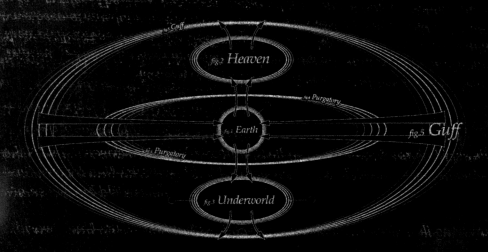

When the war between Heaven and Hell erupted, each realm began harvesting souls to recruit new warriors into their armies. Heaven and Hell sent their strongest soldiers to fight for each soul, and protect them through their ascent into the war. This not only destroyed the choice of human free-will and the promise of a peaceful afterlife, but also questioned the good nature of Heaven.

The burden of the war has taken its toll on Earth and the Guff. By retaining souls, and not allowing them to return to the Guff, the war has disrupted the balance of the universe, and started the eventual "deforestation" of humanity. Since souls can no longer return to the Guff from Heaven or Hell; Earth can not re-populate from the Guff.

The Mashiach is the only being that can break the cycle and restore balance. The Mashiach would not bring the end of the world; instead he would be the being to restart the cycle of life. The ancient Talmud reads, "The Mashiach will not arrive until there is no more soul in the body" meaning that there are a certain number of souls waiting to be born on Earth. Until they are born, they wait in a heavenly repository called "the body." The Mashiach can not return until every soul has been born into the physical world.

This demonstrates that each person is important and has a unique role which only he, with his unique soul, can fulfill. Every soul brings the Mashiach closer to being born. In early Christianity, it was thought that Jesus was the final soul from the Guff, and Armageddon would soon come, however that belief quickly died, and the concept of Guff dropped from Christian teachings.

The war between Heaven and the Underworld has robbed the Earth of souls, and kept them from returning to the Guff, thereby denying the Mashiach from returning. The Mashiach is the only being that can restore balance to the universe; however the last mortal soul must leave the Earth, before he can return.

At the moment of his death, Sebastian realizes too late that he is the Chosen one; however by sacrificing his angelic spirit to Rebeka, he becomes the last mortal soul left on Earth. His death thereby fulfills the destiny of the Mashiach to ends the war.

"If we or an Angel from heaven should preach a gospel other than the one I preached to you, let him be eternally condemned!" (Gal 1:8)

The first Angel to be banished is their former ruler, Barak "Malakh ha-mavet" - the Angel of Death. The Angel of Death, was given his power on the first day (Gen. XXXIX. 1). "Over all people have I surrendered thee the power, only not over this one which has received freedom from death " (Ex. XXXI. 18).

"In the hour of death he stands at the head of the departing one with a drawn sword. The drawn sword of the Angel of Death" (I. Chron. xxi. 15; Enoch LXii. 11), "Man, on the day of his death, falls down before the Angel of Death like a beast before the slaughterer" (Grünhut, "Likkutim," v. 102a).

There are 7 laws of Angels:
They must not dispense hope (Hebrews 11:1,6);
They must not heal the sick (James 5:16);
They must not predict the future (Galatians 1:6-9; Matthew 24:36; Mark 13: 32);
They do not know the mind of God (Romans 11:34);
They must not taste death for anyone (Hebrews 2:6-11);
May not establish war in the heavenly places (Colossians 1:20);
May not to reveal truth to heavenly places (Ephesians 3:9-10).

Each of the Angels in Ascend violates these laws for their own benefit. Ultimately, all fallen beings are driven to reclaim their former grace; to ascend to their rightful place beyond Earth. Gideon has felt the lure of the darkness, and as he slips into a life of murder, he brings his family closer to an eternity of damnation. Sebastian forsakes his right as an Angel to heal a mortal, and give hope for mankind. Seraphine foresees her future, and tries to interfere between the impending battle between the brothers.

AUTHOR NOTES

Excerpt from Seraphine's first Harvest:

PAGE 74
INTRO OF MORTAL WOMAN DYING IN CAR CRASH

Below in the city at an intersection. Smoke and flames echo above the city's towers.
A gruesome accident. A small sportscar is horribly wedged under a tanker truck.

Angle: the car driver.
She is bloodied and trapped, but alive. Flames lick up around her car.
She is terrified, dying.Suddenly, Seraphine is by the truck observing the wreckage.
No one seems to notice this morbidly curious bystander.

Angle: Seraphine from the trapped woman's POV.
Almost bird like, she tilts her head to observe the dying woman.Through the flames,
blurred by the heat, Seraphine looks much different than before:
a regal, other-worldly angel bathed in shimmering light.
[Note: again, the angel effect should be blurred, unclear. The wings and light are actually
the suit opening up to claim the soul of the dying, but we don't reveal that with
any clarity until later.]

PAGE 75
SERAPHINE HARVESTS THE WOMAN

Seraphine strides through the flame to stand by the car.

Angle: Seraphine.
She is glowing, a triumphant and supremely confident expression.
Flames obscure everything around her. She extends her hand to the woman.

SERAPHINE:
IT IS TIME.

The woman is now equal parts terrified and awed.

WOMAN IN CAR:
YOU...YOU HAVE COME...FOR ME...

Seraphine is completely calm.

SERAPHINE:
YOU CAME...TO ME.

Seraphine's wings begin to radiate a warm blue light.

WOMAN IN CAR:
PLEASE...TAKE ME. TAKE ME.

Seraphine places her hands on the woman trapped the wreckage,
as "wings" from her suit envelop the woman.
With flames all around, the two are engulfed in a sphere of light.
Their bodies merge as the woman becomes the light and illuminates Seraphine from within.

The Tanker and car explode in an inferno of light and flame.

PAGE 76
RAPE OF THE SOUL

Outside the flames, Seraphine emerges as a silhouette from the inferno.
Her suit has again returned to it's normal, skin-tight fit.

Emergency crews hardly notice Seraphine as she slowly walks away.
The woman, car, and tanker are gone...Consumed in the fire.

As Seraphine walks away, her suit fills the scene with light, dancing, shifting,
organic in the same way as the opening storm,
only this is light and brightness as opposed to darkness and ferocity.

Seraphine's face is a mask of serenity, and she looks upwards, smiling with curiosity.
The light lifts her into the air, tossing her hair, almost playing with her.
Seraphine is facinated as the dancing light radiates from her body.

Suddenly, the light explodes from within her. Seraphine is violently arched into the air,
her head and shoulders thrown back. The light is ripped from her body,
in a violent rape of the soul she is carrying. Seraphine begins to scream.

SERAPHINE:
NO! PLEASE!

The light quickly ascends toward the sky, leaving Seraphine thrown on the ground.

Alone in the darkness of the shadows left behind.

AUTHOR NOTES
BIBLICAL CONTEXT

Legion:
"If a single Angel killed 185,000 soldiers in one night, imagine what a legion of Angels can do!"
– Isaiah 37:36.

When He was arrested by the Romans,
Christ's disciple St. Peter tried to intervene, but Jesus stopped him, saying,
"Do you think I cannot call on my Father and He will at once put at my disposal more than
twelve legions of Angels?" (Matt. 26:52-53) A legion generally consisted of over
6,000 soldiers, meaning that Christ could have summoned over 72,000 angelic warriors.

When Lucifer rebelled against God in heaven, he was able to convince other Angels to join him.
In fact, in Revelation 12:4, Satan was convincing enough so that one-third of the Angels
in heaven sided with him.

"How you have fallen from heaven, son of the dawn!
You have been cast down to the earth, you who once laid low the nations!
You said in your heart, "I will ascend to heaven; I will raise my throne above the stars of God;
I will sit enthroned on the mount of assembly, on the utmost heights of the sacred mountain.
I will ascend above the tops of the clouds;
But you are brought down to the grave, to the depths of the pit
(Isa. 14:12—15, NIV).

What does "Angel" mean?
• The Greek word "Angelos" and the Hebrew "Malak". The term "Angel" means "messenger."

Can Angels fight?
• Angels killed 185,000 Assyrians, (2 Kings 19:35),
• Genesis 19:11 invoke blindness,
• Chase and pursue enemies (Psalms 35:5-6)
• destruction through plagues (Psalm 78:49)

How strong are Angels?
• Greater in power and might than man (2 Peter 2:11),
• excel in strength (Psalms 103:20),
• mighty (2 Thessalonians 1:7),

What do Angels look like?
• Held a sword, staff or chain with his hand (Numbers 22:23; Joshua 5:13; Judges 6:21; Revelation 20:10),
• Shining garments (Luke 24:4),
• Clothed in pure bright linen and chests girded with golden bands (Revelation 15:6),
• Countenance of the Angel of God, very awesome, like lightning (Judges 13:6; Matthew 28:3)

Do Angels speak a unique language?
• Yes: 1 Corinthians 13:1; 14:10-11.
• Voice like thunder: Revelation 10:3; 19:6.
• Loud voice: Revelation 5:5; 11:15.

What is an Angel's role?
• Protection, ensuring the well-being or survival of God's people:
Genesis 19:1-25; 48:16; Exodus 14:19,20; 1 Kings 19:1-8; 2 Kings 6:16; 2 Kings 19:35;
Psalms 34:7; Matthew 4:11; Acts 5:17-23; Acts 12:7-11.
• Watches man: Daniel 4:13,17; 12:1.
• Punishment, enforcing the wrath of God on the wicked:
Genesis 19:12-13; Exodus 12:23,29; Exodus 32:34: Numbers 22:22; 2 Samuel 24:17; 2 Kings 19:35;
1 Chronicles 21:15; 2 Chronicles 32:21: Psalms 78:48-5; Isaiah 37:36;
• Chases our personal adversaries providing vengeance: Psalms 35:4-6; Romans 12:19.
• Revealing God's will or announcing key events: Genesis 19:1-22;
Exodus 3:2-6; Judges 2:1-5; 13:2-23; Acts 10:5; Revelation 1:1.

How does one know if an Angel is evil?
• Evil Angels will preach a different message than what is in the Bible: Galatians 1:8.
• Truth is simple and pure devotion to Heaven: 2 Corinthians 11:3-4.

Can a fallen Angel quote scripture?
• Yes: Matthew 4:6; 1 Timothy 4:1.
• "they believe": James 2 :19.
• "they fear God": 2 Peter 2:11.

Angelic Hierarchy
• Commander of the army of the LORD: Joshua 5:14.
• ArchAngel: 1 Thessalonians 4:16; Jude 9; Revelation 12:7.
• Romans 13:1 "There Is no authority except from God & those which exist are established by God."

Cherubim:
• Cherubim warriors are 180" high / 15 feet, with a wingspan was 15 feet across (1 wing = 5 cubits)
• Body includes hands, wings, wheels and face: Ezekiel 10:12-22
• Guards: Gen. 3:24.
• Attendants: Ezekiel 10:3-22; Isa. 6:2-6; Ezek. 1:4-28; 10:3-22.
• Represented in Temple furnishings: Ex. 25:18-22; 26:1, 31; 1 Kings 6:23-35; 2 Chron. 3:7-14.
• Throne: 1 Sam. 4:4; 2 Sam. 6:2; 22:11; 2 Kings 19:15; 1 Chron. 13:6; 28:18; Ps. 18:10; 80:1; 99:1;
Isa. 37:16; Ezekiel 9-11& 4; Hebrews 9:5.

Seraphim:
• Literally means "the burning ones": Ezekiel 1:4-25.
• Six wings: Isaiah 6:2; Revelation 4:6-8.

KEITH AREM

Ascend was created by writer, producer, and creative director Keith Arem.
President of Los Angeles based PCB Productions, Arem is a leading
creator and digital post-production supervisor for the interactive community.
He served as Director of Audio for Virgin Interactive Entertainment (1994 -1998)
and Director of Audio for Electronic Arts Pacific (1998-1999). Arem holds
a Bachelors degree in Audio Engineering and Electronic Music Synthesis from
California State University Dominguez Hills.

Arem has produced and recorded over 500 commercial releases in the film,
music, and interactive industries, including: Call of Duty 2-4, Ghost Recon
Advanced Warfighter, Ultimate Spiderman, Spiderman The Movie, X-Men 2-3,
Lord of the Rings, Tony Hawk Pro Skater 2-4, Everquest 2, Splinter Cell 3,
Prince of Persia 2-3, Spriggan, Disney's Emperor's New Groove, Metal Arms,
.Hack//Sign, X-Files On-line, Ridge Racer, and Contagion's Infectant.
Arem's clients include: Sony, Activision, Microsoft, UbiSoft, Universal, Disney,
Nintendo, Boeing, Namco, Capitol, Ubisoft, Electronic Arts, and Fox.

CHRISTOPHER SHY

Artist Christopher Shy is an illustrator, painter, and writer, who has worked in
comics, games, and film since 1993. President of Studio Ronin, Shy's recent
work includes X-Men, Black Panther (Marvel Comics), Resistance (DC Comics),
and products for White Wolf, Arbor Sports, and Sims Snowboards.

Shy has completed two graphic novels for Studio Ronin and
is the creator of Man to Leaves, Seven Leaves, Syndicate Has No Face,
Hateful Youth, AunJnu, and Apokolpse Ant. Shy was voted Artist of the Year at
Origins, and spot lighted as Artist of the Year for White Wolf Games.
In 2003, Shy was chosen for the prestigious cover of Wisconsin
Review by the University of Wisconsin. Shy's clients include: Microsoft,
Marvel Comics, DC Comics, LucasArts, White Wolf Productions,
Russell Productions, UbiSoft, Red Storm, and many others.

KRISTIAN HEDMAN

As Creative Director & Art Director at PCB Productions, Kristian Hedman oversees the visual aspects of PCB Productions's original content production. Hedman is a veteran of the video game and design industries with a list of credits that spans over 13 years of creative innovation. Hedman's past and current clients include: Sony, Activision, Mattel, Virgin, Disney, Electronic Arts, and Marvel.

For Ascend, Hedman created a strong and consistent visual identity across multiple media. He created the Ascend trailer, extended and re-purposed some of the original artwork, authored the Ascend website, and designed many of the promotional assets for the project. Hedman was also responsible for the layout of this book, and several post-production tasks, including visual effects.

SCOTT CUTHBERTSON

A graduate of the University of Michigan with a degree in Film/TV Production and Communication, and a minor in English Composition, Scott Cuthbertson has been working in the entertainment industry for over 13 years. Cuthbertson has extensive experience in creative design, writing, and production management for the interactive entertainment industry, having worked for industry leaders such as Disney, AOL, Universal, and Nintendo.

Cuthbertson has lead creative development of video games for such properties as: Lilo & Stitch, Atlantis, The Emperor's New Groove, Treasure Planet, Pirates of the Caribbean, Dungeons & Dragons, and The Lord of the Rings.

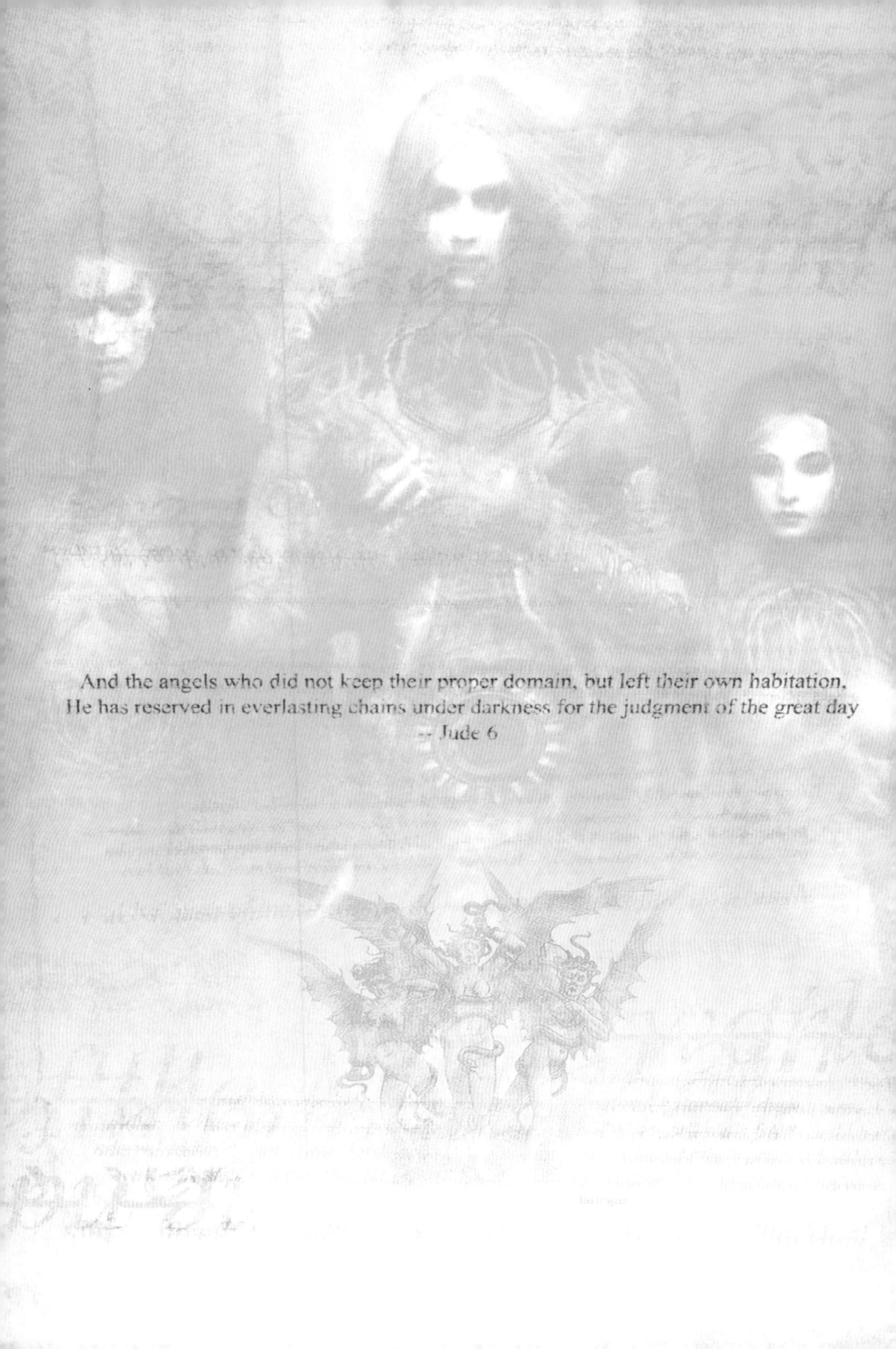

And the angels who did not keep their proper domain, but left their own habitation,
He has reserved in everlasting chains under darkness for the judgment of the great day
-- Jude 6

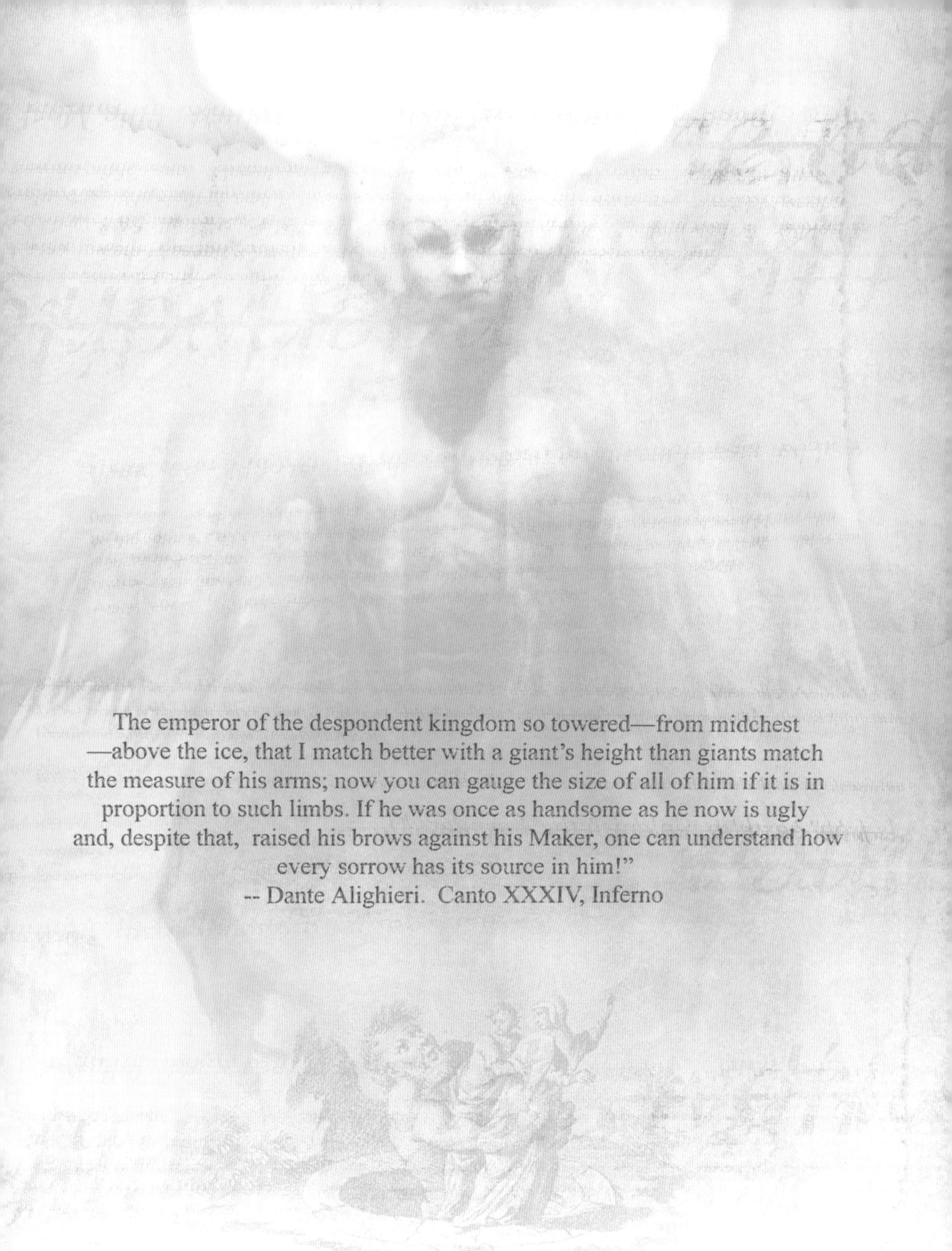

The emperor of the despondent kingdom so towered—from midchest —above the ice, that I match better with a giant's height than giants match the measure of his arms; now you can gauge the size of all of him if it is in proportion to such limbs. If he was once as handsome as he now is ugly and, despite that, raised his brows against his Maker, one can understand how every sorrow has its source in him!"

-- Dante Alighieri. Canto XXXIV, Inferno

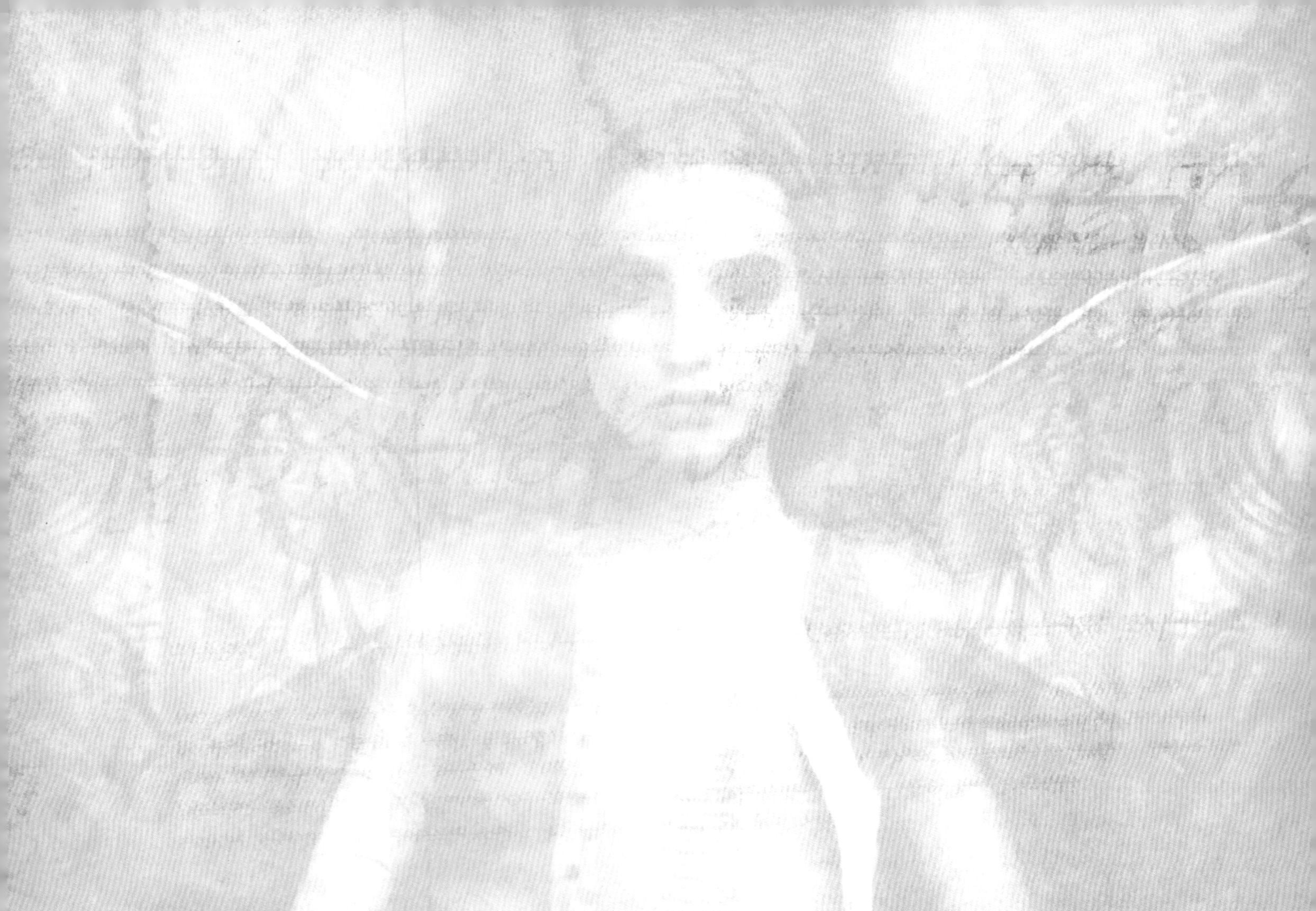

How art thou fallen from Heaven...how art thou cut down to the ground, which didst weaken the nations. For thou hast said in thine heart, I will ascend into Heaven, I will exalt my throne above the stars of God: I will ascend above the heights of the clouds; I will be like the most High, yet thou shalt be brought down to the sides of the pit.

Isaiah 14: 12-15

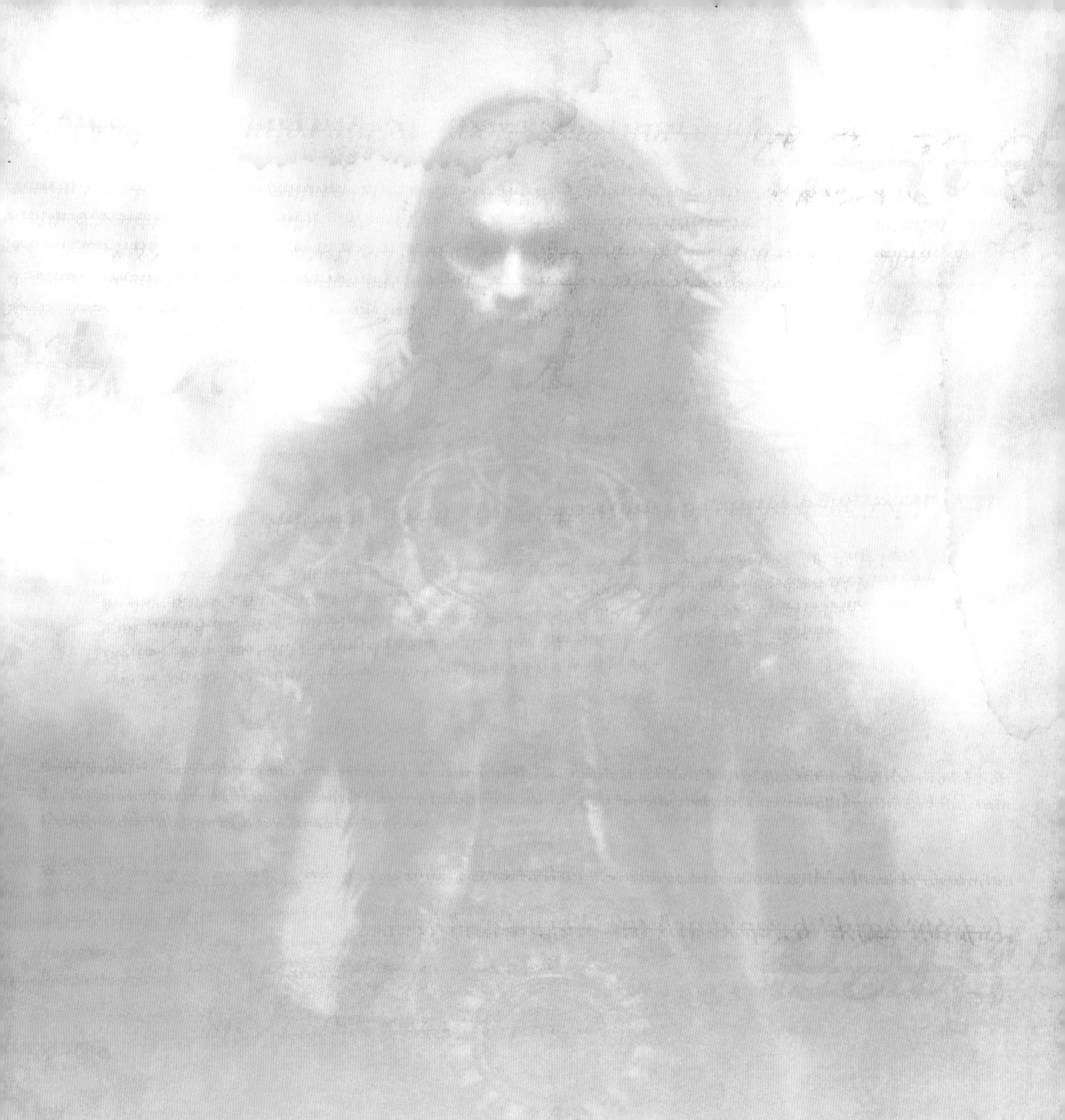

Through your widespread trade you were filled with violence, and you sinned
So I drove you in disgrace from the mount of God, and I expelled you,
Guardian cherub, from among the fiery stones.
Your heart became proud on account of your beauty and you corrupted your wisdom
because of your splendour. So I threw you to earth; I made a spectacle of you before kings.

--Ezekiel: 12-18

PRINTED IN CHINA